REEXAMINING
DEMOCRACY

REEXAMINING DEMOCRACY

Essays in Honor of Seymour Martin Lipset

Editors

Gary Marks
Larry Diamond

SAGE PUBLICATIONS
International Educational and Professional Publisher
Newbury Park   London   New Delhi

For information address:

 SAGE Publications, Inc.
2455 Teller Road
Newbury Park, California 91320

SAGE Publications Ltd.
6 Bonhill Street
London EC2A 4PU
United Kingdom

SAGE Publications India Pvt. Ltd.
M-32 Market
Greater Kailash I
New Delhi 110 048 India

Printed in the United States of America

Library of Congress Cataloging-in-Publication Data

Main entry under title:

Reexamining democracy: essays in honor of Seymour Martin Lipset /
    edited by Gary Marks, Larry Diamond.
        p.   cm.
    Includes bibliographical references and index.
    ISBN 0-8039-4641-4
    1. Democracy.   I. Marks, Gary.   II. Diamond, Larry Jay.
JC423.R33   1992
321.8—dc20   92-17317

92 93 94 95 96 10 9 8 7 6 5 4 3 2 1

Sage Production Editor: Astrid Virding

Contents

Foreword: Notes on the Young Lipset
ROBERT K. MERTON   ix

Seymour Martin Lipset and the Study of Democracy
LARRY DIAMOND and GARY MARKS   1

Part I. Theoretical Perspectives

1. Democracy in Permanently Divided Systems
JAMES S. COLEMAN   17

2. Democracy as Political Competition
KAARE STROM   27

3. Rational Sources of Chaos in Democratic Transition
GARY MARKS   47

4. On the Place of Virtues in a Pluralistic Democracy
AMITAI ETZIONI   70

5. The Concept of National Development, 1917-1989:
Elegy and Requiem
IMMANUEL WALLERSTEIN   79

Part II. Comparative Perspectives

6. Economic Development and Democracy Reconsidered
LARRY DIAMOND   93

7. Capitalism, the Market, and Democracy
   CARLOS H. WAISMAN   140

8. Interest Systems and the Consolidation of Democracies
   PHILIPPE C. SCHMITTER   156

9. Change and Continuity in the Nature of Contemporary
   Democracies
   JUAN J. LINZ   182

10. Two New Nations: Israeli and American Foreign Policies
    AMOS PERLMUTTER   208

Part III. Politics and Social Change in American Democracy

11. State Formation and Social Policy in the United States
    THEDA SKOCPOL   227

12. The Insurgent Origins of Union Democracy
    MAURICE ZEITLIN and JUDITH STEPAN-NORRIS   250

13. Class, Race, and Higher Education in America
    MARTIN TROW   275

14. Inequality and American Culture: The Persistence of
    Voluntarism
    ANN SWIDLER   294

15. "Off With Their Heads": The Confidence Gap and the Revolt
    Against Professionalism in American Politics
    WILLIAM SCHNEIDER   315

    Appendix: Publications of Seymour Martin Lipset   332

    Index   356

    About the Authors   362

Foreword

NOTES ON THE YOUNG LIPSET

PROUD claims to academic progeny are notoriously subject to dispute, often by the ascribed progeny themselves. Still, I like to think that I really was among the first on Morningside Heights to have set eyes on Seymour Martin Lipset almost half a century ago, when, as substantially more than a mere slip of a young man who had just achieved legal adulthood, he entered my classroom. Before long, he was a consequential presence. Not only did he take active part in the discussion of moot theoretical points, which, of course, were in abundant supply, but, as he has himself recorded in print, the paper he wrote for that course—on the ITU (International Typographical Union) as a striking counterexample to Michels's "iron law of oligarchy"— eventually materialized in the classic work we know as *Union Democracy*. But that superb work, written in the exciting intellectual atmosphere of the Columbia Department of Sociology and its Bureau of Applied Social Research and, rightly enough, in conjunction with the newer graduate students Martin A. Trow and James S. Coleman (each destined to come into his own world fame), did not appear for another 10 years or so.[1] In the meantime, Marty Lipset had run off to Canada to study the CCF (Cooperative Commonwealth Federation), the first mass socialist party in English-speaking America.

Marty Lipset must himself know that my describing his young self as a "consequential presence" is anything but a belated *ex post* observation. He has only to recall one of our conversations back in those early days, not long after he had taken his degree. There I was, one of his proud teachers, informing the already prolific author that his scholarly work was bound to be of consequence even if he elected to publish only a fraction of his eager scholarship. However, now that his first 20-or-so books and even more edited volumes have become enshrined in the core library of sociology and political science, he may actually have come to question the wisdom of that would-be sage advice.

Nor need I remind Marty that Robert Lynd, Paul Lazarsfeld, and I took immediate notice of this new student, for he has himself generously done so in honoring that receptive trio by dedicating his *Revolution and Counterrevolution* to "Bob, Paul and Bob for origins and encouragement." Some observers at the time might even have regarded us three teachers as actively competing for that student's attention. With Bob and Paul gone, alas, only Marty and I can recall how it was, for example, that Bob Lynd seduced him into doing the CCF study for his dissertation although I had been urging him instead to flesh out his early sketch of the ITU paper for a surely memorable dissertation. And so it was that the enduring monograph *Agrarian Socialism* preceded the appearance of the classic *Union Democracy* by half-a-dozen years.

It is a matter of further public record that after the young Marty's short stints first at Toronto and then at Berkeley, we at Columbia persuaded him to return to his alma mater, at least for a while, just as Max Weber had moved from short stints first at Berlin and then at Freiburg before returning to Heidelberg to become, in the words of Marianne Weber, "the colleague of his former teachers"—if I may be allowed so grand an analogue within the glowing context of a *Festschrift.*

All this, of course, Marty Lipset knows. But he does not know that I have long been variously enjoying the great range of his predicted consequential presence. Not alone in the most direct and obvious way by faithfully studying each new tome and article as it appears—no small achievement in itself—but by getting a quick if approximate fix on his consequentiality for other scholars the world over. Thanks to Eugene Garfield's *Science Citation Index* and *Social Sciences Citation Index,* one can track the vast array of authors who have drawn on Marty Lipset's scholarship to advance their own. To be sure, Gene Garfield himself sounded an early cautionary note (back in 1963) about the possible "promiscuous and careless use of quantitative citation data" and went on to observe that "it is preposterous to conclude blindly that the most cited author deserves a Nobel prize." Still, it is plain from the magnitudes involved that, as was evident from the start would be the case, Marty Lipset's lifelong scholarship has indeed been greatly and diversely consequential. Limiting ourselves to a readily available 20-year segment of the citation indexes, we find that Seymour Martin Lipset has been cited well over 4,000 times, with *Political Man* far out in front and *Union Democracy* next in line. In light of the continuing currency of these and his many other books, this comes as no surprise; after all, *Political Man,* to take a prime example, is now in some 15 translations. Still, in drawing upon this indicator of widespread intellectual influence, I can put these swiftly assembled numbers in further perspective: Of the nearly 3 million scientific authors cited in the SCI during that 20-year period, only 3 in 10,000 have had their work drawn upon as often.

But enough of such redundant numbers, which only confirm what this volume declares: Seymour Martin Lipset is one of the truly consequential social scientists of our time.

Robert K. Merton
Columbia University

NOTE

1. For keen depictions of that complex microenvironment as perceived by two graduate students of that time, see James S. Coleman (1980) and David L. Sills (1987).

REFERENCES

Coleman, J. S., & Lazarsfeld, P. F. (1980). The substance and style of his work. In R. K. Merton & M. W. Riley (Eds.), *Sociological traditions from generation to generation: Glimpses of the American experience* (pp. 153-174). Norwood, NJ: Ablex.

Sills, D. L. (1987). Paul F. Lazarsfeld, 1902-1976. In National Academy of Sciences, *Biographical memoirs* (Vol. 56, pp. 251-282). Washington, DC: National Academy Press.

Seymour Martin Lipset and the Study of Democracy

Larry Diamond
Gary Marks

THROUGHOUT this century, and especially since World War II, no theme has more preoccupied the fields of comparative politics and political sociology than the nature, conditions, and possibilities of democracy. And no political scientist or sociologist has contributed more to advancing our thinking about democracy—in all its dimensions, both comparatively and in the United States—than Seymour Martin Lipset. It is in some sense fitting, then, that this *Festschrift* in honor of Lipset is devoted to rethinking the character and development of democracy in the United States and the world.

There are other fruitful conjunctures that make this a timely moment of reflection and celebration. On the one hand, democracy is now resurgent in the world. More than 15 years since the onset of the "third wave" of global democratic expansion (Huntington, 1991), considerably more countries have (more or less) democratic forms of governance than ever before—some 65 in 1990, by the count of Freedom House (1991), and that number has since increased. On the other hand, the performance of many long-standing democracies, not least the United States, is proving less than satisfactory to their publics, who are demanding reform.

There is also a happy personal conjuncture—especially for the many scholars of democracy and society (including all the contributors to this volume) who have had the benefit of studying under Marty Lipset. This year marks not only a numerical milestone in his life, but a professional one as well. With his election in 1991 to the presidency of the American Sociological Association

1

(which he will assume later this year), Lipset becomes the only social scientist ever to serve as president of both the American Sociological and Political Science associations. During the first four decades of his scholarly career, he has also served as president of the World Association for Public Opinion Research, president of the International Society of Political Psychology, and vice president of the International Political Science Association—to mention only a few of the roughly 20 offices he has held in professional societies. This is not to mention the numerous distinguished awards, honorary degrees, and honorific memberships he has received. Author (or coauthor) of 21 books and scholarly articles too numerous to count, and editor or coeditor of 25 more, he is one of the most prolific social scientists of this century. No living political scientist or sociologist is more frequently cited by other scholars. Few social science books in our times have had the impact of his *Political Man,* for example, which has been published in 16 other countries, including Japan, Turkey, India, Yugoslavia, Israel, and Vietnam. Few social scientists are more admired for the range of their intellects, or more beloved for their friendship, decency, and humanity. The essays in this volume are a tribute to Marty Lipset, the scholar and the person.

Of course, no *Festschrift* could do justice to the extraordinary range of Seymour Martin Lipset's intellectual contributions. His books and articles have sought to elucidate such diverse phenomena as the political and social origins of socialism (or the absence of socialism), fascism, revolution, protest, ethnic prejudice, anti-Semitism, and political extremism; the sources and consequences of class structure, class consciousness, class conflict, and social mobility; the links among social cleavages, party systems, and voter alignments; the connections between voter preferences and electoral outcomes; the dense reciprocal relations between values and institutions; the changing character of such diverse institutions as trade unions and higher education (and even unions in higher education!); the determinants and dynamics of public opinion and public confidence in institutions; the role of religion in American life; the political behavior of American Jews; the conditions of the democratic order; and the differences among cultures, especially the contrast (which has fascinated him throughout his scholarly life) between Canada and the United States. Across this sweeping landscape of classical and pioneering issues in the social sciences, Lipset has brought a consistently lucid and strikingly accessible analytical style and a breathtaking array of sources and evidence that have made his works among the most popular and widely used, both by teachers and by researchers. More striking still, he has explored virtually every one of these issues authoritatively both across nations and with a specific focus on the United States. And he has published with equal distinction as a social historian and as an astute commentator on the politics, culture, and conflicts of our time. Few living social scientists could lay claim to such a broad and broadly honored set of works.

Yet, within this great and restless diversity of questions, issues, methods, and foci, we think there lies a core theme to Lipset's work. That core is composed of the conditions, problems, dynamics, values, and institutions of democracy, both in the United States and comparatively throughout the world. Thus we have chosen democracy as the theme of this *Festschrift.*

REFLECTIONS ON
THE CHARACTER OF DEMOCRACY

In elaborating the liberal, pluralist approach to the conditions of the democratic order that pervades his writing on the subject, Lipset has been heavily influenced by classical political thinkers, dating back to Aristotle. Indeed, he frequently acknowledges this intellectual debt, as with the selections from Aristotle that introduce *Political Man.* These passages emphasize the crucial link between political order and the rule of law; the dangers of political extremism and unfettered populism; the importance to democracy of limited inequality, a large middle class, and political moderation. These themes resonate powerfully and continuously through Lipset's writings on politics and governance and have significantly shaped his theoretical and philosophical approach.

Of course, as with any great social scientist, Lipset's thinking has been strongly influenced by a variety of preceding theorists, including Robert Michels, Talcott Parsons, Karl Marx, and, perhaps most of all, Max Weber. But with reference to the conditions of democracy, Lipset's intellectual affinity with Alexis De Tocqueville is also noteworthy. As Lipset observes in his introduction to *Political Man,* Tocqueville, struggling with many of the same momentous, nineteenth-century issues and conflicts as Karl Marx, came to very different conclusions. Rejecting the desirability or inevitability of conflict polarization and revolution, Tocqueville "deliberately chose to emphasize those aspects of social units which could maintain political cleavage and political consensus at the same time" (Lipset, 1960/1981, p. 7). This concern for the factors that contain political conflict within a framework of consensus, and so neutralize the demand for violent and revolutionary change, has been an enduring theme in Lipset's writings on democracy and society. Following Tocqueville, it has led him to an intellectual and normative interest in gradual change, political accommodation, and the sources of political legitimacy; in limiting the power of the state; and in independent, voluntary associations as one important means for controlling the state and otherwise developing the social infrastructure of a free society.

An abiding concern for avoiding the polarization of conflict, the formation of extremist political movements and preferences, or the elimination of all conflict in a state-dominated "mass society" runs through much of Lipset's writing on the conditions of the democratic order. In *Political Man* he demonstrates the importance, for these democratic ends, of historical legitimacy, effective performance, social mobility, and cross-cutting cleavages, as well as the gradual incorporation into the polity of newly mobilizing social groups. His analyses there of the dynamics of legitimacy and the effects of cleavage structure are among the clearest and most compelling in political sociology. These and related issues of democratic development are further advanced in *The First New Nation* (1963/1979), which highlights the importance of political leadership and political values, and the determinants and consequences of party systems.

One of Lipset's enduring contributions to our understanding of democratic stability is the notion of cross-cutting cleavages or pressures that reduce the intensity of political emotions and assure individuals who are in the minority on one issue that they may form the majority on other issues. In his contribution to this volume, James Coleman offers a proposal for sustaining democracy in societies where individuals are not subject to cross-cutting pressures but are, instead, encompassed within rigid ethnic or cultural cleavages that relegate some people to the position of a permanent minority. One solution to this, as Coleman notes, is to decentralize decision making within smaller geographical units so as to provide a degree of self-government to each ethnic, religious, or linguistic enclave. But the force of this solution is undercut where rigid groups are territorially enmeshed. Coleman's proposal for sustaining democracy under such circumstances is simple, but profound. In place of majoritarian decision making in the legislature, he proposes that each legislator be given a quantity of fungible votes ("kaldors"), any number of which can be bid in support of or opposition to particular legislative bills. Winners compensate losers to the extent of their original bids for or against the legislation. Hence a defeated minority is able to build its store of votes for a future occasion when it has the prospect of winning, irrespective of the relative size of its constituency. Such a system is attuned to intensity of interest as well as sheer numbers, and provides minorities with constitutional channels for gaining some of what they want. This problem of contending nationalisms and the need to protect national minorities—so fiercely salient again on the world stage—is also addressed by Juan Linz in Chapter 9.

Few, if any, scholars of the conditions of democracy have been more concerned than Lipset with various forms of conflict and competition. Democracy, according to Lipset (1960/1981), "requires institutions which support conflict and disagreement as well as those which sustain legitimacy and consensus" (p. 439). Lipset is clearly in the Schumpeterian tradition that views free competition among political parties as a defining feature of democracy. In Chapter 2 of this volume, Kaare Strom identifies two basic approaches to political competition elaborated in the Schumpeterian and Downsian traditions and proceeds to unpack democratic competition into two components: political contestability and situational competitiveness. Democratic contestability exists where the entry conditions facing potential new political parties are low. Situational competitiveness is present when the stakes of competition are high, when electoral victory is determined by party choice and performance rather than structural or random factors, and when no party is inherently favored over others. Viewed in this way, democracy is fundamentally a matter of risk induced by intense competition.

Amitai Etzioni, by contrast, emphasizes in Chapter 4 the need for shared virtues or communitarian values that bind a democratic society together, curb "contentiousness and litigiousness," and so help "to resolve differences."

Pluralism must fit within some kind of overarching normative unity; "some ultimate values must be shared" if the diversity in a democratic society is to be contained democratically. Acknowledging liberal fears that such communitarian values could lead to the kind of majoritarian political domination that concerns Coleman in his essay, or constrain individual cultural freedom to be different, he maintains, "Rights can be protected if communitarian virtues include tolerance for one another and, above all, a clear demarcation of the areas that deservedly lie in the public realm and those that ought to be left to individual choice and subgroup preferences." Moreover, Etzioni stresses that "nothing makes for more government and ultimate coercion . . . than the absence of shared morals, backed by strong commitments." To the degree that society lacks shared virtues, the maintenance of civic order must depend more and more on compulsion and coercion by the state. Turning the liberal objection on its head, Etzioni maintains that it is precisely strong collective (consensual) moral foundations that limit state intervention. These collective virtues also produce political legitimacy in a democracy "by providing . . . public accord about the nature of justice and the need for the public pursuit of the . . . common good."

In Chapter 5, Immanuel Wallerstein argues that from 1917 to 1989 the modern world-system was dominated by two rival, yet essentially similar, ideologies: Wilsonianism and Leninism. Both supported decolonization and saw national development as the key to integrating the periphery into the world-system. According to Wallerstein, the political practices of pro-American and pro-Soviet states were not that different: "Even when states had a multiparty system in formal terms, one party tended in reality to dominate the institutions and to be impervious to change of regime other than by military coup d'état." He finds the same picture of essential similarity in the importance placed on economic modernization in noncore countries within both the American and Soviet spheres of influence. Wallerstein goes on to argue that the consensus between Wilsonianism and Leninism on the importance of national economic development no longer holds, and this is so because of two developments: the revolution of 1968 and economic stagnation from 1970 to 1990. Because there are no real prospects of economic transformation in the periphery, the failure of Leninism has left Wilsonians "in a quandary," which, Wallerstein expects, will feature more dramatic North-South confrontations in the decades to come.

THE CONDITIONS OF DEMOCRACY

One of the richest and most important currents in Lipset's work has concerned the conditions of the democratic order. Very few contributions on this theme have proven more seminal and durable over time than his 1959 article in the *American Political Science Review,* "Some Social Requisites of Democracy: Economic Development and Political Legitimacy" (republished in *Political Man* as "Economic Development and Democracy"). As Larry Diamond demonstrates in Chapter 6 of this volume, Lipset's assertion of a direct relationship

between economic development and democracy has been subjected to extensive empirical examination, both quantitative and qualitative, in the last 30
years. And the evidence shows, with striking clarity and consistency, a strong
causal relationship between economic development and democracy. The relationship is not as linear as Lipset implied. It has been subject to weakening or
reversal at middle levels of development. But across a wide range of studies,
with a great variety of samples, time periods, and statistical methods, the level
of economic development—or, as Diamond has slightly reformulated it, the
level of "human development"—continues to be the single most powerful
predictor of the likelihood of democracy. Moreover, there is much historical
evidence to support Lipset's hypotheses about the causal dynamics involved:
that development promotes democracy by generating more democratic values
and attitudes, a less polarized class structure, a larger middle class, and a more
vigorous, autonomous associational life. It is these intervening variables,
Diamond shows in his reexamination both of Lipset's theory and of the
evidence, that hold the key to developing stable democracy.

   In Chapter 3, Gary Marks analyzes the transition from an authoritarian to a
more liberal regime in terms of strategic interaction between the ruling elite
and its political opposition. In contrast to correlative approaches in which
democratization is viewed as a probabilistic function of independent variables,
Marks argues that there is a region of indeterminacy in political change where
choices of key political actors are dependent on their perceptions of other
actors' strategic intentions. In the model Marks describes, regime change
depends on strategic interactions that are extremely sensitive to exogenous
factors, such as the death of a political leader or a revolution in a neighboring
state that may accentuate divisions within the ruling elite or galvanize protest
against the regime. Regime change, in Marks's view, is subject to the butterfly
effect noted in chaos theory: Very small variations in initial conditions may
have disproportionately large effects. Hence it is inappropriate to theorize
about democratization, or regime change in general, in terms of statements
having the form, "If $X_1, X_2, \ldots X_n$ then this probability of Y." Marks argues
that indeterminacy in political change does not result from the inadequacy of
our present state of knowledge, but is an inherent feature of certain kinds of
strategic interaction among actors whose choices are influenced by their anticipation of the choices of others.

   In addition to these essays, three others in this collection address aspects of
Lipset's work on the conditions of democracy. Taking up the problem of one
of Lipset's earliest and most celebrated works, *Union Democracy* (Lipset, Trow,
& Coleman, 1956), Maurice Zeitlin and his former student Judith Stepan-Norris,
in Chapter 12, challenge the notion, going back to Robert Michels, that there is
an ineluctable tendency toward oligarchy in labor unions. While they draw on
particular hypotheses put forward by Lipset, Trow, and Coleman, they do not
share the view that democracy in a labor union is an exceptional phenomenon
demanding treatment as a "deviant case." Instead of searching for functional
conditions of democracy, Zeitlin and Stepan-Norris inquire into the kinds of

political struggles that promote constitutional provisions establishing basic democratic political rights. Based upon a comparison of formal constitutions and political developments in CIO international unions in the 1940s, they find that the level of union democracy is influenced by the intensity of political struggle within the union, particularly in its founding period. Generally speaking, the stronger the internal factionalism within a union, the greater its level of constitutional democracy. Democracy tends to be stronger in unions that originated as amalgams of disparate, or even hostile, groupings rather than as unitary organizations incorporating new members, and in unions that were created from the bottom up by the efforts of independent grass-roots organizers rather than from the top down by a centralized CIO committee. Zeitlin and Stepan-Norris conclude, in Lipsetian fashion, that democracy and political conflict are symbiotically related, for, in the context of labor unions, "insurgency and democracy are inseparable."

In Chapter 7, Carlos Waisman analyzes a different problem in the relationship between economic structure and democracy—the role of capitalism, and of the specific *form* of capitalism. His concern is with the effects on democracy of a capitalist system in which private property coexists with severe impediments to the operation of the market, as a result of a highly protectionist strategy of industrialization. This constricted, "autarkic" form of capitalism gave rise to political polarization, crisis, and democratic breakdown in Argentina, Uruguay, and Chile, because it produced economic stagnation (after an initial period of "easy" growth) and highly mobilized, rent-seeking classes with a strong interest in preserving noncompetitive, protected industries. By identifying market orientation—specifically, openness to international economic competition—as an important structural condition of democracy, Waisman adds significantly to our understanding of the relationship between capitalism and democracy. By illuminating the long-term historical impact on democratic legitimacy of economic stagnation and consequent political polarization, he reinforces Lipset's arguments about the impacts of economic performance and cleavage structure on the legitimacy and stability of democracy.

Reflecting on his own reactions as a student to Lipset's "Party Systems and the Representation of Social Groups" (published in revised version in *The First New Nation*), Philippe Schmitter turns to the question of how the representation of social groups shapes the consolidation of new democracies. In the spirit of Lipset's concern in that essay for the consequences of alternative institutional arrangements, Schmitter argues, "The core of the consolidation dilemma lies in coming up with a set of institutions that politicians can agree upon and citizens are willing to support." But the consequential institutions do not involve only constitutional structures and party and electoral systems. Parties, Schmitter suggests, are today less central to the representation of interests than they were in the past. Interest associations and social movements have increased in importance, and therefore the rules structuring their involvement in the polity become a crucial issue in the contemporary process of democratic consolidation. Democratic regimes must be disaggregated analytically into "partial regimes" of governance and conflict resolution. These constitute many different types of democracy. The nature of the "representation regime"—how class, sectoral, and professional associations are structured and related to the structures of political power—will significantly affect the type and quality of democracy that emerges.

The declining centrality of political parties is one of several elements of change in democracies that concern Juan Linz in Chapter 9 of this volume. While the end of ideology strengthens the democratic prospect by eliminating rival legitimating formulas and by reducing political polarization, it also weakens democratic functioning by accentuating the decline of political parties. In the future, Linz believes, individuals moved by ideas are more likely to become mobilized by single-issue movements or "by a diffuse hostility to politics." The erosion of class barriers and the multiplication of interests in society reinforce this trend because they break down the traditional social bases of parties and increase the salience of cultural, life-style, and age-related issues. Political parties are less able to articulate coherent, sharply distinctive programs as interests become increasingly fluid and complex.

As Schmitter also observes, these various changes "are not all negative," but they will have sweeping implications for the ways that democracies function and legitimate themselves: for the recruitment of political candidates, the formation of policies, and the personalization and professionalization of politics (trends that William Schneider also addresses in his essay on U.S. politics). Some innovations could be dangerous, as may be the case (ironically) with the internal democratization of nongovernment institutions, which could "introduce into previously nonpolitical settings . . . the conflicts of the larger society," as Linz puts it. Urging us to pay closer attention to the varieties of democracy and the ways they function, Linz proposes a rich agenda for systematic cross-national research on a number of issues that determine the quality of democratic governance: the tensions and trade-offs between independent representation and party cohesion and discipline; the political impact of different electoral cycles; the values, attitudes, professional motivations, social ties, role conflicts, and coping mechanisms of today's politicians; and the sources of growing public cynicism with politics—"the confidence gap"—which, again, occupies a central place in Schneider's analysis of U.S. politics in Chapter 15. Such comparative analysis is crucial, Linz suggests, not only for improving democracy but for achieving a realistic understanding of the limits of various types of democracies, and thereby perhaps mitigating the potential for disillusionment with democracy.

AMERICAN EXCEPTIONALISM

From the time of his Ph.D. dissertation and first published book, *Agrarian Socialism: The Cooperative Commonwealth Federation in Saskatchewan* (Lipset, 1950/1971), which compared the contrasting experiences of left radicalism in Saskatchewan and the U.S. Northwest, to his forthcoming book reevaluating the reasons for the weakness of socialism in the United States (Lipset & Marks, in press), Seymour Martin Lipset has sought to explain the unique character of American politics. This project has led him to work on a range of topics, including the U.S. Constitution, political parties and electoral systems, federalism, labor unions, academic and student politics, culture, religion, law and crime, welfare, immigration, and literature, to name just a few. Marty Lipset's writings in these areas have been immensely influential, and he is sensibly regarded as a full-fledged Americanist as well as a comparativist, though he has done as much as any scholar to break down the boundary between these subfields.

Three basic themes are interwoven throughout Lipset's work on U.S. politics and society. First, he has consistently elaborated the view that the United States is exceptional, even among the English-speaking settler societies. The most striking evidence of this can be seen in the unique absence in this country of a socialist or labor party, the relative weakness of class consciousness and labor organization, and the relative paucity of welfare provision. These are topics that Lipset has explored in detail in many publications spanning the last four decades. Among these writings are some justly famous and much-cited works, including *The First New Nation* (1963/1979) and *Continental Divide* (1990), and lesser-known gems such as "Why No Socialism in the United States?" (1977).

A second theme underlying Lipset's writing is that values are a critical source of variation in national behavior. Lipset has always been extremely sensitive to the need to develop multicausal explanations for complex social phenomena, and his explanations of American exceptionalism stress a range of political variables, including characteristics of the U.S. political system and political leadership, alongside such social variables as societal stratification and immigration. At the same time, however, Lipset has given special attention to the role of culture, tracing the exceptional strength of individualism, antistatism, and egalitarianism in the United States to the country's founding period.

Third, virtually all of Lipset's writings on the United States are motivated by the conviction that an understanding of American politics and society involves a comparative perspective, which is best pursued by relating the United States to countries with which it has the most in common—that is, English-speaking developed countries, particularly Canada. As Lipset (1990) concludes in his most recent book, *Continental Divide: The Values and Institutions of the United States and Canada*: "Canadians and Americans will never be alike, but Americans can learn more about Canada, and Canadians can learn more about why Americans are as they are. And by so doing they will come to understand their own countries better" (p. 227).

These themes are variously taken up in the chapters in this volume by Theda Skocpol, Martin Trow, Amos Perlmutter, Ann Swidler, and William Schneider. Theda Skocpol reassesses the U.S. pattern of social policy, arguing that while social security provision was relatively late and weak, some aspects of welfare provision, particularly for women (and children), were relatively early and comprehensive. In place of the characterization of the United States as a "welfare state laggard," Skocpol argues that from 1900 to the 1920s "America came close to creating a pioneering maternalist welfare state." To explain this, Skocpol explores the influence of the peculiarly fragmented American state in setting institutional limits for social provision and in providing opportunities for collective action and political alliances among social groups. Here, Skocpol makes the telling point that the early extension of the franchise to all white males—but not to women—weakened working-class organization *and* created sharper gender-based lines of political differentiation than in any other industrialized society. On the one hand, working-class demands for a comprehensive regime of public social provision were weak; on the other, women reacted strongly against their political exclusion, and were able to gain some impressive maternal welfare provisions.

In Chapter 13, Martin Trow observes that mass education in the United States has reflected and reinforced individualism by providing plentiful opportunity for individual advancement. The ethos of education is "Rise out of your class, not with it," and, Trow stresses, this makes it diametrically opposed to socialism, trade unionism, and, indeed, any collectivist movement in which the life chances of an individual are tied to those of the group as a whole. Trow goes on to shed light on some of the direct and indirect links between the relatively early and broad development of education in the United States and the exceptional weakness of socialist and union movements. The negative relationship between these social phenomena is particularly evident in the period since World War II, which has seen college enrollment increase from 1.5 to 14 million and the level of union membership drop by more than half. In the final section of his chapter, Trow argues that the recent innovation of affirmative action challenges individualism in education by giving priority to racial identity. He warns of the creation of racially based group identities in education that are more inflexible than previous ethnic or class identities.

Amos Perlmutter, in Chapter 10, compares the principles of foreign policy in the United States and Israel in the periods following their independence. Although the two countries differ in many respects, not least in size and population, Perlmutter emphasizes that they share some exceptional characteristics bearing on foreign policy. Both countries saw themselves as exceptional societies that would serve as havens for persecuted people. Regimes in both countries had their origins in a revolutionary outlook: the United States as a liberal republic based on eighteenth-century republican antimonarchism, and Israel, 160 years later, as a republic based on socialism. Consequently, the foreign policies of both countries were profoundly influenced by moral precepts. However, as Perlmutter shows, ideology was pursued in the context of pragmatic concerns. In the United States, Jeffersonian and Hamiltonian approaches to foreign policy agreed on the desirability of neutrality, though they interpreted it differently and shared the goal of territorial expansion pursued through traditional power politics. Through the 1940s the major Zionist group, Mapai, and later Israel itself, pursued a policy of neutrality between the United States and the Soviet Union that reflected both principles of nonidentification and practical concerns, until in the early 1950s it became clear that Israel's future lay in closer relations with the West.

In Chapter 14, Ann Swidler reexamines the causal underpinnings of conti-nuity in American values. She offers three thought-provoking explanations for the persistence of egalitarianism and individual achievement emphasized by Lipset in *The First New Nation* and subsequent writings. First, American values may persist as a distinct national identity that continually reemerges in accounts of U.S. relations with other states. From this perspective, the events of the founding of the United States, as emphasized by Lipset, are important because they initially dramatized a national myth that defined how the national com-munity was distinctive. A second approach is to argue that durable institutions have continually re-created American values. Although Swidler is skeptical of "recurrent experience" explanations such as immigration, the frontier, or mo-bility, because of the diversity of experiences across individuals and through time, certain institutional realities have been extremely durable. The United States has always been exceptional by virtue of its decentralized institutions. This is true in education (as Martin Trow observes), in religion, and in politics generally (as Theda Skocpol and William Schneider both observe, in different ways). As a result, most Americans have a deep-seated sense that life chances are dependent on individual exertion and that "status-group competition is not unified and hierarchical, but multiplex and open." Finally, unique American values may be explained in terms of the persistence of collectively established ways of organizing action. Even though their experiences vary, Americans continue to view the individual as the subject and the object of social change. Swidler interprets this belief as a myth, a society's way of organizing the sacred, that provides a paradigm for collective action in a way that is relatively invulnerable to individual disconfirmation. By posing difficult questions about causality and developing some interesting lines of explanation, Swidler adds significantly to our understanding of American values.

In Chapter 15, an analysis of the recent attack on professionalism in U.S. politics, William Schneider identifies a tension in American values between the devotion to democratic principles and the increasing cynicism Americans feel about politicians and elected governments. This "confidence gap"—which was first documented in the widely celebrated book of that title by Lipset and Schneider (1983)—places "politician" (along with "business and labor leader") among the least trusted and respected professions. This is nothing new, as Schneider's time-series data show, but public cynicism concerning government and politicians has reached historic proportions in recent years. Voter disgust with incumbent politicians of both parties is increasingly manifest in the 1991 election results, in the growing movement for statutory limits on the terms of elected legislators, and in the widespread conviction that the Congress "can't get anything done." Rising voter anger is not merely cyclical, Schneider argues, but the product of long-term trends in American public life. Politics has become more personalized, less substantive, and government and politicians have lost credibility. As Linz also observes in this volume, parties are declining, and politicians have gone "into business for themselves," marketing their person-alities rather than their principles and beliefs. The consequences, according to

Schneider, have been "rampant careerism, the need for huge amounts of money to market the image, and the increasing power of special interests," all of which lead to negative campaigning and voter cynicism. The very need that Linz observes for some kind of balance between independent representation and party cohesion is lost, as politicians "become a core of individualist professionals focused on their own careers and goals." While these features of American politics—fierce individualism, suspicion of power—might be regarded as a part of the American character, they represent in their current incarnation a serious deterioration in the quality of democratic governance, in the capacity of democratic institutions "to solve policy problems." And this, in turn, generates other dangers for U.S. democracy, such as the illusory panacea of term limits and the antiestablishment populism of former Ku Klux Klan leader David Duke. The answer, argues Schneider, is to attack the real problem—uncompetitive elections—with campaign reforms that level the playing field between incumbents and challengers.

CONFLICT AND DEMOCRACY

Befitting his self-description as an "apolitical Marxist" as well as one deeply influenced by Tocqueville, Lipset has always had a profound appreciation of the importance of political conflict in democracy. In his efforts to comprehend the forces that shape regimes, he has analyzed the sources of a diverse array of conflicts, on both the left and the right (as well as in the center) of the political spectrum. Characteristically, his analysis of left voting in *Political Man* is subtitled "The Expression of the Democratic Class Struggle." Democracy, from this standpoint, facilitates—and constrains—conflicts that are an inherent feature of political life. It should be noted that Lipset maintains this perspective even in the context of predicting an "End of Ideology," by which he means a decline in the intensity of the traditional left-right cleavage, rather than the emergence of an overarching consensus on major economic or political issues, such as the distribution of wealth or the trade-off between economic growth and the quality of life.

The conceptualization of democracy as a means of channeling or structuring, not eradicating, conflict runs throughout this *Festschrift*. The contributors to this volume largely follow in the tradition of Lipset (and, before him, Tocqueville) in recognizing that "stable democracy requires the manifestation of conflict" and at the same time mechanisms to contain conflict and preserve social cohesion (Lipset, 1960/1981, p. 1). However, they disagree about the best means of institutionalizing conflict and about the right balance between conflict and consensus.

A number of the contributors to this book are concerned with the means for containing conflict or reducing its potential for intense polarization. This is the challenge that occupies Coleman in his search for an institutional arrangement to compensate and protect ethnic and other groups that find themselves in the position of a permanent minority. It motivates Etzioni's appeal for the importance of shared virtues to a democratic community. For Diamond, as for Lipset, it is precisely by reshaping the class structure and so mitigating the potential for conflict polarization that economic development contributes most significantly to democracy. Waisman's emphasis on the importance to democracy of an internationally open, market-oriented economy ultimately comes down to the same concern: reducing the proclivity to zero-sum class conflict and thus political polarization. For Schmitter, the increasing centrality of interest associations in modern democracy is significant in part because of their role in conflict mediation and resolution.

Linz welcomes to some extent the changes that are eroding the traditional bases for polarized conflict in party politics, but, like William Schneider for American politics, he is also concerned with the reverse side of the "balance"— the need for some clear lines of conflict in politics, and hence for political parties with some degree of programmatic coherence. Without such substantive, policy conflict, politics can descend, as Schneider maintains it has in the United States, into a miasma of individual political agendas that leave major problems unaddressed and voters cynical and disillusioned.

Strom sees competition—that is, structured conflict between political parties—as the core ingredient of democracy. Marks considers the conflict between an authoritarian regime and its opposition, and their interactive evaluation of the costs of toleration versus suppression (for the regime) and of compliance versus challenge (for the opposition), to be the critical variable underlying transitions to democracy. Skocpol maintains that conflict has been crucial in reshaping policy outcomes in American political development. Because class conflict was strongly inhibited by the pattern of U.S. state formation, and in particular by the early democratization of the franchise for white males, comprehensive public social provisions were not achieved; but because the political exclusion of women motivated a strong reaction on their part, American women were able to win significant provisions for maternal welfare. Zeitlin finds that the strength of democracy in individual American labor unions during the 1930s and 1940s is intimately linked to the institutionalization of factional conflict during their founding period.

The contributors to this *Festschrift* present a diverse array of foci and perspectives on democracy and society. Befitting the pluralism that Lipset has much embraced—not only in his scholarship and thinking but in his treatment of colleagues and students—no grand theme or conclusion runs through these essays. Each, however, reexamines an important aspect of the problem of democracy, challenging important assumptions along the way. In that sense, each is true to the spirit of Lipset's enormous contribution to scholarship.

REFERENCES

Freedom House. (1991). *Freedom in the world: Political rights and civil liberties 1990-1991.* New York: Author.

Huntington, S. P. (1991). *The third wave: Democratization in the late twentieth century.* Norman: University of Oklahoma Press.

Lipset, S. M. (1959). Some social requisites of democracy: Economic development and political legitimacy. *American Political Science Review, 53,* 69-105.

Lipset, S. M. (1971). *Agrarian socialism: The Cooperative Commonwealth Federation in Saskatchewan* (rev. ed.). Berkeley: University of California Press. (Original work published 1950; first rev. ed. published 1968)

Lipset, S. M. (1977). Why no socialism in the United States? In S. Bialer & S. Sluzar (Eds.), *Sources of contemporary radicalism* (Vol. 1, pp. 31-149, 346-363). Boulder, CO: Westview.

Lipset, S. M. (1979). *The first new nation: The United States in historical and comparative perspective.* New York: Norton. (Original work published 1963)

Lipset, S. M. (1981). *Political man: The social bases of politics* (2nd ed.). Baltimore: Johns Hopkins University Press. (Original work published 1960)

Lipset, S. M. (1990). *Continental divide: The values and institutions of the United States and Canada.* New York: Routledge.

Lipset, S. M., & Marks, G. (in press). *Why is there no socialism in the United States? A comparative perspective.* Cambridge, MA: Belknap.

Lipset, S. M., & Schneider, W. (1983). *The confidence gap: Business, labor and government in the public mind.* New York: Free Press.

Lipset, S. M., Trow, M. A., & Coleman, J. S. (1956). *Union democracy: The internal politics of the International Typographical Union.* New York: Free Press.

PART I

THEORETICAL
PERSPECTIVES

1

Democracy in
Permanently Divided Systems

James S. Coleman

STRUCTURAL CLEAVAGE

I N studying the history of the International Typographical Union (ITU), Seymour Martin Lipset discovered a structural change in the ITU. The union, which at that time (1949) was composed only of compositors and mailers, had not always been so. Around the end of the nineteenth century, the union was composed of a number of printing trades, including printing pressmen, bookbinders, photoengravers, stereotypers, electrotypers, type founders, and mailers, along with the compositors, who were in the majority. One by one, these minority crafts seceded from the ITU. Only the mailers, who were much lower paid, and whose union if alone would have been quite weak, remained within the ITU.

As Lipset points out in his account of the historical description of the ITU in *Union Democracy* (Lipset, Trow, & Coleman, 1956, chaps. 2, 3), the existence of the separate crafts created a structural problem in a highly democratic union, in which many decisions were made by referendum. The crafts constituted distinct subgroups in the ITU, with differing interests, all relatively fixed in size and with permanent membership. Many of the democratically decided actions involved these subgroup interests. Because the compositors were in the majority, the other crafts would be outvoted, and their interests would be ignored.

In an attempt to hold these crafts within the ITU, each craft was given a vice presidency, thus representing the craft's interests in the union's executive. However, because a large fraction of policies of the ITU were made through direct referendum, the numerical superiority of the compositors continued to lead to decisions that ignored other crafts' interests.

The structural problem of the ITU can be seen vividly in contemporary political upheavals. So long as Yugoslavia was under Tito's rule, the republics remained united. Since Tito, the movement toward democratic rule has been accompanied by extensive strife between Serbia, in a majority, and Croatia and Slovenia, permanent minorities in Yugoslavia as a whole.

More generally, two sorts of events are creating the problem of structural cleavage in democratic systems: the integration of the European Community in 1992 to create a supranational economic and political system, and the emergence of Eastern Europe and the Soviet Union as democratically oriented political entities free from the yoke of communism.

These two events create difficult problems for the design of political institutions. In the area of social choice, regarded broadly, the most serious of these problems is that of taking action decisively without fragmenting. This problem can be seen in the difficulty of bringing the federation of countries that constitute the European Community into being as a federation that can act. The problem can also be seen in the challenges to nation-states by the ethnic, cultural, and linguistic enclaves within them, challenges in countries as differently organized as Canada and the Soviet Union.

VOTING BY CLASS

Various approaches have been used to address the problems created by rigid and permanent structural cleavages in democratically governed systems. One is voting by class. An example is the governance structure of German universities instituted by legislatures following the student uprisings of 1968. In different *Länder,* the systems differed somewhat, but they all had the following character: Voting was specified to be by class, with three classes designated— professors, assistants, and students. Each class had a specified proportion of the total representation in the university's governing body, for example, in some *Länder,* 1/3, 1/3, 1/3. This voting by classes seems quite natural, whereas it would seem quite unnatural to have voting in any way other than by classes. But natural or not, voting by classes raises a question of principle: What is the principle that leads to voting by classes?

A mental experiment can suggest something about the principle: Suppose the number of students dwindled by half; should the representation of students be reduced by half? Suppose the number of students doubled; should the representation of students be doubled? Most of us would answer no in both cases; it seems appropriate that the representation of students, professors, and assistants be independent of the numbers of each, but instead dependent on something about the roles or functions that students, professors, and assistants play in the university. In effect, the imagery that seems appropriate in this case is that of a system with functionally differentiated parts, not the imagery of a population of citizens, each with the same citizen rights. Each part should have a voice in determining the direction of the system, independent of the number of persons who occupy that part.

Voting by class, however, seems suited only for sociopolitical systems in which there are functionally differentiated parts, such as a university, or some other type of formal organization. For German and Scandinavian business corporations, for example, codetermination laws have created systems of democratic governance in which shareholders, managers, and nonmanagement employees are treated as distinct classes in election of representatives to a governing board. Such systems cannot, however, solve the problem of rigid and permanent cleavages among functionally similar subgroups, as among crafts in the ITU or republics in Yugoslavia. In such settings, a permanent majority can exercise permanent oppression of the minority.

DEVOLUTION OF DECISIONS

One possible direction is suggested by looking for patterns that have evolved in nation-states that have two or more linguistic subgroups. There are many, but I will consider only Switzerland, with four linguistic groups, Belgium with two, and Canada with two. Switzerland has had a long history of stability and successful democracy, despite its fulfilling all the conditions for majority oppression of the minority and for secession. The linguistic subgroups are nearly territorially distinct and thus without constraints on secession. Furthermore, the German-speaking portion of Switzerland contains a majority of the population, so the potential for tyranny of the majority is as great as for the ITU described earlier.

The apparent means by which Switzerland has avoided the degeneracy of fragmentation and secession is through localization of many decisions at the level of the canton. Switzerland is a federation of cantons, which share some policies but are independent with respect to many others. Throughout Switzerland's history, it was never more than a federation, never under a single ruler. Thus devolution of decisions from a single center was never necessary.

Belgium and Canada have not been so successful. Both have been marked by internal strife between linguistic groups: the French and English in Canada, and the French and Flemish in Belgium. Both have been under central rule, and the existence of a strong central government has created conflict initiated by minority citizens who feel oppressed: the French Quebecoise in Canada, and the Flemish in Belgium (who, although in the numerical majority, have traditionally been a minority in political and economic power).

In both Canada and Belgium, the conflicts have led to what may be regarded as an evolutionary change: decentralization of many functions to local levels. This has given Quebec some measure of independence and has given greater autonomy to the Flemish, Walloon, and Brussels (mixed French and Flemish speaking) sections of Belgium. In the Soviet Union as well, the desperate moves to save the Union consisted of granting a large measure of autonomy to the republics. In the Soviet Union these moves were not successful, and whether the decentralization in Canada and Belgium will be successful in maintaining the nation-state remains to be seen. The Swiss example suggests that, in principle, this can be an effective means for maintaining a linguistically heterogeneous state.

If these moves, and others like them, are successful, the direction they suggest is one in which the idea of the "nation-state" is separated into its two components, representing the two different bases of organization: the nation as a primordial group, grounded in ethnicity, religion, and language; and the state as a constructed social system, a federation of semisovereign nations. These two components of "nation" and "state" were never wholly compatible; the nation-state as a way of organizing the world may contain inherent instabilities when governance is democratic.

I have described one possible direction for constitutions of the 1990s confronted with a linguistically or ethnically heterogeneous state (such as Yugoslavia or Czechoslovakia) and for federations of nations, such as the European Community or the former Soviet Union. (It may well be that in 10 or 15 years, the European Community and the former Soviet republics will come to be very similar confederations, beginning from two very different starting points.) Under certain circumstances, however, the federal solution does not solve the problem. Consider Yugoslavia: The Croatians are restive under the dominance of Serbia and demand independence. But within Croatia is an enclave of Serbians, who in a sovereign or semisovereign Croatia become an oppressed minority. Similarly, in the republics of the Soviet Union, a deliberate policy of the Communists was to overcome ethnic homogeneity within a republic, by resettling Russians or other "foreign" ethnic groups in a republic. Thus devolution of decision-making power to the republics creates a new problem like the one it was designed to solve. This problem can be described as the problem of inherently heterogeneous states: states with rigid and encompassing cleavages among groups that are so territorially enmeshed that decentralization of decisions cannot eliminate the cleavage.

THE GENERAL WILL
VERSUS A CLASH OF INTERESTS

There is a view of democracy that contrasts greatly with that implicit in the introduction of structure exemplified by class voting or decentralized decision making. This is the idea that there is a single unitary system, that there is an objectively correct action for this system to take, and that democratic decision making is the process of discovering this action. This view arose at the time of the French Revolution. A central issue of the revolution was the demand for replacing the voting by estates in the national assembly with voting by head, in which each delegate's vote would count equally. Underlying this demand was the idea that, following Rousseau, there was a "general will," and that the task of collective decision making was to discover the general will.

The practical question of how to discover the general will was addressed by others deeply involved in the activities of the times, with procedures for voting and for aggregating votes into a decision of the collectivity. The work of two of these theorists, Jean Charles de Borda and the Marquis de Condorcet, has survived. Borda's solution was to have each individual rank the outcomes, to give numbers to the rankings, add up the numbers, and choose that outcome whose summed ranks placed it in first position. This is known today as the Borda count for arriving at a social choice.

The contribution of Condorcet (who wrote the first constitution of the Revolution and was later imprisoned and killed by that Revolution) is more diversified and more theoretically consistent with the idea of a general will waiting to be discovered. Condorcet found that with pairwise comparisons of alternatives, selecting a winner in each comparison could lead not to a simple order of outcomes with the overall winner at the top, but to a cycle, in which outcome A defeats B, outcome B defeats C, but outcome C defeats A. This is the Condorcet paradox, a problem that has led to an enormous body of work designed to find a solution for the paradox. One solution is that of Condorcet himself, and the rationale behind the solution shows its close correspondence to the Rousseauian idea of the general will. Condorcet's solution was to break the cycle at the weakest link. (For example, if A defeated B by five votes, B defeated C by three votes, and C defeated A by seven votes, then the cycle would be broken at the "B defeats C" link, resulting in C defeats A, who defeats B.) The rationale behind this solution was a rationale of "minimizing errors" in identifying the general will. Condorcet's solution assumes with Rousseau that there is an objectively correct outcome of the collectivity, that the aim of the casting of votes is to discover the objectively correct outcome, and that each voter in casting a vote is judging what outcome is correct.

The contrast between this conception of democratic decision making and that based on cleavages among interest groups can be seen in Ostrogorski's (1902/1964) characterization of democracy in Britain and democracy in the United States. Democracy in Britain, as he saw it, was democracy in which two subgroups within a governing class projected somewhat different views of the future path of the country. The voting population, consisting not only of the governing class but of those who would be governed, selected between these views. The principle by which the governing class functioned was the principle of noblesse oblige, the idea of serving selflessly for the good of the country as a whole. Political parties differed only in their beliefs about what was best for the country as a whole. Leaders of both parties saw themselves as administering to the interests of all segments of society, to the common interest. The system could be seen as a democratic extension of an aristocratic system, with many of the characteristics of an aristocracy. One might call it a patrician democratic system. Obviously, Ostrogorski's characterization of British democracy is only relative; since the time of the early Whigs and Tories, reflecting the landed gentry and urban business, the parties have differed in the groups they attracted and thus in the interests they reflected.

Ostrogorski found a different conception of democracy in the United States. Here was a clash of interests. Different factions were distinguished by their differing interests. Party platforms and candidates' positions were expressed in terms of the interests of particular subgroups in the country. There was no governing class, no conception of noblesse oblige. In their place was a contest between interests, with the outcome of the contest depending on which interest, or coalition of interests, was stronger. This form of democracy has nothing in common with aristocracy. One might call it an interest-based democratic system.

IS VOTING APPROPRIATE IN INTEREST-BASED DEMOCRACY?

The casting of votes may be seen as appropriate for discovery of the general will, but in permanently divided systems, in which there are rigid divisions without cross-cutting cleavages, a different means of making decisions democratically may be more workable. One such means is suggested by a principle introduced by Nicholas Kaldor (1939), a British economist. Economists were engaged in a debate over whether it was possible to decide whether a policy was economically beneficial for a country when that policy benefited some and hurt others. The debate was carried on by use of an example: repeal of the Corn Laws in Britain, which provided tariff protection for grain producers. The question was whether an economist could give a policy prescription, to the effect that repeal of the Corn Laws would make the country better off or would not. Roy Harrod (1938), an economist, argued that because the gain to the community as a whole would exceed the loss to the grain producers, repeal of the tariff was beneficial, even though some would experience a loss. He held that the economist must carry out an interpersonal comparison of utility, balancing the interests of those who gain against those who lose, and counting each equally. Lionel Robbins (1938), on the other hand, argued that such interpersonal comparison was invalid, because there were no economic processes through which the comparison occurs. No inference was possible by the economist about which policy was better, because some gained at the expense of others, and one person's losses could not be compared with another's gain. Note that this is exactly the situation of fixed and rigid cleavages; the economists were arguing whether under such circumstances, when some would be clearly hurt and others clearly benefited, social choice was possible.

In this setting, Kaldor (1939) proposed a way out by use of a "compensation principle." He pointed out that in considering whether to adopt a new economic policy or to retain the old, if the new policy were economically superior to the old, it would make some parties sufficiently better off that they could compensate those who were made worse off and still themselves be better off than before. If the policy would bring about an absolute economic gain, such compensation could in principle be paid so that everyone was at least as well off as before, and some were better off. If no such compensation were in principle possible, then the policy would be inferior to the status quo. Policies that met the criterion could be, if compensation were paid, Pareto optimal moves, but policies that did not meet the criterion could never be Pareto optimal.

Kaldor did not contemplate actual compensation to those who lost as a result of the policy; the principle served merely as a criterion for whether the policy was beneficial. More significant from the present perspective, no one has noted that compensation might be important for another reason: to prevent irreconcilable conflict that could divide the society. Another practical element was also neglected: Suppose, by application of Kaldor's compensation principle, it was clear that Britain would be better off if the Corn Laws were repealed. But suppose also that the grain producers were stronger politically than those who favored repeal, despite a greater efficiency if the tariff were repealed, that is, despite the fact that compensation could be paid to eliminate their losses. Then, unless there were a way for compensation to actually be paid, the Corn Laws would not be repealed, and Britain would remain worse off than if they were repealed.

Both of these problems would be overcome if compensation were actually carried out. First, consider legislation that was efficient—that is, the benefits to those who gain outweigh the losses to those who lose. In the case where those who would gain from the legislation were in control of the social choice, the requirement for compensation would reduce conflict and fragmentation and facilitate passage of other efficient legislation the losers might otherwise block. In the case where those who would lose from the legislation were in control of the social choice, then compensation would bring into being the legislation, which would otherwise fail. Now consider a case of legislation that was not efficient: The benefits to those who gain are less than the losses to those who lose. If those who would lose were in control, then, because sufficient compensation could not be paid, the legislation would fail as it should. But if those who would gain were in control of the social choice, then the potential losers would pay sufficient compensation to bring about defeat of the legislation, which would otherwise pass despite its inefficiency.

What Kaldor's idea suggests more generally is that there may be an avenue toward elimination of a fundamental problem of democracies: oppression of the minority by the majority. If the winners in a legislative action were required to compensate the losers, then there would be no true losers; if an action had sufficient power behind it to pass, compensation would result in it being favored by all. If no pattern of compensation could lead all to favor it, this would indicate that the action did not have more support than the status quo.

This implies that with compensation, a legislative action should be required to pass with unanimity. Only those actions that pass the unanimity test are certain to be an improvement over the status quo. Such reasoning, or reasoning very allied to it, was the basis of an argument at the turn of the century by Knut Wicksell (1896/1958) concerning legislation for taxation. Wicksell argued that every public service to be financed by taxation should be voted on in the same legislative action as the taxation to pay its cost. Unanimous approval would be required; if a given distribution of the tax burden did not secure unanimous approval, then a portion of the tax on those who opposed it should be shifted to those who favored it. If the service-and-tax was socially beneficial, then some distribution of taxation could be found that would gain unanimous approval. Absence of unanimous approval would mean that there was more interest opposed to the action than there was favoring it, and it should thus not be enacted.

Wicksell's proposal was never put into effect because of some obvious defects, such as the incentive not to cast a sincere vote but to understate one's interest in the public service in order to shift the tax burden to others. Nonetheless, the principle has from the beginning been seen as an appropriate principle for balancing costs and benefits when they are unequally distributed among persons.

Kaldor's compensation principle can be seen as a generalization of Wicksell's taxation principle. In Wicksell's principle, the costs and benefits are contained in the same legislative action, and the only balancing occurs through redistributing the costs contained in the act. Kaldor compensation is applicable to legislative acts in which some persons experience only benefits, others experience only costs, and possibly some experience both. Any redistribution of benefits is outside the act itself, away from those who are benefited by the act toward those who are harmed by it.

However, if such redistribution is to occur voluntarily, there must be some means by which legislators who want to get legislation passed can shift benefits from their own constituents to others in order to gain their support. When we look at legislatures empirically, we find that something very much like this already happens for certain types of legislation. For legislation that benefits one district or a few specific districts, such as locating government facilities in a particular district, there has long been "logrolling," in which legislators agree to vote for projects in each others' districts. In a legislature with majority rule, it is necessary to get such agreements covering half the legislators' districts, for half is sufficient to secure passage of the legislation. But, as Buchanan and Tullock (1962) point out, this does not ensure, as Wicksell's taxation principle or Kaldor's compensation does, that the legislation is socially beneficial. The majority who are benefited by getting projects that benefit constituents of all funded projects can exploit the minority, who get no projects but bear a portion of the costs.

An extension of logrolling is carried out in the Congress of the United States through creation of a very large "omnibus bill" containing many projects, each of interest to one or a few specific constituencies. Packaged together in a single bill, the Kaldor (or Wicksell) efficiency criterion would be satisfied if the decision rule were unanimity. But when the decision rule is majority, the efficiency criterion is not satisfied, and a minority can be exploited. Again, our interest here in these criteria is not in order to ensure that only economically efficient legislation passes; it is to overcome the problems of tyranny of the majority, fragmentation, conflict, and impasse in social choice.

Logrolling and omnibus bills are not the only instances in which legislators whose constituencies would gain by legislation shift benefits from their own constituents to others in order to gain passage of the legislation. It is sometimes the case that legislation to remove tariffs on agricultural products is accompanied by a payment of some sort (for example, payment to keep land out of production) to farmers who would lose by the tariff removal. Another even more frequent example is something like the omnibus bill: When the original legislation would benefit only a minority, amendments are added to the bill that extend the benefits (at a cost to all, including the original beneficiaries) to cover a majority sufficient to secure passage of the legislation.

However, despite the fact that legislatures tend to carry out those transactions that overcome inaction and reduce conflict that would lead to impasse, these transactions can just as easily lead away from efficient legislation as toward it, and toward conflict rather than away. A major reason for these consequences is the majority decision rule, which means that compensation need be paid not to all but only to a majority, which is sufficient for passage. The result is both majority tyranny over the minority and legislative outcomes that are inefficient. A second reason these transactions involving legislation are defective is that compensation must be contained in legislation; it cannot be paid outside the legislative decisions themselves. Despite this, legislators attempt to create currency to facilitate these transactions, particularly through the use of a kind of credit system: "I will support you on this bill, but I want you to remember it later in the legislative session when I expect to have legislation for which I will need support." This sort of negotiation is less frequent in a parliamentary system than in a congressional one; however, it can be expected to be quite important in the parliament of the European Community, where the relevant actors in many cases will be the country delegations.

DEMOCRACY WITHOUT VOTES

Negotiation of the sort that will prove necessary in the European Community, in democratic states with permanent and rigid cleavages—such as Yugoslavia, Canada, Belgium, and Israel—and in the reconstituted Soviet Union may be facilitated by collective decision making that does not have votes at all. First, consider that each legislator is provided not with a vote on each issue as it arises but with an account of "political money," which I will give a name: not dollars, pounds, or Deutschmarks, but "kaldors," after the inventor of the compensation principle. The kaldors in a legislator's account are fungible; they can be used on any legislation as it arises. As a bill arises, each legislator places a "bid" in kaldors on that legislation, pro or con. After all bidding is in, the bill passes if more kaldors have been bid positively than negatively; it fails otherwise. If the bill passes, those who bid against it are compensated, each by the number of kaldors bid. Compensation is paid from the bids of the winners. If the bill fails, compensation occurs in the reverse direction. Thus the winning of a desired outcome on that legislation is at a cost to the winners of depleting their kaldor accounts, whereas the losers have increments to their accounts. The incentive of all is to bid exactly in accord with their individual interests (or, if they want to risk a utility loss, to bid higher than that amount if they expect to be on the losing side). The procedure is approximately incentive compatible, a term that implies no one has an incentive to misstate his or her interests.

With such accounts of political money, legislators who represent minority interests would not be subject to continual oppression from the majority. By building up their accounts on issues in which they have some interest and bid those interests but lose, they come to be in a position to employ their kaldors, with a good likelihood that they will win, on issues on which they have very strong interests and the majority's interest is less strong. At some point in succession of actions, there will be an action in which their interests outweigh those of opponents in a numerical majority. With such a system of accounts, legislators who have accumulated kaldors will be able to express the intensity of those interests and obtain the outcome favoring them.

Something like this system of accounts has been described by Mueller, Tollison, and Willett (1974). So far as I know, no constitution has prescribed anything like this method of making social choices, and no legislative body has established rules of this sort. One possible reason is that there are biases against conceiving of social choices in terms of conflicting interests, biases that are particularly strong at the time of constitution construction. Constitutions are designed at a time when common interests are especially strong, favoring the "general will" conception of a democracy. They are designed by persons most likely to regard themselves as acting in the common interest and most likely to see themselves in the majority in future deliberations, both tendencies producing bias against a conflicting-interests conception of social choice. In addition, both at the time of constitutional design and later, the common-interest conception of a democracy is more socially acceptable than the conflicting-interests conception and thus more likely to be put forward.

Will democracy without voting, designed to facilitate decision making in systems with permanent majorities through compensation of the losers, be brought into being? Certainly the crude patterns of logrolling, omnibus bills, and compensatory amendments found in current legislation indicate the value of some institution other than voting with majority rule. Whether institutions incorporating the Kaldor principle will be brought into being remains to be seen.

REFERENCES

Buchanan, J., & Tullock, G. (1962). *The calculus of consent.* Ann Arbor: University of Michigan Press.

Harrod, R. F. (1938). Scope and method of economics. *Economics Journal, 48,* 383-412.

Kaldor, N. (1939). Welfare propositions of economics and interpersonal comparisons of utility. *Economics Journal, 49,* 549-552.

Lipset, S. M., Trow, M. A., & Coleman, J. S. (1956). *Union democracy: The internal politics of the International Typographical Union.* New York: Free Press.

Mueller, D. C., Tollison, R. D., & Willett, T. D. (1974). On equalizing the distribution of political income. *Journal of Political Economy, 82,* 414-422.

Ostrogorski, M. (1964). *Democracy and the organization of political parties.* Chicago: Quadrangle. (Original work published 1902)

Robbins, L. (1938). Inter-personal comparisons of utility. *Economics Journal, 48,* 635-641.

Wicksell, K. (1958). A new principle of just taxation. In R. A. Musgrave & A. T. Peacock (Eds.), *Classics in the theory of public finance* (pp. 72-118). New York: St. Martin's. (Original work published 1896)

2

Democracy as Political Competition

Kaare Strom

WHEN *Political Man* appeared more than three decades ago, it was instantly recognized as a seminal contribution to the study of the social preconditions of democracy. The topic was one of intense scholarly interest at the time, as well it should be at any time. But *Political Man* was more than a work of contemporary relevance; it was also a statement of personal concern. As Lipset (1981) points out, "the book illustrates my basic intellectual concerns and personal values more fully than my previous publications" (p. x). And the themes taken up in *Political Man* have made their mark on much of Lipset's subsequent scholarship as well.

Democracy and its preservation, then, were the concerns that motivated this work of comparative political sociology. Yet, for better or worse, *democracy* has come to mean many different things to a lot of different people. Several radically different models or conceptions have been developed, and this diversity of conceptions is also clearly reflected in the empirical literature on democracy's preconditions, on processes of transformation, and on democratic crises and breakdowns. These differences in conceptualization often have major and predictable implications for the analytical and normative conclusions that are drawn in the literature on contemporary democracies. The struggle over the definition of the "D word" has clearly been a battle in the war over our conception of the good society. And it was Lipset's role in this larger picture, as much as his empirical analysis of democracy's preconditions, that came to gain him a central place in the scholarly debate.

In Chapter 2 of *Political Man,* Lipset defines democracy as

a political system which supplies regular constitutional opportunities for changing the governing officials, and a social mechanism which permits the largest possible part of the population to influence major decisions by choosing among contenders for political office. (p. 27)

Lipset's conception focuses on contestation, or competition, for office as a key feature of democratic politics; as he has subsequently put it, elections express the "democratic class struggle." In thinking about democracy in these terms, Lipset (1981, p. 27) explicitly acknowledges his debt to Joseph Schumpeter. In standing in the Schumpeterian tradition, he was hardly alone. In another influential book in this tradition, Robert A. Dahl (1971) identifies competition, which he also refers to as public contestation, as one of the two defining properties of polyarchy (or democracy).

Influential as the Schumpeterian school was in the 1950s and 1960s, it was hardly uncontroversial. In the decades that followed, it came in for considerable criticism among students of democracy. The *competitive model of democracy,* with which Schumpeter was associated, became a favorite target for scholars committed to participatory, communitarian, or unitary democratic ideals. At the same time, Anthony Downs's (1957) *An Economic Theory of Democracy* became an increasingly important focal point for those interested in analytical results concerning political competition and democracy. With his more precise formulations and more rigorous results, Downs became a convenient benchmark for many of those who were interested in extending or criticizing the competitive model of democracy.

Despite the general interest in competitive democracy, however, discussions of political competition and its consequences generally have proceeded without a clear and explicit conception of their subject. Although political competition is frequently discussed, it is rarely defined with any precision. Hence it is unclear exactly what the competitive model (or models) of democracy implies.

In this analysis, I revisit the competitive model of democracy that informed the early work of Lipset and many others. I identify two different approaches within this tradition, represented by Downs and Schumpeter, respectively. After a discussion of the results, merits, and limitations of the Downsian and Schumpeterian models, I suggest an alternative conceptualization of political competition. This alternative conception, I maintain, owes much to Schumpeter and represents an attempt to reintroduce some of his most important concerns into the current debate. I will also show how this conception of political competition captures essential concerns in the recent literature on transitions to democracy and redemocratization. Thus the basic conception of democracy that motivated so much scholarship nearly a generation ago may well prove its relevance to contemporary concerns in political science. Before political competition can be reconceptualized, however, it behooves us to consider its place in the existing literature on democracy.

DEMOCRACY AS POLITICAL COMPETITION

Lipset's conception of democracy places him within a venerable tradition. The competitive model of democracy has been highly influential normatively and analytically during the post-World War II period. More precisely, we could call the competitive model of democracy a posttotalitarian conception, a reaction to Nazi and Stalinist brutalities of the 1930s and 1940s.

Competition and Political Parties

Because it characterizes a broad range of social interactions, competition is a fitting subject for the social sciences. But although political scientists, sociologists, and anthropologists so frequently refer to the effects of competition on their subject matters of choice, the analysis of competition clearly has been most rigorously developed in economics. Hence students of political competition have often borrowed extensively from the conceptual apparatus of economics (see Demsetz, 1982; Scott, 1970; Stigler, 1972).

Although competition affects a wide range of political actors and arenas, most of the interest among political scientists has focused on party system representation (see Ware, 1987). These are the institutions that guarantee popular rule. According to G. Bingham Powell (1982), "The competitive electoral context, with several political parties organizing the alternatives that face the voters, is the identifying property of the contemporary democratic process" (p. 3). Much of the literature on political parties and party systems shares this view of political competition. As David Robertson (1976) puts it, "To talk, today, about democracy, is to talk about a system of competing political parties" (p. 1). And in Giovanni Sartori's (1976) influential work, it is precisely interparty competition that defines the boundaries of democracy. Single-party authoritarianism begins "where competition ends" (p. 217).

Political competition is commonly taken to be a powerful determinant of party behavior. As Renate Mayntz (1961) puts it in her classic study of German party organization:

> Competition between rival parties is essential to a democratic political system. This competition is expected not only to stimulate political interest and a large election turn-out (something which a single party in a totalitarian country can also do), but it is also expected to stimulate citizens to make politically responsible choices. To be a serious rival force, able to compete successfully, every party must seek to be an effective organization. To this end, processes such as recruiting members, training officers, allocating tasks, and activities serving organizational maintenance must be sustained at significant levels. (p. 139)

This focus on political parties as the agents or vehicles of political competition is widespread in the literature and guides the presentation here.

The Downsian Model

Downs's work is particularly beholden to economic equilibrium analysis. Applying a rational-choice model of oligopolistic behavior, he derives his famous result that parties, in a two-party system with a one-dimensional issue space under complete information, will converge to the position of the median voter. In his simplest and most powerful model, the *median voter result* is the equilibrium outcome. Downs's median voter result has a number of implications that frequently have been taken as desirable properties of political competition.

Voter Effectiveness

The median voter result implies that any party that deviates ever so slightly from the ideal point of the median voter inevitably goes down to electoral defeat. If we accept the Downsian assumptions as a measure of electoral competitiveness, then perfect competitiveness implies that the voters are maximally effective vis-à-vis the parties. In other words, the parties will be perfectly constrained by the popular will. Downs thus offers us a model of perfectly responsive political parties.

Representativeness

The argument concerning representativeness is closely related to the previous point. If the distribution of voters along the left-right axis (or whatever interpretation we give Downs's unidimensional space) is symmetric (e.g., a normal distribution), then the median voter position will minimize the aggregate policy distance between the government and the voters.[1] Since both parties, and hence implicitly the government, converge to this position, the preferences of the electorate will thus be represented in the best possible way.[2] According to Downs, the *efficiency* of electoral representation is thus maximized. Of course, voters are in reality unlikely to be perfectly symmetrically distributed. If deviations from symmetry are small, however, the median voter position will still be a highly efficient representation of popular preferences.[3]

Nonexploitation

Exploitation here refers to the use by political leaders of their office for private gain (literally or figuratively) rather than for the pursuit of the public interest. The greater the competition for votes, the less opportunity party leaders will have to pursue their own interests (assuming that these are different from the preferences of the median voter). Voters will, according to Downs, base their electoral verdicts on the behavior of the parties in the near past (retrospective voting). Any party that in government offends even small groups of voters easily falls from grace.

Moderation

Assuming a plausible voter distribution, the median voter result implies that parties will be especially concerned with winning the support of centrist voters.

Therefore, it could be argued that Downs's model of competitive democracy ensures moderate parties and governments. At the very least, extremist parties and governments are unlikely. To the extent that political moderation is desirable, we find here another favorable consequence of Downsian party competition.

Continuity

Party convergence also implies policy continuity between successive governments, even if these are formed by different parties. This is because both parties converge in equilibrium and because this position tightly constrains their behavior in government. Hence all governments should pursue identical policies. The only cause of policy differences between governments would be changes in voter preferences over time.

The Schumpeterian Model

Writing at a time when democracy was gravely threatened, Schumpeter (1942/1987) set out to define a "realistic" and, in some sense, minimal conception of democracy. In Schumpeter's words, "the democratic method is that institutional arrangement for arriving at political decisions in which individuals acquire the power to decide by means of a *competitive struggle* for the people's vote" (p. 269; emphasis added). The Schumpeterian model of democracy can thus be characterized as *competitive elitism* (Held, 1987).

Schumpeter (1942/1987) wrote in large part in response to what he saw as the unrealistic expectations "classical" theorists of democracy had harbored concerning the role of ordinary citizens in the political process. In his view, extensive citizen participation was not only unlikely but even potentially quite dangerous.[4] Schumpeter saw the proper role of the ordinary citizen as much more circumscribed. The electorate must have a choice at regular intervals between at least two competing parties with different policy platforms.[5] Competitive elections, then, are the principal protective mechanism that allows voters to check the threat of tyranny.

Between elections, Schumpeter saw no active role for the electorate. This, he believed, is where "the classical doctrine" had gone wrong. This doctrine, which "realizes the common good by making the people itself decide issues through the election of individuals who are to assemble to carry out its will" (p. 250), is unrealistic for two fundamental reasons. First, ordinary citizens are not sufficiently informed and rational to carry out the tasks this model prescribes for them. This shortcoming stems not so much from the inherent imperfections of the human condition as from the fact that citizens very rarely are more than amateurs and part-time participants in politics. This lack of experience and professional training makes the classical doctrine of democracy a pie in the sky. Second, even if individual citizens were perfectly rational and informed, there would not necessarily be any way to aggregate their opinions

and interests into the "general will" presumed by Rousseau and other "classical" theorists of democracy. Here, of course, Schumpeter essentially anticipates
the impossibility theorems developed by Arrow (1951) and others in the social
choice tradition.

The task we can realistically expect ordinary citizens to perform, then, is no
more than to choose between competing teams of leaders, to "produce government." Yet it is important that this choice be as free and unrestricted as possible.
Democracy requires that everyone be "free to compete for leadership by
presenting himself to the electorate" (Schumpeter, 1942/1987, p. 272). Although political competition, like economic competition, may be far from
perfect, it is this mechanism that protects citizens from the potential tyranny
of their masters.

Schumpeter recognizes that his theory of democracy rests on a number of
preconditions. In order for this model of democracy to work, a number of
conditions must be fulfilled. First, the human material of politics, the caliber
of politicians, must meet certain standards of qualification and moral character.
Second, the effective range of political decisions should not be extended too
far. That is to say, political leaders must not exceed the competence of the
government or raise the stakes of the political game too high. Third, the
government must have at its disposal a professional and well-trained bureaucracy with a strong esprit de corps. Fourth, there must be "democratic self-con-
trol," that is, some deference by voters toward political leaders and by the
opposition toward the government. Elected representatives must be allowed to
be trustees rather than pure delegates, and the opposition must refrain from
pouncing on government embarrassments in a way that might discredit democracy. Finally, competitive democracy requires a large measure of tolerance for
differences of opinion (Schumpeter, 1942/1987, pp. 289-296).

Although these preconditions may be in keeping with the "realism" of the
Schumpeterian doctrine of democracy, they do restrict the applicability of his
model. Operationally, it may also be difficult to judge whether or not these
conditions are met in a given case. By introducing these concerns, Schumpeter
therefore complicates his case substantially.

THE CRITIQUE OF COMPETITIVE DEMOCRACY

Since its heyday in the 1950s, the competitive model of democracy has been
subjected to a variety of criticisms. Parts of this critical literature have been
narrowly technical and limited in their concerns, whereas some critics have
developed much more radical and sweeping indictments. We can distinguish
among (a) an *analytical* critique, which questions the validity of the Downsian
model under less restrictive assumptions; (b) an *applicability* critique, which
raises the problem of whether any benefits of competition are likely to be
realized in the political "markets" Downs and Schumpeter describe; (c) an
argument concerning the *insufficiency* of political competition as a guarantee

of good government; and (d) a critique that sees political competition as a *perversion* of the proper relationships among democratic citizens. Let us briefly consider these critiques in order.

Analytical Critiques of Competitive Democracy

This literature, which in part is highly technical, is primarily concerned with the validity of the Downsian results concerning party convergence and voter participation. Critics have questioned the Downsian assumptions of information certainty, the unidimensionality of his political space, the postulation of vote maximization as the parties' objective function, his neglect of the effects of party activists, and the assumption of sincere voting (see, e.g., Aldrich, 1983; Aranson, Hinich, & Ordeshook, 1974; Barry, 1970; Enelow & Hinich, 1984; Robertson, 1976; Wittman, 1983). Under many alternative sets of assumptions, the basic Downsian results no longer hold. The ultimate robustness of the Downsian model is still a matter of controversy within the spatial voting literature.

The Inapplicability of Market Models

The spatial voting literature rarely develops any broad normative critique of the Downsian model of party competition. Other critics have argued, however, that the process of party competition cannot properly be understood through the use of these and similar economic analogies. These critics have focused in part on the inapplicability of the concept of perfect competition, with its concomitant salutary effects, to the realm of political representation. For one thing, economists tend to assume *price* competition, which has no clear analogy in politics. It would be difficult to apply the concept of price to many of the phenomena with which we associate political competition, as politics is not commonly characterized by homogeneous goods markets. Second, the model of perfect competition posits a world of extreme *decentralization,* where the number of players approaches infinity and where no player has any control over the plans of any other (Demsetz, 1982, p. 8). That is to say, the choices of one player are independent of those of any other. David Miller (1983, p. 148) challenges what he sees as an unrealistic assumption in Downs: that parties behave as perfect competitors. In reality, he argues, parties may well collude to produce policies that are undesirable to the voters.

The Downsian model has essentially been borrowed from the economic theory of oligopoly behavior. But if parties are oligopolists, then the benefits of perfect competition may not obtain. Oligopolistic markets allow producers to neglect consumer preferences to a significant extent (Macpherson, 1977). It is true that Schumpeter explicitly recognizes the discrepancies between the contest for votes and the perfect competitive equilibria often posited by economists. Even so, however, the possibility of party collusion and exploitation of the voters leaves Schumpeter's analysis uncomfortably dependent on his ad hoc preconditions, discussed above.

The Insufficiency of Political Competition

These considerations naturally lead us toward a third body of literature, one critical of the competitive model of democracy. Peter Bachrach (1967) maintains that no democratic theorist has found elite competition in itself sufficient to solve the problem of power in a democracy. As in Schumpeter, elite consensus is typically stipulated as an additional prerequisite to contain the exercise of power by those in leadership positions. Arend Lijphart's (1975, 1977) seminal work can in large part be seen as empirical corroboration of this argument.

Whereas Bachrach (1967) focused on the insufficiency of competitive democracy on the "producer" side, others have identified limitations on the "consumer" side. It is not normatively obvious that all voter preferences should be accorded the same weight (Elster, 1983). This is especially important to the extent that voting is a *private* act whose motives need not stand up to the scrutiny of public debate. Thus a voter's ideal point may be determined by sadism, stupidity, or socially unacceptable prejudices (Elster, 1983; Goodin, 1986; Sen, 1979). While it is true that Downs assumes voters to be motivated by self-interest rather than sadism, champions of competitive democracy have generally neglected the problem of "laundering" political preferences (Goodin, 1986).

Competitive Democracy as a Perversion

Macpherson (1977) goes further in his critique of the demand side of the competitive model. This market-based model, he contends, is sensitive only to *effective* demand, and effective demand depends on the financial resources each voter commands. This resource dependence creates inequalities among voters and apathy among those least well endowed. For these reasons, Macpherson prefers a participatory, rather than competitive, model of democracy. Bachrach's (1967) conclusion is equally critical.

Jane Mansbridge (1983) formulates a different, but related, alternative to the competitive model she identifies and criticizes as *adversary democracy*. Her favored alternative is *unitary democracy,* which is characterized by a stress on common social interests, *equal respect* as an egalitarian ideal, *consensus* as a decision rule, and a greater degree of face-to-face contact in the decision process than what characterizes competitive democracy.

These theorists, then, stress the systematic inferiority of competitive democracy to alternative forms of democracy. Their rejection of competitive ideals (at least in some contexts) is commonly linked to a belief that the competitive process may actually pervert the political instincts and preferences of individuals and distort social interests.

AN ALTERNATIVE CONCEPTION
OF POLITICAL COMPETITION

Thus the competitive model of democracy is a controversial normative model of decision making in modern polities. Even if parts of the "antielitist" critique are based on a misrepresentation of the competitive model, there is clearly room for skepticism concerning its applicability and normative power. Yet it is difficult to see any promising alternative to the competitive model when it is seen as Schumpeter intended it: as a *minimal* model designed especially for "difficult" collective decisions, that is, for situations in which there is urgency about making a definitive decision; the options are well defined and well known; individual preferences are strong, conflicting, and firmly held; and decision costs are potentially high (see Buchanan & Tullock, 1962).

In this section, therefore, I propose an alternative conception of political competition that is more beholden to the Schumpeterian than to the Downsian tradition, yet also allows us to relate our concept of political competition to more contemporary modes of analysis in the social sciences, such as game theory. In so doing, I have to complicate the analysis by identifying different elements of political competition. Thus I distinguish between *political contestability* and *situational competitiveness*. Finally, in the Schumpeterian spirit, I seek to capture more directly the importance of actors and strategies in the competitive process. This, of course, is precisely what a more game-theoretic approach affords us.

The economic notion of perfect price competition may not be the most appropriate analogy for political scientists. In politics, we are more commonly interested in identifying competitive behavior in situations where there is no equivalent to price and where player choices are interdependent. These circumstances call for a somewhat different approach to the study of competition. It may be more fruitful and intuitively plausible to analyze competition in game, rather than market, terms. Game theory affords us a simple and analytically powerful way to consider political situations in which choices are interdependent.

Political Contestability and Concentration

In its most fundamental sense, a competitive society is an open one. And much of the normative attraction of political competition must lie in its relationship to a political marketplace of ideas that is open and free for all. In more technical parlance, we can refer to this aspect of competition as *political contestability*. This concept, of course, has a direct and obvious economic analogy. In its economic meaning, contestability denotes markets where entry and exit are free, demand is met, existing firms make nonnegative profits, and there are no incentives for potential entrants (Baumol, Panzar, & Willig, 1982). In contestable markets there may be few firms, but the potential for competition protects consumers and keeps producers efficient. Contestability is a necessary but not sufficient condition for perfect competition.

We can take contestability in a political sense to refer more broadly to entry and exit conditions. The easier it is to "throw one's hat into the ring" and join the contest for office, the more contestable the political "market" (Strom, 1989). Note that contestability clearly is implicit in Schumpeter's concern with freedom to compete for leadership. In electoral politics, contestability is determined by such institutional factors as electoral laws, party finance, and the costs of campaigning. It is useful to think of political contestability as a background condition favoring competitive *behavior*. In terms that will be explained below, contestability is particularly likely to promote player indeterminacy, since ease of entry is likely to go together with ex ante equality of opportunity.

But contestability presumably has other and more direct effects. One is its impact on political *concentration,* that is, the extent to which political contests are dominated by few and large players. In electoral politics, party system *fragmentation* or *fractionalization* is defined in precisely such terms (Rae, 1971). The degree of fractionalization is argued to be an important determinant of party system dynamics and stability (Sartori, 1976). Just as in the economic realm, fractionalization is often taken as an indirect measure of systemic competitiveness.

Situational Competitiveness

Yet contestability and concentration hardly exhaust the meaning of political competition. In order to understand the dynamic behavior that Schumpeter so forcefully stressed in his analysis, we need to capture situational competitiveness and the incentives it gives to players once they are in the "game."

Let us therefore think of political competition as existing between multiple (two or more) players, whose payoffs depend on the combination of their individually adopted strategies and the state of nature. Each set of strategies, combined with a state of nature, yields some outcome characterized by a particular distribution of payoffs. Choices are interdependent because outcomes are affected by every player's choice. Competitiveness then pertains to the strategies, states of nature, and payoffs of particular games.

In these terms, situational competitiveness has three dimensions: payoff variability, strategy determinacy, and player indeterminacy. *Payoff variability* refers to the variation of payoffs to the various players across their sets of strategies. The more variation, the greater the competitiveness. *Strategy determinacy* refers to the extent to which strategy choice, rather than states of nature, affects payoffs for each player. The more strategy choice matters relative to states of nature, the more competitive the game. *Player determinacy* refers to the extent to which the payoff distribution systematically favors certain players over others. The less any player is so favored over his or her opponents, the higher the level of competitiveness.

Let us elaborate this conception by considering some applications and some very simple examples, applying the concept of situational competitiveness to partisan electoral contests in representative democracies. I assume for simplicity that there are just two parties and that each party has only two strategies from which to choose. These strategies may, for example, be policy positions. In Figure 2.1, the players are designated 1 and 2 and their strategies a_1 and a_2 (for Player 1) and b_1 and b_2 (for Player 2), respectively. In the payoff matrix, the payoffs to Player 1 are always listed first. For simplicity, all games in Figure 2.1 are constant sum, as the payoffs consistently sum to 100.

Think of Players 1 and 2 as two parties contesting an election in which there will inevitably be one winner and one loser. We simplify by assuming that the value of winning is equal to 100 for each party and that the value of losing is $0.$[6] Each set of strategy pairs is associated with a probability distribution over the outcomes. Thus, in Game A, the strategy set (a_1, b_1) leads to victory for Player 1 with probability .8 and consequently gives Player 2 a 20% chance. In Game B, on the other hand, the same strategy set gives Player 1 a .6 probability of winning, whereas Player 2 has a .4 probability (a 40% chance). Assuming that each player is risk neutral, this gives strategy set (a_1, b_1) an expected value to Player 1 of 80 in Game A and 60 in Game B. Conversely, the expected values to Player 2 are 20 in Game A and 40 in Game B. Let us now discuss situational competitiveness on the basis of the simple examples in Figure 2.1.

Payoff Variability

As noted, *payoff variability* refers to the variation in payoffs to each player across his or her set of strategies. The greater this variability, the more competitive the game. Compare, for example, Games A and B. These two games are similar in that the same strategy sets produce the same likely winners. However, because of differences in the probability distributions, the expected values of the various strategy sets differ systematically between them. In Game A, both players face a set of expected values that range from 20 to 80. The payoff variability in Game B, again identical for both players, is the much narrower range from 40 to 60. The increment in payoff is 60 in Game A, as opposed to only 20 in Game B. Consequently, Game A is more competitive than Game B.

Payoff variability is more commonly referred to as the *stakes* of the game. Game A is more competitive than Game B because there is more at stake for both players. In the examples in Figure 2.1, I have made the somewhat unrealistic assumption that winning counts equally for both parties. In a more realistic setting, payoff variability depends on institutional characteristics such as decision rules, as well as on the value each party places on winning elections. If we were to measure the stakes of electoral contests in the real world, we would therefore want to take into account the institutional rules by which votes get translated into control over policy, office benefits (spoils), and other scarce goods that parties value (see Strom, 1990). Lijphart's (1984) influential distinction between *Westminster* and *Consensus* democracies is precisely one between high and low degrees of competitiveness in this sense. In Westminster democracies, electoral majorities are worth a great

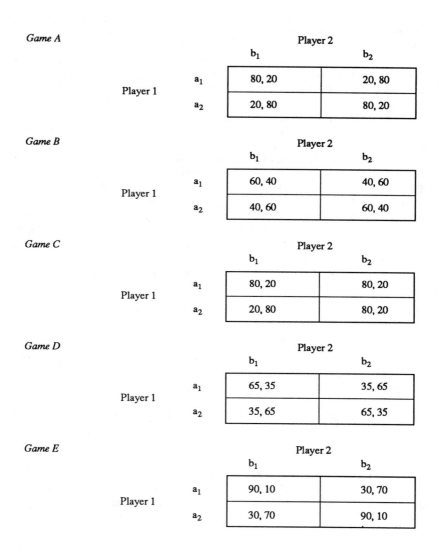

Figure 2.1. Illustrative Games

deal more than they are in Consensus systems. This is because majority parties have much greater control over policy decisions and office benefits in Westminster democracies than elsewhere.

Strategy Determinacy

Strategy determinacy is the degree to which outcomes (here "probabilities of winning") are determined by strategic choices rather than by random factors.[7] The more the players' own choices shape the terrain of competition, the greater the strategy determinacy. In a state of perfect strategy determinacy, outcomes would be fully determined by the strategies of the actors, leaving nothing to chance. Obviously, political contests need not be that simple, and outcomes may depend on exogenous states of nature as much as on player strategies. The greater the effect of states of nature relative to strategies, the lower the strategy determinacy.

In order to illustrate the meaning of strategy determinacy, let us make some simplifying assumptions about the games in Figure 2.1. We treat the payoffs (probabilities of winning) as if they were determinate outcomes. Let us then think of nature (uncertainty) as intervening in the following way. There are two possible payoff distributions, each represented by one of the games in Figure 2.1. Nature chooses randomly between these two sets of outcomes in such a way that each has a probability of .5. Let us assume that Game B represents one possible payoff configuration and that the other is either Game A or Game D. We can then compare the game where nature chooses randomly between B and D with the game where the choice is between B and A. Contrary to the discussion of payoff variability, we limit the discussion to equilibrium strategies.[8] This simplifies the analysis but requires a brief description of the equilibria in the games in Figure 2.1.

Game C is the only game in the figure that has an equilibrium in pure strategies, namely, the strategy pair (a_1, b_1). This is an equilibrium in which Player 1 gets an expected payoff of 80 and Player 2 a meager 20. None of the other four games has an equilibrium in pure strategies. However, each of these games has essentially the same equilibrium in mixed strategies. This equilibrium is for both players to randomize between both strategies with probability .5 for each. In Games A, B, and D, both players can get expected payoffs of 50 by randomizing between their two strategies with equal probability. In Game E, Player 1 can obtain an expected payoff of 60 by the same kind of random choice, whereas Player 2 can do no better than an expectation of 40.

Thus the lottery over A and B has the same expected value for both players as that over B and D. However, the state of nature clearly has a larger impact on the payoffs in the former case. There, the expected value of the payoff to each player varies by 20 points according to the state of nature, whereas in the lottery between B and D, the range of variation is only 5. Because nature (chance) is a more important determinant of the expected payoffs in the lottery between B and A, the lottery between B and D is more strategy dependent and thus more competitive.

In the real world of electoral politics, strategy determinacy reflects the degree to which electoral results are decided by the choices and performance of the relevant parties, rather than by politically random events. Examples of the latter might be the weather on election day, deaths or sex scandals among leading public figures, international crises, or exogenous shocks in the economy. The more such events rule elections, the less competitive the electoral process. If we were studying survey data, we might similarly see strategy determinacy as consistent with issue voting rather than, for example, with voting on the basis of family ties or subcultural identification.

Player Indeterminacy

The third and final component of situational competitiveness is player indeterminacy, or the equivalence of payoff distributions across players. The more equal the odds facing each player, the more competitive the situation. A high degree of player indeterminacy need not require that all players face identical payoff schemes or even similar strategy sets. Rather, player indeterminacy requires the *expected payoffs* for all players to converge.[9] Thus parties can be highly competitive without being interchangeable in the same sense that two tennis players with very different fortes can be closely matched. Note that player indeterminacy thus is defined ex ante and not ex post. Competitiveness in this sense does not require equality of results, only equality of opportunity.

In Figure 2.1, Game A has a higher degree of player indeterminacy than either Game C or Game E, both of which favor Player 1, though in different ways. As mentioned above, Game C has a pure strategy equilibrium that gives Player 1 a payoff of 80 versus only 20 for Player 2. In Game E, the expected payoff to Player 1 is 60 and to Player 2, 40.

The extension of player indeterminacy to real-world politics is straightforward. The more equal the preelectoral chances of all parties, the more competitive the contest. Lack of such equality of opportunity may be due to campaign resources, constraints of past policy decisions on the range of credible policy positions, or the advantages or burdens of incumbency (Rose & Mackie, 1983; Strom, 1985). Institutions such as electoral laws or public subsidies may also systematically discriminate against particular parties. Player indeterminacy is indeed captured in some of the most common empirical measures of interparty competition, such as the closeness of electoral victories. Turnover rates or previous victory margins are common proxies for the ex ante uncertainty of electoral contests (Schlesinger, 1955, 1960; see also Ferejohn, 1977; Meltz, 1973; Patterson & Caldeira, 1984).

POLITICAL COMPETITION
AND COMPETITIVE BEHAVIOR

The different elements of political competition have distinctive constraining effects. *Situational competitiveness* forces each player to select a strategy with care and, in the process, to consider the likely behavior of known adversaries.

In the electoral context, this means aiming to please the voters at least as much as any competitor. *Political contestability* constrains each player also to take into account the options of any *potential* competitors. For those who deal in votes, that means pleasing the voters enough to keep out new parties and candidates. Thus situational competitiveness forces parties to select their strategies efficiently in the short run, whereas contestability keeps them honest (or at least responsive) in the longer run.

There is a simpler way to summarize the meaning of political competition. Competition is fundamentally a matter of risk. The more competition, the greater the risk. Competition means that one's actions have consequences and that some of these consequences are more desirable than others. Different strategies are likely to lead to different payoffs, but one may never be sure exactly which consequences will flow from which actions. Hence life under competition is inherently risky.

One particular risk is especially important in shaping political competition— that is, to put it bluntly and imprecisely, the risk of *failure*. The great and profoundly uncomfortable virtue of competition is that it makes failure commonplace. Whether in the economic or the political "marketplace," each player knows that failure always lurks just around the corner. The more intense the competition, the more acute the threat of failure. And just as the moral acceptance and regulation of economic failure (bankruptcy) were critical to the development of capitalism, so the toleration and protection of temporary political losers (oppositions) have been critical to the establishment of democracy (see Dahl, 1966, 1971).

Thus competition is inherently discomforting. And just as every capitalist would like to escape competition and be a lazy monopolist, so every politician would like to be unchallenged. Indeed, as Schumpeter argues, it is in the efforts to escape from the "knife-edged" world of perfectly competitive equilibria that the real dynamics of competition lie (see Nelson & Winter, 1982). Thus innovation and anticipation are born of competition and reflect efforts to escape a situation where failure is so perilously close. As in capitalist markets, these dynamics may in the long run be the greatest benefit of political competition.

DESIGNING COMPETITIVE DEMOCRACY

One of the great and pleasant surprises of the late 1970s and especially the 1980s was the establishment, or frequent reestablishment, of democracy across large parts of the world. This process started in Southern Europe, spread to South and Central America, and finally engulfed Eastern Europe. In the 1990s it seems likely to involve parts of Africa as well. These dramatic and highly consequential processes have spurred a renewed scholarly interest in the nature and preconditions of democracy.

The recent literature on transitions to democracy has occasioned a heightened concern with the meaning of democracy and democratization itself. And, interestingly, in this process the key role of political competition has been rediscovered. In his collaborative work with Diamond and Linz, Lipset stresses the competitive nature of democracy more clearly than ever:

> Democracy . . . denotes a system of government that meets three essential conditions: meaningful and extensive *competition* among individuals and organized groups (especially political parties) for all effective positions of government power . . . , a highly inclusive level of *political participation* in the selection of leaders and policies . . . and a level of *civil and political liberties* . . . sufficient to ensure the integrity of political competition and participation. (Diamond, Linz, & Lipset, 1988, p. xvi)

But Lipset is in no way alone in reaffirming his commitment to this competitive model of democracy. Philippe Schmitter (1986), for example, similarly identifies the existence of autonomous groups, capable of defending their interests through participation in collective action, as a precondition of democracy, noting that

> such participation is accomplished in large part consensually through political parties which *compete to win electoral majorities,* ally with others in dominant coalitions, or enter into consociational arrangements. (p. 6; emphasis added)

Adam Przeworski (1986) defines democracy in terms even closer to the concept of political competition developed above:

> Democracy constitutes a set of stable relations between the actions of particular groups and the effects of these actions upon them. Conflicts are organized in a specific manner and their outcomes bear some relation to the particular combinations of strategies pursued by various actors. Characteristic of a democracy is that each group has some choice of strategies and that strategies have consequences. . . . In a democracy, no one can win once and for all: even if successful at one time, victors immediately face the prospect of having to struggle in the future. . . . Outcomes of democratic conflicts are not simply indeterminate within limits. They are uncertain. (p. 57)

Note that Przeworski here identifies democracy with all three elements of situational competitiveness. In stressing that "strategies have consequences," he invokes payoff variability. His specification that outcomes bear some relation to strategies refers to strategy determinacy. And his insistence that no player can win once and for all at least indirectly echoes player indeterminacy. Finally, his conception of democratic conflict as intrinsically *uncertain* mirrors the focus above on risk.[10]

Przeworski (1986) describes democratization as "a process of institutional-izing uncertainty" and adds that "it is this very act of alienation of control over outcomes of conflicts that constitutes the decisive step toward democracy" (p. 58). Thus democracy is not only described analytically in very familiar terms, but the introduction of competitive risks (or uncertainty) is even prescribed as an avenue toward a regime type he and his coauthors clearly favor. The competitive model of democracy has regained center stage analytically as well as normatively.

But should we in the interest of democratization always favor an increase in contestability, payoff variability, strategy determinacy, or player indetermi-nacy? And if we have the choice, in which direction should we move first? Students of democratization tell us that there may be a favored sequence in which the transition to democracy can take place. Some inequality of opportu-nity (player determinacy) may be desirable in the early stages of that process (Przeworski, 1986, p. 60). Specifically, O'Donnell and Schmitter (1986) argue, parties of the right and center-right must be "helped" to do well (p. 62). And as the same authors point out, under a variety of circumstances democratization may be secured through pacts, which "tend to reduce competitiveness as well as conflict" (p. 38).

Pacts are essentially ex ante agreements to preclude certain outcomes. Thus pacts may reduce payoff variability, as when consociational institutions are created (Lijphart, 1975, 1977). They tend to limit strategy determinacy as well when they impose on the electoral contestants a grand coalition or a rotation scheme (O'Donnell & Schmitter, 1986, p. 41). Pacts might even inhibit con-testability by discriminating against "unwelcome voters and/or unwilling par-ties."[11] The general purpose of pacts is to "move the polity toward democracy by undemocratic means" (O'Donnell & Schmitter, 1986, p. 38). We may safely take "undemocratic" here to refer to restrictions on competitiveness. Whatever the institutional means, it is clear that although the road to democracy is one toward greater competitiveness, the route may be both circuitous and long.

CONCLUSIONS

The study of democracy and democratization has in recent years returned to the prominent place it occupied in political science at the time *Political Man* was published. And not only has the academic theme returned with a vengeance, but the very conceptions and analytical frameworks that characterized much of the best literature of that day have been rejuvenated.

In the 1960s and 1970s, the competitive model of democracy came in for substantial criticism, much of it justified. This analysis has shown that it is necessary to distinguish between two distinct strands of competitive demo-cratic theory, associated with Anthony Downs and Joseph Schumpeter, respec-tively. These two traditions differ both in their conception of competition and in their presentation. I have argued that it is possible to reconstruct a model of political competition that borrows more heavily from the Schumpeterian tradition and frames political contests in terms of strategic interaction.

Through examples and references to the literature, I have shown how this framework allows us to capture the interaction of political parties and other competing groups. An examination of authoritative recent works on democracy and democratization shows that these are exactly the terms in which democracy and democratization have been analyzed. Thus political competition has been restored to its proper place as a key part of good government.

NOTES

1. We assume here that parties will be reliable in government, that is, that their policies will be consistent with their campaign promises. Downs (1957) argues that the prospect of future elections will constrain parties to behave in this way.

2. This argument assumes that it is admissible to compare the "utilities" of different persons along one and the same political dimension. This is controversial in economic theory but widely accepted in political theory and practice.

3. If the distribution of voters is *asymmetric*, then the mean (rather than median) voter position will constitute the most efficient collective representation of their preferences. Yet the discrepancy between the mean and the median voter position is likely to be small in most plausible voter distributions.

4. The related, but more qualified, position that sudden *increases* in popular participation could destabilize democracy was, of course, to become one of the most controversial theses in *Political Man* (Lipset, 1981, pp. 227-229). Thus Lipset shares with Schumpeter not only a basic conception of the democratic order but a concern with the potential excesses of a participatory society.

5. Note that this precondition implicitly rules out the Downsian world of policy convergence.

6. Strictly speaking, the payoffs to each player depend on both the objective outcomes and the subjective values the players put on these outcomes, and it is problematic to compare payoffs across players. The game representations should therefore be seen as simplifying illustrations only.

7. It is important to distinguish this concept from another possible meaning we could give to the notion of strategy determinacy, namely, the degree to which one player's choice of strategy is determined regardless of what the other players do. The latter would be the case if there exist dominant strategies in the game. I thank James D. Morrow for bringing this point to my attention.

8. It would be theoretically appropriate but computationally more unwieldy to include out-of-equilibrium strategies in the analysis of strategy and player determinacy. Such a choice is most appropriate where the equilibria are particularly fragile or where there is incomplete information. In a full account of situational competitiveness, we should probably consider all undominated strategies. Dominated strategies, however, can reasonably be ignored. Dominated strategies are strategies for which there is at least one alternative that is better regardless of the strategy choice of the other player(s). None of the substantive conclusions in these examples would change if we considered all strategies rather than just those in equilibrium.

9. As in the case of strategy determinacy, we might ideally want to consider player indeterminacy across all undominated strategies.

10. In the technical literature, risk and uncertainty have somewhat different meanings, in that uncertainty pertains to states of nature that are in principle knowable, whereas risk cannot be eliminated ex ante. Real-world political competition probably always includes both risk and uncertainty.

11. This consideration is again reminiscent of Schumpeter's and Lipset's concern with the dangers of excessive participation.

REFERENCES

Aldrich, J. H. (1983). A Downsian spatial model with party activism. *American Political Science Review, 77*, 974-990.

Aranson, P., Hinich, M. J., & Ordeshook, P. C. (1974). Election goals and strategies: Equivalent and nonequivalent candidate objectives. *American Political Science Review, 68*, 135-152.

Arrow, K. A. (1951). *Social choice and individual values*. New York: John Wiley.

Bachrach, P. (1967). *The theory of democratic elitism*. New York: Lieber-Atherton.

Barry, B. (1970). *Sociologists, economists, and democracy*. Chicago: University of Chicago Press.

Baumol, W. J., Panzar, J. C., & Willig, R. D. (1982). *Contestable markets and the theory of industry structure*. New York: Harcourt Brace Jovanovich.

Buchanan, J. M., & Tullock, G. (1962). *The calculus of consent*. Ann Arbor: University of Michigan Press.

Dahl, R. A. (Ed.). (1966). *Political oppositions in Western democracies*. New Haven, CT: Yale University Press.

Dahl, R. A. (1971). *Polyarchy*. New Haven, CT: Yale University Press.

Demsetz, H. (1982). *Economic, legal, and political dimensions of competition*. Amsterdam: North-Holland.

Diamond, L., Linz, J. J., & Lipset, S. M. (1988). Preface. In L. Diamond, J. J. Linz, & S. M. Lipset (Eds.), *Democracy in developing countries* (pp. xix-xxvii). Boulder, CO: Lynne Rienner.

Downs, A. (1957). *An economic theory of democracy*. New York: Harper & Row.

Elster, J. (1983). *Sour grapes*. Cambridge: Cambridge University Press.

Enelow, J. M., & Hinich, M. J. (1984). *The spatial theory of voting: An introduction*. Cambridge: Cambridge University Press.

Ferejohn, J. A. (1977). On the decline of competition in congressional elections. *American Political Science Review, 71*, 166-176.

Goodin, R. E. (1986). Laundering preferences. In J. Elster & A. Hylland (Eds.), *Foundations of social choice theory* (pp. 75-101). Cambridge: Cambridge University Press.

Held, D. (1987). *Models of democracy*. Cambridge: Polity.

Lijphart, A. (1975). *The politics of accommodation* (2nd ed.). Berkeley: University of California Press.

Lijphart, A. (1977). *Democracy in plural societies: A comparative exploration*. New Haven, CT: Yale University Press.

Lijphart, A. (1984). *Democracies*. New Haven, CT: Yale University Press.

Lipset, S. M. (1981). *Political man: The social bases of politics* (expanded ed.). Baltimore: Johns Hopkins University Press.

Macpherson, C. B. (1977). *The life and times of liberal democracy*. Oxford: Oxford University Press.

Mansbridge, J. (1983). *Beyond adversary democracy.* New York: Basic Books.

Mayntz, R. (1961). Oligarchic problems in a German party district. In D. Marvick (Ed.), *Political decision-makers: Recruitment and performance.* New York: Free Press.

Meltz, D. B. (1973). An index for the measurement of inter-party competition. *Behavioral Science, 18*(1), 60-63.

Miller, D. (1983). The competitive model of democracy. In G. Duncan (Ed.), *Democratic theory and practice* (pp. 133-155). Cambridge: Cambridge University Press.

Nelson, R. R., & Winter, S. G. (1982). *An evolutionary theory of economic change.* Cambridge, MA: Harvard University Press.

O'Donnell, G., & Schmitter, P. C. (1986). *Transitions from authoritarian rule: Tentative conclusions about uncertain democracies.* Baltimore: Johns Hopkins University Press.

Patterson, S. C., & Caldeira, G. A. (1984). The etiology of party competition. *American Political Science Review, 78,* 691-707.

Powell, G. B., Jr. (1982). *Contemporary democracies.* Cambridge, MA: Harvard University Press.

Przeworski, A. (1986). Some problems in the study of the transition to democracy. In G. O'Donnell, P. C. Schmitter, & L. Whitehead (Eds.), *Transitions from authoritarian rule: Comparative perspectives* (pp. 47-63). Baltimore: Johns Hopkins University Press.

Rae, D. W. (1971). *The political consequences of electoral laws* (rev. ed.). New Haven, CT: Yale University Press.

Robertson, D. (1976). *A theory of party competition.* London: John Wiley.

Rose, R., & Mackie, T. T. (1983). Incumbency in government: Asset or liability? In H. Daalder & P. Mair (Eds.), *Western European party systems: Continuity and change* (pp. 115-137). Beverly Hills, CA: Sage.

Sartori, G. (1976). *Parties and party systems.* Cambridge: Cambridge University Press.

Schlesinger, J. A. (1955). A two-dimensional scheme for classifying the states according to degree of inter-party competition. *American Political Science Review, 49,* 1120-1128.

Schlesinger, J. A. (1960). The structure of competition for office in the American states. *Behavioral Science, 5*(3), 197-210.

Schmitter, P. C. (1986). An introduction to Southern European transitions from authoritarian rule: Italy, Greece, Portugal, Spain, and Turkey. In G. O'Donnell, P. C. Schmitter, & L. Whitehead (Eds.), *Transitions from authoritarian rule: Southern Europe* (pp. 3-10). Baltimore: Johns Hopkins University Press.

Schumpeter, J. A. (1987). *Capitalism, socialism, and democracy* (6th ed.). London: Unwin Hyman. (Original work published 1942)

Scott, A. (1970). *Competition in American politics: An economic model.* New York: Holt, Rinehart & Winston.

Sen, A. (1979). Personal utilities and public judgments: Or what's wrong with welfare economics? *Economic Journal, 89,* 537-558.

Stigler, G. J. (1972). Economic competition and political competition. *Public Choice, 18,* 91-106.

Strom, K. (1985). Party goals and government performance in parliamentary democracies. *American Political Science Review, 79,* 738-754.

Strom, K. (1989). Inter-party competition in advanced democracies. *Journal of Theoretical Politics, 1,* 277-300.

Strom, K. (1990). A behavioral theory of competitive political parties. *American Journal of Political Science, 34,* 565-598.

Ware, A. J. (1987). *Citizens, parties and the state.* Cambridge: Polity.

Wittman, D. (1983). Candidate motivation: A synthesis of alternative theories. *American Political Science Review, 77,* 142-157.

3

Rational Sources of Chaos in Democratic Transition

Gary Marks

A crisis of legitimacy is a crisis of change. Therefore, its roots must be sought in the character of change in modern society. Crises of legitimacy occur during a transition to a new social structure, if (1) the status of major conservative institutions is threatened during the period of structural change; (2) all the major groups in the society do not have access to the political system in the transitional period, or at least as soon as they develop political demands.

—S. M. Lipset
Political Man: The Social Bases of Politics

IN his seminal analysis of the requisites of democracy, Seymour Martin Lipset focused on the influence of the level of wealth, industrialization, urbanization, and education, in which significant change is measured over years, or even decades (Lipset, 1959). Other social scientists who have built on Lipset's work have emphasized the role of interest group pluralism, civil society, elite culture, ethnic cleavages, religion, state structure, and the distribution of the instruments of violent coercion, where change is, if anything, even

AUTHOR'S NOTE: I would like to thank Steven Genco, Peter Lange, Kaare Strom, and Michael Taylor for helpful comments on an earlier version of this chapter, and Kira Nam for research assistance. This chapter was written while I was a fellow at the Center for Advanced Study in the Behavioral Sciences. I am grateful for financial support provided by a grant from the National Science Foundation (No. BNS-8700864).

more glacial (Bollen & Jackman, 1985; Dahl, 1971, 1989; Diamond, Linz, & Lipset, 1988-1989; Huntington, 1984, 1991). Yet the implantation of democratic institutions and practices is notoriously a chaotic affair, full of sudden and unpredictable shifts in behavior and decisive watersheds where decisions made at particular moments in time appear to shape the possibilities of democracy for years to come.[1] Why is this? Why are periods of political stasis, where the existence of the ruling oligarchy appears to be overdetermined, interrupted by episodes of political turmoil, indeterminacy, and apparent chaos?

The commonsensical response is that the indeterminacy of such episodes reflects their complexity, the diversity and large number of relevant political actors, their multiple interactions, their incomplete information, and rapidly shifting goals. But in this matter I do not think common sense is a sure guide. Although indeterminate outcomes are often the result of complex systems, they may also be the result of very simple systems. Strategic interaction, even under radically simplified circumstances, may produce outcomes that are tumultuous and unpredictable.

In this chapter, I analyze one such example of strategic interaction that lies at the heart of political change in authoritarian political systems. The strategic interaction is typical of scenarios of political discontinuity, revolutionary as well as evolutionary, having the following characteristics: (a) The institutions of the existing regime fail to regularize and contain political activity, but become themselves a locus of political struggle; (b) political power is contested by two or more groups, each of which is composed of actors having heterogeneous preferences or incomplete information about the responses of other actors in the same group; and (c) choices made within one group influence the choices of the other group.

The model set forth here attempts to capture essential features of strategic interaction within and between a ruling elite and political opposition in the setting of an authoritarian regime. Each of these groups has two courses of action: The ruling elite may decide to suppress or tolerate the political opposition; the political opposition may decide to abide by the imposed rules of the regime or to operate outside of those rules and challenge the regime. A subgame takes place within each group. The ruling elite is composed of two factions that may have contrasting preferences for suppression versus toleration, and the political opposition is made up of N-individuals who must individually decide whether to abide by the rules imposed by the regime or challenge the regime in protest.

The general payoffs of the first round of the iterated game between the ruling elite and political opposition are set out in Figure 3.1.[2] The ruling elite makes the first move, either to tolerate or to suppress the political opposition, and the political opposition responds either by accepting the rules of the political system or by challenging them. This order of moves is repeated an indeterminate number of times in a supergame until the elite either is toppled or abandons or bargains away its monopoly of government control and the oligarchy is superseded by a different regime.

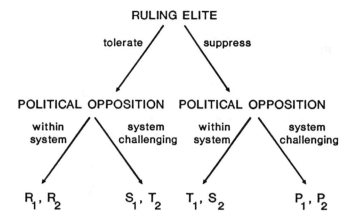

Figure 3.1. Game Between Ruling Elite and Political Opposition

The payoffs in this game are constrained in two fairly obvious ways:

Assumption 1: The ruling elite always prefers the political opposition to operate within the political system than to challenge the political system ($R_1 > S_1$; $T_1 > P_1$). As the dominant group in the society, the ruling elite wants the political opposition to accept the status quo, or at least acquiesce to it. Even if the political opposition is small and can challenge only weakly, the ruling elite would prefer not to have to deal with a political opposition mobilized against it.

Assumption 2: The political opposition always prefers the ruling elite to tolerate rather than suppress it ($R_2 > S_2$; $T_2 > P_2$). Toleration provides the opposition with more space to mobilize followers and to formulate, voice, and press political demands.[3] The opposition may also place an intrinsic value on expanded civil rights as a result of elite toleration.

The game described here has two sets of scenarios. The first set is made up of cases in which the ruling elite selects a particular course of action irrespective of the response of the political opposition. If the elite prefers its worst case under toleration (S_1) to its best case under suppression (T_1), then the elite will tolerate no matter what the political opposition does. If the elite prefers its worst case under suppression (P_1) to its best case under toleration (R_1), then the elite will suppress no matter what the political opposition does. Elite choice in these cases is nonstrategic in the sense that the decision to tolerate or suppress has nothing to do with the elite's interaction with the political opposition as modeled in Figure 3.1.[4]

The second set of scenarios involves strategic interaction between the ruling elite and political opposition. These are cases in which the elite prefers toleration followed by opposition restraint, or suppression followed by opposition restraint, to any alternative in which the opposition challenges the political system.[5] For example, the elite may prefer to tolerate, but only if the opposition does not respond by challenging the political system. If the opposition does challenge, the elite prefers to suppress. A distinguishing characteristic of this type of scenario is that the anticipated response of the political opposition is critical to the choice made by the ruling elite.

Which scenario best describes a regime at any particular time depends on the preferences of the elite. Following Robert Dahl (1971), we must examine the respective costs of toleration and suppression for the elite. However, we cannot conclude, with Dahl, that "the more the costs of suppression exceed the costs of toleration, the greater the chance for a competitive regime" (p. 15). While this statement is valid for the extremes, in nonstrategic scenarios where the costs of suppression are greater (or lower) than the costs of toleration no matter what the opposition does, it is invalid in the intermediate zone conceptualized by the second set of scenarios. If the costs of toleration and suppression are close enough in size so that the response of the political opposition may tip the balance, we have to probe the strategic interaction of elite and opposition rather than calculate the relative costs of elite toleration and suppression. The following section examines the costs of toleration and suppression from the standpoint of the ruling elite; analysis of the consequences of strategic interaction follows.

COSTS OF TOLERATION AND SUPPRESSION

We can distinguish two ideal typical motivations for elite suppression that in practice usually coexist in varying degrees. Suppression may be adopted as an end in itself because the ruling elite regards its domination as intrinsically good, or it may be adopted as a means toward other goals valued by the elite. Where the ruling elite's monopoly of power is its overriding goal, the suppression of opposition, no matter what it entails, will be preferable to toleration. This was most nearly the case for the Nazi regime. The concentration of political power under the Nazi party and Hitler were overriding goals in themselves and not simply means that might be dispensed with if better means were found. Toleration of political opposition was abhorred not because of its consequences, but because it was viewed as bad in itself. No matter what the elite expected of the political opposition, it would suppress.[6]

If all ruling elites were in this mold, then democratic transitions could come about only if the elite was coercively displaced. However, many ruling elites have an instrumental view of the benefits of monopolistic control of government. They enjoy the diverse benefits of power, but they also prize other things, such as their material life-style, their control over the means of production, the privileges conferred on their religious institutions, and their social status.

Under these circumstances, what are the costs of tolerating political opposition? Two variables stand out in importance. First, the ruling elite has a particular stake in governance, both because it enjoys ruling and because this enables it to make authoritative decisions on matters regarding its interests. As Adam Przeworski (1986) points out, a distinguishing characteristic of a democracy, in contrast to an authoritarian regime, is that there is uncertainty about substantive outcomes. As a political elite takes steps toward democracy, it reduces its hold on the state as an instrument for achieving its preferred objectives.

The elite's stake in governance may vary widely. In some cases, the worst that an elite can expect under a strategy of toleration is an unpleasant loss of status and political power that leaves its economic base and religiocultural values secure. In other cases, the call for toleration of political opposition fuels deep-seated fears within the ruling elite about its economic viability, the continued existence of hallowed institutions, or even personal survival.

Second, although toleration increases the elite's uncertainty about its capacity to maintain its monopoly of governmental power, the degree of uncertainty varies. A political elite will have some estimation of its prospective capacity to protect its basic interests both by building institutional safeguards into the emerging democratic process and by actively competing in it, and this will enable the elite to discount possible outcomes by the estimated likelihood of their occurrence. Combining these variables, we can summarize the costs of toleration for a ruling elite as *the costs of losing monopolistic control of the government* multiplied by *the probability of losing that monopoly as a result of liberalizing the regime.*

The costs of losing monopolistic control of government may be partially offset by the collective benefits of liberalization. Although democracy involves uncertainty about policy choices, it institutionalizes highly predictable procedures about how governments are chosen (Linz & Stepan, 1989, p. 47). Democratization may also offer enhanced legitimacy. A democracy, more than any other type of regime, is based on the inclusion of diverse interests rather than their exclusion, on institutionalizing conflicts rather than suppressing them, and on the distinction between the regime as a stable set of rules governing the polity and particular governments that are responsible for policy and that can be democratically removed from office at regular intervals. In addition to the diverse benefits of enhanced regime stability and legitimacy, liberalization may also offer the ruling elite the prospect of international recognition and economic aid.

Suppression, on the other hand, holds out the promise that the ruling elite may sustain its monopoly of governmental control by quashing the opposition or intimidating it into passivity. The largest and most obvious cost of suppression is that of possible failure. If the elite is unable to maintain internal cohesion, if its control over the coercive apparatus breaks down, or if the opposition proves too determined or strong, the consequences for the elite are likely to be harsh. Suppression creates a brutal, zero-sum game of winners and losers in which the stakes are extremely high: coercive domination for the winner and loss of freedom, country, or even life for the loser. But unless the elite is internally divided (a possibility examined below), the chances that it will be defeated are extremely small. In most situations, the ruling elite's control of the state and the instruments of organized coercion give it a high probability of success against all but the most militarized oppositions.

But the costs of suppression are not limited to possible defeat. The stronger the political opposition, the more extensive and brutal the level of suppression necessary and the greater the accompanying social dislocation. Although some totalitarian rulers may actually relish repression, such measures may be extremely distasteful for leaders who have a shred of decency. Whatever the elite's normative view of violent suppression, it is certain to disrupt the economy and threaten the flow of international investment, aid, and trade.

In addition, suppression raises the stakes of political conflict, because, as Seymour Martin Lipset (1983) has argued, it reinforces radicalism among the opposition (see also Marks, 1989). Suppression tends to drive even moderate groups that would otherwise press for piecemeal reform toward radical demands. This is so for several reasons: Repression arouses feelings of deprivation and resentment among the target group; injustice is likely to be felt all the more acutely when those subject to it are explicitly denied the chance to defend themselves through their own organizational efforts; and repression cuts off political channels of upward mobility and prestige for opposition leaders. If the elite wishes to change its strategy at some time in the future to one of toleration, it will find that it is dealing with a radicalized opposition that is likely to demand the prosecution of the elite for the crimes it has committed. Thus one of the costs of suppression is that it narrows strategic options of the elite in the future.

The relative weight of these costs and benefits will vary across regimes, through time, and across subgroups within the elite. In some cases, the costs of toleration greatly outweigh the costs of suppression irrespective of whether the opposition is acquiescent or challenges the regime. This might occur in regimes where the opposition is so weak that the costs of suppression are negligible. Primitive patrimonial regimes where there are very few associations or politically mobilized communities may fall into this category.

Nonstrategic suppression is also found in societies where the political opposition is strong, but the ruling elite's basic interests are tied directly to its domination of the state. To the extent that the ruling class views its life chances as depending exclusively on its monopoly of government, the costs of toleration will be extremely high. Such an outlook may be structurally determined or even overdetermined. Landed aristocracies clinging to traditional or labor-repressive agrarian practices in feudal regimes are likely to oppose democracy for economic, cultural, and social reasons as well as for political reasons. Under such circumstances, the struggle for integration of new strata into the polity

> took the form of defining the place in the polity of the old preindustrial upper
> classes, the church, the business strata, and the working class . . . in which

the enduring economic struggle among the classes overlapped with the issues concerning the place of religion and the traditional class structure. Such controversies usually were perceived in "moral" terms involving basic concepts of right versus wrong, and hence they were much more likely than economic issues to result in sharp ideological cleavages and even civil war. (Lipset, 1963, p. 269)

This was the case in the *ancien régimes* of the larger European societies before 1848 and in some societies, such as Austria-Hungary, until World War I. In these societies, the allocation of political authority structured the allocation of economic, social, and cultural values in the society as a whole. Even when the ruling elite faced considerable political opposition and the costs of suppression were correspondingly high, suppression might be undertaken whatever the anticipated response if the stake of the ruling elite in monopolistic control of government was sufficiently great. The exercise of political authority was a vital ingredient in the efforts of the landed aristocracy to extract an economic surplus from peasants and sustain the aristocracy's social and cultural hegemony.[7] The same can be said for Germany under the Second Empire and for the coffee republics of Central America, in which peasants were formally free but effectively dominated by ruling elites through labor-repressive methods of agricultural production (Moore, 1966; Weeks, 1986). In Germany, the *Junker* ruling class monopolized government both to sustain their hegemony over the peasantry and to maintain tariffs that protected agriculture from international competition. In much of Central America, particularly in El Salvador and Guatemala, "governments served as the direct agents of landed property, and state repression played a central role in the day-to-day operation of the large estates" (Weeks, 1986, p. 37).

Such regimes may be stable if the political opposition comes to accept that it is unable to topple the ruling elite coercively and to believe that the elite is unlikely to change its preference for suppression under any conceivable circumstances. In terms of the model of protest elaborated in the next section, even if it is in the interest of the opposition as a whole to challenge the regime, it may not be in the interest of individual opponents of the regime to take the risks of doing so. This depends above all on the effectiveness of the ruling elite in imposing costs on individuals who protest and on whether opponents of the regime believe that by challenging they can alter the elite's strategy in the next round. If the ruling elite is both effective and stubborn, the equilibrium in this game is suppression, followed by an opposition strategy of political activity that is within the limits imposed by the ruling elite.

This scenario is not uncommon among authoritarian regimes for extended periods of time. The ruling elite is determined to suppress the opposition in the present and in the foreseeable future. The opposition becomes convinced that it can do nothing to alter this state of affairs. To mount a popular campaign of resistance would be both ineffective and foolhardy. Although there may be some extraordinarily courageous persons who speak out against the injustices committed by the regime, the sensible course of action is to lie low and turn one's energy to other matters until the situation changes. The regime appears cast in stone. The ruling elite maintains a tight grip on the political arena, signaling its absolute preference for suppression by the decisiveness and brutality with which it deals with any brave enough to challenge it.

The paths from nonstrategic suppression to strategic suppression are diverse and have been much analyzed. Economic growth, urbanization, the growth of the middle class, the spread of education, demands for participation, and the like may increase the ability of the opposition to mobilize politically and gradually shift the preferences of the elite away from suppression in favor of toleration, depending on the response of the opposition. Once suppression is recognized by the actors involved to be strategic—that is, conditional on the response of the political opposition—political stability can no longer be taken for granted. Single episodes, such as a mass demonstration in which it first becomes clear that this many protesters may find safety in numbers, or a refusal to obey an order to repress that indicates for the first time that there is a split within the ruling elite, may, at a single stroke, transform the possibility for political transition. The impact of such episodes may be felt for years or decades into the future. Once the web of self-fulfilling expectations about the stability of the regime is broken, what previously was regarded as inevitable becomes the subject of intense political conflict. Regimes that just a short time before seemed to be cast in stone may crumble rapidly. The working assumption that serves social scientists well in normal periods of social development—namely, that to explain large divergences in outcome one must find large systematic differences in cause—is no longer sustainable. Critical outcomes can be traced to nonsystematic and unpredictable events, such as the failure of the regime in some foreign policy venture, the assassination of an opposition leader, or the death of the leader of the regime.

The dynamics of transformation of authoritarian regimes appear fundamentally different from the dynamics that give them stability. Regime transformation is not simply the absence or obverse of regime stability, but has its own distinctive logic. In the remainder of this essay, I explore the properties of such episodes, analyzing strategic interactions between the ruling elite and political opposition in authoritarian regimes.

TOLERATION AND STRATEGIC INTERACTION

In the first set of scenarios, elite strategy can be conceptualized as a function of the costs of toleration versus the costs of repression. In the second set of scenarios, we cannot simply compare the costs of alternative choices for the ruling elite.[8] Interaction between the ruling elite and political opposition opens up a vortex of strategic responses, responses to anticipated responses, responses to anticipated responses to anticipated responses, and so on, which can lead to multiple, rather than single, equilibria. Game theory demands that we simplify real-life situations in order to model them, but in doing so there is no guarantee that outcomes will be uniquely determined by the preferences of the actors involved. In the type of scenario depicted below, game theory helps us fathom the sources of political chaos: extreme dependence of outcomes on tiny—and effectively unmeasurable—changes in initial conditions.

There are three logically possible scenarios in which toleration results from strategic interaction between the ruling elite and political opposition, given Assumption 1 (the ruling elite prefers that the political opposition abide by rather than challenge the political system) and Assumption 2 (the political opposition prefers the ruling elite to tolerate rather than suppress) and assuming that the ruling elite moves first:

1. The elite prefers suppression followed by opposition acquiescence to any other outcome, but if the opposition challenges under suppression, the elite prefers to tolerate no matter what the opposition response.[9]
2. The elite prefers toleration followed by opposition activity within the system to any other outcome, but if the opposition challenges under toleration, the elite prefers to suppress no matter what the opposition response.[10]
3. The elite prefers toleration followed by opposition activity within the system to suppression followed by the system challenging political activity, but in every other case it prefers suppression.[11]

In these scenarios the political opposition can induce elite toleration by convincing the ruling elite that it will challenge the regime under suppression (Scenario 1), by convincing the ruling elite that it will act within the system under toleration (Scenario 2), or by doing both (Scenario 3). Of these scenarios, the third is the most difficult to achieve and the most theoretically interesting. If the conditions for elite toleration are met under this scenario, then they will necessarily be met in each of the other scenarios where toleration is a possible outcome. The payoffs in the one-shot version of Scenario 3 are depicted in Figure 3.2.

The situation here is described in accounts of democratic transitions that stress the benefits of opposition mobilization followed by restraint once the ruling elite has made real steps toward democracy. In his overview of the contribution of labor movements to democratization, Samuel Valenzuela (1989) argues that

a combination of high labor and popular mobilization at certain critical moments of breakdown of the authoritarian institutions (that is, when the option for a course of redemocratization becomes possible but state elites have not yet committed themselves to it), followed by the decline of that mobilization and by the willingness and capacity of the labor movement's union and political leaderships to show restraint when the political agenda shifts in favor of redemocratization, would seem to provide the ideal mix in

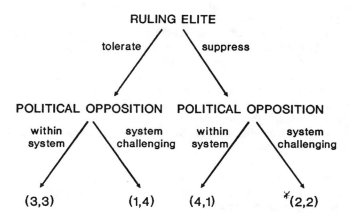

Figure 3.2. Prisoner's Dilemma

terms of labor's contribution to ensuring the latter's success. (p. 450; see also Diamond, 1989)

If we assume that the political opposition is motivated by continuing grievances (as discussed below) so that it prefers to challenge the political system even under toleration, the scenario is a prisoner's dilemma in which the players select their strategies sequentially rather than simultaneously. Both the ruling elite and political opposition prefer the *tolerate/act within the system* outcome (R_1, R_2) to *suppress/challenge* (P_1, P_2), yet the ruling elite will not choose to tolerate because it expects the political opposition to respond by challenging. In a one-shot game, the equilibrium is *suppress/challenge*. However, when the scenario is iterated, the Pareto optimal outcome of *tolerate/act within the system* can result if the ruling elite adopts a "tit-for-tat" strategy, making toleration conditional on the restraint of the political opposition. For its part, the political opposition may desist from maximizing its short-term gain from challenging the political system if it realizes that this will incur retaliation in the form of elite suppression in the next round.

The feasibility of cooperation as a result of a tit-for-tat strategy is influenced by two factors that cannot be discussed at length here: the cardinal (not merely the ordinal) size of the payoffs and the rate at which they are discounted by the players through time (Taylor, 1987). The greater the preference of the ruling elite for toleration followed by opposition acquiescence (R_1) relative to suppression $(P_1$ or $S_1)$, the less the ruling elite has to lose if it gets suckered by the

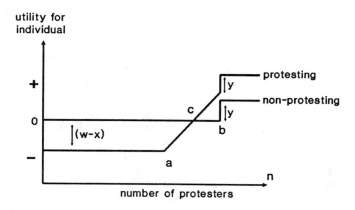

Figure 3.3. Individual Utility for Protesters and Nonprotesters Under Suppression

opposition and the more willing it will be to risk toleration. By the same logic, the greater the preference of the political opposition for toleration followed by acquiescence (R_2) relative to suppression (P_2 and S_2), the greater the incentive for the political opposition to select its second-best outcome under toleration in this round to sustain elite toleration in the future. The lower the discount rate (i.e., the proportion added to a future payoff to compensate for delaying receipt by one period), the less the temptation for the political opposition to challenge the system in this round, thereby gaining an immediate benefit, but sacrificing elite toleration in future rounds.

Before we investigate further the conditions under which liberalization may take place in this scenario, we need to examine the response of the political opposition, relaxing the assumption that it is a unitary actor and conceiving it instead as an N-person subgame.

Opposition Strategy Under Suppression

To illustrate the models described below, I use Schelling (1978) diagrams representing how individual payoffs for protesting and nonprotesting vary with respect to the number of those protesting in a group of $n + 1$ individuals (n is the number of "others" for each individual). The horizontal axis measures the number of those protesting (from 0 to n) and the vertical axis measures individual utility along each curve. Hence, in Figure 3.3, if the number protesting is less than a (i.e., is to the left of a), a person choosing to protest will face a penalty (reading off the curve for protesting individuals) and a person choosing not to protest will have a zero payoff (reading off the curve for nonprotesting individuals).

On balance, it seems sensible to assume that individuals within the opposition place a *positive* value (w) on engaging in protest. This runs counter to collective choice models that assume that rational individuals will free ride rather than participate in mass movements, but an assumption of positive value appears sound on theoretical and empirical grounds. The assumption that individuals place a positive value on protest is consistent both with models that explain protest as a result of private benefits and with models that view individuals as having preferences reflecting the collective benefits of their political activity (Elster, 1989, chap. 1; Finkel, Muller, & Opp, 1989; Muller & Opp, 1986; Tarrow, 1983, p. 23). Previous theorizing has focused on protest in democratic settings. In an authoritarian political setting—as dealt with in this chapter—we may assume that the positive value of protest for individuals will be enhanced by the satisfaction of expressing deeply held convictions for decency and self-respect. The reverse side of imposed conformity in an authoritarian regime is a deep psychological need on the part of ordinary people publicly to voice the disapproval they always felt but were unable to act on. Such protest, across regimes in South America and Eastern Europe, has been described in terms of self-healing, catharsis, and rebounding from apathy, orientations that are rewarding for those who participate (Ash, 1990; Di Palma, 1990; O'Donnell, 1986b).

Further, I assume that ruling elite suppression poses costs (x) for those engaging in collective protest that outweigh the selective benefits. When the number of protesters reaches a high enough level (a), protesters begin to find safety in numbers, and the cost facing the individual who wishes to join in protest begins to decline. The regime is perfectly capable of repressing, say, 1,000 or perhaps even 10,000 protesters, but at some level the sheer number of protesters begins to strain the capacity of the state repressive apparatus to arrest or physically harm the individuals involved. As the number of protesters further increases, the curve describing the utility for the protest swings upward, cutting the curve for nonprotest at the point where the selective benefits of protest outweigh the costs imposed by the regime.

Finally, when the number of protesters reaches some level (b), collective protest becomes system challenging, and both protesters and nonparticipants reap the resulting collective gains (y) or losses (z). These collective gains or losses reflect the strategic costs and benefits of the political opposition conceived as a unitary actor. When it is in the strategic interest of the opposition to punish the ruling elite for suppression by engaging in challenging political activity, mass protest will have a collective benefit. Where challenging political activity in response to toleration is expected to lead the elite to suppress in the next round, mass protest will impose a collective cost for the opposition.

This model does not allow us to predict the unique choices of opponents of the regime. There are two equilibria and they are drastically different: Either everyone in the political opposition will protest or no one will. The situation is an N-person assurance game. It is impossible to estimate the number of individuals within the political opposition who will protest under elite suppression without knowing how individuals themselves evaluate that number. If an individual is assured that enough other players will protest, then he or she will do the same. Otherwise, it is rational to act within the system. In the scenario set out in Figure 3.3, the number of people who must protest to make protest beneficial for each participant is c, which is the point at which the individual payoff from protesting swings into the positive. This is the critical mass necessary to generate mass protest. If an individual believes that more than c individuals will engage in protest, then that person stands to lose if he or she does not follow suit. If an individual believes that the number of protesters will be less than c, then he or she will suffer by participating.

The point at which critical mass is reached is partly determined by the regime. The regime may increase the size of w, the individual cost of protest, by, for example, killing rather than arresting protesters, or it may shift the point at which protesters begin to find safety in numbers (a) to the right by mobilizing more troops, or, finally, it may deny protesters the collective good of strategic influence (y) because it prefers suppression even if the opposition challenges it. If the regime succeeds in pushing c beyond n, which is the total number of individuals in the opposition, then it is never in the interest of individuals to protest. Under all other circumstances, information about intentions is critical.

If there is to be protest under suppression, individuals must be assured that they will act as a group large enough to provide them with safety. The issue is one of coordination. Community ties, social networks of various kinds, and formal organizations may play a decisive role (Oberschall, 1973; Tilly, 1978). However, the necessary assurance does not have to be provided collectively. Individuals may take their cues from their neighbors in the manner of individuals in a school of fish, or may coordinate their behavior around a focal point or incident that provides a common cause, time, and place for protest (Schelling, 1960, p. 90).

The model set out here is obviously an extreme simplification. Reality will be much more complicated: Individuals are heterogeneous, having varying vulnerability to the costs imposed by the regime and reaping varying selective benefits from protest. It is quite possible that some people may be willing to protest even if no one else does, whereas others may demand varying levels of assurance. However, the same basic feature—dual equilibria—is a logical feature of models that are more complex than the one presented here. The critical element producing dual equilibria is that the curve for protest dissects the curve for nonprotest, and this results from the basic assumption that when the number of participants is low, protest is less desirable than nonprotest for some proportion of individuals, while at a higher level of participation protest becomes more desirable than nonprotest for some proportion of individuals.

Dual equilibria are consistent with discontinuities of protest in authoritarian regimes. In many cases, the revolutions in East Germany and Czechoslovakia being the most recent, the number of people engaging in protest did not increase incrementally over time, but rose sharply once expectations about the number of protesters and the costs of protest shifted.[12] Such expectations appear

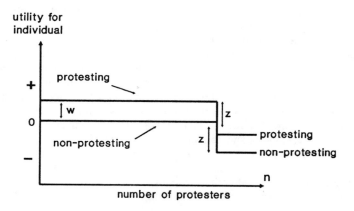

Figure 3.4. Individual Utility for Protesters and Nonprotesters Under Toleration

extraordinarily sensitive to external impeti that produce in people's minds an expectation that protest will take place. For example, the murder of Aquino in the Philippines created the expectation that mass protest would accompany his funeral. When individuals realized they could find safety in numbers that strained the repressive capacity of the state, each new occasion that coordinated expectations saw mass protest. This kind of scenario is frequently determined by pivotal episodes where very small and unpredictable impeti have very large consequences for collective protest.

Opposition Strategy Under Toleration

The model describing the strategic situation facing individuals in the political opposition under toleration, illustrated in Figure 3.4, differs from that just discussed in two respects. First, the regime is no longer repressive and does not impose negative sanctions on those who protest. Second, when protest takes place in numbers sufficient to challenge the regime (at *b*), the political opposition suffers a collective bad (*z*), because it risks unleashing elite suppression in the future. The resulting model is based on the continued assumption that protest provides individuals with selective benefits. In the period immediately following suppression this appears reasonable, although alternatives exist, some of which I discuss below.

The critical task for the political opposition in this scenario is to *limit* protest despite the penchant of individual oppositionists to protest previously bottled-up anger, grievances, and demands. The elite has decided to tolerate the opposition, but in the early stages of democratic transition the elite still retains economic and social privileges, disproportionate political power, control of the military, and responsibility for the brutalities it has previously committed. Yet at the very moment when individuals in the political opposition have the freedom to protest these injustices, to try to bring about radical change by mounting mass demonstrations, political strikes, and so on, they come face-to-face with the paradox of collective action: What is rational for them as individuals is irrational for the group as a whole.

The problem of providing restraint under elite toleration is that no rational individual will do so, because his or her individual sacrifice makes little or no difference. Communitarian norms are unlikely to be of much help. Given previous experience of suppression, the community response is likely to be one of collective anger and indignation. Leaders of the opposition are saddled with the task of trying to stem a tide of protest that they have helped build up under suppression.

If the political opposition is too small to mount a challenge to the regime under toleration (i.e., if $n < b$), then the dilemma does not exist. The weakness of the opposition nullifies the elite's fear of the consequences of opposition challenge under toleration, although such a situation would be double-edged, for it would also reduce the cost of suppression for the elite. This possibility reveals that there is no iron link between strength of political opposition and likelihood of toleration. Although a weak opposition reduces the cost of suppression for a ruling elite, it simultaneously reduces the cost of toleration.[13]

Where the opposition is strong, its ability to provide the collective good of restraint under toleration is positively related to its organizational coverage, coherence, and ideological cohesion. The more extensive the coverage of an organization, the more it can internalize the collective benefits that result from its restraint (Olson, 1982). An organization that encompasses a significant proportion of a group is better able to act in that group's collective interest. If, as is likely, the political opposition is made up of more than one group or party, the transition process is helped if they are not numerous and ideologically split. If there are many opposition groups, the problem of coordination at the individual level is replicated at the group level. If there are ideological splits, it will be more difficult to agree on a policy of restraint. Restraint on the part of some groups in an attempt to stabilize the transitional political system and assure the elite may involve unacceptable losses of support to opposition groups that outbid them for popular support while free riding on their restraint. If, as discussed below, pact negotiations take place between the ruling elite and political opposition, the fewer the number of opposition parties, the more streamlined the process of negotiation between the opposition and the ruling elite (Gunther, 1992). A coherent and ideologically cohesive political opposition is therefore not only more capable of providing reliable expectations that undergird protest in a suppressive regime, but more able to provide the ruling elite with credible assurance that if it tolerates political opposition, the political opposition, for its part, will not challenge the political system.

Why should the ruling elite believe leaders of the opposition when they promise to act "responsibly" if the elite liberalizes the regime? If the elite retains the capacity to suppress the opposition after having tolerated it, then they have a kind of insurance in the event that the opposition defects or leaders cannot control followers. However, this insurance is weakened by two considerations. First, the discount rate for both political opposition and ruling elite is likely to be high. In a situation where the stakes encompass ruling elite monopoly of government and the future of the regime, the present and near future are likely to loom large relative to the more distant future. Second, suppression will be more costly for the ruling elite following a period of toleration. A likely effect of opening political space for political opposition is a flowering of opposition activity among those who had previously kept quiet out of fear. Political parties, political clubs, trade unions, issue groups of diverse kinds, newspapers, and so on will flourish as repressive disincentives to group activity weaken and as new possibilities of communication alert individuals and groups to their diverse common interests (O'Donnell & Schmitter, 1986b). It is far more costly for a ruling elite to try to suppress its political opponents after the first step toward liberalization than prior to that step.

Given this, an explicit agreement, or pact, between a ruling elite and political opposition may play a critical role in assuaging elite fears that the opposition may use its newfound freedom to challenge the political system and in strengthening the elite's hand even if the opposition does challenge. A pact may involve substantive concessions on the part of the opposition on policy. For example, a pact may guarantee the legal status of elite landholdings, foreign corporations, or private property in general, or it may involve a promise on the part of the opposition to limit prosecution of past crimes committed by the ruling elite. In this way a pact may provide the ruling elite with assurances that reduce the stakes of political conflict if it tolerates the opposition. Procedurally, a pact may shape the rules of political competition by, for example, specifying the constitutional role of the military, the character of the electoral system, or the conditions under which constitutional reform is possible. In this way, the pact shapes the terrain of political competition in favor of the ruling elite, providing the elite with the prospect of influence over posttransition outcomes.

Pacts are extremely useful in transition scenarios, but they rest on preconditions similar to those of tit for tat. They demand either that the political opposition be weakly organized, thus giving wide scope for elite bargaining without fear of widespread protest, or that the opposition be organized in a few coherent, ideologically cohesive bodies capable of negotiating and implementing pacts (O'Donnell, 1986a). Moreover, pacts between ruling elites and political oppositions are recent innovations. Only when democracy is conceived as an explicit goal of political development does it make sense to bargain about the means and institutional configuration of the resulting democratic regime. Pactmaking as the path to democracy is, therefore, a response of elites who have been able to learn from the experience of earlier transitions to democracy.[14]

A critical assumption in the subgame elaborated here is that individuals within the political opposition receive identical selective benefits when they protest. When we refine the model, making it a little more realistic by adding a dynamic element of preference change over time and by allowing for the fact that selective benefits vary across individuals, an elite strategy of tit for tat produces toleration even in the absence of some of the conditions set out above.

So far, I have assumed that individuals in the political opposition respond to toleration by protesting pent-up demands and grievances because they gain selective benefits by doing so. This seems a sensible assumption for the round following a shift from suppression to toleration, but it may describe only the immediate response to toleration, not the response in future rounds if toleration is sustained. Consider the logical implications if protest under toleration involves a small but negative cost arising from commitment of time and energy and, further, that selective benefits derived from protest progressively decline in size if toleration is sustained. Even if protest entails collective benefits for some constituency, individuals face an incentive to free ride rather than participate. Under these circumstances, the ruling elite realizes that system-challenging protest is most dangerous in the very short term; further down the road, antisystem anger and retribution will decay if a liberalized regime is institutionalized. In this model, toleration itself shapes preferences for protest. Taking up the famous phrase used in the *Times* to describe the way in which suffrage extension in Britain in 1867 would shape working-class political activity, this can be described as the "Angels in Marble" effect.[15]

Consider, also, the consequences of relaxing the assumption that all political opponents of the regime have an identical preference for protest and, instead, assume that there is a normal distribution of selective benefits of protest for individuals around some mean (w_{mean}) and that protest also involves some small uniform cost of time and energy, as above. In this case, the size of w_{mean} becomes critical in determining the number of protesters under toleration. The greater the sense of injustice and the deeper the grievances felt by the opposition, the higher we would expect w_{mean} to be. Conversely, at some level of w_{mean}, a regime that had not so brutally abused the political opposition could expect a level of protest that, although perhaps high, would not reach the threshold at which it is system threatening. The same result might be accomplished by time and generational turnover even in cases where the regime has engaged in brutal repression (O'Donnell & Schmitter, 1986b). For example, General Franco's regime systematically killed tens of thousands of political opponents during and after the Spanish Civil War, but by the 1970s most of the generation who had suffered through those years were no longer politically active, with the result that the political opposition was able to negotiate with the elite in good faith (Gunther, Sani, & Shabad, 1986).

INTRA-ELITE POLITICS

Let us inject an external shock into this scenario that exacerbates and drives into the open a fundamental, though formerly latent, tension within the elite. As a result of, say, the transparent failure of the elite in a foreign policy adventure or the death of a unifying authoritarian leader, the ruling elite is riven

Table 3.1 Subgame Between Hardliners and Softliners

		Softliners	
		Tolerate	Suppress
Hardliners	Tolerate	3, 4*	1, 1
	Suppress	2, 2	4, 3*

Payoffs: 4 = best; 3 = second best; 2 = second worst; 1 = worst.
*Nash equilibria.

into two groups: hardliners who wish to suppress the opposition and softliners who prefer to tolerate the opposition. While hardliners and softliners differ in their preference for suppression versus toleration, their preferences are identical in one vital respect. Both groups realize that if they cannot agree on a single course of action they will be very severely punished. Softliners who defect from hardliners bent on suppression are themselves a likely target; hardliners who suppress without the active participation of the elite risk defeat. This subgame within the ruling elite is set out in Table 3.1.

This game has a key characteristic of the game of chicken.[16] If either of the actors is able to convince the other that nothing will deter it from its preferred strategy, then that will be the outcome. If softliners are convinced that hardliners will suppress no matter what they do, their effective choices are either to go along or to pay the dire penalty of breaking ranks. Similarly, once hardliners believe that softliners are committed irrevocably to toleration, they will choose to join them rather than suppress alone. This game has multiple equilibria in both the single-shot and iterated versions, and these are starred in Table 3.1. The outcome is determined by the expectations of each actor concerning the strategies of the other, the expectations of each about the other's expectations, and so on. Hardliners and softliners are driven into a realm of bluff and counterbluff, of attempts to precommit one's strategy to force the other's hand. It is a game that turns on the ability to make credible threats, to nurse and manipulate a reputation for toughness, and to seize the initiative.

The cardinal values of the payoffs constrain such strategies. The more painful disunity is for any one faction relative to the other, the greater the disincentive for that faction to precommit. If, for example, hardliners monopolize coercive resources and are only mildly punished if they suppress without softliner support, whereas softliners are severely punished if their strategy diverges from that of the hardliners, a threat on the part of softliners to tolerate no matter what is likely to sound hollow. As O'Donnell and Schmitter (1986b) emphasize, softliners must have support within the military to press effectively for liberalization.

An interesting and critical feature of this subgame is that it is intimately linked to the subgame within the political opposition. The threat of opposition mobilization under continued suppression is an important resource for softliners, allowing them to argue for toleration as a practical adaptation to societal pressures as well as on ethical terms. But, as I have stressed above, the likelihood of system-challenging opposition mobilization is not a game against inert nature. The probability of it's happening cannot be evaluated independently of the struggle within the ruling elite itself. The collective good of system-challenging protest for the political opposition is devalued if softliners are weak and the prospects of toleration correspondingly dim. Conversely, opposition protest may be sparked if softliners are effective and the ruling elite badly split. This is to say that the subgames within the ruling elite and political opposition are not isolated but mutually feed into each other. Expectations about the strategic choices in one subgame directly influence strategic choices in the other. Hence the indeterminacy of each subgame is magnified by its interaction.

CONCLUSION

This chapter models a simple strategic interaction between a ruling elite, composed of two potential factions, and a political opposition, composed of N-individuals. Each actor has two, and only two, choices. The ruling elite, and factions within it, chooses to tolerate or suppress the political opposition; the political opposition, and individuals within it, responds by acting within the political system or by challenging the political system.

Real situations are, of course, more complicated. Instead of two factions within the ruling elite, there may be three or more. The preferences of individuals within the political opposition will be diverse, not uniform. Also, decision making within the elite and opposition will not be as rational as assumed here. The potential use of a model such as this rests in how much it can aid us in understanding systems that, inevitably, are more complex than those in the model. Has the model captured salient aspects of a range of situations that, although different from the model in some respects, are similar in others? I have presented some evidence for the robustness of my conclusions across different sets of assumptions, but readers will no doubt come to their own conclusions about the heuristic value of the model applied to cases they know well.

One further motive for making the model as simple as possible is to reveal the minimal conditions for chaos in regime transformations. If one finds indeterminacy in a relatively simple system, then it should also be present if one adds additional elements to the model in an effort to replicate individual cases (or sets of cases) more precisely. If one begins with a very complex picture of the process of regime transformation, then the temptation is to believe that indeterminacy is the result of precisely this complexity. The corresponding fallacy is that simpler scenarios, specifically scenarios in which the number of actors or factions is smaller, are more deterministic.

Under a variety of assumptions concerning individual preferences, the decisions of individual opponents of the regime about whether to protest or not

have the structure of an N-person assurance game. Either every opponent of
the regime protests or nobody does, depending on the information individuals
have about the intentions of others. These intentions are extremely sensitive to
public cues or demonstration effects. The death of the leader of the ruling elite,
reports of a revolution in a neighboring state, the murder of an opposition
leader—these are the kinds of cues that transform the possibilities of opposition
response to suppression, not by directly altering preferences, but by changing
expectations about how others will respond. The phenomenon is in some
interesting respects similar to that of creating a focal point that has an effect
on the strategy of opponents of the regime simply because it coordinates
expectations (Schelling, 1960).

In this context, game theorizing alerts us to situations in which outcomes are
embedded in intentions, evaluations of intentions, evaluations of evaluations,
and so forth. Metagames, in which players try to shape such evaluations, take
a variety of forms. In the model I have analyzed here, metagames within the
ruling elite and political opposition are intimately connected. The struggle
between hardliners and softliners to precommit their strategies credibly, and
thereby to force the other's hand, is constrained by the expected response of
the political opposition. At the same time, a split within the ruling elite may
provide a powerful cue for individuals in the opposition to protest.

These dynamics stand in sharp contrast to the situation under nonstrategic
suppression, where the ruling elite is determined to suppress irrespective of the
response of the political opposition. This type of scenario is determined by the
relative costs of toleration and suppression for the ruling elite and is likely to
be stable and predictable in the short term. The model analyzed in this essay
reveals that scenarios of democratic transition in which there is strategic
interaction between the ruling elite and political opposition have fundamentally
different properties. Outcomes of such scenarios are highly sensitive to extremely small changes in relevant variables and are correspondingly unstable
and indeterminate.

Hence indeterminacy is not simply a by-product of inadequate knowledge about
extremely complex and fluctuating preferences, groups, or social systems; rather,
it is an essential feature of strategic interaction in contested political systems where
constraining expectations generated by established norms and institutions break
down. The source of the inability of social scientists to predict political outcomes
is, therefore, not to be found in complexity or in transient weaknesses of theory or
insufficient data, but is inherent in certain types of situations, of which the scenarios
analyzed in this chapter provide an illustration.

NOTES

1. The term *chaos* was initially developed in the physical sciences in reference to
"irregular, unpredictable behavior of deterministic, nonlinear dynamical systems" (Roderick

Jensen, quoted in Gleick, 1987, p. 306). Applying *chaos* to social systems, I define the term with reference to a distinguishing characteristic of chaotic systems in the physical sciences: *sensitive dependence on initial conditions.*

2. Figure 3.1 follows conventional notation. In prisoner's dilemma, R, S, T, and P symbolize Reward, Sucker, Temptation, and Penalty, respectively.

3. This is to exclude fringe groups or terrorists who prefer repression in the short term in order to provoke radical resistance to the ruling elite. The political influence of such groups on elite decisions to tolerate or suppress is, in most cases, marginal. Spain is a case in point.

4. Here my terminology departs from conventional game theory, which describes elite choice in this kind of scenario as "dominant strategy." I describe such choice as "non-strategic" to emphasize that, within the context of the model, it is independent of other players' strategies.

5. These situations are given by $R_1 > P_1$ and $T_1 > S_1$ in addition to the inequalities specified in Assumption 1.

6. Juan Linz (1975) has observed that repression itself was a goal of this type of regime: "A frightening and rationally difficult to explain characteristic of Nazi and Stalinist terror was the degree to which it was unnecessary and even dysfunctional for the achievement of the goals those systems had set themselves, the extent to which it had become an evil end in itself" (p. 228).

7. Where landed aristocracies rooted in feudal institutions dominated government—as was the case in the larger countries of Europe—the surest path, and perhaps the only path, to democracy was via revolution (Moore, 1966). However, revolution was not necessary for democratization in the smaller societies where there were not enough large estates to produce a strong landed aristocracy (Castles, 1973; Stephens, 1989) and where, as a consequence, the ruling elite did not view monopoly of government as necessary for its economic survival.

8. George Tsebelis (1989) makes a similar point in the context of evaluating decision-theoretic and game-theoretic explanations.

9. The minimal conditions for this scenario are, given Assumptions 1 and 2, $T_1 > R_1$ and $S_1 > P_1$. In this scenario, the elite's preference ordering is therefore $T_1 > R_1 > S_1 > P_1$.

10. The minimal conditions for this scenario are, given Assumptions 1 and 2, $R_1 > T_1$ and $P_1 > S_1$. In this scenario, the elite's preference ordering is therefore $R_1 > T_1 > P_1 > S_1$.

11. The minimal conditions for this scenario are, given Assumptions 1 and 2, $R_1 > T_1$ and $P_1 > S_1$. In this scenario, the elite's preference ordering is therefore $T_1 > R_1 > P_1 > S_1$.

12. For an insightful discussion of protest in Eastern Europe using game-theoretic concepts, see Bunce and Chong (1990).

13. This is to take issue with Dahl (1971), who maintains that it is axiomatic that "the likelihood that a government will tolerate an opposition increases as the resources available to the government for suppression decline relative to the resources of an opposition" (p. 48).

14. Earlier pacts, such as the elite settlement of 1688-1689 in England or the Swedish settlement of 1809, facilitated but were not directly linked to the creation of a democratic regime (Burton, Gunther, & Higley, 1992).

15. This is merely to suggest one property of a dynamic model. Another would be that sustained suppression increases selective incentives for protest up to some point. This would lower the critical mass necessary for opposition protest. However, a suppressive regime might counter by increasing the severity of suppression, thereby raising the costs of protest.

16. The game is not strictly a game of chicken, which is characterized by $T > R > S > P$ for both players.

REFERENCES

Ash, T. G. (1990). Eastern Europe: The year of truth. *New York Review of Books, 18.*

Bollen, K. A., & Jackman, R. W. (1985). Economic and noneconomic determinants of political democracy in the 1960s. *Research in Political Sociology, 1,* 27-48.

Bunce, V., & Chong, D. (1990, August). *The party's over: Mass protest and the end of communist rule in Eastern Europe.* Paper presented at the annual meeting of the American Political Science Association, San Francisco.

Burton, M., Gunther, R., & Higley, J. (1992). Introduction: Elite transformations and democratic regimes. In J. Higley & R. Gunther (Eds.), *Elites and democratic consolidation in Latin America and Southern Europe.* Cambridge: Cambridge University Press.

Castles, F. G. (1973). Barrington Moore's thesis and Swedish political development. *Government and Opposition, 8,* 313-330.

Dahl, R. A. (1971). *Polyarchy: Participation and opposition.* New Haven, CT: Yale University Press.

Dahl, R. A. (1989). *Democracy and its critics.* New Haven, CT: Yale University Press.

Diamond, L. (1989). Beyond authoritarianism and totalitarianism: Strategies for democratization. *Washington Quarterly, 12,* 141-163.

Diamond, L., Linz, J. J., & Lipset, S. M. (1988-1989). *Democracy in developing countries* (4 vols.). Boulder, CO: Lynne Rienner.

Di Palma, G. (1990). *Transitions: Puzzles and surprises from West to East.* Paper presented at the Conference of Europeanists, Washington, DC.

Elster, J. (1989). *The cement of society: A study of social order.* Cambridge: Cambridge University Press.

Finkel, S. E., Muller, E. N., & Opp, K.-D. (1989). Personal influence, collective rationality, and mass political action. *American Political Science Review, 83,* 885-904.

Gleick, J. (1987). *Chaos: Making a new science.* New York: Viking.

Gunther, R. (1992). Spain: The very model of the modern elite settlement. In J. Higley & R. Gunther (Eds.), *Elites and democratic consolidation in Latin America and Southern Europe* (pp. 38-80). Cambridge: Cambridge University Press.

Gunther, R., Sani, G., & Shabad, G. (1986). *Spain after Franco: The making of a competitive party system.* Berkeley: University of California Press.

Huntington, S. P. (1984). Will more countries become democratic? *Political Science Quarterly, 99,* 193-218.

Huntington, S. P. (1991). Democracy's third wave. *Journal of Democracy, 2,* 12-34.

Linz, J. J. (1975). Totalitarian and authoritarian regimes. In F. I. Greenstein & N. W. Polsby (Eds.), *Handbook of political science: Vol. 3. Macropolitical theory* (pp. 175-411). Reading, MA: Addison-Wesley.

Linz, J. J., & Stepan, A. (1989). Political crafting of democratic consolidation or destruction: European and South American comparisons. In J. Linz & A. Stepan (Eds.), *Democracy in the Americas: Stopping the pendulum* (pp. 41-61). New York: Holmes & Meier.

Lipset, S. M. (1959). Some social requisites of democracy: Economic development and political legitimacy. *American Political Science Review, 53,* 69-105.

Lipset, S. M. (1963). *Revolution and counterrevolution: Change and persistence in social structures.* New York: Basic Books.

Lipset, S. M. (1981). *Political man: The social bases of politics* (expanded, rev. ed.). Baltimore: Johns Hopkins University Press. (Original work published 1960)

Lipset, S. M. (1983). Radicalism or reformism: The sources of working-class politics. *American Political Science Review, 77,* 1-19.

Marks, G. (1989). *Unions in politics: Britain, Germany, and the United States in the nineteenth and early twentieth centuries.* Princeton, NJ: Princeton University Press.

Moore, B., Jr. (1966). *Social origins of dictatorship and democracy: Lord and peasant in the making of the modern world.* Boston: Beacon.

Muller, E. N., & Opp, K.-D. (1986). Rational choice and rebellious collective action. *American Political Science Review, 80,* 471-489.

Oberschall, A. (1973). *Social conflict and social movement.* Englewood Cliffs, NJ: Prentice-Hall.

O'Donnell, G. (1986a). Introduction to the Latin American cases. In G. O'Donnell, P. C. Schmitter, & L. Whitehead (Eds.), *Transition from authoritarian rule: Latin America* (pp. 3-18). Baltimore: Johns Hopkins University Press.

O'Donnell, G. (1986b). On the fruitful convergences of Hirschman's *Exit, voice, and loyalty* and *Shifting involvements*: Reflections from the recent Argentine experience. In A. Foxley et al. (Eds.), *Development, democracy, and the art of trespassing: Essays in honor of Albert O. Hirschman* (pp. 249-268). Baltimore: Johns Hopkins University Press.

O'Donnell, G., & Schmitter, P. C. (Eds.). (1986a). *Transition from authoritarian rule: Southern Europe.* Baltimore: Johns Hopkins University Press.

O'Donnell, G., & Schmitter, P. C. (1986b). *Transitions from authoritarian rule: Tentative conclusions about uncertain democracies.* Baltimore: Johns Hopkins University Press.

Olson, M. (1982). *The rise and decline of nations.* New Haven, CT: Yale University Press.

Przeworski, A. (1986). Some problems in the study of transition to democracy. In G. O'Donnell, P. C. Schmitter, & L. Whitehead (Eds.), *Transition from authoritarian rule: Comparative perspectives* (pp. 47-63). Baltimore: Johns Hopkins University Press.

Schelling, T. C. (1960). *The strategy of conflict.* Cambridge, MA: Harvard University Press.

Schelling, T. C. (1978). *Micromotives and macrobehavior.* New York: Norton.

Stephens, J. D. (1989). Democratic transition and breakdown in Western Europe, 1870-1939: A test of the Moore thesis. *American Journal of Sociology, 94,* 1019-1077.

Tarrow, S. (1983). *Struggling to reform: Social movements and policy change during cycles of protest.* Ithaca, NY: Cornell University, Center for International Studies.

Taylor, M. (1987). *The possibility of cooperation.* Cambridge: Cambridge University Press.

Tilly, C. (1978). *From mobilization to revolution.* Reading, MA: Addison-Wesley.

Tsebelis, G. (1989). The abuse of probability in political analysis: The Robinson Crusoe fallacy. *American Political Science Review, 83,* 77-91.

Valenzuela, J. S. (1989). Labor movements in transitions to democracy: A framework for analysis. *Comparative Politics, 21,* 445-472.

Weeks, J. (1986). An interpretation of the Central American crisis. *Latin American Research Review, 21,* 31-53.

4

On the Place of Virtues in a Pluralistic Democracy

Amitai Etzioni

THE VIRTUE OF VIRTUES

IF a community recognizes a set of moral values and commitments as compelling, as virtues, these become the foundations of moral discourse in that community. Other statements, new moral claims, and so on—as long as they are not absorbed into the set of shared virtues—have no or little standing. And, while there are frequently differences in interpreting the exact meanings and implications of prevailing virtues—for instance, how much is due to charity?—virtues do provide sound and shared foundations for consensus formation, community endeavors, public policies, *and* moral standing. For example, in the traditional European Jewish *shtetl,* studying the scriptures was accorded high virtue. It left little doubt as to which activities were to be extolled and merited the seat nearest the preferred Eastern (oriented to Jerusalem) wall of the synagogue. It was not a question of the rights of one subgroup versus those of others, but a communitywide recognition of the virtue of commitment to the scriptures.

Also, in communities that subscribe to shared virtues (or communitarian values), contentiousness and litigiousness are curbed, as relatively clear and shared criteria are available to resolve differences. Finally, the cynicism of "anything goes as long as it satisfies a deal among the interpreted parties" is avoided.

THE FEAR OF CONSENSUAL MORALITY

Despite all these apparent merits, the concept of virtues troubles many who are committed to democratic values. While some of their misgivings are

AUTHOR'S NOTE: I am indebted to Brad Wilcox and Sharon Pressner for research assistance.

misplaced or overstated, they point to considerations and measures that those who wish to embrace the language of virtue best attend to.

One frequently raised objection to the notion of virtues (as well as to communitarian values), is that they are "majoritarian" ("Communitarian really means majoritarian," according to Ira Glasser; quoted in *Business Week,* September 3, 1990, p. 56). That is, once a community comes to share a set of values, these will be used to suppress dissent and minorities, to violate individual and civil rights. (The lack of a secure place for individual and minority rights is a criticism leveled against Alasdair MacIntyre, one of the champions of the language of virtues [Thigpen & Downing, 1987, p. 643; see MacIntyre, 1984].) While historically this fear grows out of the roots of the American existence, a society fashioned by dissenters escaping dogma, it is a legitimate concern for all democracies.

Actually, there are two versions of the concern that are often intertwined and mutually reinforcing but should be kept apart for both analytical and policy purposes. One concerns the polity, the other the community. Within the polity, it is feared that a government will follow a simplistic notion of democracy: It will impose public policies and rules that the majority favor without regard to other rights (e.g., imposing prayers in schools). In the words of John Rawls, "A public and workable agreement on a single and general comprehensive conception [of the good] could be maintained only by the oppressive use of state power" (quoted in Hollenbach, 1989, p. 79). Although this is not a problem necessarily or exclusively caused by the concept of virtues, it can be exacerbated by the elevation of shared consensus to the status of virtues. Historically, this happened in the United States when abortion and divorce were morally condemned and difficult to obtain legally.

Even when the government is not involved, and when there are no votes and hence no "majoritarian" positions or threat, a parallel concern is raised, and not without reason: It is argued that when a community shares one set of virtues that are strongly endorsed and urged upon the members, even without the power of law, only through the community mechanisms of social pressure and ostracism, these can exert great pressures on those who deviate, whether they are gay or conscientious objectors or individuals who refuse to join a strike or boycott and so on. Salem during the witch trials, Geneva during the heyday of Calvinism provide historical cases in point. More recently, the press has referred to the dangers of neopuritanism, which they characterize as excessive public concern over personal behavior (*London Economist,* July 20, 1991; *Time,* August 12, 1991).

Libertarians and laissez-faire conservatives hence tend to favor a community without a set of overarching values, and build instead on the social (not merely economic!) merits of a world in which individuals are the only judges of their own conduct, each choosing what is best and hence personally right for him or her, from how much to work, to whether or not to have a family, to riding a motorbike without a helmet, and even to using addictive substances.

Michael Novak maintains that democracy has value in much the same way that capitalism does: Both work on the principles of aggregating individual choices. Arguing that the common good is too complex for the government or any other large social institution to grasp, Novak believes that government should not attempt to legislate morality, or what is "good for society." David Hollenbach (1989) summarizes Novak's view of the polity this way:

> Thus the best path toward the common good is not one that proceeds by intending the good society as a whole. Rather, the free market institutions of democratic capitalism create the conditions in which an invisible hand will coordinate the pursuit of individual self-interest . . . in a way that maximizes the social good. (p. 72)

And just as there are a series of personal values that sustain a capitalist system—individual virtues such as hard work, thrift, ingenuity, discipline, and mutual respect—there are also individual virtues that sustain a democracy, such as toleration of one another and commitment to liberty. These democratic virtues are justified on the grounds of enlightened self-interest, as are the capitalist virtues. In sum, for classical liberals such as Novak and modern liberals such as Hook, democracy and the virtues that give life to it have value in a systemic fashion: They promote the private pursuit of fulfillment for the ultimate repository of "virtue"—the individual. For that reason, a democratic polity may foster democratic virtues even as it avoids social or communitywide virtues.

As I see it, we should not scrap the quest for shared virtues and communitarian values, and the social mechanisms to affirm them, because nothing makes for more government and ultimate coercion (that is, the demon libertarian and laissez-faire conservatives properly fear) than the absence of shared morals, backed by strong commitments. Once virtues are eroded, social and civic order must, by default, rest more and more on government regulation, controls, and police force. Thus if a community ceases to define drug abuse and alcohol abuse, violence, and greed as unacceptable behavior, it is left solely to the state to protect citizens from these abuses and from one another, an often untenable task. Communities require moral foundations to minimize the role of the government and make those roles it must play possible and properly circumscribed.

Moreover, a community without value commitments is a jungle of warring or selfish parties—indeed, no community at all. Banfield (1958) depicted such a village in his *The Moral Basis of a Backward Society*. In this village, the poverty and backwardness, he concludes, is largely explained by the villagers' inability to act together for their common good, or for any end transcending the immediate interest of each family (p. 10). In short, *what is clearly needed is a political and moral conception that accommodates the protection of minorities' and individuals' rights without giving up the concept of communitarian virtues.*

COMMUNITARIAN VIRTUES AND DEMOCRACY

Communitarians believe that the invisible hand cannot hold a nation together by itself. Moreover, they argue that the libertarian view leads to an insidious complacency about the moral and spiritual health of the republic. Communitarians point out, for instance, that the libertarian faith in one present-day democratic virtue—the right to privacy—provides no legitimate grounds for the prohibition of racial discrimination in private housing, businesses, and clubs. In the communitarian view, communities and the political institutions representing them must make ethical and social issues a common concern, especially given the continuing erosion of central values and social institutions, such as the family, in the postmodern era.

In contrast to the individual-driven faith of libertarians, communitarians argue that persons are social creatures. Personal fulfillment is contingent on social ends and interaction. Virtue, therefore, is not a private affair; virtue signals appropriate conduct in society. And as virtue is a social affair, it also becomes a political concern because, in the words of Aristotle, "a state exists for the sake of a good life, and not for life only" (quoted in Hollenbach, 1989, p. 77).

Virtue serves two important communitarian purposes. First, as a commonly held moral compass, virtue provides persons and social institutions with direction as they grapple with the political, economic, and social issues of the day. Second, a consensus about virtue also legitimates the polity itself by providing, to paraphrase Cicero, public accord about the nature of justice and the need for the public pursuit of the *summum bonum,* the common good. Given virtue's central place, communitarians maintain that the polity must make the moral health of the community its concern and take appropriate social, political, and legal steps to support virtues and the social institutions, such as the family, that sustain them.

PROTECTING RIGHTS

American institutions already reflect an ingenious answer to the need to combine consensus making and the moral power of virtues with a democratic polity. Instead of allowing unrestrained sway to policies that reflect majorities, we have the well-known "balancing" institutions, whose task is not only to curb one another to limit the general power of each but specifically to protect the rights of individuals and minorities. The same protection is, of course, accorded by the courts, above all the U.S. Supreme Court, and the Constitution itself not only as a force that directs law enforcement, regulatory, administrative, and other agencies, but as a moral/social normative factor. (William Galston, in an important paper presented at the 1991 meeting of the American Political Science Association, provides an excellent discussion of that point, especially by pointing out the role that "supermajoritarian" requirements built into American democracy play in this country. That is, for a number of significant political measures, simple majorities cannot define what is of merit or virtue while, say, overriding a presidential veto.)

In short, the U.S. political system is far from a simple democratic government if one means by that, as it is all too often put, the rule of the majority, or of the people by the people for the people. Constitutional democracy is, of course, characterized in part by defining areas over which "the people" or the majority may not set policies, whatever its size.

COMMUNITARIAN PLURALISM?

The fall of Rome is usually the metaphor of choice for harbingers of imminent cultural, social, and political collapse. Communitarians maintain (along with Cicero and Augustine) that the fall of Rome was precipitated by a decline in the sense of public virtue. Modernity, they add, is destined to go Rome's way if the libertarian insistence on individual free choice and state "neutrality" when it comes to matters of virtue, such as protecting the family, continues. Theologian David Hollenbach shares many of the communitarian fears and draws upon one of the greatest "fall of Rome" theorists, Augustine, to outline his vision of the role that virtue should play in a democratic polity. But Hollenbach is also concerned about the tradition of oppression and discrimination in premodern republics; he thus sees a third way between the shoals of libertarianism and authoritarianism.

Augustine's City of God, according to Hollenbach, is the perfect republic. There, citizens are united by a common conception of faith, virtue, and the public end. This, however, is just the kind of polity—a community of faith—that makes liberals apoplectic. Augustine, however, disarms this criticism by suggesting that citizens in a republic should not confuse the City of God with the City of Man. Man's highest hopes for fulfillment must lie with heaven: To make an earthly republic the repository of man's final hopes for the *summum bonum* would be idolatrous. Therefore, the civil realm should (and can) be only the realm of the proximate and the possible good.

An earthly approximation of the good, for Hollenbach, may be found when a community defines a plurality of "common goods." This plurality of common ends and virtues, supported by social mores and the force of law, will provide the community with an integral sense of unity without giving undue emphasis to any one virtue. Hollenbach (1989) cites Jeffrey Stout to make the case that "no sphere [of historical existence] can rightly occupy the position of be-all-end-all in our lives without throwing the rest out of proper proportion—neither vocation, nor family, nor voluntary association, nor private projects, nor politics" (p. 84). Rather, every sphere that contributes in a meaningful way to virtue that the community holds high is entitled to social and political support. By rejecting a unitary relationship between religion and politics while encouraging a plurality of common ends, Hollenbach hopes to meet communitarian hopes while allaying libertarian fears.

THE LIMITS OF PLURALISM

Many, like Hollenbach, argue that pluralism sustains the delicate balance between the will of the majority and consensual virtues and the constitutional safeguards. On the community level, it is argued, if there is no one orthodoxy but several competing truths, the fervor of each will be restrained, and people of different moral persuasions and commitments will find their own sets of virtues (various religions or sets of secular moral values). And, regarding the polity, it is often suggested that if various politically active groups advance different sets of values, no one majoritarian position will arise. Policies then would reflect compromises among the various positions advanced.

However, as I see it, pluralism and virtues do not accommodate each other readily because pluralism mitigates commitments and provides no moral foundations for communitywide consensus per se, no overarching values and criteria for working up differences other than such mechanical and uncommitting notions as splitting the differences and nose count. On the contrary, when there are a number of value commitments, all of which are considered legitimate, all commitments become relative and weak, and there remain only practical, not principled, grounds for community building, shared values, and policies. In effect, this "de-ideologizing" is precisely what the opponents of virtues and proponents of pluralism seek.

It might be argued that in a society in which little is done on a shared basis, as in a frontier society in which those who seek change can go and find their ways in unsettled territories, there is no need for community values, consensus, and virtues. There can be little doubt, however, that for a society such as that in the contemporary United States, which has a long list of matters to which it must attend collectively, such as defense, public safety (crime), the environment, and global competitiveness, a society that has lost the basic moral/social foundations of a shared social and civic order, pluralism per se will not suffice.

PLURALISM WITHIN UNITY:
VIRTUES WITH RIGHTS

As Seymour Martin Lipset (1960) writes, "The stability of any given democracy depends . . . upon the effectiveness and the legitimacy of its political system" (p. 77). Both the effectiveness and legitimacy of a democratic society depend on a measure of unity. Yet many democratic societies, especially the United States, confront the fact of ethnic, religious, and social pluralism. How can we then sustain an effective and legitimate republic?

An answer is to be found in the concept of pluralism within unity. It recognizes that diversity cannot be unlimited and that some ultimate values must be shared for the diversity to be contained. These provide the foundations for shared policies and criteria for settling conflicting claims. These virtues include, first of all, a set of ultimate values such as compassion for the poor, concern for the viability of the family, and concern for the environment. (The fact that these values are fuzzy at the edges is not necessarily detrimental, because as long as the basic commitments stand, societies have various ways to work out the specific meanings of such values; this ceases to be the case when the values are directly challenged or their basic meaning is contested.)

Second, the shared values or virtues are to include a legitimation of democracy and tolerance of diversity within the shared framework and of individual standings and hence certain basic rights (Langan, 1990). This point should be stressed: Individual rights do not rest on individuals, somehow born or endowed with them, but on a community-shared morality that legitimates and otherwise sustains them. In the polity, community values and virtues take the form of recognizing a public interest or interests above and beyond the plurality of special ones. Both of these points deserve some elaboration.

The first issue is frequently raised in discussions of bicultural education. Pluralists stress the merits of allowing, even encouraging, people of different ethnic, cultural, and racial backgrounds, especially immigrants, not only to learn in their own language and traditions—say, Spanish—rather than be forced to shift right away and learn all subjects in English, but also to maintain separate traditions and learning (e.g., Black English) and to maintain parallel tracks of values and commitments, without a commitment to a shared, overarching educational program. Thus in Miami, a Cuban American can complete 12 years of school in a Spanish program without ever mingling with other Americans or learning about American core values, at least not without a strong Hispanic orientation. These educational programs are compatible with the concept of a "rainbow" society, in which a variety of equally legitimate "colors," with different traditions and virtues, are to coexist alongside one another.

I suggest that such unbounded pluralism, one that cuts into ultimate values and shared virtues, is not compatible with maintaining a moral, social, and civic order, with providing a community with a set of criteria for sorting out differences and forming consensus, and hence is incompatible with the democratic process. Pluralism is compatible with community and virtue as long as it is limited to maintaining *sub*traditions, as long as all recognize areas of *communalities that frame the community* as well as mutual tolerance and respect of the various plural traditions. Thus no sociopolitical difficulties arise if various groups adhere to different folk dances, songs, food tastes, religious beliefs, and social manners (say, at weddings and funerals). No melting pot is needed here. However, when these groups cease to share a commitment to one community, society, or nation, the unity that needs to contain pluralism is strained.

For example, in a debate with a representative of a major Hispanic group on William F. Buckley, Jr.'s television show *Firing Line,* I suggested that while it is fine for various ethnic groups in the United States to maintain their languages as second languages (from Hebrew to Japanese), they all need to learn English. The Hispanic representative argued that we all live in a Hispanic hemisphere and hence we should all first learn Spanish; then those who wish may learn English on the side. This notion cuts into the bonds of unity. (Language often has this power—it still divides Belgium and Canada, and, whereas the Swiss make do with several, they are only following a thousand years of warfare among the various language-loyal cantons.)

In the same vein, later in the same debate the representative of the Hispanic group declared that should the United States engage in war in Latin America— say, Nicaragua (this program took place before the U.S. intervention in Panama)—Hispanic Americans ought to refuse to fight. Similarly, some black Americans opposed participating in the war in the Persian Gulf because they saw it as a black-against-black confrontation. At a Harlem rally, the Reverend Al Sharpton proclaimed, "We will not fight our brothers in the Middle East" (quoted in *New Yorker*, March 18, 1991).

Typically, communities cannot tolerate pluralism on these issues when sizable groups are involved (they can and do tolerate a few conscientious objectors). Ravitch (1991) put it well:

> If there is no overall community, if all we have is a motley collection of racial and ethnic cultures, there will be no sense of the common good. Each group will fight for its own particular interests, and we could easily disintegrate as a nation, becoming instead embroiled in the kinds of ethnic conflicts that often dominate the foreign news each night. (p. 36)

There is no clearly established list of what belongs in the share frame versus in which areas pluralism is welcome or essential. Indeed, the specific list may differ from one community to another (e.g., many European countries include Good Samaritan laws, we do not; Glendon, 1990-1991, p. 10) as long as the realm of virtues is sufficiently powerful to provide a containing capsule to the centrifugal forces of the various plural parts. A shared set of basic moral values, a language, some shared national symbols and values, a commitment to mutual tolerance, and a commitment to democracy, as a "good" and not merely as a procedural device, seem to be essential and found in most if not all functioning democracies. These shared values are noticeably absent in other societies as different as the Soviet Union was from Nigeria. The jury is out about India, where the weak set of shared virtues is reflected in massive intergroup violence and frequent violations of individual rights.

In the polity, the same issue arises with reference to the concept of the public interest. Unbounded pluralists have argued that there is no need for a concept of public interest and that none is possible (Truman, 1964, p. 50). Politics, they argue, is an extension to society from a market concept, as special interest groups vie with one another over the direction of public policies (Key, 1958, p. 166). The state is merely a point that reflects the results of the relative power of the various special inputs (Milbrath, 1963, p. 345). While it is true that the notion of public interest is often raised, unbounded pluralists argue that these statements are mere ideological ones that each special interest group mouths to advance its particular cause (Horowitz, 1979, p. 4); that public interest cannot even be defined.

In contrast, I argue that a concept of public interest, recognizing that some virtues rest in the commons, is needed to correct and balance the political centrifugal forces, as it is necessary in the community to balance the moral/social effects of pluralism there (Etzioni, 1984). Moreover, one can determine when a group advances the needs of its members and when it serves the public at large according to who benefits from the action. Thus the Sierra Club, a leading environmentalist group, on the basis of its stated goals, is clearly a public interest group. On the other hand, if it really does dedicate itself, as Tucker (1982) argues, to gaining privileges for its upper-middle-class members, such as untrammeled mountains to ski on, it clearly is a special interest group.

In conclusion, communitarian virtues—virtues shared and underwritten by a community—are not incompatible with true democracy. Rights can be protected if communitarian virtues include tolerance for one another and, above all, a clear demarcation of the areas that deservedly lie in the public realm and those that ought to be left to individual choice and subgroup preferences. Moreover, various political mechanisms, especially the Constitution, serve to sustain the creative tension between spheres of commonality and social virtues and spheres of individuality and personal virtues.

REFERENCES

Banfield, E. (1958). *The moral basis of a backward society.* Glencoe, IL: Free Press.

Etzioni, A. (1984). *Capital corruption: The new attack on American democracy.* New Brunswick, NJ: Transaction.

Galston, W. (1991, August). *Liberal purposes, democratic processes, and social justice.* Paper presented at the annual meeting of the American Political Science Association, Washington, DC.

Glendon, M. A. (1990-1991). Does the United States need "Good Samaritan" laws? *The Responsive Community: Rights and Responsibilities, 1*(2).

Hollenbach, D. (1989). The common good revisited. *Theological Studies, 50.*

Horowitz, I. L. (1979, September/October). Interest groups and the patriotic gore. *Humanist.*

Key, V. O., Jr. (1958). *Politics, parties, and pressure groups* (4th ed.). New York: Cromwell.

Langan, J. (1990, December). *The moral dimension: One or many?* Paper presented at the annual meeting of the Association for Social Economics, Washington, DC.

Lipset, S. M. (1960). *Political man: The social bases of politics.* Garden City, NY: Doubleday.

MacIntyre, A. (1984). *After virtue: A study in moral theory* (2nd ed.). Notre Dame, IN: Notre Dame University Press.

Milbrath, L. W. (1963). *The Washington lobbyists.* Chicago: Rand McNally.

Ravitch, D. (1991). Pluralism vs. particularism in American education. *The Responsive Community: Rights and Responsibilities, 1*(2).

Thigpen, R. B., & Downing, L. A. (1987). Liberalism and the communitarian critique. *American Journal of Political Science, 31,* 637-655.

Truman, D. B. (1964). *The governmental process: Political interests and public opinion.* New York: Alfred A. Knopf.

Tucker, W. (1982). *Progress and privilege: America in the age of environmentalism.* Garden City, NY: Anchor.

5

The Concept of
National Development, 1917-1989
ELEGY AND REQUIEM

Immanuel Wallerstein

S INCE at least the sixteenth century, European thinkers have been discussing how to augment the wealth of the realm, and governments have sought or were adjured to take steps to maintain and enhance this wealth. All the debates about mercantilism centered on how to be certain that more wealth entered a state than left it. When Adam Smith wrote *The Wealth of Nations* in 1776, he was concerned with attacking the notion that governments could best enhance this wealth by various restrictions on foreign trade. He preached instead the notion that maximizing the ability of individual entrepreneurs to act as they deemed wisest in the world market would in fact result in an optimal enhancement of the wealth of the nation.

This tension between a basically protectionist versus a free trade stance became one of the major themes of policy-making in the various states of the world-system in the nineteenth century. It often was the most significant issue that divided the principal political forces of particular states. It was clear by then that a central ideological theme of the capitalist world-economy was that every state could, and indeed eventually probably would, reach a high level of national income and that conscious, rational action would make it so. This fit in very well with the underlying Enlightenment theme of inevitable progress and the teleological view of human history that it incarnated.

By the time of the First World War, it was also clear that a series of countries in Western Europe plus the white settler countries in the rest of the world had indeed become, in our contemporary parlance, "developed," or at least were well on their way to doing so. Of course, by the standards of 1990, all of these countries (even Great Britain) were far less "modern" and wealthy than they became later in the century, but by the standards of the time they were doing magnificently. The First World War was the shock it was precisely because, among other things, it seemed a direct menace to this generalized prosperity of what we today call the core zones of the world-economy.

The year 1917 is often taken to be an ideological turning point in the history of the modern world-system. I agree that it was this, but not quite in the way it is usually argued to be. On April 2, 1917, President Woodrow Wilson addressed the Congress of the United States and called for a declaration of war against Germany. He argued: "The world must be made safe for democracy." That same year, on November 7, the Bolsheviks assaulted the Winter Palace in the name of the workers' revolution. The great ideological antinomy of the twentieth century, Wilsonianism versus Leninism, may be said to have been born in 1917. I shall argue that it died in 1989. I shall further argue that the key issue to which both ideologies addressed themselves was the political integration of the periphery of the world-system. And finally, I shall argue that the mechanism of such integration was, both for Wilsonianism and for Leninism, "national development," and that the essential dispute between them was merely about the path to such national development.

WILSON, LENIN, AND NATIONAL SOVEREIGNTY

Wilsonianism was based on classical liberal presuppositions. It was universalist, claiming that its precepts applied equally everywhere. It assumed that everyone acted on the basis of rational self-interest and that therefore everyone in the long run was reasonable. Hence peaceful and reformist practice was plausible. It placed great emphasis on legality and on form.

Of course, none of these precepts was new. In 1917, in fact, they seemed quite old-fashioned. Wilson's innovation (not invention) was to argue that these precepts applied not only to individuals within the state but to nation-states or peoples within the international arena. The principle of self-determination, the centerpiece of Wilsonianism, was nothing but the principle of individual freedom transposed to the level of the interstate system.

The transposition of a theory that had been intended to apply only at the level of individuals to the level of groups is a very tricky proposition. A harsh critic, Sir W. Ivor Jennings (1956), said of Wilson's doctrine of self-determination: "On the surface it seemed reasonable: let the people decide. It was in fact ridiculous because the people cannot decide until somebody decides who are the people" (p. 56). Ay, there's the rub, indeed! Still, it was obvious that, when Wilson was talking about the self-determination of nations, he was not worrying about France or Sweden. He was talking about the liquidation of the Austro-Hungarian, Ottoman, and Russian Empires. And when Roosevelt picked up the same theme a generation later, he was talking about the liquidation of the British, French, Dutch, and other remaining imperial structures. The self-determination of which they were speaking was the self-determination of the peripheral and semiperipheral zones of the world-system.

Lenin pursued very similar policy objectives under the quite different slogans of proletarian internationalism and anti-imperialism. His views were no doubt based on other premises. His universalism was that of the world working class, the soon-to-be singular class that was slated to become literally identical with the "people." Nations or peoples had no long-run place in the Marxian pantheon; they were supposed eventually to disappear, like the states. But nations or peoples did have a short-run, even middle-run reality that not only could not be ignored by Marxist parties but was potentially tactically useful to their ends.

The Russian Revolution denounced the Russian Empire in theory and provided for the same self-determination of nations/peoples as did Wilson's doctrines. If much of the "empire" was retained, it was scrupulously insisted that this took the form of a voluntary federation of republics, the USSR, with plenty of room for formal autonomy of peoples, even within each of the republics. And when all hope was abandoned for the mythical German revolution, Lenin turned at Baku to proclaiming a new emphasis on the "East." Marxism-Leninism in effect was moving from its origins as a theory of proletarian insurrection against the bourgeoisie to a new role as a theory of anti-imperialism. This shift of emphasis would only grow with time. In the decades that would come, it is probable that more people read Lenin on *Imperialism: The Last Stage of Capitalism* than read the *Manifesto*.

Wilsonianism and Leninism emerged thus as rival doctrines for the fealty of the peoples of the peripheral zones. Because they were rivals, each placed great emphasis in its propaganda on its differences from the other. And, of course, there were real differences. But we should not be blind to the deep similarities as well. The two ideologies not only shared the theme of the self-determination of nations; they also believed it was immediately (if not always urgently) relevant to the political life of the peripheral zones. That is, both doctrines favored what later came to be called "decolonization." Furthermore, by and large, even when it came to the details of "who was a people" that had this hypothetical right to self-determination, the proponents of both doctrines came up with very similar lists of names. There were, to be sure, minor tactical scuffles related to passing considerations of the world *rapport de forces,* but there was no important example of fundamental empirical disagreement. Israel was on both lists, Kurdistan on neither. Neither was to accept the theoretical legitimacy of the Bantustans. Both found no theoretical reason to oppose the eventual realities of Pakistan and Bangladesh. It could not be said that fundamentally different measuring rods were being used to judge legitimacy.

To be sure, there were differences about the road to self-determination. Wilsonians favored what was termed a "constitutional" path, that is, a process of gradual, orderly transfer of power arrived at by negotiations between an imperial power and respectable representatives of the people in question. Decolonization was to be, as the French would later put it, *octroyée,* that is, given. Leninism came of a "revolutionary" tradition and painted a more insurrectional path to "national liberation." Independence was not to be *octroyée* but *arrachée,* that is, taken. This would be incarnated in the later Maoist injunction of the need for "protracted struggle," which came to be widely repeated and, more important, to be part of the fundamental strategy of movements.

One should not exaggerate even this difference. Peaceful decolonization was not unacceptable in Leninist doctrine, merely improbable. And revolutionary nationalism was not inherently inconsistent with Wilsonian ideas, merely dangerous and thus to be avoided whenever possible. Still, the debate was real because it masked another debate: who was to lead the struggle for self-determination. And this was important, in turn, because it would presumably determine the "postindependence" policies. Wilsonians saw the natural leadership of a national movement to lie in its intelligentsia and bourgeoisie—educated, respectable, and prudent. They foresaw a local movement that would persuade the more "modern" sectors of the traditional leadership to join in the political reforms and accept a sensible, parliamentary mode of organizing the newly independent state. Leninists saw the leadership to lie in a party/movement modeled on the Bolshevik party, even if it did not accept the whole Leninist ideological canon. The leaders might be "petty bourgeois," provided they were "revolutionary" petty bourgeois. When it came to power, the party/movement was supposed to become a party/state. Here, too, one should not exaggerate the difference. Often, the respectable intelligentsia/bourgeoisie and the so-called revolutionary petty bourgeoisie were in reality the same people, or at least cousins. And the party/movement was almost as frequently a formula of "Wilsonian" movements as of "Leninist" ones. As for the postindependence policies, neither the Wilsonians nor the Leninists worried too much about them as long as the struggle for self-determination was ongoing.

WILSON, LENIN, AND NATIONAL DEVELOPMENT

What then of the postdecolonization practice? Surely here the Wilsonian-Leninist antinomy would reveal its importance. In one major respect, there was no question that the two paths to independence tended to correlate with opposite postindependence policies. This was in the domain of foreign policy. In all world issues in which the United States and the USSR were locked in Cold War battle, the states outside the core zones tended to lean in one direction or the other. Some states were considered and considered themselves "pro-Western," and other states considered themselves to be part of a world progressive camp that included the USSR.

There was, of course, a long continuum of positions, and not all states were consistent over time. Nonalignment was itself a major movement. Still, when the chips were down, on unimportant matters like voting for resolutions in the General Assembly of the United Nations, many votes were easily predictable. The United States and its allies on the one hand and the USSR and the so-called socialist bloc on the other spent much diplomatic energy on trying to push wavering states in one direction or the other. Wilsonian versus Leninist propaganda was incessantly purveyed, directly through government media and indirectly through scholarly discourse.

A close look at the internal realities of the various states reveals, however, that in both the political and the economic arenas there was less difference than the theory or the propaganda would suggest. In terms of the actual political structures, most of the states most of the time were either one-party states (de facto or de jure) or military dictatorships. Even when a state had a multiparty system in formal terms, one party tended in reality to dominate the institutions and to be impervious to change of regime other than by military coup d'état. The corollary of such structures tended to be a low level of civil rights—a powerful police structure, arbitrary arrests of opposition figures, a government-controlled press, and a long list of intellectuals in exile. There was very little difference in this regard to be found among states employing a Wilsonian rhetoric and those employing a basically Leninist rhetoric.

Nor was much more difference to be located in the economic arena. The degree to which private local enterprise was permitted has varied, but in almost all Third World states there has been a large amount of state enterprise and in virtually no state has state ownership been the only property form. The degree to which foreign investment has been permitted has no doubt varied more. In the more "pro-Western" states it has been encouraged, indeed solicited, albeit quite frequently in the form of joint ventures with a state corporation. In the more radical, or "progressive," states, foreign investment has been dealt with more cautiously, although seldom totally repudiated. Rather, it has been the case that investors from OECD countries have themselves been reluctant to invest in such countries because of what they considered higher political risk.

Finally, the aid picture has not been too different. Virtually all Third World countries have actively sought to obtain aid in the form of both direct grants and loans. To be sure, the aid-giving donors tended to correlate their assistance with the foreign policy stance of the potential recipients. A long list of countries received aid primarily from OECD countries. A smaller list received aid primarily from socialist bloc countries. A few countries self-consciously sought to emphasize the Nordic countries (plus the Netherlands and Canada) as aid sources. A large number of countries were ready to accept aid from multiple sources. In the end, most of the aid took the same form: personnel and tied grants, intended to support military structures and to fund so-called development projects.

What was most alike in all these countries was the belief in the possibility and urgent importance of "national development." National development was operationally defined everywhere as "catching up." Of course, it was assumed by everyone involved that this was a long and difficult task. But it was also assumed that it was doable, provided only that the right *state* policies were pursued. The state policies advocated, of course, covered the whole ideological gamut from facilitating the unrestricted flow of capital, commodities, and even labor across the national frontiers at one extreme to total state control of productive and exchange operations within largely closed frontiers at the other. There were, of course, a very large variety of in-between positions.

What was common, however, to the programs of all the noncore state members of the United Nations—from the Soviet Union to Argentina, from India to Nigeria, from Albania to St. Lucia—was the overall state objective, increasing the wealth of the nation and "modernizing" its infrastructure. What was also common was an underlying optimism about this objective. What was further common was the sense that this objective could be best pursued by full participation in the interstate system. When any state was excluded even partially—as was the People's Republic of China for many years—it worked very hard to regain its unquestioned status of full membership.

In short, what has to be seen is that the Wilsonian-Leninist ideology of the self-determination of nations, their abstract equality, and the developmentalist paradigm incarnated in both variants of the ideology were overwhelmingly and virtually unfailingly accepted as the operational program of the political movements of the peripheral and semiperipheral zones of the world-system. In this sense, the USSR itself was the first test case of the validity of the analysis and the workability of the recommendations. The postrevolutionary state was formally structured—a federation of states, most of which contained autonomous subunits—to respond precisely to the juridical formula of self-determination. When Lenin launched the slogan "Communism equals the Soviets plus electricity," he was putting forward national (economic) development as the prime objective of state policy. And when Khrushchev, decades later, said that the Soviet Union would "bury" the United States by the year 2000, he was venting supreme optimism about "catching up."

These themes grew stronger in the interwar years—in Eastern and Central Europe, in Latin America, in India, and elsewhere (Chandra, 1991; Love, 1988). The original great boast of the USSR was that, in the 1930s, at a time of world economic depression, there was not only no unemployment in the USSR but also a program of rapid industrialization.

After 1945, the world chorus on the possibilities of national development grew stronger. The relatively rapid reconstruction of Western Europe and Japan (after massive wartime destruction of infrastructure) seemed to demonstrate that, with will and investment, it was possible to upgrade technology rapidly, and thus raise the overall standard of living. All of a sudden, the theme of economic development became pandemic among politicians, journalists, and scholars. The forgotten corners of already industrialized states (the American South, southern Italy, and so on) were targeted for "development." The Third World was to develop as well—partly through self-help, partly with the assistance of the more advanced "developed" countries. The United Nations would officially proclaim the 1970s the "development decade."

In the universities of the world, development became the new intellectual organizing theme. A liberal paradigm, "modernization theory," was elaborated in the 1950s, to be countered by a *marxisant dependista* counterparadigm elaborated in the 1960s. This was, of course, essentially the updating of the Wilsonian-Leninist antinomy. Once again, in practice, the specific recommendations for state policy may have been polar opposites, but both sets of theories involved specific recommendations for state policy. Both sets of applied practitioners, who advised the governments, were confident that, if their recommendations were implemented, national development would in fact follow and the countries in question would eventually catch up.

We know what happened in the real world. From roughly 1945 to 1970, there was considerable practical effort to expand the means and level of production around the world. It was in this period that gross national product and GNP per capita became the principal measuring tools of economic growth, which itself had become the principal indicator of economic development.

This period was a Kondratieff A-period of exceptional amplitude. The amount of growth varied considerably around the world, but on the whole the figures were upward everywhere, not least of all in the so-called socialist countries. This same period was a period of the political triumph of a large number of movements in the Third World that had evolved the strategy of struggling for state power in order thereby to implement policies that would guarantee national development. Everything therefore seemed to be moving in the same positive direction: worldwide economic expansion, the fulfillment state by state of the Wilsonian-Leninist vision, and the almost universally upward growth rates. Developmentalism was the order of the day; there was a worldwide consensus about its legitimacy and its inevitability.

This consensus, however, suffered two shocks from which it has not recovered and, I am arguing, will not recover. The first was the worldwide revolution of 1968. The second shock was the worldwide economic stagnation of the period 1970-1990, the economic failure of almost all the governments of the peripheral and semiperipheral zones, and the collapse of regimes in the so-called socialist states. Events of 1968 broke the ideological crust. The 1970s and 1980s removed the rest of the ideological covering. The gaping sore of the North-South polarization has been uncovered and exposed to view. At the moment, in desperation, the world is muttering incantations about the market as remedy, as though this could solve anything. But market medicine is mercurochrome and will not prevent further deterioration. It is highly unlikely that most states now abandoning "socialist" slogans in favor of "market" slogans will see a significant improvement in the 1990s in their standard of living. After all, the vast majority of noncore states who adhered to market slogans in the 1980s did quite poorly. Reference is always made to the rare "success" stories (the current hero is South Korea), neglecting the much larger number of failures and the fading of earlier so-called success stories, such as Brazil.

The main issue, however, is not whether specific state policies have or have not led to economic development. Rather, it is whether or not there will continue to be widespread belief in the likelihood of economic development as the result of any particular state policies.

THE PARADIGM NOT WORKING

The worldwide revolution of 1968 grew out of a sense that national development had not occurred; it was not yet the consequence of feeling that the objective itself was an illusion. There were two main themes that were common to all the uprisings (east and west, north and south), whatever the local details. The first was a protest against U.S. hegemony in the world-system (and the collusion of the USSR in that hegemony). The second was a protest against the inefficacy of the so-called Old Left movements that had come to power in the world in multiple versions—social democracy in the West, communism in the East, national liberation movements in the South. These movements were attacked for not having truly transformed the world, as they had promised in their mobilizational days. They were attacked for being too much a part of the dominant world-system, too little antisystemic (Wallerstein, 1991).

In a sense, what those who participated in the various uprisings were saying to the "Old Left" political movements is that their organizational activities had achieved the formal political objectives they had historically set themselves, most notably state power, but that they had distinctly not achieved the greater human equality that had been said to be the purpose of achieving the state power. The worldwide attraction during this period of "Maoism" was due to the fact that it expressed in the most vigorous possible way this double rejection: of U.S. hegemony (and Soviet collusion) and of inefficacious "Old Left" movements in general. However, Maoism represented the argument that the fault lay in the poor leadership of the "Old Left" movements, those who were in Maoist terminology the "capitalist roaders." Hence it was implied that, were the movements now to reject the "capitalist roaders," were they to have a "cultural revolution," then at last the objective of national development would in fact be achieved.

The significance of the worldwide revolution of 1968 was not in the political change it brought about. By 1970, the uprisings had been suppressed or had fizzled everywhere. Nor was the significance in the new ideas it launched. Maoism had a short career in the 1970s but disintegrated by mid-decade, and first of all in China. The themes of the new social movements—cultural nationalism of "minorities," feminism, ecology—have had somewhat more staying power than Maoism but have yet to find a firm ideological footing. The significance of 1968 was rather that it punctured the consensus around Wilsonianism-Leninism by questioning whether the developmentalist ideology had in fact achieved anything of lasting importance. It sowed ideological doubt and corroded the faith.

Once the faith was shaken, once the consensus viewpoint was reduced to the status of merely one viewpoint amid others in the arena (even if still the one most widely held), it was possible for day-by-day reality to have the effect of stripping that ideology bare. This is what happened in the next two decades. The world economic stagnation, the Kondratieff B-phase, has thus far been played out in two major dramas. The first was the OPEC oil price rise of the 1970s. The second was the debt crisis of the 1980s.

The OPEC oil price rise was thought at first to give renewed credence to the possibilities of national development. It seemed to be a demonstration that primary producers in the South, by concerted action, could significantly affect the terms of trade. An initial hysteria in Western public opinion abetted such an interpretation. It did not take long for a more sober assessment to take hold. What had really happened? The OPEC countries, under the leadership of the shah of Iran and the Saudis (the leading friends of the United States, be it noted) raised the price of oil dramatically, thereby drawing a significant percentage of world surplus into their hands. This represented a very significant drain on national accounts for all Third World and socialist countries that were not themselves oil producers, at a time when the world market for their own exports was weakening. The drain on the national accounts of the major industrialized countries was also important but far less significant as a percentage of the total and more temporary since these countries could more easily take steps to restructure their energy consumption.

What happened to the world surplus funneled through the oil-producing countries? Some of it, of course, went into the "national development" pro- grams of oil-producing states, such as Nigeria, Algeria, Iraq, Iran, Mexico, Venezuela, and the USSR. Some of it went into heavy luxury consumption in oil-producing states, which meant it was transferred to the OECD states as the purchasing of commodities, as investment, or as individual capital flight. And the remaining money was placed in U.S. and European banks. The money that was placed in the banks was then refunneled to Third World and socialist states (including even the oil-producing states) as state loans. These state loans solved the immediate problems of the balance of payments of these states, which were in particularly bad shape precisely because of the oil price rise. With the state loans, the governments were able to stave off for a time political opposition by using the money to maintain imports (even while exports were falling). This in turn sustained world demand for the manufactured goods of the OECD coun- tries and thus minimized the effects on them of the world economic stagnation.

Even during the 1970s, a number of Third World states began nonetheless to feel the effects of a decline in the growth rate combined with an exhaustion of monetary and social reserves. By the 1980s, the effects were felt everywhere (with the exception of East Asia). The first great public expression of the debt crisis was Poland in 1980. The Gierek government had played the 1970s like everyone else, borrowing and spending. But the bill was coming due, and the Polish government sought to reduce it by increasing internal prices, thereby making the Polish working class assume the burden. The result was Gdansk and Solidarnosc. Solidarnosc could then incarnate Polish nationalism (and hence both anti-Russianism and anticommunism). But Polish nationalism was not new. It was the debt crisis that made the difference. In 1982, Mexico announced it could not service its debt. And now at last the world acknowledged it had a "debt crisis." It is noteworthy that it was in relatively strong and relatively industrialized countries outside the core—Poland and Mexico— where the collapse started, or at least where it attracted attention.

The 1980s saw a cascade of economic difficulties for peripheral and semi-peripheral countries. In virtually all, two elements were the same. The first was popular discontent with the regime in power, followed by political disillusionment. Even when regimes were overthrown—whether by violence or by collapse of a rotting regime, whether they were military dictatorships or Communist parties or one-party African regimes—the pressure for political transformation was more negative than affirmative. It was less out of hope than out of despair that the changes occurred. The second common element was the hard financial face of the OECD countries. Faced with their own economic difficulties, they exhibited little patience for the financial dilemmas of Third World and socialist governments. The latter were handed harsh IMF conditions to fulfill, given risible assistance, and subjected to sermonizing about the virtues of the market and privatization. Gone were the Keynesian indulgences of the 1950s and 1960s.

In the early 1980s, the Latin American countries saw a wave of dismantling of developmentalist military dictatorships and discovered "democracy." In the Arab world, developmentalist secular regimes were under sharp attack from Islamists. In Black Africa, where one-partyism was once the sustaining structure of developmentalist hopes, the myth had become ashes in the mouth. And in Eastern and Central Europe, the dramatic transformations of 1989 came as a great surprise to the world, although they were clearly inscribed in the events of 1980 in Poland.

In the Soviet Union, where in some senses the developmentalist trek began, we have witnessed the disintegration of the CPSU and of the USSR itself. When developmentalism failed in Brazil or Algeria there was still the argument possible that it was because they had not followed the political path of the USSR. But when it fails in the USSR?

ELEGY AND REQUIEM

The story of 1917-1989 deserves both elegy and requiem. The elegy is for the triumph of the Wilsonian-Leninist ideal of the self-determination of nations. In these 70 years, the world has been largely decolonized. The world outside Europe has been integrated into the formal political institutions of the interstate system.

This decolonization was partly *octroyée*, partly *arrachée*. In the process, an incredible political mobilization was required across the world, which has awakened consciousnesses everywhere. It will be very difficult ever to put the genie back in the bottle. Indeed, the main problem is how to contain the spreading virus of micronationalism as ever-smaller entities seek to claim peoplehood and therefore the right to self-determination.

From the beginning, however, it was clear that everyone wanted self-determination primarily in order to make their way to prosperity. And from the beginning the road to prosperity was recognized as a difficult one. As I have argued, this has taken the form of the search for national development. And this search for a long time found itself relatively more comfortable with Leninist than with Wilsonian rhetoric, just as the struggle for decolonization had found itself relatively more comfortable with Wilsonian rhetoric.

Because the process was in two steps—first the decolonization (or comparable political change), then the economic development—it meant that the Wilsonian half of the package was always waiting for its Leninist fulfillment. The prospect of national development served as the legitimation of the world-system's overall structure. In this sense, the fate of Wilsonian ideology was dependent on the fate of Leninist ideology. To put it more crudely and less kindly, Leninist ideology was the fig leaf of Wilsonian ideology.

Today the fig leaf has fallen, and the emperor is naked. All the shouting about the triumph of democracy in 1989 around the world will not long hide the absence of any serious prospect for the economic transformation of the periphery within the framework of the capitalist world-economy. Thus it will not be the Leninists who sing the requiem for Leninism but the Wilsonians. It is they who are in a quandary and who have no plausible political alternatives. This was captured in the no-win dilemmas of Mr. Bush in the Persian Gulf crisis. But the Persian Gulf crisis is only the beginning of the story.

As the North-South confrontations take ever more dramatic (and violent) forms in the decades to come, we shall begin to be aware how much the world will miss the ideological cement of the Wilsonian-Leninist ideological antinomy. It represented a glorious but historically passing panoply of ideas, hopes, and human energy. It will not be easy to replace. Yet it is only by finding a new and far more solid utopian vision that we shall be able to transcend the imminent time of troubles.

REFERENCES

Chandra, B. (1991). Colonial India: British versus Indian views of development. *Review, 14,* 81-167.

Jennings, W. I. (1956). *The approach to self-government.* Cambridge: Cambridge University Press.

Love, J. L. (1988). Theorizing underdevelopment: Latin America and Romania, 1860-1950. *Review, 11,* 453-496.

Wallerstein, I. (1991). 1968: Revolution in the world-system. In I. Wallerstein, *Geopolitics and geoculture: Essays in the changing world-system* (pp. 65-83). Cambridge: Cambridge University Press.

PART II

COMPARATIVE
PERSPECTIVES

6

Economic Development and Democracy Reconsidered

Larry Diamond

IRST published in the *American Political Science Review* in 1959, Seymour Martin Lipset's essay "Some Social Requisites of Democracy: Economic Development and Political Legitimacy" has proved one of the most controversial, durable, and frequently cited articles in the social sciences. Asserting a broad and multistranded relationship between economic development levels and democracy, it broke new ground in what came to be known (quite often disparagingly) as "modernization theory" and became an essential reference point, typically the *starting point,* for all future work on the relationship between political systems and the level of economic development.

Lipset's general argument was simply "that democracy is related to the state of economic development. The more well-to-do a nation, the greater the chances that it will sustain democracy" (Lipset, 1960, p. 31).[1] To demonstrate his argument, he classified the countries of Latin America, Europe, and the English-speaking democracies into two sets of two groups each, based on their experience with democracy: for Europe, North America, Australia, and New Zealand, stable democracies versus unstable democracies and dictatorships; for Latin America, democracies and unstable dictatorships versus stable dictatorships. Within each region or set, he then compared the two groups of regimes on a wide range of indicators of socioeconomic development: income, communications, industrialization, education, and urbanization. Not surprisingly (from the perspective of anyone having even the most casual acquaintance with the profusion of analyses that have followed), he found that within each regional set, the more democratic countries had consistently and often dramatically higher mean levels of development than did the less democratic countries.

AUTHOR'S NOTE: This essay has benefited from the suggestions, criticisms, and research assistance of Yongchuan Liu.

Lipset's analysis can be and has been criticized on a number of conceptual and methodological grounds. It is a static analysis of data from a single time point, although it does classify regimes on the basis of their experience over long periods (25 to 40 years). Like other theories in the modernization or "liberal" school, it assumes linearity, ignoring the possible negative impact on democracy "that the processes of changing from one developmental level to another might have" (Huntington & Nelson, 1976, p. 20). It establishes only correlation, not causality, yet it does assume and infer that democracy is the consequence of these various developmental factors. It shows the correlation of democracy with a wide range of developmental variables, but it does not present a truly multivariate analysis in which the independent causal weight or correlational significance of each variable is established by controlling for the other variables. Of course, Lipset was writing before the social sciences began employing multiple regression analysis (not to mention dynamic analyses such as event history). But even with the methods of the time, no attempt was made to control for other factors (except region) or to test them in interaction with one another. However, Lipset did emphasize—and demonstrate with data from Lerner's (1958) study of modernization in the Middle East—that the various developmental variables "are so closely interrelated as to form one major factor which has the political correlate of democracy."

There was also a problem of substantive interpretation that has been less frequently noted. Although the decomposition of the sample into two parts can be justified as an attempt to control for cultural and regional variation, it produced a striking anomaly that Lipset did not analyze: On 11 of the 15 development variables for which he presented data, the European *nondemocracies* (and unstable democracies) had higher mean levels of development than did the Latin American *democracies* (and unstable dictatorships). In fact, on most dimensions, these differences were quite large, often as large as the differences between the more and less democratic groups *within* regions. Only on urbanization did the more democratic Latin American group rank consistently more "developed" on average than the more authoritarian European group, and these differences were relatively small.

At first glance, it would be tempting to attribute this anomaly to the non-comparability of the criteria for dichotomizing the two sets of countries. As a result, the *less* democratic European category—"unstable democracies and dictatorships"—overlapped conceptually to a considerable degree the *more* democratic Latin American category—"democracies and unstable dictatorships." However, conceptual overlap does not entirely account for the anomaly. Of the 7 Latin American "democracies and unstable dictatorships," 5 (Brazil, Chile, Argentina, Costa Rica, and Uruguay) had democratic systems in 1959 (and those in Chile, Costa Rica, and Uruguay had been in place for at least 10 years). Of the 17 European "unstable democracies and dictatorships," 10 were stable dictatorships (most of them Communist).[2] Had Lipset compared these two conceptually distinct categories—Latin American democracies and European dictatorships—he would have found the latter to have notably higher levels of economic development than the former, significantly qualifying his asserted relationship between economic development and democracy.[3] For example, the 10 European dictatorships had an average literacy rate in 1960 of 87%, compared with 80% for the 5 Latin American democracies. Their per capita GNPs averaged $598, compared with $428 for the Latin American democracies. On a particularly valuable index of development not available when Lipset was writing, the "physical quality of life," the mean level for the European dictatorships was 8 points higher than that for the Latin American democracies: 89 versus 81.[4] Had the comparison been broadened to "Third World democracies," including India and Sri Lanka in particular, the gap with European dictatorships would have been even more striking.

This modest reinterpretation of Lipset's analysis also heightens the strength of his relationship in a different sense. Within Europe, there is a clear step pattern among the three groups of countries that emerge when, in addition to the "stable democracies," we separate "unstable democracies" and "dictatorships." As expected, the mean development level increases substantially with each step toward stable democracy.[5] As will be shown later, a more striking stepwise progression is apparent when one examines the relationship between development and a more refined typology of regime democraticness.

Thus the data around 1960 offer some impressive support for Lipset's thesis of a direct relationship between economic development and democracy, but within Lipset's comparative data were also some strong indications of the limits to this relationship. Region (and all it stands for in terms of cultural and social conditions) was an important intervening variable (most of the stable European dictatorships were in *Eastern* Europe). That development level was hardly completely determinative was also indicated by the considerable overlap in ranges of development levels between the more and less democratic groups within each region. On every developmental variable, there were countries in the less democratic group with a higher level of development than countries in the more democratic group.[6]

In fact, what Lipset showed in his famous article—and all he intended or claimed to show—was a correlation, a (linear) causal *tendency*. Before even presenting his main thesis, he conceded that "a syndrome of unique historical circumstances" can give rise to a political regime form quite different from what would be favored by "the society's major (developmental) characteristics" (p. 28). Moreover, once having arisen for whatever unique historical reasons, "a political form may persist under conditions normally adverse to the *emergence* of that form" (p. 28).

In this chapter, I reevaluate Lipset's thesis on the relationship between socioeconomic development and democracy more than 30 years after its formulation. This is certainly a propitious moment to undertake such a reassessment. For one thing, there are many more democracies in the world today, especially among the less developed countries. In the midst of this "third wave" of democratization in the world, there were in 1990, by Huntington's (1991, p. 26) count, 58 democracies in states with populations greater than 1 million, compared with only 36 in 1962, when the second wave of democratization came to an end.[7] This democratic expansion follows a "second reverse wave" of democratic breakdowns in the 1960s and 1970s that was seen by a number of political scientists, especially those working with the "bureaucratic-authoritarian" model (Collier, 1979; O'Donnell, 1973), to negate Lipset's thesis. Today, that reverse wave has itself passed, and European decolonization has been almost entirely completed (bringing more than 70 new states into the world since Lipset first published his article in 1959). With many more states, over 30 more years of regime change and persistence, and an impressive accumulation of social science research addressed to this thesis, the time is ripe for a reevaluation.

A GENERATION OF QUANTITATIVE ANALYSIS

Since Lipset's essay appeared, a vast number of quantitative studies, using a wide range of methods, have examined the relationship between democracy and many different dimensions of socioeconomic development. Almost all of them have found a positive relationship, and the weight of the evidence suggests that, in the conclusion of one of the more systematic and sophisticated studies, "level of economic development appears to be the dominant explanatory variable" in determining political democracy (Bollen & Jackman, 1985, p. 42).

Cross-Tabulations

A number of scholars over the years have done cross-tabulations of economic development and democracy for a variety of samples and time points, and all of them have strongly supported Lipset's thesis. While this method is unable to establish causality, much less to model its paths or determine its linearity, it can clearly demonstrate interdependencies among variables. Various cross-tabulations have done this rather strikingly for the overall relationship between economic development and democracy. Using an approach similar to Lipset's but even more comprehensive, Coleman (1960) divided 75 "modernizing political systems" into three categories—competitive, semicompetitive, and authoritarian regimes—which he then related to 11 different indicators of national wealth (economic development), industrialization, urbanization, and education. In each of his two regional sets, Latin America and Africa-Asia, the ranking of regime types conformed almost perfectly to the expected pattern: Countries with competitive regimes had the highest levels of development, semicompetitive countries the next highest, and authoritarian countries the lowest. Remarkably, on only one variable (unionization) did the development data deviate even slightly from the expected step pattern.[8] Cross-tabulating the same three regime types with five "stages" of economic development (for 89 countries at all levels of development), Russett (1965, cited in Dahl, 1971, p. 65) found that all of the 14 countries in the highest stage ("high mass consumption") were democratic, 57% in the next highest stage, but only 12% to 33% in the lower three stages. Significantly also for Lipset's thesis, Russett justified his classification of countries into broad development stages by demonstrating high intercorrelations among the various dimensions of social and economic development. (These high intercorrelations have also been found by Cutright, 1963; Olsen, 1968; Powell, 1982; and virtually all other such analyses.)

Cross-tabulating Russett's same five stages of development with the 29 polyarchies that he identified in 1969, Dahl (1971, p. 66) found again that all highest-level countries are polyarchies, with the proportion dropping to 36% in the second-highest ("industrial revolution") group, and negligible below that (only 2 of the 57 countries in the three lowest development groups qualified as polyarchies in 1969). This led Dahl to offer an important and influential extension of Lipset's hypothesis, which he stated in the form of two propositions:

Proposition 1: "There exists an upper threshold, perhaps in the range of about $700-800 GNP per capita (1957 U.S. dollars), above which the chances of polyarchy . . . are so high that any further increases in per capita GNP [and associated variables] cannot affect the outcomes in any significant way."

Proposition 2: "There exists a lower threshold, perhaps in the range of about $100-200 GNP per capita, below which the chances for polyarchy . . . are so slight that differences in per capita GNP or variables associated with it do not really matter" (pp. 67-68).

A recalculation by Diamond (1980, p. 91; see also Lipset, 1981, p. 471), using Freedom House data for 1977 and per capita GNP figures for 1974, again divided the countries for which there were data (now 123) into five quintiles of economic development. Three-fourths of the 25 wealthiest countries were democratic (or "free" by the rating of Freedom House); the remainder were Arab oil or communist states. A third of the countries in the second category (with per capita GNPs ranging from $740 to $2,320) were democratic. Below the 50 richest countries, there were only 4 democracies among the remaining 73 states (about 5%).

Finding a similar pattern in 1981, Huntington (1984) was led to extend Dahl's extension one step further. If so many cross-tabulations at successive points in time kept showing with such consistency apparent upper and lower thresholds for the likelihood of democracy, then it made sense to conceptualize the developmental space between them as "a zone of transition or choice, in which traditional forms of rule become increasingly difficult to maintain and new types of political institutions are required to aggregate the demands of an increasingly complex society and to implement public policies in such a society" (p. 201). If Huntington's logical extension of the theory is correct, most democratic transitions should be occurring at this middle level of economic development because "in poor countries democratization is unlikely; in rich countries it has already occurred" (Huntington, 1991, p. 60). In fact, Huntington has demonstrated this to be the case with the democratic transitions of the third wave: "About two-thirds of the transitions were in countries between roughly $300 and $1,300 in per capita GNP (1960 dollars)." Counting all 31 countries that experienced either democratization or significant political liberalization between 1974 and 1989, Huntington found half of them to lie in the middling range of $1,000-$3,000 per capita GNP in 1976. Amazingly, "three-quarters of the countries that were at this level of economic development in 1976 and that had nondemocratic governments in 1974 democratized or liberalized significantly by 1989" (Huntington, 1991, pp. 62-63). These transitions "corrected" many of the most anomalous locations of more developed countries with respect to regime type: By 1990, Spain, Portugal, Greece, Poland, Hungary, and Czechoslovakia had all become democratic, and the Soviet Union and Bulgaria were at least heading in that direction.

The cross-tabulations to date have been conducted with a very simple categorization of regimes into democracies and nondemocracies, at most including semidemocracies. The real world, of course, presents a more continuous range of variation on the principal dimensions of democracy—competition, participation, and liberty.[9] These dimensions are closely (though not perfectly) captured by Freedom House's annual survey of political rights and civil liberties in every country of the world. Each country is rated from 1 to 7 on each of those two measures, with 1 being *most free* and 7 *most authoritarian* (Freedom House, 1991, pp. 53-54).[10] Using this combined 13-point scale of what I will call "political freedom," I have proposed a typology of seven regime types, moving in step fashion from the most highly closed and authoritarian to the fully liberal and institutionalized democracies (Diamond, 1991). Cross-tabulating these regime types with economic development levels enriches our understanding of the pattern of association at this moment of peak democratic expansion in world history.

Table 6.1 presents a cross-tabulation of per capita GNP in 1989 (broken down into the World Bank's four national income groups) and regime type in 1990 for 142 countries (unfortunately, a number of communist countries are omitted because of lack of GNP data). It shows, once more, a strong apparent relationship between economic development and democracy. Two aspects of this cross-tabulation (and that in Table 6.2) add to its importance for cumulative research. First, as just noted, it examines the association with seven regime types rather than just two or three. And second, the data have been tested for statistical significance with two forms of the chi-square test, both of which show the association to be highly significant at the .0001 level.

Looking first at income groups, we see in Table 6.1 that more than 83% of the high-income countries have competitive, essentially democratic regimes (that is, one of the three most democratic regime types). Four countries in this income group have highly authoritarian regimes, but they are all Persian Gulf oil states whose incomes vastly overstate their real levels of socioeconomic development. Outside the Gulf, Singapore is the only high-income country that

Table 6.1 Freedom Status (1990) and Per Capita GNP (1989)

Regime Type	High Income	Upper- Middle Income	Lower- Middle Income	Low Income	Total
State hegemonic, closed (13-14)	2	2	2	13	19
	10.5%	10.5%	10.5%	68.4%	100.0%
	6.7%	11.1%	4.1%	28.9%	13.4%
State hegemonic, partially open (11-12)	2	3	3	18	26
	7.7%	11.5%	11.5%	69.2%	100.0%
	6.7%	16.7%	6.1%	40.0%	18.3%
Noncompetitive, partially pluralist (10)	0	1	5	5	11
	—	9.1%	45.4%	45.4%	100.0%
	—	5.5%	10.2%	11.1%	7.7%
Semicompetitive, partially pluralist (7-9)	1	3	14	6	24
	4.1%	12.5%	58.3%	25.0%	100.0%
	3.3%	16.7%	28.6%	13.3%	16.9%
Competitive, partially illiberal (5-6)	1	1	12	1	15
	6.7%	6.7%	80.0%	6.7%	100.0%
	3.3%	5.5%	24.5%	2.2%	10.6%
Competitive, pluralist, partially institutionalized (3-4)	5	6	12	1	24
	20.8%	25.0%	50.0%	4.1%	100.0%
	16.7%	33.3%	24.5%	2.2%	16.9%
Liberal democracy (2)	19	2	1	1	23
	82.6%	8.7%	4.3%	4.3%	100.0%
	63.3%	11.1%	2%	2.2%	16.2%
Total	30	18	49	45	142
	21.1%	12.7%	34.5%	31.7%	100.0%
	100.0%	100.0%	100.0%	100.0%	100.0%

SOURCE: Freedom House (1991), World Bank (1991, table 1).
NOTE: Chi-square measures are significant beyond the .0001 level by both the Pearson and likelihood ratio methods. Numbers in parentheses after regime type represent the range of scores on the Freedom House combined scale of "political freedom." The first figure in each cell is the raw number of cases; the second figure is the row percentage; the third figure is the column percentage.

is not democratic. Interestingly, there is less difference than we would expect between the upper-middle- and lower-middle-income countries. It is in fact the *upper*-middle-income countries that have the higher proportion of very authoritarian (state hegemonic) regimes, but four of these five are again Arab oil states (the other is Romania, which has since experienced further political opening). The two groups have the same proportion of democracies (about half of the total), but the upper-middle-income countries, as expected, have a higher proportion of more fully democratic states. In accord with Lipset's thesis and all its extensions, only three low-income countries are democratic—India, Gambia, and the Solomon Islands (in ascending order of democraticness)—and the latter two have populations of fewer than 1 million, a size that seems more conducive to democracy.[11] Two other low-income countries—Sri Lanka and Pakistan—were democratic in recent years, but deteriorated to semidemocratic status. (Haiti lasted in the "democratic" category during 1991 for all of 8 months.) Strikingly, large proportions (almost 70%) of the two most authoritarian regime forms were concentrated in the low-income group of countries.

Per capita national income, or gross national product, is the development variable most often tested in association with democracy (whether by cross-tabular, correlational, or multivariate analysis). However, it has a number of drawbacks and limitations, including the difficulty in estimating the money incomes of communist countries (without the benefit of market prices) and of many developing countries (where so much economic activity takes place in the informal economy), as well as the exaggerated development levels indicated for the principal oil-exporting states. In addition, the *mean* national income of a country tells us nothing in itself about its distribution, and because money income can be far more unequally distributed than years of life expectancy or schooling, per capita figures for GNP are less reliable indicators of average human development in a country than are national averages for the latter nonmonetary types of measures. These problems are attenuated when we examine indices of development that either exclude monetary measures, such as the Physical Quality of Life Index (PQLI),[12] or combine per capita GNP with such nonmonetary indicators of human welfare as literacy and life expectancy.

Just such a measure, the Human Development Index (HDI), has been developed by the United Nations Development Program (UNDP) (1991). It represents an unweighted average of three (standardized) measures: adult literacy, life expectancy, and (the log of) per capita GDP.[13] It has the advantage of availability for almost all countries in the world (capturing a number of countries not included in Table 6.1), and greater validity in indicating real levels of human well-being. As is readily apparent in Table 6.2, the relationship between democracy and development is even stronger when the HDI is used as the development indicator and the universe of nations is decomposed into five development levels instead of four.[14] In particular, some of the most glaring anomalies fade or disappear. All of the 20 most developed countries are concentrated among the two most democratic regime types, and 85% of them fall into the *most* democratic regime type. More significantly, in comparison with the cross-tabulation for per capita GNP, the HDI shows a more perfect step pattern of association with regime democraticness through the middle levels of development. The medium-high countries have a higher proportion of democracies, and especially of more fully democratic democracies, than do the medium countries, which are scattered across all regime types, with semi-competitive regimes being the mode. Medium-development countries, in turn, are more democratic than the medium-low countries, which range from state

Table 6.2 Freedom Status and Human Development Index, 1990

Regime Type	Human Development Index					
	High (Top 20)[a] .993-.951[b]	Medium- High (21-53) .950-.80	Medium (54-97) .796-.510	Medium- Low (98-128) .499-.253	Low (129-160) .242-.048	Total
State hegemonic, closed (13-14)	0 — —	2 9.1% 6.25%	7 31.8% 16.3%	2 9.1% 7.7%	11 50.0% 35.5%	22 100.0% 14.5%
State hegemonic, partially open (11-12)	0 — —	3 10.3% 9.4%	6 20.7% 14.0%	7 24.1% 26.9%	13 44.8% 41.9%	29 100.0% 19.1%
Noncompetitive, partially pluralist (10)	0 — —	0 — —	3 27.3% 7.0%	5 45.4% 19.2%	3 27.2% 9.7%	11 100.0% 7.2%
Semicompetitive, partially pluralist (7-9)	0 — —	6 24.0% 18.8%	10 40.0% 23.3%	6 24.0% 23.0%	3 12.0% 9.7%	25 100.0% 16.4%
Competitive, partially illiberal (5-6)	0 — —	3 18.75% 9.4%	7 43.8% 16.3%	6 37.5% 23.1%	0 — —	16 100.0% 10.5%
Competitive, pluralist, partially institutionalized (3-4)	3 12.0% 15.0%	13 52.0% 40.6%	8 32.0% 18.6%	0 — —	1 4.0% 3.2%	25 100.0% 16.4%
Liberal democracy (2)	17 70.8% 85.0%	5 20.8% 15.6%	2 8.3% 4.6%	0 — —	0 — —	24 100.0% 15.8%
Total	20 13.2% 100.0%	32 21.1% 100.0%	43 28.3% 100.0%	26 17.1% 100.0%	31 20.4% 100.0%	152 100.0% 100.0%

SOURCE: Freedom House (1991), United Nations Development Program (1991, table 1).
NOTE: Chi-square measures are significant beyond the .0001 level by both the Pearson and likelihood ratio methods. Numbers in parentheses after regime type represent the range of scores on the Freedom House combined scale of "political freedom." The first figure in each cell is the raw number of cases; the second figure is the row percentage; the third figure is the column percentage.
a. Numbers in parentheses in row are the range of country rankings on Human Development Index.
b. Numbers in row are the range of scores on the Human Development Index.

hegemonic to somewhat democratic and yet are still more democratic than the overwhelmingly authoritarian low-development countries. Of the 57 countries that are low or medium-low in development, only 1, tiny Gambia, scores even in the second most democratic regime type (see the appendix to this chapter).[15] At the authoritarian end of the scale of regimes, the association also works in reverse much more regularly than for per capita GNP. The highest proportion of state hegemonic regimes (77%) is found among the low-development countries, followed again in step pattern by the medium-low countries (35%), the medium (30%), and the medium-high (6%).

As a comparison of the two tables suggests, the HDI shows a substantially higher correlation (.71) with the combined index of political freedom than does per capita GNP (.51). (The correlation between the two development measures is .66, which means they are strongly associated but that more than half of the variance of each is explained by other factors.) Two important conclusions should be drawn from these two correlations. First, it is a country's mean level of "human development" or physical quality of life, more than its per capita level of money income, that better predicts its likelihood of being democratic and its level of political freedom. This is consistent with multivariate statistical analyses that have shown the PQLI to be even more strongly associated with democracy than per capita GNP. It also is consistent with the logic of Lipset's argument, as I will argue in the final section of this chapter. One reason the HDI correlates with the freedom index more closely than does per capita GNP is that many democracies in the developing world rank significantly higher on the HDI than they do on per capita GNP; this gap is especially large for Chile Costa Rica, Uruguay, Mauritius, Jamaica, the Dominican Republic, and (semi-democratic) Sri Lanka (UNDP, 1991, Table 1). In other words, the physical quality of life for their citizens (in life expectancy, literacy, and so on) is significantly beyond what would be predicted purely by their level of economic development.[16]

Second, the moderate correlation between per capita GNP and political freedom (lower than those found in many earlier studies discussed shortly) may indicate that the relationship between economic development and democracy has weakened somewhat in the last 30 years as the number of democracies, especially in the middle ranges of development, has grown, especially in the last few years. Although differences in the measures of democracy are obviously important here, I believe the more important factor has been real change in the world, "globalization of democracy, in terms of the near-universalization of popular demands for political freedom, representation, participation, and accountability" (Diamond, 1992a). While this change may be eroding, or at least temporarily challenging, what both Dahl and Huntington identified as a lower development threshold for the viability of democracy, it only reinforces the upper threshold, as evidenced both in the universality of democracy among the high-HDI countries and by the fact that above about $6,100 per capita (1989), only three countries were undemocratic in 1990 (Singapore, Kuwait, and the United Arab Emirates).

Interestingly, many of the countries whose placement in Table 6.2 is roughly as predicted by the overall correlation are recent arrivals to their regime type—that is, products of the third wave of democratization. One could argue, with Huntington (1991), that two historic changes account for this: the relatively swift and sudden collapse of a *non*developmental barrier to democratization in Eastern Europe and the Soviet Union—the authoritarian intransigence of the Soviet Communist party—and the sheer passage of time, enabling "political development" in countries such as Spain, Portugal, Greece, South Korea, and Taiwan to catch up to their levels of socioeconomic development. In fact, Huntington (1991) argues, "In considerable measure, the wave of democratizations that began in 1974 was the product of the economic growth of the previous two decades" (p. 61).[17]

Multivariate Analyses[18]

Cutright's (1963) study was the first to use correlational analysis to test the Lipset hypothesis. His index of democratic stability correlated most highly with his index of communication development (.81), but measures of urbanization, education, and industrialization also showed high positive zero-order correlations with political development (.69, .74, and .72, respectively) and even higher intercorrelations with one another. The multiple correlation of these four aspects of socioeconomic development with Cutright's democracy index was .82 (meaning they accounted for about two-thirds of the variance)—giving strong support to Lipset's thesis of a broad, multistranded association between development and democracy.

Cutright labeled his regime index "political development" but in combining measures of multiparty competition and stability, he was correctly seen to be measuring "democratic stability" and in later writings he referred to the same index as "political representation."[19] This index was subsequently used (partially or entirely) in a number of other quantitative studies (Coulter, 1975; Cutright & Wiley, 1969; Olsen, 1968), so it is important to acknowledge Bollen's (1980, pp. 374-375; 1990, pp. 15-17) objection that combining measures of stability with measures of democracy raises important conceptual and methodological problems: By averaging out possible sharp swings in levels of democracy, the researcher may obstruct the study of political change and confound the interpretation of correlations.

Using both the Cutright index of political representation and an alternative index that did not incorporate stability over time,[20] Olsen (1968) found results strikingly similar to Cutright's on a larger sample of countries (115 as opposed to 77). Both Cutright's scale and Olsen's own showed consistently strong correlations with a number of different (multivariable) dimensions of socioeconomic development, ranging from .59 to .71. In addition, Olsen found that his 14 socioeconomic variables collectively had a multiple correlation with political development/democracy almost identical to what Cutright found (.83 for the Olsen index and .84 for the Cutright index). Given the quite different composition of the two political indices (and particularly their difference in incorporating the stability dimension), it is all the more striking that their correlations with the various development indices were virtually identical (Olsen, 1968, p. 706; see also Table 6.3 in this chapter).

In 1969, Cutright and Wiley took an important methodological step by examining only those countries that were continuously self-governing from 1927 to 1966 (excluding the effects of colonial rule and foreign occupation). Dividing these 40 years into four successive decades, they examined the relationship between democracy and socioeconomic development in each decade and applied a "cross-lagged" correlational test. In doing so, they found not only a consistently strong positive association between democracy and social and economic development in each decade, but grounds for inferring a causal path from economic development in particular to democracy. The additional finding that changes in political representation (in effect, democracy) occurred only where social security provisions were low and literacy high led them to modify Cutright's earlier presumption of a simple linear relationship. The provision of social security (and, more broadly, the meeting of economic expectations and needs) appeared to give stability to all constitutional forms. This finding anticipated in some ways that of Hannan and Carroll (1981), discussed below.

By the late 1960s, other scholars were also becoming concerned with attempting to establish causality. McCrone and Cnudde (1967) built on the earlier work of Lerner (1958), Lipset (1960), and Cutright (1963) in testing different causal paths among the variables using the Simon-Blalock method (which infers causality from the patterning of cross-sectional correlations over time). The model that they found best fit Cutright's data begins with urbanization, which increases education and also has a small direct effect on democratization. Education, in turn, they found, stimulates the expansion of communication media, which then has a large direct effect on democratization.[21] More direct evidence for this causal path was produced by Winham's (1970) longitudinal study of the United States, which used as an indicator of democracy in each decade the Cutright representation index combined with a measure of participation (the average percentage of the population who voted in presidential elections). Winham also found positive correlations between communication, urbanization, education, and democratization strikingly similar to Cutright's, but by using time-lagged correlations over a long span of time, Winham was able to infer more persuasively that socioeconomic development had a causal effect on democratic development. Specifically, he found that the data pointed to the causal priority of education and especially (again) communication.[22]

Using similar time-lagged correlations for 36 European, North American, and Latin American nations, Banks (1970) found a very different pattern. His scale of democratic performance (measuring how the chief executive is elected, the effectiveness of the legislature, and the extent of the franchise) was positively correlated with socioeconomic development throughout the period 1868 to 1963, but he inferred from the patterning of time-lagged correlations that if there was a causal relationship between development and democratic performance it was more likely that it ran in the reverse direction. This method is open to serious question, however, raising doubts about the findings of all the studies that employed it.[23]

Jackman (1973) developed a more continuous measure of democratic development, merging simple categorical measures of the presence of democratic structures with the continuous measures of participation and freedom of the press in 1960. Comparing linear with curvilinear models of the effects of economic development (per capita energy consumption) on his scale of democratic performance, he found two curvilinear models to fit much better than the linear one.

Jackman's contribution was significant in part because it tested a scale of democracy that was not "contaminated" with a measure of stability over time. In fact, Jackman subsequently showed that the heavy reliance on political stability in Cutright's (1963) measure of political representation could produce a spurious analytical result (in this case, concerning the relationship between political democracy and social equality; Jackman, 1975, pp. 86-87; see also Bollen, 1980, p. 382).[24]

However, Jackman's democracy measure was itself flawed in another common respect, including as one of four equally weighted components voter turnout rates (among adults of voting age). This same practice, which confuses the democraticness of the regime with the democratic behavior of its individual citizens, flaws the design of Coulter's (1975) study of the determinants of "liberal democracy," which is further (but less seriously) flawed by its use of Cutright's index as a measure of competitiveness. One should be cautious about interpreting the results from studies employing measures of such questionable validity unless those studies present (as Coulter's does in places) evidence for individual components of the democracy measure that are more valid than the scale as a whole.[25]

A methodologically and conceptually much sounder measure of democracy is Bollen's scale of political democracy for 1960 and 1965.[26] Using this scale, Bollen and Jackman (1985) produced one of the clearest and most frequently cited quantitative studies of the determinants of democracy. It employed several different multiple regression models (ordinary and weighted least squares) to estimate the effects on political democracy in 1960 and 1965 of several independent variables that figure prominently in the literature on determinants of democracy: economic development (as measured by the log of per capita GNP), ethnic pluralism (as indicated by Taylor & Hudson's, 1972, widely used measure of ethnolinguistic fractionalization), the percentage of the population that is Protestant, prior history as a British colony, and recent passage to nationhood (the latter two both dichotomous variables). Bollen and Jackman found that most of their noneconomic variables did have significant effects on democracy (negatively for cultural pluralism—though significantly so only for 1965—positively for Protestantism and British colonial heritage). However, economic development level explained more of the variance by itself than did a regression with all the other variables collectively. And they found that "a good portion (about 50%) of the effects of cultural pluralism and Protestantism are, in fact, effects of economic development" (p. 39). Reinforcing Jackman's earlier finding, they found (by using the logarithmic functional form for the per capita GNP variable) that the effect of economic development is nonlinear, "such that the impact of development on democracy is most pronounced at lower levels of development and declines thereafter" (p. 39).

In previous studies, Bollen (1979, 1983) had found consistently strong positive effects on democracy of the level of economic development, no significant relationship between the timing of development and democracy, positive effects of Protestant culture, negative effects of state control over the economy, and negative effects of peripheral and semiperipheral (dependent) status in the world economy (even after controlling for economic development). Using a panel analysis that regressed several of these independent variables (in 1960) and political democracy in 1960 on democracy in 1965, Bollen (1979) was able to demonstrate the significance of socioeconomic development even in accounting for changes in levels of democracy between 1960 and 1965.

Two other innovative analyses published around the same time as Bollen's also found significant positive effects on democracy of economic development level, but with important caveats. Using panel regression analysis for two periods of time (1950 to 1965 and 1960 to 1975) on two measures of centralization of power (regimes with less than two genuine parties and military regimes), Thomas, Ramirez, Meyer, and Gobalet (1979) found "substantial and significant" negative effects of economic development (per capita GNP) on centralist regimes, but also that these effects were reduced (for party centralization) in a sample of new nations only (p. 197). Further, because two measures of national economic dependence were independently associated (positively) with political centralism (i.e., authoritarianism) while other modernization variables, such as education and urbanization, were not, Thomas et al. concluded that world system theory had more validity than modernization theory (associated with Lipset) (pp. 200-201).[27]

Hannan and Carroll (1981), studying explicitly for the first time regime *change* (from 1950 to 1975) with the event history method, found that economic development (per capita GNP) inhibits movement from *all* political regime forms (one-party even more than multiparty) but also encourages transitions to the multiparty form. Like Thomas et al., they found "no evidence that modernizing experiences and institutions [e.g., education] affect rates of change in political forms" (p. 30), but they also found no effects of economic dependency on regime stability or change. The crucial finding of Hannan and Carroll was that high levels of economic development tended to promote the stability not only of democracy but of all types of regimes. However, that finding was based on the experience of the 1950-1975 period. Were the analysis to be reconducted today, after the pervasive breakdown of communist one-party states in the Soviet Union and Eastern Europe and the transitions in newly industrializing countries such as South Korea and Taiwan, it would probably show a very different effect of economic development on one-party regimes in recent years.

The most recent and in some ways most comprehensive statistical analysis has been undertaken by Lipset himself in collaboration with two graduate student colleagues. Reexamining the Bollen and Jackman data for 1960 and 1965 and adding their own panel regression analysis for the 1970s and 1980s using the combined Freedom House scale of civil and political liberties, Lipset, Seong, and Torres (1991) continued to find "that economic development is the single most important predictor of political democracy when controlling for other variables" (p. 12). Testing nonlinear models on a sample of developing countries, they found a consistently good and significant fit for an N-curve relationship, such that economic development increases the chances for democracy up to a lower-middle level of per capita GNP, then decreases the odds in a middle range (between $2,346 and $5,000 in 1980), while stabilizing the chances for democracy at a very high probability in the higher-income range.

Multiple regression analyses I conducted previously with Lipset, Seong, and others uncovered another significant and distinctive finding. In a number of different regressions, the Physical Quality of Life Index had consistently positive effects on political freedom, usually highly significant statistically (and sometimes even more so than per capita GNP). For example, when the 1984 political freedom index was regressed on six different time-lagged indicators of socioeconomic development, the only two factors that emerged as significant were per capita GNP (lagged back in time quite substantially to 1965) and the PQLI in 1970. The latter effect was substantially larger and more significant statistically, while urbanization, education, and communication showed no independent effect (possibly because of multicollinearity among the independent variables). In a similar regression for 72 developing countries only, the PQLI was again powerful and highly significant in its positive effect, while per capita GNP showed no independent effect at all. The substantial and statistically significant correlations in both samples (.67 and .42) between 1965 per capita GNP and 1970 PQLI suggested that the latter could be a critical intervening variable in the relationship between development and democracy.

In related regressions employing shorter (5- and 10-year) time lags, this causal path was given considerable support. We tested five different models of the per capita income-PQLI-democracy relationship (three with successive 5-year time lags and two with successive 10-year time lags) each on two different samples of nations (one global, one less developed countries only). In each of these 10 regressions, the PQLI exhibited powerful positive effects on political freedom, significant at the .001 level. Also, per capita GNP had very powerful (and again always highly significant) positive effects on PQLI 5 or 10 years later. The direct effects of per capita GNP on democracy were always positive but weaker than those of PQLI and were statistically significant only about half the time. Economic dependence never showed direct significant effects, while military expenditures sometimes showed significant negative effects on democracy. Figure 6.1 presents the findings for one of the causal paths tested. In all, the evidence gave substantial support to the thesis that the contribution of economic development to democracy is substantially mediated through improvements in the physical quality of life.[28]

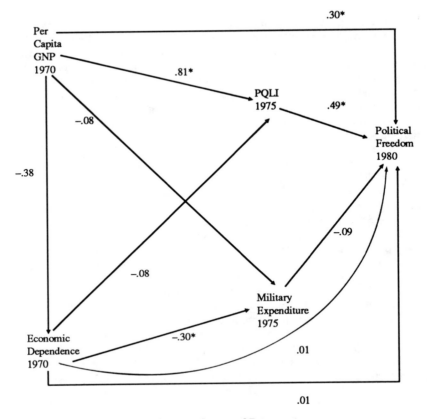

Figure 6.1. Causal Model of Determinants of Democracy

NOTE: Figures are the standardized regression coefficients for the paths indicated; $n = 88$; $r^2 = .62$. $*p < .001$.

Weighing the Evidence

Reviewing this accumulation of quantitative evidence over three decades of social science research, what are we able to conclude? The following general-izations appear warranted:

1. There is a strong positive relationship between democracy and socioeconomic development (as indicated by both per capita income and measures of physical well-being).
2. This relationship is causal in at least one direction: Higher levels of socioeco-nomic development generate a significantly higher probability of democratic government.
3. It also appears to be the case that high levels of socioeconomic development are associated with not only the presence but the stability of democracy.[29]

4. The relationship between socioeconomic development and democracy is not unilinear but in recent decades has more closely resembled an "N-curve"—increasing the chances for democracy among poor and perhaps lower-middle-income countries, neutralizing or even inverting to a negative effect at some middle range of development and industrialization, and then increasing again to the point where democracy becomes extremely likely above a certain high level of economic development (roughly represented by a per capita income of $6,000 in current U.S. dollars).

5. The causal relationship between development and democracy may not be stable across time but may itself vary across periods or waves in world history. The current wave of global democratic expansion may be weakening or eroding Dahl's (1971) hypothesized "lower threshold" of per capita GNP below which the chances for democracy are "slight"—although democracy would still be less likely at this income level than at any other above it. Even more so, the current wave may be moderating or eliminating the reverse relationship between democracy and development at middle levels of development.

6. The level of socioeconomic development is the most important variable in determining the chances of democracy, but it is far from completely determinative. Other variables exercise influence, and a number of countries (still) have regime forms that appear anomalous in terms of their level of development.

7. Although per capita national income appears to be the one independent variable that has most reliably and consistently predicted the level of democracy, this is likely a surrogate for a broader measure of average human development and well-being that is in fact even more closely associated with democracy. Lipset's thesis may thus be slightly reformulated: *The more well-to-do the people of a country, on average, the more likely they will favor, achieve, and maintain a democratic system for their country.*

It is important to emphasize here the extraordinary consistency with which the central premise of Lipset's thesis has stood up through all manner of tests. Although different studies and research designs yield different angles of inference and interpretation, virtually all demonstrate a consistent and strong positive relationship between the level of economic development and democracy (or, in one case, a negative relationship between economic development and authoritarian regimes). The effects of economic development are not only powerful and consistent but often literally overwhelming. In 44 regressions for various sets of nations (each including all countries for which data were available) over two different time periods and on two different types of authoritarian regimes, alternating into their regressions 11 different control variables, Thomas et al. (1979, Table 11B) found that economic development had a significant negative effect in 43 of the 44 equations. Of these 43 effects, 24 were significant beyond the .01 level, 16 were at the .05 level, and 3 were at the .10 level. In those 44 regressions, the 11 other independent variables showed significant effects only four times (less than 10% of the times they were tested).[30]

As is indicated by the summary of their principal features in Table 6.3, this common finding of a strong positive relationship between economic development and democracy is virtually the only one these various studies have in common. Given the considerable variation in quantitative methods, in countries and years tested, in the measures of democracy employed, and in the vast array of different regression equations (testing more than 20 different independent variables), this must rank as one of the most powerful and robust relationships in the study of comparative national development. Further, there are strong methodological and theoretical grounds for inferring that this relationship is indeed causal (without precluding the very real possibility of reciprocal causation). Several of the studies employ panel or dynamic designs, and, as will be shown below, there is considerable evidence (especially historical) to support Lipset's arguments about the specific mechanisms by which economic development favors democracy.

In a survey of some of these same quantitative studies and the comparative historical critiques of the Lipset thesis, Rueschemeyer (1991) arrives at a similar conclusion:

> There is a stable positive association between social and economic development and political democracy. This cannot be explained away by problems of operationalization. A whole array of different measures of development and democracy were used in the studies under review, and this did not substantially affect the results.
>
> This result cannot be invalidated either by arguing that it may not apply to certain regions of the world. Nor can it be explained by diffusion from a single center of democratic creativity, though some associations of democracy with former British colonial status as well as the proportion of Protestants were found by Bollen (1979). It also cannot be explained by a particularly close correlation between development and democracy at the highest levels of development, because samples consisting only of less developed countries exhibited substantially the same patterns. Finally, the close concatenation of level of development and democracy cannot be accounted for by a special association between early modernization and democracy since the explicit inclusion of measures of the timing of development did not significantly affect the relationship between level of development and democracy. (pp. 25-26)

Rueschemeyer is nevertheless left unsatisfied, as are many readers, with the insights that these many studies generate, for although they show that there is clearly a positive relationship between development and democracy, and even enable us to infer causality, most of them tell us little about why development tends to generate democracy, how it does so, and under what circumstances it fails to do so, or does the reverse. While some of the more recent quantitative studies, especially those using panel regression, dynamic, and path-analytic methods, have begun to generate insights of this kind, we remain heavily

Table 6.3 Quantitative Studies of the Correlates and Determinants of Democracy

	Cutright (1963)	Olsen (1968)	Cutright and Wiley (1969)	Jackman (1973)	Bollen (1979, 1983)	Bollen and Jackman (1985)	Thomas, Ramirez, Meyer, and Gobalet (1979)	Hannan and Carroll (1981)	Diamond et al. (1987)	Lipset, Seong, and Torres (1991)
Method used	Correlation	Correlation	Cross-lagged correlations	Multiple regression	Multiple regression and panel regression	Multiple regression	Panel regression	Event history	Panel regression	Multiple regression
Years analyzed	1940-1960	1940-1960	1927-1936, 1937-1946, 1947-1956, and 1957-1966	1960	1960 and 1965	1960 and 1965	1950-1965 and 1960-1975	1950-1975	1965-1975, 1975-1985, and 1965-1985	1960, 1965, 1975, 1980, and 1985
Scope and number of cases	77 (every region but Africa)	115 (independent nations)	40 (independent from 1927 to 1966)	60 (non-communist)	28-99, 94-100 (+4 75% random samples)	97-109	Global (49-102) and new nations (15-37)	90 countries and 206 transitions	Global (80-100) and less developed countries (62-72)	66-104 former colonies
Democracy variable	Index of political representation (includes stability)	(1) Scale of "political modernization" and (2) Cutright index	Cutright index with a franchise index	Jackman index (democratic structures and participation and press freedom)	Bollen index (1960 and 1965)	Bollen index (1960 and 1965)	Categorical: state centralism (military and 1-party regimes)	Categorical regime index (4 types)	Freedom House scale of political freedom	Bollen index (1960 and 1965) and Freedom House (1973-1985)

Continued

Table 6.3 Continued

	Cutright (1963)	Olsen (1968)	Cutright and Wiley (1969)	Jackman (1973)	Bollen (1979, 1983)	Bollen and Jackman (1985)	Thomas, Ramirez, Meyer, and Gobalet (1979)	Hannan and Carroll (1981)	Diamond et al. (1987)	Lipset, Seong, and Torres (1991)
Economic development measure	Per capita GNP, energy consumption, and others	(Log) Per capita GNP, energy consumption; labor diversity	Energy consumption per capita	(Log) energy consumption per capita	(Log) energy consumption per capita	(Log) per capita GNP	(Log) per capita GNP	(Log) per capita GNP	(Log) per capita GNP and PQLI	(Log) per capita GNP
Effects										
Economic										
development	+ ($r = .68$)	+ (1) $r = .62$ (2) $r = .68$	+	+	+	+	+	+	+/+	+
Education	+ ($r = .74$)	+ (1) $r = .61$ (2) $r = .69$	+ (literacy)				0	0	0	
Urbanization	+ ($r = .69$)	+ (1) $r = .59$ (2) $r = .60$					0	0	0	
Communication	+ ($r = .81$)	+ (1) $r = .60$ (2) $r = .68$							0	
Transportation		+ (1) $r = .71$ (2) $r = .70$								

Cultural pluralism		–	0	–
Protestant (% of population)		+		
Timing of development	+			
Economic dependence	0 – (world system position)	0	– (export partner concentration and investment dependence)	0 (export partner concentration and investment dependence)	0/– (trade dependence)
Military expenditure (% GNP)				–/0
Combined correlation of all socio-economic development variables	+ (r = .82)	+ (1) r = .83 (2) r = .84		–

NOTE: Plus sign indicates a statistically significant positive effect on democracy (or negative effect on authoritarianism); minus sign indicates a significant negative effect on democracy; 0 indicates that the variable was tested and did not show a *statistically significant* effect.

dependent for the answers to these questions on the evidence from case study
and comparative historical analysis.

HISTORICAL CASE
AND COMPARATIVE EVIDENCE

I will not attempt here to present in any systematic fashion the many critiques
of the Lipset thesis that have derived from (qualitative) historical and comparative
analysis. However, it will be useful to summarize a few of the principal challenges
so as to examine *their* durability 15 years into the progress of the "third wave" of
global democratization. I will then examine each of the causal mechanisms asserted
by Lipset to undergird the democracy-development relationship.

Challenges to Lipset

Probably the most forceful challenge to the Lipset hypothesis—and to the
entire "modernization" school with which it was associated—came from the
dependency school that emerged in the late 1960s and 1970s and the affiliated
perspective of world-system theory. Much dependency thinking posited a
negative relationship of economic dependency to democracy. These theorists
argued that the dependent capitalist developing states were captured by elites
in alliance with and serving the interests of dominant countries and corporations abroad. This exclusionary alliance required political repression of popular
mobilization to maintain low wage levels and high profit levels (Evans, 1979;
Fernandes, 1975). In an enormously influential analysis, O'Donnell (1973)
argued that at a certain stage of economic development in contemporary Latin
America, further development produced not democracy but "bureaucratic-authoritarian" dictatorship. This stage came roughly when the opportunities for
"easy" import-substituting industrialization through production of light consumer goods became more or less exhausted and countries needed to "deepen"
their industrialization to produce capital goods. This deepening necessitated
reducing popular consumption to generate higher domestic investment and
attract foreign investment. This in turn required demobilization (typically with
brutal repression, at least initially) of militant trade union movements and
populist parties and politicians. To pursue this strategy of dependent capitalist
development, military coups brought to power coalitions of civilian and military technocrats, supported by large-scale domestic and international capital.

This perspective also had its proponents outside the radical dependency
school. In explicit criticism of Lipset and other modernization theorists who
argued, in effect, that "all good things go together," Huntington and Nelson
(1976) asserted that there were basic trade-offs at different stages of development among three key goals: growth, equity, and (democratic) participation. At
low levels of industrialization, or what they called Phase I, equity and partici-

pation conflict. A key requirement for reducing inequality in these more agrarian societies—land reform—in turn requires (though is not assured by) an authoritarian regime. If democracy is chosen, democratic participation will be dominated by rural and urban elites; their rule might produce economic growth, but not greater equity. When countries begin to industrialize and develop strong trade unions and other popular sector movements (roughly akin to the approach of the capital goods era in the O'Donnell thesis), a different conflict emerges, one between participation and economic growth. A participatory (democratic) regime in this phase would be dominated by populist parties and movements making so many demands for distribution that they would choke off economic growth. The choice in this phase is therefore between a "populist" democracy and a "technocratic" (read bureaucratic-authoritarian) dictatorship.

In urging a historical, "genetic" approach to the study of democracy, Rustow (1970) issued one of the earlier and more influential challenges to the Lipset thesis. Democracies, he suggested, had existed at low levels of economic development historically (e.g., the United States in 1820, France in 1870, and Sweden in 1890). The only true prerequisites of democracy, he argued, were a sense of national unity and some kind of elite commitment to a democratic transition, often arising not out of any intrinsic valuing of democracy but out of a stalemated conflict for which democracy seems to offer the best chance of resolution (p. 352).

As I will argue in conclusion, Rustow was right that no particular level of economic development is a *pre*requisite of democracy (it would be difficult, for that matter, to specify any level of national unity as an absolute *pre*requisite of democracy). But the analogy to nineteenth-century low-income democracies is inappropriate for several reasons. In his own reassessment of his famous thesis, Lipset (1981) observes:

> These and other early democracies had . . . the historical advantage of having formed their political institutions prior to the emergence of a worldwide communications system which might make it apparent that other countries were much wealthier than they, and before the appearance of electorally significant popular movements that demanded more equal distribution of worldly goods. (p. 475)

Thus they had the advantage of gradual development. They did not have to meet the simultaneous or overlapping crises of integration, legitimation, penetration, participation, and distribution that have confronted developing countries in the post-World War II era (Binder, 1971; Diamond, 1980; LaPalombara & Weiner, 1966). In particular, they benefited from a favorable historical sequence in which the institutions of competition developed first among a limited stratum of political participants and gradually incorporated a wider and wider range of citizens. Historically, this has been the path most likely to produce a "system of mutual security" and trust between contending elites, but in an age of instant

communication and universal franchise it is no longer open to emerging
democracies (Dahl, 1971). Thus new democracies emerge in less developed
countries with increasingly high levels of social and political mobilization, in
which social and economic demands are liable easily to overwhelm the capacity
of poor states to meet them and in which nascent participatory institutions may
be ill equipped to incorporate and respond to historically marginalized groups
(Huntington, 1968).

More to the point is Rustow's (1970) concern with taking a genetic or
historical approach. In doing so, we inevitably find that history is not moved
by some hidden economic hand, but by people and the variety of interests,
values, and unique historical factors that motivate them. Yet changing social
and economic conditions—including economic development and its consequences—powerfully frame those interests and values and conjunctures. Behind the contending elite values and interests, strategies and calculations,
divisions and pacts that take the lead in elite-centered theories of democratic
transition (Burton & Higley, 1987; Higley & Burton, 1989; O'Donnell &
Schmitter, 1986; Rustow, 1970), one may frequently discern the facilitating
effects of long periods of social and economic development.

Socioeconomic Development as a "Cause" of Democracy

In his original essay, Lipset (1960) hypothesized a number of historical and
sociological processes by which economic development generated a greater
likelihood of democracy. First, economic development gives rise to a more
democratic political culture, due in part to increased education. Citizens come
to value democracy more and to manifest a more tolerant, moderate, restrained,
and rational style with respect to politics and political opposition (pp. 39-40).
This moderation of political conflict is also advanced by several interrelated
changes in the class structure that accompany economic development. Higher
levels of income and economic security at the mass level temper the intensity
of the "class struggle, by permitting those in the lower strata to develop longer
time perspectives and more complex and gradualist views of politics" (p. 45).
Among the upper strata as well, attitudes change; with rising national income,
the upper classes are less likely to regard the lower classes as "vulgar, innately
inferior" and hence utterly unworthy of political rights and the opportunity to
share power (p. 51). More generally, Lipset argued that increased wealth
reduces the overall level of objective inequality, weakening status distinctions,
and, most important, increasing the size of the middle class (pp. 47-51).
Economic development also tempers the tendency of the lower classes to
political extremism by exposing them to cross-pressures in a more complex
society (p. 50). Finally, with respect to class, Lipset suggested that economic
development would reduce the premium on political power by reducing the
costs of socioeconomic redistribution and by generating attractive income and
career alternatives to positions in the state (pp. 51-52). Independent of these

changes in class structure, Lipset maintained, in a Tocquevillean vein, that economic development would also contribute to democracy by giving rise to a large number of voluntary, intermediary organizations that collectively increase political participation, enhance political skills, generate and diffuse new opinions, and inhibit the state or other domineering forces from monopolizing political resources.

It is beyond the scope of this essay to consider systematically the historical and comparative evidence for each of these processes. Hence what follows is a more illustrative sketch of the very substantial and compelling accumulation of empirical data since Lipset first articulated these arguments.

Political Culture

Lipset (1960) cited a number of studies suggesting a strong relationship between education, socioeconomic status, and modernization on one hand and democratic values and tendencies on the other. Subsequent survey evidence has added further support to Lipset's argument that educated individuals tend to be more tolerant of opposition and of minorities, and more committed to democracy and participation. In their study of five national political cultures, Almond and Verba (1963) found that educational attainment had "the most important demographic effect on political attitudes." Within each of the five nations, more educated people were found to be better informed politically and more broadly opinionated, more likely to follow politics, and more likely to engage in political discussion and to join and become active in organizations (with obvious implications for the development of civil society), more confident of their capacities to influence government, and more likely to manifest trust in other people. Inkeles (1969) found in his six-country comparative study of modernization that education in particular, and mass media exposure as well, contributed significantly to a syndrome of "active citizenship," with attitudinal, informational, and behavioral consequences similar to those found by Almond and Verba.

Of course, as Almond and Verba concede, the fact that educated people are much more inclined to participate tells us nothing in itself about the content of that participation, and Huntington (1968) warns that such social mobilization, in the absence of adequate political institutionalization, can actually lead to political instability and praetorianism. However, Inkeles's syndrome of individual modernity, of which active citizenship is one dimension, also includes such other democratic orientations as efficacy, respect for minority rights, and "freedom from absolute submission to received authority" (Inkeles & Smith, 1974, p. 109), and this larger syndrome is also advanced by education and contact with other modernizing institutions, such as the factory and mass media. Inkeles (1978) subsequently established that the level of economic development of the nation has a substantial independent effect on individual modernity. More to the point for Lipset's thesis, Inkeles and Diamond (1980) showed that this effect of the national context held quite strongly for a number of discrete elements of democratic political culture, even when socioeconomic status was to some extent controlled. Surveying a large number of comparative studies, they computed, in each case, a rank order correlation between the average scores of country samples (within socioeconomic or occupational groups) on certain types of attitudes and values and the per capita GNPs of their countries. The median rank order correlations were .76 for measures of antiauthoritarianism (or tolerance), .85 for trust, .55 for efficacy, and .60 for personal satisfaction (which has strong potential implications for political legitimacy). Recently, Inglehart (1990) has shown (with comparative survey data from more than 20 mainly European countries) that life satisfaction and interpersonal trust are highly correlated not only with economic development but with stable democracy.[31]

A very different type of quantitative evidence derives from Powell's (1982) comparative study of 29 countries that had democratic regimes for at least five years during the period 1958-1976. Grouping his sample into four levels of modernization in 1965, he found a modest association between participation (voting turnout) and development level, increasing sharply from the lowest development groups to the second highest but leveling off after that. His truly stunning behavioral evidence, however, concerned political violence: The median annual death rate from political violence was dramatically higher among the six least developed countries—India, Sri Lanka, the Philippines, Turkey, Costa Rica, and Jamaica—than among any of the other groups.[32] Not coincidentally, these six countries together experienced the greatest democratic instability of any of the four development levels, and in every case (except stable Costa Rica) political violence played a major role. In that deadly political violence is an obvious—indeed, the *ultimate*—behavioral manifestation of intolerance and lack of moderation, it is certainly consistent with Lipset's theory that it is the poorest nations that experience the greatest amount of it. Powell states that "insofar as containment of violence is a measure of democratic performance, the poorer nations seem to be much more difficult to govern as democracies" (p. 41).[33]

There is also (less precise) historical evidence that attitudes and values may change in response to socioeconomic development. Booth and Seligson (1992) were "startled to discover" that despite the long experience of authoritarian rule in Mexico and the general assumptions about the authoritarian character of Mexican political culture, their sample of urban working-class and middle-class Mexicans "manifested high levels of support" for civil liberties and extensive rights of participation and dissent. These democratic inclinations were broadly distributed, despite their also being modestly correlated with education and class standing. Booth and Seligson speculate that a number of factors—diffusion from the United States, long experience with the rhetoric and forms of constitutionalism, and disillusionment with the ruling party—may account for this. However, an equally if not more compelling explanation would look to the cultural impact of a quarter century of relatively rapid growth in per capita GNP, averaging 3.0% annually between 1965 and 1989, and probably affecting the urban working and middle classes most intensively.[34]

Elsewhere in Latin America, case studies discern evidence of socioeconomic development's producing democratic value change, at least among important class groups. Just as highly undemocratic attitudes and values in Peru and the Dominican Republic were fostered by poverty and inequality, rapid socioeconomic change in these two countries helped to breed, among new business and professional elites and other educated middle-class groups, a stronger value on democratic participation and a more acute appreciation of the need for social and political accommodation (Diamond & Linz, 1989; McClintock, 1989; Wiarda, 1989). As a result of the socioeconomic reforms under the Velasco military regime in Peru (1968-1975), which reduced inequality and oligarchic power, and also as a result of dramatically increased access to television and secondary and university education, lower- and middle-class groups in Peru became more politically active, informed, and sophisticated, and manifested, in a number of surveys during the 1980s, historically high levels of democratic attitudes (McClintock, 1989).

Class Structure and International Diffusion

The Peruvian case also indicates that the effects of socioeconomic development on political culture are heavily mediated through changes in the class structure. In fact, these changes—the growth of the middle class and more specifically of a commercial and industrial bourgeoisie; the enlargement, unionization, and improved incomes of the working class; and the migration of the rural poor to cities and consequent disruption of clientelistic and feudalistic relations in the countryside—are heavily interrelated in time and logic. Their interactive effect in stimulating democratization in Taiwan is depicted succinctly by Cheng (1989):

> Rapid growth . . . had liberalizing consequences that the KMT had not fully anticipated. With the economy taking off, Taiwan displayed the features common to all growing capitalist societies: The literacy rate increased; mass communication intensified; per capita income rose; and a differentiated urban sector—including labor, a professional middle class, and a business entrepreneurial class—came into being. The business class was remarkable for its independence. Although individual enterprises were small and unorganized, they were beyond the capture of the party-state. To prevent the formation of big capital, the KMT had avoided organizing business or picking out "national champions." As a result, small and medium enterprises dominated industrial production and exports. As major employers and foreign exchange earners, these small and medium businesses were quite independent of the KMT. (p. 481)

Democratization in Taiwan was particularly advanced by "the newly emerging middle-class intellectuals who had come of age during the period of rapid economic growth," who were connected through family and social ties to the emergent bourgeoisie, and whose training abroad in law and the social sciences heavily disposed them to "Western democratic ideals" (Cheng, 1989, p. 483).

Taiwan is unique in many senses, and theoretically it stands out here for having achieved rapid economic growth while at the same time significantly improving the distribution of income and thus accelerating the democratic impact of development by diffusing it more rapidly to the lower strata. Typically, income inequality is aggravated during the early phase of industrialization. However, where this effect does not become too severe and where the material conditions of all class groups improve at least in absolute terms, economic development is eventually likely to have political consequences similar to those Cheng identifies for Taiwan. Even at a much lower stage of economic development, brisk economic growth (averaging 6.4% annually in GDP during the 1980s) generated pressure for democratization in Pakistan. Particularly important were the emergence (as in northern India) of rural and small-town entrepreneurs, the general improvement of the rural economy, the diminishing power of the traditional rural landed elite, rapid urbanization, and a better-organized and more active trade union movement. Moreover, development may be expected to deepen and invigorate democracy over time in Pakistan by propelling into politics a new, better-educated generation from rural elite families, thus broadening the base of political parties long dominated by urban elite families, most of whom fled India at the time of partition (Rose, 1989).

Of course, whatever impact economic development has on democracy will be more decisive to the extent that it thrusts a country into higher *levels* of development, and to the extent that it occurs rapidly, because "rapid economic growth creates rapidly the economic base for democracy" and may also generate "stresses and strains" that wear thin the fabric of authoritarian rule (Huntington, 1991, p. 69). This was a critical underlying factor, Huntington (1991) argues, in the democratic transitions in Portugal, Spain, and Greece in the mid-1970s, whose (per capita) economic growth rates in the quarter century before their transitions averaged 5-6% annually (p. 68). Such vigorous and sustained development rapidly expanded the middle classes while at the same time raising expectations, heightening inequality in some cases (especially Brazil), and generating frustration, discontent, and political mobilization (for democracy).

As Huntington recognizes in an important, if subtle, qualification of Lipset's thesis, the burgeoning middle classes are not *always* prodemocratic and may even actively support authoritarian rule under conditions of social polarization and threat such as those prevailing in Brazil and the Southern Cone of South America during the late 1960s and early 1970s. However, one irony of the combination of effective authoritarian rule and rapid economic development is that it eliminates (albeit often at tragic human cost) these conditions of class polarization and insurgency, rendering the authoritarian regime "dispensable," in the language of O'Donnell and Schmitter (1986, p. 27). Thus what has been considered for some years now a critical factor in elite-centered theories of democratic transition (very much opposed in spirit to Lipset's structural approach)—change in the strategic interests and behavior of crucial middle-class groups—often springs from the very structural factor emphasized by Lipset: economic development.

These changes in both the alignment of the bourgeoisie and the culture and structure of society more generally have had a powerful impact in motivating democratic transition in South Korea. Rapid economic growth—averaging 7% annually in per capita GNP since 1965—had democratizing consequences similar to those in Taiwan, even though industrialization proceeded with greater concentration of capital and repression of labor. Indeed, in both countries, an important incentive for democratization was not only the increasing contact of urban middle classes with Western democratic values, but the realization— quite powerful for a country where industrialization is so heavily led by exports—that "democratization is the necessary ticket for membership in the club of advanced nations" (Han, 1989, p. 294).

These indirect effects of economic development in "internationalizing" a country's elite and its values have probably always been present, but they are more intensive today than ever before. In an era of satellite communications, jet travel, and increasing global interdependence, "economic development in the 1960s and 1970s both required and promoted the opening of societies to foreign trade, investment, technology, tourism, and communications. . . . Autarchy and development were an impossible combination" (Huntington, 1991, p. 66). Further contributing to this internationalizing impact of development has been the increasing salience of formal and informal supranational structures, such as the European Community, that regard democracy (*explicitly* in the case of the European Community) as a prerequisite of membership (Diamond, 1992a; Huntington, 1991). This growing interconnectedness adds an additional dimension to the impact of socioeconomic development. So does the rapid improvement in the technology of communication, transportation, and information storage and retrieval, which has had two very strong prodemocratic effects: radically decentralizing and pluralizing flows of information, and producing more powerful, immediate, and pervasive diffusion effects than ever before, reaching well beyond the elite sector. Where the dominant themes and images conveyed are democratic, as they have been in world culture for more than a decade, so will be the political consequences.

State and Society

Lipset argued that economic development alters the relationship between state and society to favor the emergence and maintenance of democracy. One way it does so, he suggested, is by reducing nepotism and bureaucratic corruption and, more generally, by altering the zero-sum nature of the electoral struggle. Reformulating Lipset slightly, a major reason democracy is less viable in less developed societies is because the "proportion . . . of wealth that the government or local elective bodies absorb and distribute is greater, and [therefore it becomes] harder . . . to secure an independent position and an honest living without relying in some respect or other upon public administration" (Mosca, 1896/1939, p. 143). While it may not be literally true that the state absorbs and distributes more wealth in less developed countries than in industrialized ones, it is certainly the case that at low levels of development, swollen states control a vastly greater share of the most valued economic opportunities (jobs, contracts, licenses, scholarships, and development largess) than they do at higher levels of development. As Mosca (1896/1939) presciently foresaw, this is yet another reason democracy requires "a large [middle] class of people whose economic position is virtually independent of those who hold supreme power" (p. 144).

In the post-World War II era, the pressures and prevailing models in the world system, and the insecurities of peripheral status in that system, have induced underdeveloped new nations to build centralized, resource-intensive states (Meyer, 1980). As a result of this state expansion in the quest for rapid development, control of the state itself has become the principal means of personal accumulation and hence the principal determinant of class formation (Diamond, 1987; Sklar, 1979). Both through legitimate state employment and contracting and through all manner of illegitimate diversion of public funds, manipulation of state resources became the easiest, most common, and least risky means of accumulating personal wealth. Throughout Africa and in much of Asia, Latin America, and the Middle East, this process gave rise to what Sklar (1965) termed, following Mosca, a "political class," in the sense that "political power is the primary force that creates economic opportunity and determines the pattern of social stratification" (pp. 203-204).

This distorted relationship between state and society has been one of the most fundamental causes of democratic breakdown in Africa and Asia following decolonization because it has generated many of the other factors superficially identified with democratic malfunctioning. It entrenched political corruption as the chief instrument of upward class mobility, draining democratic states of economic resources and political legitimacy. Both through the perverting effects of systematic rent seeking and through the pervasive impediments to productive enterprise generated by gross excesses in state ownership, regulation, taxation, and staffing, statism depressed and obstructed economic growth. By crowding economic competition out of the private sector, it prevented the emergence of an autonomous, productive (rather than parasitic) bourgeoisie. By subjecting virtually all developmental activity to state mediation and control, it made community as well as individual advancement dependent on control of the state, heightening inequality and political tensions among ethnic and regional groups. Because of the latter inducement to group conflict, and because of the enormous premium for individuals on control of the state, it induced pervasive fraud and violence in the electoral struggle for power. Indeed, Powell's (1982) finding that deadly political violence is strongly negatively associated with economic development tells us a good deal more about the effects of statism in this context than about intrinsic features of the political cultures, as I have argued elsewhere for the case of Nigeria (Diamond, 1988a, 1988c).

Collectively, these consequences of statism—corruption, abuse of power, economic stagnation and crisis, ethnic conflict, electoral fraud, and political violence—heavily explain the failures of democracy thrice in Ghana, twice in Nigeria and Uganda, and more generally throughout the African continent (Chazan, 1988; Diamond, 1988b; Kokole & Mazrui, 1988). Outside of Africa as well, these perverse consequences of statism have contributed to the three breakdowns or interruptions of democracy in Turkey (Ozbudun, 1989), the ethnic polarization and consequent democratic deterioration in Sri Lanka (Phadnis, 1989), and the broad decline in democratic performance (including rising levels of corruption, party decay, group conflict and political violence) in India (Brass, 1990; Kohli, 1990). Certainly, swollen states conducive to rent seeking are not inevitably a consequence of low levels of economic development; Singapore and Taiwan have developed rapidly while managing largely to avoid this syndrome, and Botswana has even done so within a democratic framework. Nor is statism absent at higher levels of development. However, statism is uniquely toxic to democracy at low levels of development precisely because it places such a high premium on control of the state. As Lipset (1960) argued, "If loss of office means serious losses for major power groups, they will seek to retain or secure office by any means available" (p. 51).

Civil Society

There is abundant historical evidence to support the hypothesized linkage between a vigorous associational life and a stable democracy. One could begin, of course, by citing Tocqueville's (1840/1945) seminal study *Democracy in America,* as Lipset did. Tocqueville was perhaps the first to note the symbiotic, mutually reinforcing relationship between participation in civil society and participation in political life, depicting associations as "large free schools" where political interests were stimulated and political and organizational skills enhanced (p. 124). This effect has been particularly apparent in less developed countries such as India and Costa Rica, where both organizational activity and partisan political participation have been more vigorous than would be expected from their levels of development (Booth, 1989; Das Gupta, 1989). Increasingly, civic organizations in the developing world are devoted to the political mobilization and empowerment of groups, such as women, young people, and the poor, traditionally excluded from power (Diamond, 1992b).

Second, as Lipset and other pluralists have argued, a vibrant associational life—and, more generally, a robust and pluralistic civil society[35]—checks and balances the power of the state. Related to this, a vibrant associational life makes for a pluralistic competition of interests, and provides poor and disadvantaged groups the capacity to relieve or redress the injustices they face. With the deterioration in the party system and the quality of political leadership, India's vigorous civil society has become an increasingly crucial (if turbulent) instrument of democratic accountability, interest articulation, social reform, and political renewal (Shah, 1988).

Third, a strong civil society may provide an indispensable bulwark against the consolidation of authoritarian rule and a catalyst for its demise. The "resurgence" of civil society has been a crucial factor in transitions from authoritarian rule in Southern Europe and Latin America (O'Donnell & Schmitter, 1986). The mobilization of independent media and organizations has been similarly significant in pressuring for democratic change in the Philippines (Bautista, 1992; Pascual, 1992), Nigeria (Ekpu, 1992; Nwankwo, 1992), and South Africa (Heard, 1992; Schlemmer, 1991; Slabbert, 1991). Democratic change in Taiwan during the 1980s was stimulated and advanced by a host of social movements—of consumers, workers, women, aborigines, farmers, students, teachers, and the environmentally concerned—breaking free of traditional deference or state intimidation and control to seek both specific demands and long-range goals (Gold, 1990). In Eastern Europe, the Soviet Union, and China, the growth of autonomous organizational, cultural, and intellectual life has been a crucial factor in undermining the cultural hegemony and monopoly of information, then the political legitimacy, and ultimately the viability of the communist party-state (Lapidus, 1989; Nathan, 1990; Sadowski, 1992; Starr, 1988; Weigle & Butterfield, 1991). Most recently in Africa, protests mobilized by autonomously organized urban groups—students, churches, trade unions, civil servants, lawyers and other professionals—have focused sweeping discontent on demands for regime change, making "a direct connection between chronic economic and political malaise and the absence of democracy" (Chazan, 1991, p. 52; see also Joseph, 1991; Kuria, 1991).

One can imagine other positive consequences for democracy of a vigorous and pluralistic associational life. To the extent that they are democratic in their internal procedures of governance, voluntary associations may socialize their members into democratic values and beliefs and help to recruit and train new political leaders for the arena of formal democratic politics. More focused research is necessary to determine whether associations do (as a by-product of their other pursuits) perform these roles, but the emergence of civic organizations focused explicitly on these goals is significant (Barros, 1992; Martini, 1992; Pascual, 1992).

Although voluntary associations and other elements of civil society do not *inevitably* contribute to democracy and may even oppose it (depending on their purposes and ideologies), it is clear, on balance, that the increasing size, pluralism, and resourcefulness of civil societies around the world have been major factors in the growth of democracy in recent decades. Numerous factors may affect the number, character, and strength of autonomous organizations in society, but it is also clear that *one* factor—socioeconomic development—contributes substantially to their growth. From Taiwan to China, from the Soviet Union to South Africa, and from Brazil to Thailand, economic development has had some strikingly similar effects: physically concentrating people into more populous areas of residence while at the same time dispersing them into wider, more diverse networks of interaction; decentralizing control over information and increasing alternative sources of information; dispersing literacy, knowledge, income, and other organizational resources across wider segments of the population; and increasing functional specialization and interdependence and so the potential for functionally specific protests (e.g., transit strikes) to disrupt the entire system. These effects would figure to be, and probably are, more rapidly experienced within the context of a market economy, but they have registered intensely in communist systems as well with the expansion of education, industry, and mass communications.

CONCLUSIONS AND IMPLICATIONS

This review of the evidence more than three decades later has demonstrated that Lipset (1960) was broadly correct both in his assertion of a strong causal relationship between economic development and democracy and in his explanations of *why* development promotes democracy. Needless to say, this relationship is not entirely predictive, nor is it necessarily linear. But that does not negate the validity of the overall relationship that Lipset hypothesized.

The preceding discussion suggests five conclusions and some obvious policy implications. First, socioeconomic development promotes democracy in two senses. Where democracy already exists, sustained development contributes significantly to its legitimacy and stability, especially in the early life of the regime (Diamond, Linz, & Lipset, 1990, 1992, chap. 5). Where democracy does not exist, it leads (sooner or later) to the eventually (if not initially) *successful* establishment of democracy. However, it is difficult to predict at what point in a country's socioeconomic or historical development the democratic moment will emerge. Below Dahl's (1971) higher threshold of development, many factors continue to intervene to structure the probability of a democratic regime, and these are, as Huntington has suggested, heavily a matter of political institutions and political leadership and choice. Nor should we dismiss the importance of such "political crafting" for the successful democratization of countries near or above the threshold (Linz & Stepan, 1989).

Second, notwithstanding Hannan and Carroll's (1981) findings for the 1950-1975 period, socioeconomic development does not produce the same enduringly legitimating effects for authoritarian regimes that it does for democratic ones. Rather, it presents the former with an inescapable dilemma. If authoritarian regimes "do not perform, they lose legitimacy because performance is their only justification for holding power. However, . . . if they do perform in delivering socioeconomic progress, they tend to refocus popular aspirations around political goals for voice and participation that they cannot satisfy without terminating their existence" (Diamond, 1989, p. 150; also Huntington, 1991, p. 55). The latter pattern of change was crucial to the transitions in Spain, Taiwan, and South Korea, is very far along in Thailand, and is beginning to register in Indonesia.

Third, it is not economic development per se and certainly not mere economic growth that is the most important developmental factor in promoting democracy. Rather, it is the dense cluster of social changes and improvements, broadly distributed among the population, that are vaguely summarized in the term *socioeconomic development*. Most important here are improvements in the physical quality and dignity of people's lives: access to potable water, safe and sanitary neighborhoods, and basic health care; literacy and advanced (probably at least some secondary) education; sufficient income to provide at least minimally adequate food and clothing and shelter for one's family; and sufficient skills to obtain a job that provides that income. Of course, the standards for what constitutes the decent and "minimally adequate" change over time and across cultures. But these basic material dimensions of "human development," as summarized in the UNDP (1991) index, better predict the presence and degree of democracy than does the level of per capita national wealth. Economic development provides a structural context in which human development can occur, but to the extent that its benefits are grossly maldistributed (or that its correlates, like urbanization, only alter the form and scale of human squalor), it may do little to promote democracy or may even generate stresses and contradictions that are hostile to democracy. For the democratic prospect, one aspect of economic development overrides all others in importance: reducing the level of absolute poverty and human deprivation.

There are several reasons democracy is so closely related to the physical quality of life. First, these conditions generate the circumstances and skills that permit effective and autonomous participation. Second, when most of the population is literate, decently fed and sheltered, and otherwise assured of minimal material needs, class tensions and radical political orientations tend to diminish. Thus, as Lipset (1960) has observed, "a belief in secular reformist gradualism can be the ideology of only a relatively well-to-do lower class" (p. 45).

Third, human beings appear to frame their values at least partly in response to what psychologist Abraham Maslow (1954) termed a "hierarchy of needs." Recent comparative research indicates that physiological needs, for physical security and material sustenance, do take precedence over "higher-order" needs of a more social, intellectual, and aesthetic nature (even though such research gives no support to Maslow's assumption of a predictable, panhuman hierarchy beyond the physiological needs; Inglehart, 1990, p. 152). Thus, while the satisfaction of lower-order needs does not automatically increase the salience of individual needs for political freedom and influence, it makes the valuing of those needs more likely.

Fourth, economic development produces or facilitates democracy *only* insofar as it alters favorably four crucial intervening variables: political culture, class structure, state-society relations, and civil society. This is also the finding of perhaps the only cross-national quantitative analysis to combine indicators of both national development and individual attitudes, namely, that conducted by Inglehart (1990, p. 44). In addition to change in the occupational structure, Inglehart identifies a powerful cultural factor mediating the relationship between economic development and stable democracy—a "civic culture" syndrome consisting of interpersonal trust, life satisfaction, and political moderation.

Finally, it is important to emphasize as well that democracy can occur at low levels of development if the crucial mediating variables are present. Economic development is not a *pre*requisite of democracy. In fact, Lipset wrote of it as a "requisite," meaning literally something that is essential but does not necessarily have to exist in advance. In a much-neglected passage of his famous essay, he anticipated a crucial element of democratic experience in the contemporary developing world: "A premature democracy which survives will do so by (among other things) facilitating the growth of other conditions conducive to democracy, such as universal literacy, or autonomous private organizations" (p. 29).

Those developing countries that have maintained democracy for long periods of time have done just that. They have inherited or developed political cultures that emphasize tolerance, inclusion, participation, and accommodation, as has been the case (more or less) with India, Costa Rica, Botswana, Venezuela after 1958, and Chile and Uruguay before their polarization in the late 1960s and again in very recent years. Many of them have, as noted earlier with regard to India and Costa Rica, developed vibrant civil societies. And perhaps most of all, they have performed reasonably well in delivering human development. The 10 developing countries (above 1 million population) that have maintained more or less continuous democracy since 1965 reduced their infant mortality by a median annual rate of 3.25% from that year until the late 1980s, compared with a median annual reduction rate of 2.3% among 10 of the most prominent continuous dictatorships in that period. These democracies have survived in large part because they have substantially improved the quality of life for their citizens (Diamond et al., 1992, chap. 5).[36]

This suggests that democracy is not incompatible with development and that in fact the causal trend *can* be reversed, with democracy leading to development. Although cross-national studies of the effects of democracy on economic development are inconclusive (Sirowy & Inkeles, 1990), there remain strong theoretical grounds for expecting that political participation, liberty, accountability, and pluralism "would be conducive to economic achievements by industrious persons, particularly entrepreneurs," and to improvements in basic human needs as well (Sklar, 1987, pp. 709, 711). Indeed, with the spectacular failures of development in Africa over the past quarter century, many Africans now believe that democracy is essential for development (Ake, 1991). To formalize slightly Lipset's argument about "premature" democracies, poor countries can maintain democracy, but only if they deliver broad and sustained (not necessarily rapid) socioeconomic development, especially "human development."

The policy implications of this are rather obvious. First, giving priority to basic human needs is not only sensible from the standpoint of economic development policy and intrinsically more humane, it is also more likely to promote or sustain democracy than more capital-intensive strategies that view basic health and literacy needs as "consumption" that must be deferred.

Second, in no country should democracy absolutely be ruled out as a possibility. Certainly, in very poor countries it is less likely, especially in its complete institutional configuration, but since "democracy comes to every country in fragments or parts" (Sklar, 1987, p. 714), development policy should try to encourage the institutionalization of as many parts or features of democracy as possible, as early as possible. A careful reading of Lipset's thesis reveals that economic development promotes democracy only by effecting changes in political culture and social structure. Even at modest levels of economic development, countries can achieve significantly democratic cultures and civil societies and significant reductions in absolute poverty. If social and political actors, private and public, focus on these intermediate goals, they stand a good chance of developing democracy "prematurely."

APPENDIX:
RANKING OF COUNTRIES BY FREEDOM STATUS AND HUMAN DEVELOPMENT INDEX IN 1990

Regime Type	High (Top 20) .993-.951	Medium-High (21-53) .950-.800	Medium (54-97) .796-.510	Medium-Low (98-128) .499-.253	Low (129-160) .242-.048
State hegemonic, closed (13-14)		Kuwait[48] Albania[49]	Cuba[62] China[82] North Korea[74] Iraq[91] Libya[76] Saudi Arabia[69] Syria[72]	Myanmar[106] Vietnam[99]	Afghanistan[157] Angola[147] Burundi[139] Cambodia[140] Chad[152] Ethiopia[141] Liberia[132] Malawi[138] Mauritania[148] Somalia[149] Sudan[143]
State hegemonic, partially open (11-12)		Qatar[50] Brunei[42] Bahrain[51]	Iran[92] Lebanon[88] Oman[86] Romania[58] United Arab Emirates[56] Maldives[93]	Ghana[121] Kenya[113] Tanzania[127] Zambia[118] Lesotho[107] Indonesia[98] Swaziland[104]	Mali[156] Togo[131] Mozambique[146] Guinea-Bissau[151] Guinea[158] Niger[155] Burkina Faso[154] Central African Republic[142] Djibouti[153] Bhutan[144] Sierra Leone[160] Uganda[134] Yemen[130]

Regime Type	High (Top 20) .993-.951	Medium-High (21-53) .950-.800	Medium (54-97) .796-.510	Medium-Low (98-128) .499-.253	Low (129-160) .242-.048
Noncompetitive, partially pluralist (10)			Jordan[83] Fiji[71] Surinam[55]	Zimbabwe[111] Cape Verde[109] Comoros[126] Ivory Coast[122] Sao Tome/ Principe[112]	Bangladesh[136] Nigeria[129] Benin[150]
Semicompetitive, partially pluralist (7-9)		Malaysia[52] Mexico[45] Yugoslavia[34] Bulgaria[33] USSR[31] Singapore[37]	Sri Lanka[75] Tunisia[90] Mongolia[87] Colombia[61] Peru[78] South Africa[57] Guyana[89] El Salvador[94] Paraguay[73] Gabon[97]	Egypt[114] Morocco[108] Guatemala[103] Pakistan[120] Algeria[102] Madagascar[116]	Nepal[145] Senegal[135] Haiti[125]
Competitive, partially illiberal (5-6)		South Korea[35] Antigua/ Barbados[46] Bahamas[28]	Philippines[84] Thailand[66] Turkey[70] Nicaragua[85] Panama[54] Brazil[60] Dominican Republic[80]	Bolivia[110] Honduras[100] India[123] Namibia[105] Papua New Guinea[117] Vanuatu[101]	
Competitive, pluralist, partially institutionalized (3-4)	France[10] Germany[14] United Kingdom[11]	Chile[38] Cyprus[26] Mauritius[47] Argentina[43] Israel[21] Uruguay[32] Venezuela[44] Czechoslovakia[27] Hungary[30] Poland[41] Dominica[53] Portugal[36] Greece[24]	Grenada[64] West Samoa[81] Botswana[95] Ecuador[77] Jamaica[59] St. Lucia[68] St. Vincent[79] Belize[67]		Gambia[159]

Regime Type	High (Top 20) .993-.951	Medium-High (21-53) .950-.800	Medium (54-97) .796-.510	Medium-Low (98-128) .499-.253	Low (129-160) .242-.048
Liberal democracy (2)	Australia[9] Canada[2] Italy[18] Japan[1] Spain[20] Sweden[4] USA[7] Austria[17] Belgium[16] Denmark[12] Finland[13] Iceland[3] Luxembourg[19] Netherlands[18] New Zealand[15] Norway[6] Switzerland[5]	Costa Rica[40] Trinidad/ Tobago[39] Ireland[23] Barbados[22] Malta[29]	St. Christopher-Nevis[65] Solomon Islands[96]		

SOURCE: United Nations Development Program (1991, Table 1).
NOTE: Superscript numbers represent the rank of the country on the Human Development Index, with 1 being highest.

NOTES

1. All page references are to the version of the essay reprinted in *Political Man* (Lipset, 1960) as Chapter 2, "Economic Development and Democracy," and specifically to the 1963 Anchor Books edition of *Political Man,* which has the same page numbers as the 1981 expanded edition.

2. The 10 European stable democracies in 1960 were Albania, Bulgaria, Czechoslovakia, Hungary, Poland, Portugal, Romania, Spain, USSR, and Yugoslavia.

3. He would also have avoided the methodological problem, emphasized by Bollen (1980, 1990), of confounding two distinct phenomena, democracy and stability, in a single measure.

4. These figures (rounded to whole numbers) were computed for this chapter by Yongchuan Liu. Data on per capita GNP in 1960 were missing for four communist East European dictatorships, but the mean difference between the two groups is too substantial to be suspect because of this.

5. On literacy, the stepwise increase in mean levels is from 87.1% for dictatorships to 94.8% for unstable democracies to 98.5% for stable democracies. Mean per capita GNP levels progress from $598 to $1,026 to $1,479. PQLI scores proceed from 89.2 to 92.8 to 98.6. A similar stepwise increase is apparent on the PQLI among the three Latin American country groups: "stable dictatorships," "unstable democracies," and "democracies." However, as there are only two countries in the middle category (Colombia and Mexico, both semi-democracies), that *n* is too small to permit reliable comparison.

6. In fact, as Cutright (1963) observes, "the spread in the values on almost every indicator [of socioeconomic development] is so extreme that it appears that it would be very difficult to place a single nation in either the democratic or non-democratic category knowing, for example, only its score on the number of telephones" (p. 254).

7. Huntington includes in this count some states, such as Guatemala, El Salvador, and Romania, that are better labeled semidemocratic. By a more cautious calculation, sensitive to the distinction between semidemocracy and democracy, I estimate the number of democracies in 1990 at 44 in states of more than 1 million and 65 total (Diamond, 1992a).

8. Authoritarian Latin American countries had higher rates of unionization than did semicompetitive regimes in that region, but this may have been due to state corporatist control of such unions.

9. I define *democracy* here in terms of these three dimensions, as articulated by Diamond, Linz, and Lipset (1990, pp. 6-7), drawing from Dahl (1971).

10. The two ratings (which actually summarize a more detailed "raw point score" of from 0 to 44) are then aggregated into three broad categories: *free, partly free,* and *not free.* These categories do not entirely overlap with other groupings of countries into, for example, democracies, semidemocracies, and authoritarian/totalitarian regimes. While "free" states roughly correspond to the generally accepted standards for polyarchy or democracy among social scientists, the "partially free" states include many that cannot be considered even semidemocratic. See also Gastil (1990).

11. One of the most striking correlates of democracy in the contemporary world (when most of the remaining European colonies have become independent) is the much greater incidence of democracy among "ministates" of less than 1 million population. Such states were much more likely to be democratic in 1990 (57%) than were states with more than 1 million population (34%) (Diamond, 1991).

12. The PQLI is an unweighted index of three measures: adult literacy, infant mortality (i.e., death rates before the age of 1 year), and life expectancy at age 1 year. Each measure is standardized on a scale of 0 to 100 (Morris, 1979).

13. The measure is thus similar to the PQLI. For each of the HDI's three components, maximum and minimum values are identified among all the country scores in the world, and the difference between these values is established as the range of "deprivation" on the measure: from 0 (total deprivation) to 1 (no deprivation). The three deprivation scores are then simply averaged. Per capita GDP measure is not only logarithmically transformed but capped at the poverty line, so a country's mean income above the poverty line does not contribute anything to its score on the HDI. This further neutralizes pure wealth differences and emphasizes broad improvements in human welfare.

14. In doing so, I have not exactly followed the United Nations' four groupings of countries; rather, I looked for natural breaking points, leaving groupings of unequal number but more substantive meaning. In any case, since the selection of cutoff points was done independent of the location of countries on the cross-tabulated variable (regime type), this method of decomposing the sample should be no more biased than any other.

15. The appendix to this chapter contains a complete listing of the countries in the cells of Table 6.2.

16. Significantly also, the five high-income countries in the world that are not democratic—semicompetitive Singapore and the state hegemonic regimes in Saudi Arabia, Kuwait, the United Arab Emirates, and Qatar—all rank significantly lower on HDI than on per capita GNP (out of 160 countries, 11 places lower for Singapore and from 26 to 43 places lower for the Persian Gulf oil states).

17. This is precisely why multiple regression analyses of the effects of socioeconomic development may be most informative when they employ independent variables that are lagged at least 5 to 10 years behind the time of the dependent variable, democracy.

18. This review has benefited from the insights of a similar recent review by Rueschemeyer (1991).

19. Although the index later came to be termed and accepted as one of "political representation," it actually is a better measure of the presence of multiparty competition. It awarded 2 points for each year in which there was a parliament with representatives from two or more parties, with the minority holding at least 30% of the seats (1 point if there were multiple parties in parliament but less than 30% for the minority), and 1 point for each year the country was ruled by a chief executive who was the product of a competitive election. The study covered 21 years at the time, so a country could obtain up to 63 points, putting a heavy emphasis on the time dimension (Cutright, 1963, p. 256).

20. Olsen's (1968) combined index of what he called political development consisted of five measures that tapped substantially (though not exclusively) important dimensions of democracy: executive functioning (including interest aggregation); legislative functioning (including legislative effectiveness, interest aggregation, and civilian control of politics); number, stability, and interest aggregation of political parties; power diversification (constitutionality of government, number of autonomous branches, and breadth of political recruitment); and citizen influence (freedom of the press and of group opposition).

21. This seemed to give particular support to Lerner's (1958) emphasis on the causal primacy of expanding communication, but Lerner's dependent variable was not democracy but political participation more generally.

22. However, what Winham (1970) is explaining here is not really "democratization" or "democraticness" in the same sense as the cross-sectional studies are testing. Because the score on Cutright's (1963) measure was relatively constant from 1830 to 1960 in the United States (see Winham's Table 3), it is mainly expansion in electoral participation that Winham was measuring and explaining over time.

23. The cross-lagged correlation method can be unreliable for drawing causal inferences. It attempts to infer causation by determining whether or not the correlation between, say, economic development at Time 1 and democracy at Time 2 is stronger than that between democracy at Time 1 and economic development at Time 2. However, even if the latter correlation exceeds the former, structural equations methods suggest that the former causal path (development $\rightarrow$ democracy) may still be the stronger one if democracy is much less stable over time than development (Diamond, 1980, pp. 93-94).

24. Bollen (1980, p. 384) subsequently demonstrated this again, showing that while Jackman's democracy measure and Bollen's own (rather similar) one paralleled the Cutright measure in showing a strong relationship to the level of development, Cutright's measure also was significantly related to the timing of national development, while neither the Bollen nor the Jackman measure showed any significant relationship.

25. Coulter (1975) should have seen his data as suspect when the Soviet Union obtained the highest score of 85 countries on his measure of "participation" (Table 1.1)! Needless to say, his measure did not require that voting be in *democratic* elections. Not surprisingly, this dimension of his liberal democracy index correlates weakly with the other two (.20 with competitiveness and .19 with public liberties) and with measures of socioeconomic development or "mobilization." Also not surprisingly, Coulter finds weaker correlation coefficients between socioeconomic development indicators and liberal democracy and weaker regression coefficients for the effects of the former (Table 2.1) than have a number of other researchers. While his general finding—that economic development (per capita GNP) is the modern-

ization variable most strongly associated with democracy—accords with other evidence, his scale is too compromised for us to invest much confidence in this finding. Of his three dimensions of democracy, the one that is substantively valid, public liberties, is—not coincidentally—also the one best predicted by economic development level in his multiple regression analyses. Perhaps even more interesting is that, in examining *rates* of change in development levels (which few researchers have done), Coulter found that "economic-development rate is the most important factor in the regression equation when explaining public liberties; the other four rates have little influence" (p. 28).

26. Bollen's measure of political democracy, used in a number of other studies as well, is an index of six components. Three are indicators of political liberties—press freedom, freedom of group opposition, and government sanctions (censorships, curfews, political arrests and bans, and so on)—and the other three are measures of popular sovereignty—fairness of elections, executive selection, and legislative selection. Each of the six components was linearly transformed to a range from 0 to 100 and weighted equally.

27. This inference against modernization theory is questionable in general and in any case not reasonably applied to Lipset's thesis because he argued that the various dimensions of socioeconomic development were so intercorrelated as to form one broad syndrome, and per capita GNP is obviously the strongest indicator for that syndrome. The fact that education and urbanization did not add independent causal weight, when controlling for per capita GNP, thus does not discredit or falsify the Lipset thesis. Moreover, of the 12 regressions that included one or the other economic dependence measure (export partner concentration or the log of per capita foreign investment), only 3 showed significant effects on political centralism (i.e., authoritarianism). All of these 3 were positive, but in 3 other regressions the effect was weakly negative.

28. The time lags tested were 1965-1970-1975, 1970-1975-1980, 1975-1980-1985, 1960-1970-1980, and 1965-1975-1985. The measure of economic dependence tested was international trade as a proportion of GNP, while military expenditures were treated as a proportion of the national budget. The 10 path models also tested other modernization variables (urbanization, secondary education, and radios per 1,000 population), but because few of these showed significant effects and, when entered together with other development variables, generated serious problems of multicollinearity, they were not included in the final regressions. As in most other research of this kind, per capita GNP was transformed logarithmically. In addition to Kyoung-Ryung Seong, Jingsheng Huang assisted in this analysis.

29. This is most persuasively indicated by Hannan and Carroll's (1981) event history analysis, showing that per capita GNP has a very strong and significant effect in inhibiting transitions away from multiparty regimes (pp. 28-29).

30. As noted earlier, the effect of economic development on authoritarianism was less often statistically significant in a sample of new nations. For Thomas et al. (1979), that effect, however, remained consistently negative and "substantively significant; the lack of statistical significance most likely is due to the dramatic loss of cases" (p. 197).

31. The correlations with economic development of the nation were .67 for life satisfaction and .53 for trust. Life satisfaction correlated .85 with the number of years a nation had functioned continuously as a democracy.

32. During the 1967-1976 period, it was 4.5 per million population among that group, compared with 1.3 among the next development level and 0 at the two highest levels.

33. Had Powell (1982) been less strict in his criteria for the sample, including some African countries, such as Nigeria, which experienced electoral competition more briefly and superficially, his observed association would probably have been even more striking. Interestingly, the association between riots and development level was much weaker, with

median yearly riots per million people actually highest among the more rapidly modernizing countries, such as Greece, Chile, and Uruguay (which all broke down during this period), as Huntington's (1968; Huntington & Nelson, 1976) theory would predict.

34. This rate exceeded the average during that period for any of the World Bank's four income groups and was well in excess of that (2.3%) for middle-income countries (World Bank, 1991, Table 1).

35. By *civil society* I mean the entire social arena of organized groups (whether based on functional interests, civic purposes, religion, or ethnicity) and of social movements, mass media, intellectual currents and centers, and artistic and symbolic modes of expression that are autonomous from the state but relate or speak to the state (see Chazan, 1991, pp. 4-9; Diamond, 1992b, p. 7; Stepan, 1988, pp. 3-4). As Chazan (1991) has suggested, *civil society* also implies notions of pluralism and partiality: that no group seeks to represent the totality of an individual's interests, and thus that there must be multiple conveyors of interest and meaning in society.

36. The 10 countries are India, Sri Lanka, Costa Rica, Colombia, Venezuela, Jamaica, Trinidad and Tobago, Botswana, Mauritius, and Papua New Guinea.

REFERENCES

Ake, C. (1991). Rethinking African democracy. *Journal of Democracy, 2,* 32-44.
Almond, G., & Verba, S. (1963). *The civic culture.* Boston: Little, Brown.
Banks, A. S. (1970). Modernization and political change: The Latin American and Amer-European nations. *Comparative Political Studies, 2*(4).
Barros, M. J. de. (1992). Mobilizing for democracy in Chile: The crusade for citizen participation. In L. Diamond (Ed.), *The democratic revolution: Struggles for freedom and pluralism in the developing world* (pp. 73-88). New York: Freedom House.
Bautista, F. B. (1992). The Philippine alternative press and the toppling of a dictator. In L. Diamond (Ed.), *The democratic revolution: Struggles for freedom and pluralism in the developing world* (pp. 145-166). New York: Freedom House.
Binder, L. (1971). Crises of political development. In L. Binder, J. Coleman, J. LaPalombara, L. Pye, S. Verba, & M. Weiner (Eds.), *Crises and sequences in political development* (pp. 3-72). Princeton, NJ: Princeton University Press.
Bollen, K. (1979). Political democracy and the timing of development. *American Sociological Review, 44,* 572-587.
Bollen, K. (1980). Issues in the comparative measurement of political democracy. *American Sociological Review, 45,* 370-390.
Bollen, K. (1983). World system position, dependency and democracy: The cross-national evidence. *American Sociological Review, 48,* 468-479.
Bollen, K. (1990). Political democracy: Conceptual and measurement traps. *Studies in Comparative International Development, 25,* 7-24.
Bollen, K., & Jackman, R. (1985). Political democracy and the size distribution of income. *American Sociological Review, 50,* 438-457.
Booth, J. A. (1989). Costa Rica: The roots of democratic stability. In L. Diamond, J. J. Linz, & S. M. Lipset (Eds.), *Democracy in developing countries: Latin America* (pp. 387-422). Boulder, CO: Lynne Rienner.
Booth, J. A., & Seligson, M. A. (1992). Paths to democracy and the political culture of Costa Rica, Mexico and Nicaragua. In L. Diamond (Ed.), *Political culture and democracy in developing countries.* Boulder, CO: Lynne Rienner.

Brass, P. R. (1990). *The politics of India since independence.* Cambridge: Cambridge University Press.

Burton, M., & Higley, J. (1987). Elite settlements. *American Sociological Review, 52,* 295-307.

Chazan, N. (1988). Ghana: Problems of governance and the emergence of civil society. In L. Diamond, J. J. Linz, & S. M. Lipset (Eds.), *Democracy in developing countries: Africa* (pp. 93-140). Boulder, CO: Lynne Rienner.

Chazan, N. (1991, August). *Voluntary associations, civil society and democracy in Africa: Patterns and comparative implications.* Paper presented at the seminar "Democracy versus authoritarianism in the Third World," Institute of World Economy and International Relations, Moscow.

Cheng, T. (1989). Democratizing the quasi-Leninist regime in Taiwan. *World Politics, 41,* 471-499.

Coleman, J. S. (1960). Conclusion: The political systems of developing areas. In G. A. Almond & J. S. Coleman (Eds.), *The politics of developing areas.* Princeton, NJ: Princeton University Press.

Collier, D. (1979). Overview of the bureaucratic-authoritarian model. In D. Collier (Ed.), *The new authoritarianism in Latin America* (pp. 19-32). Princeton, NJ: Princeton University Press.

Coulter, P. (1975). *Social mobilization and liberal democracy.* Lexington, MA: Lexington.

Cutright, P. (1963). National political development: Measurement and analysis. *American Sociological Review, 28,* 253-264.

Cutright, P., & Wiley, J. A. (1969). Modernization and political representation: 1927-1966. *Studies in Comparative International Development, 5,* 23-44.

Dahl, R. A. (1971). *Polyarchy: Participation and opposition.* New Haven, CT: Yale University Press.

Das Gupta, J. (1989). India: Democratic becoming and combined development. In L. Diamond, J. J. Linz, & S. M. Lipset (Eds.), *Democracy in developing countries: Asia* (pp. 53-104). Boulder, CO: Lynne Rienner.

Diamond, L. (1980). *The social foundations of democracy: The case of Nigeria.* Unpublished doctoral dissertation, Stanford University.

Diamond, L. (1987). Class formation in the swollen African state. *Journal of Modern African Studies, 25,* 567-596.

Diamond, L. (1988a). *Class, ethnicity, and democracy in Nigeria: The failure of the first republic.* London: Macmillan.

Diamond, L. (1988b). Introduction: Roots of failure, seeds of hope. In L. Diamond, J. J. Linz, & S. M. Lipset (Eds.), *Democracy in developing countries: Africa* (pp. 1-32). Boulder, CO: Lynne Rienner.

Diamond, L. (1988c). Nigeria: Pluralism, statism, and the struggle for democracy. In L. Diamond, J. J. Linz, & S. M. Lipset (Eds.), *Democracy in developing countries: Africa* (pp. 33-91). Boulder, CO: Lynne Rienner.

Diamond, L. (1989). Beyond authoritarianism and totalitarianism: Strategies for democratization. *Washington Quarterly, 12,* 141-163.

Diamond, L. (1991, March). *Ripe for diffusion: International and domestic factors in the global trend toward democracy.* Paper presented at the annual meeting of the International Studies Association, Vancouver.

Diamond, L. (1992a). The globalization of democracy: Trends, types, causes and prospects. In R. Slater, B. Schutz, & S. Dorr (Eds.), *Global transformation and the Third World.* Boulder, CO: Lynne Rienner.

Diamond, L. (1992b). Introduction: Civil society and the struggle for democracy. In L. Diamond (Ed.), *The democratic revolution: Struggles for freedom and pluralism in the developing world* (pp. 1-27). New York: Freedom House.

Diamond, L., & Linz, J. J. (1989). Introduction: Politics, society, and democracy in Latin America. In L. Diamond, J. J. Linz, & S. M. Lipset (Eds.), *Democracy in developing countries: Latin America* (pp. 1-58). Boulder, CO: Lynne Rienner.

Diamond, L., Linz, J. J., & Lipset, S. M. (1990). Introduction: Comparing experiences with democracy. In L. Diamond, J. J. Linz, & S. M. Lipset (Eds.), *Politics in developing countries: Comparing experiences with democracy* (pp. 1-38). Boulder, CO: Lynne Rienner.

Diamond, L., Linz, J. J., & Lipset, S. M. (1992). *Democracy in developing countries: Persistence, failure, and renewal.* Boulder, CO: Lynne Rienner.

Ekpu, R. (1992). *Newswatch* and the struggle for press freedom in Nigeria. In L. Diamond (Ed.), *The democratic revolution: Struggles for freedom and pluralism in the developing world* (pp. 181-200). New York: Freedom House.

Evans, P. (1979). *Dependent development: The alliance of multinational, state, and local capital in Brazil.* Princeton, NJ: Princeton University Press.

Fernandes, F. (1975). *A Revolucao Burguesa no Brasil.* Rio de Janeiro: Zahan Editores.

Freedom House. (1991). *Freedom in the world: Political rights and civil liberties 1990-1991.* New York: Author.

Gastil, R. D. (1990). The comparative survey of freedom: Experiences and suggestions. *Studies in Comparative International Development, 25,* 25-50.

Gold, T. (1990). The resurgence of civil society in China. *Journal of Democracy, 1*(1), 18-31.

Han, S. (1989). South Korea: Politics in transition. In L. Diamond, J. J. Linz, & S. M. Lipset (Eds.), *Democracy in developing countries: Asia* (pp. 267-304). Boulder, CO: Lynne Rienner.

Hannan, M. T., & Carroll, G. R. (1981). Dynamics of formal political structure: An event-history analysis. *American Sociological Review, 46,* 19-35.

Heard, A. (1992). The struggle for free expression in South Africa. In L. Diamond (Ed.), *The democratic revolution: Struggles for freedom and pluralism in the developing world* (pp. 167-179). New York: Freedom House.

Higley, J., & Burton, M. (1989). The elite variable in democratic transitions and breakdowns. *American Sociological Review, 54,* 17-32.

Huntington, S. P. (1968). *Political order in changing societies.* New Haven, CT: Yale University Press.

Huntington, S. P. (1984). Will more countries become democratic? *Political Science Quarterly, 99,* 193-218.

Huntington, S. P. (1991). *The third wave: Democratization in the late twentieth century.* Norman: University of Oklahoma Press.

Huntington, S. P., & Nelson, J. M. (1976). *No easy choice: Political participation in developing countries.* Cambridge, MA: Harvard University Press.

Inglehart, R. (1990). *Culture shift in advanced industrial countries.* Princeton, NJ: Princeton University Press.

Inkeles, A. (1969). Participant citizenship in six developing countries. *American Political Science Review, 63,* 1120-1141.

Inkeles, A. (1978). National differences in individual modernity. *Comparative Studies in Sociology* (Vol. 1). Greenwich, CT: JAI.

Inkeles, A., & Diamond, L. (1980). Personal qualities as a reflection of level of national development. In F. Andrews & A. Szalai (Eds.), *Comparative studies on the quality of life* (pp. 73-109). London: Sage.

Inkeles, A., & Smith, D. H. (1974). *Becoming modern: Individual change in six developing countries.* Cambridge, MA: Harvard University Press.

Jackman, R. W. (1973). On the relation of economic development to democratic performance. *American Journal of Political Science, 17,* 611-621.

Jackman, R. W. (1975). *Politics and social equality: A comparative analysis.* New York: John Wiley.

Joseph, R. (1991). Africa: The rebirth of political freedom. *Journal of Democracy, 2*(3), 11-24.

Kohli, A. (1990). From majority to minority rule: Making sense of the "new" Indian politics. In M. M. Bouton & P. Oldenburg (Eds.), *India briefing 1990* (pp. 1-24). Boulder, CO: Westview.

Kokole, O. H., & Mazrui, A. A. (1988). Uganda: The dual polity and the plural society. In L. Diamond, J. J. Linz, & S. M. Lipset (Eds.), *Democracy in developing countries: Africa* (pp. 259-298). Boulder, CO: Lynne Rienner.

Kuria, G. K. (1991). Confronting dictatorship in Kenya. *Journal of Democracy, 2*(3), 115-126.

LaPalombara, J., & Weiner, M. (Eds.). (1966). *Political parties and political development.* Princeton, NJ: Princeton University Press.

Lapidus, G. (1989). State and society: Toward the emergence of civil society in the Soviet Union. In S. Bialer (Ed.), *Politics, society, and nationality: Inside Gorbachev's Russia* (pp. 121-147). Boulder, CO: Westview.

Lerner, D. (1958). *The passing of traditional society.* New York: Free Press.

Linz, J. J., & Stepan, A. (1989). Political crafting of democratic consolidation or destruction: European and South American comparisons. In R. A. Pastor (Ed.), *Democracy in the Americas: Stopping the pendulum* (pp. 41-61). New York: Holmes & Meier.

Lipset, S. M. (1959, March). Some social requisites of democracy: Economic development and political legitimacy. *American Political Science Review,* pp. 69-105.

Lipset, S. M. (1960). *Political man: The social bases of politics.* Garden City, NY: Doubleday.

Lipset, S. M. (1981). *Political man: The social bases of politics* (expanded ed.). Baltimore: Johns Hopkins University Press.

Lipset, S. M., Seong, K.-R., & Torres, J. C. (1991). *A comparative analysis of the social requisites of democracy.* Unpublished manuscript, Stanford University, Hoover Institution.

Martini, M. R. de. (1992). Educating for democracy in Latin America: The experience of Conciencia. In L. Diamond (Ed.), *The democratic revolution: Struggles for freedom and pluralism in the developing world* (pp. 29-52). New York: Freedom House.

Maslow, A. (1954). *Motivation and personality.* New York: Harper & Row.

McClintock, C. (1989). Peru: Precarious regimes, authoritarian and democratic. In L. Diamond, J. J. Linz, & S. M. Lipset (Eds.), *Democracy in developing countries: Latin America* (pp. 335-386). Boulder, CO: Lynne Rienner.

McCrone, D. J., & Cnudde, C. F. (1967). Toward a communications theory of democratic political development: A causal model. *American Political Science Review, 61,* 72-79.

Meyer, J. W. (1980). The world polity and the authority of the nation-state. In A. J. Bergesen (Ed.), *Studies of the modern world system* (pp. 109-137). Beverly Hills, CA: Sage.

Morris, M. (1979). *Measuring the condition of the world's poor: The Physical Quality of Life Index.* New York: Pergamon.

Mosca, G. (1939). *The ruling class: Elementi di scienza politica.* New York: Free Press. (Original work published 1896)

Nathan, A. J. (1990). Chinese paths to democracy. *Journal of Democracy, 1*(2), 50-61.

Nwankwo, C. (1992). The civil liberties organisation and the struggle for human rights and democracy in Nigeria. In L. Diamond (Ed.), *The democratic revolution: Struggles for freedom and pluralism in the developing world* (pp. 105-123). New York: Freedom House.

O'Donnell, G. (1973). *Modernization and bureaucratic-authoritarianism: Studies in South American politics.* Berkeley: University of California, Institute of International Studies.

O'Donnell, G., & Schmitter, P. C. (1986). *Transitions from authoritarian rule: Tentative conclusions about uncertain democracies.* Baltimore: Johns Hopkins University Press.

Olsen, M. E. (1968). Multivariate analysis of national political development. *American Sociological Review, 35,* 699-712.

Ozbudun, E. (1989). Turkey: Crises, interruptions, and reequilibrations. In L. Diamond, J. J. Linz, & S. M. Lipset (Eds.), *Democracy in developing countries: Asia* (pp. 187-230). Boulder, CO: Lynne Rienner.

Pascual, D. (1992). Building a democratic political culture in the Philippines. In L. Diamond (Ed.), *The democratic revolution: Struggles for freedom and pluralism in the developing world* (pp. 53-72). New York: Freedom House.

Phadnis, U. (1989). Sri Lanka: Crises of legitimacy and integration. In L. Diamond, J. J. Linz, & S. M. Lipset (Eds.), *Democracy in developing countries: Asia* (pp. 143-186). Boulder, CO: Lynne Rienner.

Powell, G. B., Jr. (1982). *Contemporary democracies: Participation, stability and violence.* Cambridge, MA: Harvard University Press.

Rose, L. (1989). Pakistan's experiments with democracy. In L. Diamond, J. J. Linz, & S. M. Lipset (Eds.), *Democracy in developing countries: Asia* (pp. 105-143). Boulder, CO: Lynne Rienner.

Rueschemeyer, D. (1991). Different methods—Contradictory results? Research on development and democracy. In C. C. Ragin (Ed.), *Issues and alternatives in comparative social research* (pp. 9-38). Leiden, Netherlands: Brill.

Russett, B. M. (1965). *Trends in world politics.* New York: Macmillan.

Rustow, D. A. (1970). Transitions to democracy. *Comparative Politics, 2,* 337-363.

Sadowski, C. (1992). Autonomous groups as agents of democratic change in communist and post-communist eastern Europe. In L. Diamond (Ed.), *Political culture and democracy in developing countries.* Boulder, CO: Lynne Rienner.

Schlemmer, L. (1991). The turn in the road: Emerging conditions in 1990. In R. Lee & L. Schlemmer (Eds.), *Transition to democracy: Policy perspectives 1991* (pp. 14-23). Cape Town: Oxford University Press.

Shah, G. (1988). Grass-roots mobilization in Indian politics. In A. Kohli (Ed.), *India's democracy: An analysis of changing state-society relations* (pp. 262-304). Princeton, NJ: Princeton University Press.

Sirowy, L., & Inkeles, A. (1990). The effects of democracy on economic growth and inequality: A review. *Studies In Comparative National Development, 25,* 126-157.

Sklar, R. L. (1965). Contradictions in the Nigerian political system. *Journal of Modern African Studies, 3,* 201-213.

Sklar, R. L. (1979). The nature of class domination in Africa. *Journal of Modern African Studies, 17,* 531-552.

Sklar, R. L. (1987). Developmental democracy. *Comparative Studies in Society and History, 29,* 686-714.

Slabbert, F. van Z. (1991). The basis and challenges of transition in South Africa: A review and a preview. In R. Lee & L. Schlemmer (Eds.), *Transition to democracy: Policy perspectives 1991* (pp. 1-13). Cape Town: Oxford University Press.

Starr, S. F. (1988). Soviet Union: A civil society. *Foreign Policy, 70,* 26-41.

Stepan, A. (1988). *Rethinking military politics.* Princeton, NJ: Princeton University Press.

Taylor, C. L., & Hudson, M. C. (1972). *World handbook of political and social indicators.* New Haven, CT: Yale University Press.

Thomas, G. M., Ramirez, F., Meyer, J. W., & Gobalet, J. G. (1979). Maintaining national boundaries in the world system: The rise of centralist regimes. In J. Meyer & M. Hannan (Eds.), *National development and the world system* (pp. 187-209). Chicago: University of Chicago Press.

Tocqueville, A. de. (1945). *Democracy in America* (Vol. 2). New York: Vintage. (Original work published 1840)

United Nations Development Program. (1991). *Human development report 1991.* New York: Oxford University Press.

Weigle, M. A., & Butterfield, J. (1991). *Civil society in reforming communist regimes: The logic of emergence.* Unpublished manuscript.

Wiarda, H. J. (1989). The Dominican Republic: Mirror legacies of democracy and authoritarianism. In L. Diamond, J. J. Linz, & S. M. Lipset (Eds.), *Democracy in developing countries: Latin America* (pp. 423-458). Boulder, CO: Lynne Rienner.

Winham, G. R. (1970). Political development and Lerner's theory: Further test of a causal model. *American Political Science Review, 64,* 810-818.

World Bank. (1991). *World development report 1991: The challenge of development.* Oxford: Oxford University Press.

7

Capitalism, the Market, and Democracy

Carlos H. Waisman

DEVELOPMENT AND DEMOCRACY

THE democratic revolution under way in the contemporary world has placed the question of the socioeconomic determinants of democracy at the center of our intellectual and practical agendas. In particular, the collapse of single-party and military authoritarian regimes in societies with substantial industrialization and high levels of urbanization and education, in Eastern and Central Europe and in the Southern Cone of Latin America, has reintroduced the issue that Seymour Martin Lipset formulated in his classic 1959 essay: the relationship between economic development and democracy.

Today a "great transformation," similar in some crucial ways to the one that concerned Karl Polanyi, is the counterpart of this process of democratization. In the East, but also in the South, a radical process of economic liberalization is taking place alongside the democratic revolution: Government firms are being privatized; markets for goods, labor, and capital are being generated, deepened, or deregulated; and autarkic or semiautarkic economies are being integrated into world markets. A discussion of the socioeconomic determinants of democracy in the world today, therefore, leads directly into one of the classic issues of political sociology: the relationship between capitalism and liberal democracy.

This relationship is still problematic. All liberal democracies in the contemporary world have existed in capitalist societies, and all noncapitalist economies have had nondemocratic polities, but not all capitalist societies have had liberal democratic polities. The twin economic and political transformations mentioned above support the proposition, formulated by Lipset a generation ago, of a direct relationship between development and democracy, and even the thesis, implied or stated by a long line of social theorists beginning with Adam

Smith and Karl Marx, of a correspondence, or "elective affinity," between liberal democracy and capitalism. However, the relationship between development and democracy is direct, but, as has been noted many times, it is not linear.

In the period following World War II, societies placed at the two extremes of the development distribution (per capita product and associated variables) clearly fit the hypothesis of a direct relationship. The poorer societies—the exceptions of India and of the more recent democracies in the less developed countries of Latin America notwithstanding—have been mostly inhospitable to liberal democracy. At the other extreme, the evidence of highly industrialized nations fully agrees with the proposition as well: Nondemocratic regimes in societies of this type have been externally imposed, as in Czechoslovakia and the former German Democratic Republic. And an examination of the record of highly industrialized societies, even as early as the decades after World War I, would show the Nazi regime in Germany as a lonely exception.

But in societies characterized by middle levels of these "development" variables, this relationship appeared to break down. These societies were especially vulnerable to different types of nonliberal regimes: Italian fascism, Spanish and Portuguese traditional authoritarianism, and bureaucratic-authoritarian regimes in Greece, the Southern Cone countries (Argentina, Chile, and Uruguay), and Brazil were all established, or persisted, in societies having substantial levels of several or all the "development" variables, and consequently high levels of political mobilization.[1]

Sociologists and political scientists have accounted for instability, and its sequels, dictatorship and revolution, in societies in the middle of the development scale mainly in terms of a model that strictly (and fruitfully) applies to societies during the onset of capitalism and mass political mobilization, or, more specifically, to societies in which precapitalist agrarian structures and premobilizational political systems break down during the growth of a market economy and political mobilization. This is the differentiation-integration paradigm, of Durkheimian and Parsonian inspiration, that underlies analyses of the "crises and sequences" school of political development and mobilization and institutionalization theories, such as those formulated by Karl Deutsch, Gino Germani, and Samuel Huntington in the 1960s. Dependency and world-systems theories—formulated explicitly as attempts to understand the evolution of societies on the basis of an alternative paradigm, emphasizing external factors and processes—did not put forward any specific models or hypotheses for the explanation of political institutions and their change, except for some ad hoc analyses (Waisman, in press).

The differentiation model focuses, at the macro level, on the breakdown of preindustrial social and political structures and on the processes leading to the institutionalization of a market economy and a mass-participation polity. At the micro level, the units of analysis are the individuals and groups released from premodern structures and newly absorbed, or not absorbed at all, by the new ones—the victims of the institutional gap produced by social differentiation. Clearly, a model of this sort is of limited use for understanding political instability, dictatorship, and revolt in societies whose social structure is wholly or predominantly capitalist and whose polity is based on high levels of mobilization.

This is the case, inter alia, of the countries of the Southern Cone in the last half century. Argentina and Uruguay have had social structures based almost exclusively on capitalist relations of production since the time of their large-scale incorporation into world markets. Precapitalist social relations were of secondary significance, or were eliminated altogether, in Chile in the decades following World War II. As for political institutions, these countries had, up to the Depression of the 1930s, long-lasting, "modern" liberal democratic polities, with high levels of pluralism and expanding participation. In Argentina and Chile, substantial proportions of the agrarian population were integrated into labor markets and subsequently incorporated into the polity following the 1930s. However, in neither case were these processes the ultimate cause of the breakdown of liberal democracy and the establishment of authoritarian regimes in the 1960s and 1970s.[2] Rather, instability and dictatorship were largely—in these two countries as well as in Uruguay—the result of economic institutions that produced, in thoroughly "modern" societies, stagnation and social and state structures not conducive to stable democracy.

Why these fully capitalist economies were inhospitable to the institutions of political liberalism is important not only for understanding the cases in question, but for clarifying the general relationship between capitalism and democracy. My argument in this chapter is based on these three South American cases. I will argue that our comprehension of the relationship between capitalism and democracy can be improved by distinguishing between the two dimensions of "capitalism": private ownership of the means of production and a market economy. The two go together in the advanced capitalist economies, but at lower and middle levels of development, there have been cases of economies based on private property with substantial limitations to the operation of market mechanisms. The autarkic capitalist economies that emerged in the countries of the Southern Cone of Latin America in the postwar period are cases in point.

Capitalist economies of this type have been especially prone to political polarization and the emergence of nonliberal regimes because, like the state socialist ones, they tended to stagnate after an initial period of "easy" growth during which large and powerful middle and working classes came into being. As in socialist countries, stagnation generated political and economic change, with or without an intervening political conflict, for in some cases this change reflected a preemptive strategy of elites eager to forestall what they saw as an impending polarization.

The argument is, therefore, that the relationship between capitalism and democracy is mediated by the strength of markets. Autarkic economies generate obstacles to liberal democracy that are not present in market-oriented economies. Put differently, a market economy, once institutionalized, is conducive to a stable liberal democracy, but private ownership of the means of production, in a context of substantial restrictions on the operation of market mechanisms, is not.[3]

DEVELOPMENT AND CAPITALISM

The proposition that fully capitalist social structures, like those of autarkic capitalist countries, would tend to have nondemocratic polities because of their lack of economic dynamism cannot be easily reconciled with the classical sociological theories of capitalism. These theories have presupposed, at least for normal times and states of the system, a correspondence between capitalists' individual rationality, usually presented as a system of action oriented toward the maximization of profits, and collective or systemic rationality (i.e., economic growth).

Liberal theories of capitalism, such as Adam Smith's and Max Weber's, postulated that, as capitalists pursue individual wealth, developmental consequences would follow for the society (greater welfare for the noncapitalist classes, the rationalization of social life, and so on). Marx, from a different perspective, also assumed that, except in the final period of systemic crisis, the growth of productive forces would be the objective consequence of capitalists' behavior. The same expectation is echoed by contemporary viewpoints, ranging from the popular "trickle-down" models of development based on the old assumption of a commonality of interests between General Motors and general welfare, to academic analyses such as Fred Block's (1987, chap. 3) conception of the relationship between state and ruling class, where, regardless of their ideology, the best choice for state managers is to maintain "business confidence," that is, to gain the support of capitalists in order to keep the gross national product up and unemployment down. In general, sociological theorists and contemporary sociologists have assumed that a social structure based on capitalist relations of production will be a sufficient condition, at least in the long run and in spite of cyclical variations, for economic growth (except, again, for Marxists, at the final point in the development of the capitalist system).

Many apparent exceptions to this proposition are not real ones, for some low-growth or stagnated societies in the capitalist world economy are cases in which either precapitalist social relations have been frozen or subsumed into capitalism or growth has been blocked by some type of international dependence. The first scenario consists of societies in whose social structure precapitalist relations of production have persisted (most typically, countries with large peasant populations, as in parts of Central America and the Andean region for much of this century). As for the second scenario, while economic dependency is undesirable from the standpoint of the subordinate country's autonomy, it does not necessarily block development (the claims of dependency theory notwithstanding) and more often than not leads to growth. But some forms of economic dependency do induce stagnation, such as "specialization" in the production for export of commodities whose overall developmental potential is low, because they do not require skilled capitalists and workers or complex technology or because their producers have little market power. Plantation economies are the classic example of this case (Baldwin, 1956).

Yet, economic performance has varied among societies with thoroughly capitalist social structures and lacking the crippling types of dependency noted above. This indicates that it is necessary to specify the conditions under which the proposition linking a capitalist social structure and economic growth holds. More concretely, the relationship between capitalists' individual rationality and collective or systemic rationality needs to be specified.

In classical theory, monopolies and, most often in the real world, looser cases of collusion among small numbers of capitalists are situations in which capitalists' search for profit may not produce economic growth. Given that there is nothing in capitalists' genes or culture that renders them risk seekers, a more valid understanding of capitalist rationality is gained when we add the search for security to the profit motive. Capitalists strive for both, and the best possible outcome from their point of view is when both gain and security are maximized, that is, when revenue has the characteristics of rent rather than of profit. In the real conditions of capitalist society, such an outcome is seldom realized, regardless of the degree of concentration.

As Joseph Schumpeter (1950, pp. 84-85) has pointed out, oligopoly will not by itself abolish competition and retard economic growth if new technology, new sources of supply, and new types of organization are possible. Under capitalism, the only situation in which such barriers to entry could be major and permanent is when they are created and enforced by noneconomic agents, the most important of which is, of course, the state. And there is a case in which this happens: that of autarkic industrialization based on import substitution. As we have seen, this was the path of industrialization followed in the postwar period by Southern Cone and other Latin American countries. In general, such a policy was initiated by an autonomous state, but, once institutionalized, it generated a web of vested interests—mainly a rent-seeking capitalist class,[4] but also reaching down to segments of the middle and working classes—whose survival depended on the maintenance of market restrictions.

MODELS OF CAPITALIST DEVELOPMENT

This type of autarkic industrial development differs from that more oriented toward world markets, which was followed by the same Southern Cone countries before the Depression (under the form of a less protected kind of industrialization for domestic consumption), and by other countries of the capitalist periphery (in particular, those that developed manufacturing for export). The export-oriented variant of open industrialization, exemplified by the newly industrializing countries of Southeast Asia, became the paradigmatic alternative to the autarkic variant followed in the Latin American countries referred to above and others in the region. It will be useful to label these two models autarkic and competitive and, by way of abbreviation, Model 1 and Model 2. (I call the first *autarkic* because its goal was industrial self-sufficiency, a goal that was never achieved because the substitution of imports required, in turn, imported machinery and other inputs.) The institutionalization of each has long-term economic and political implications. What follows is an abstract sketch of these implications.

Model 1 generates an economy prone to stagnation, and, if realized in full, it leads to a polity prone to illegitimacy and thus to instability or authoritarianism. The intervening variables in relation to political effects are sociological: the degree of mobilization and the sociostructural factors that cause it.

The long-term result of autarkic, import-substituting industrialization is economic stagnation, or at least stagnating tendencies, because this pattern of growth is based on the transfer of resources from the export sector, which is internationally competitive, to manufacturing, which produces for the internal market only. The latter sector usually survives only behind high protective barriers, for most of its output is relatively poor in quality and/or highly priced.[5] Advanced import-substituting industrialization commits most labor and capital to production for the captive domestic market. Once this market is saturated for a specific commodity, capitalists producing it are more likely to diversify into the substitution of another commodity (sometimes through backward linkage) than to export and try to compete with more efficient and established producers. This pattern inevitably leads to sharp economic fluctuations caused by balance-of-payment crises and eventually to low growth rates, as a consequence of massive misallocation of resources.

Except in rare situations where the surplus obtained by the agrarian or mining export sector is so large that it can provide virtually unlimited subsidies to advanced noncompetitive manufacturing (e.g., in small oil-rich nations), the economy eventually comes to a standstill and may even retrogress. Data for Argentina, Chile, and Uruguay over the last 30 years are clear in this respect. Per capita gross domestic product in Argentina grew by an annual average of 2.9% in the 1960s and .9% in the 1970s, but it declined at a rate of 2.4% in the 1980s. The average rates of economic growth in Chile were 2.1%, .9%, and .9%, respectively, and in Uruguay, .5%, .3%, and –.7%.[6]

The economy may weaken and decline, but capital keeps growing and concentrating, as hothouse capitalists increase their ability, sometimes in alliance with rent-seeking unions, to appropriate and institutionalize various privileges, including very high tariff and nontariff barriers, cheap credits from government banks, subsidized inputs, guaranteed demand through government contracts, export subsidies, and export markets assured by bilateral trade agreements. The result is that the strongest capitalists reap very high profits with low risk.

Illegitimacy is a long-term outcome of autarkic industrialization. It is produced by an explosive combination of factors: a stagnant economy and a society made up of highly mobilized and organized social groups, the urban lower classes and the intelligentsia in particular.

Among the factors responsible for the mobilization of the working class and the urban poor is the size of the labor reserve, by which I mean the actual reserve of labor for specific occupations. If the labor reserve is small, as is often the case for skilled occupations or for occupations requiring some education, or if it is effectively absorbed by the process of industrialization (as was the case in Argentina and Uruguay), there will be a structural propensity for the development of strong unions and/or, depending on other conditions (e.g., a strongly organized radical Left, as in Chile), mass radical parties. The mobilization of these groups is likely to destabilize the system, once stagnation becomes apparent.

Usually, import-substituting industrialization also delegitimates the regime from above. Industrialization, urbanization, state growth, and the expansion of education produce a large professional, commercial, and bureaucratic middle class that controls considerable economic and cultural resources and therefore has a high potential for political mobilization. Whereas the mobilization of the working class is strongly influenced by structural characteristics, such as the size of the labor reserve, middle-class entry into politics is largely the consequence of this "internal" resource endowment.

The activation of the petty bourgeoisie, however, is not necessarily a threat to the ruling classes. In fact, co-optation is a typical elite response to the development of a large middle class, and an extensive system of higher education is usually a part of the co-optation package.[7] If this system is in place when stagnating tendencies appear in the economy, as was the case in Argentina and Uruguay, the mass mobilization of the intelligentsia (especially students and frustrated professionals and intellectuals) is inevitable. Such mobilization frequently strengthens and consolidates radical organizations. Where conditions favorable to lower-class activation are also present, the stage is set for mass radicalism and ultimately for a revolutionary situation and its likely consequence—military rule or, in a few cases, successful revolution.

But even before stagnation sets in, Model 1 generates a social structure conducive to political institutions quite different from those that existed in advanced capitalist countries (early as well as late developers) at similar levels of industrialization. At first, autarkic industrialization usually combines an autonomous state with a very weak, very dependent manufacturing bourgeoisie. In this setting, the state may also seek to develop corporatist mechanisms to control labor, which may be successful only as long as there is a surplus available for redistribution (a likely occurrence before stagnating tendencies appear) and if a radical intelligentsia is absent or weak. Argentina in the 1940s and 1950s exemplifies a developmental path of this type (Waisman, 1987). On the other hand, the case of Chile in the 1950s and 1960s reveals that corporatist mechanisms of labor control are less likely where there is a strong Left (Sigmund, 1977; Stallings, 1978). Over time, as stagnation sets in, corporatism breaks down due to the impossibility of continuing redistributive policies. Also, the state weakens as it is penetrated by increasingly powerful rent-seeking capitalists and distributional coalitions involving capital and labor.

Model 2, on the other hand, in its export-led form but also in the variant of a less protectionist industrialization for the domestic market, does not seem to create structural barriers to continued economic growth or to stable liberal democracy. The bourgeoisie it generates will, of course, try to be as rent seeking as the industrialists in Model 1, whose rents were granted by the state, or their predecessors, the pre-Depression dominant classes (i.e., the agrarian or mining bourgeoisie, whose rents were based on the monopoly of natural resources). However, industrialists in Model 2 are less likely than these other bourgeoisies to succeed in becoming a rentier class, for the rent they may secure will be temporary and contingent as long as they are exposed to market forces in their own societies (as a result of open industrialization for the domestic market— e.g., in Argentina before the Depression) or outside (as a result of export-oriented industrialization, even when this pattern of development is combined with restrictions on the entry of foreign competition, as in South Korea in the last two decades). Because this model compels the domestic bourgeoisie to compete internationally, it is not inherently prone to stagnation, as hothouse capitalism is. Consequently, the capitalist class generated by export-led industrialization is likely to be more autonomous vis-à-vis the state than its counterpart, the rent-seeking pseudobourgeoisie of autarkic development.

Finally, if industrialization promoted by Model 2 is successful, pressures for democratization and high growth rates may lead to the extension of participation to the lower classes. Export-led industrialization in South Korea and Taiwan took place under authoritarian regimes, but the presence of these regimes owed more to political factors, such as their position in the front line of the Cold War and their intense conflict and competition with their communist twins, than to pressures inherent in their model of industrialization.

In sum, Model 2 appears to be free of the self-limitations of autarkic development and to be compatible with the hegemony of the local capitalist class. Thus Model 2 countries are similar in certain key respects to "core" countries, where the eventual establishment of stable democracy was facilitated by high rates of industrialization. In some of these countries, industrialization also took place under nondemocratic regimes established as a consequence of social or cultural legacies or of the tensions accompanying the dissolution of precapitalist social structures.

This does not mean, of course, that Model 2 necessarily produces either sustained economic growth or political liberalization. In addition to policy choices, economic growth is a function of a country's resource endowments, of its supply of social and cultural capital in relation to those of its competitors, and of its adaptability in the face of economic and technological change in the markets in which it is involved. No one can guarantee that competitive industrialization will be successful or that initial success can be maintained indefinitely. However, the risks of stagnation associated with export-led growth based on manufacturing, the most successful type of Model 2, are much lower than in primary export economies, as in Latin America before the Depression. The reason for this is that most of these economies were highly specialized; that is, they focused on exporting one or two major commodities and thus were extremely vulnerable to market fluctuations. Export manufacturing, in contrast, is likely to be more diversified and to allow for easier transfers of capital and labor in response to changes in demand.

As for the potential for liberal democracy, Model 2 generates a social structure that is compatible with a polity of this type, and economic growth is an excellent fuel for hegemony and thus for stable democracy. Of course, compatibility does not mean inevitability, for political institutions are also

determined by noneconomic factors (including, in the beginning of industrialization, those highlighted by the differentiation-integration model) and by
international pressures and interactions.

AUTARKY AND ILLEGITIMACY

An interesting characteristic of Model 1 is that the society it generates is
intrinsically unstable, and yet it is, like Marx's Asiatic mode of production,
highly resistant to structural change. On one hand, autarkic industrialization
leads, as we have seen, to a stagnated economy and an illegitimate polity and
hence to economic and political instability. On the other hand, this type of
industrialization also impedes a switch to Model 2 because such a change of
direction is against the immediate interests of both capitalists and workers.

There are two reasons for this. The first is that hothouse capitalists and, in
many cases, unions share a basic objective with the state elite: to extract rents
from the society. A paradox of autarkic industrialization is that it generates
predatory ruling classes: a state elite whose policies do not favor development,
and a capitalist class not interested in the expansion of capitalism. The image
of an autonomous state in Latin American countries (especially in the case of
the authoritarian regimes in the Southern Cone and Brazil in the 1970s and
early 1980s) is erroneous. In many of these societies, the state may have
controlled and regulated every area of economic activity, but it was hardly
autonomous, for it was the arena in which rent-seeking elites, sometimes
involved in distributional coalitions with other groups, pursued their objectives
and aimed at using the state as their instrument.[8]

The second reason for blockage is the typical collective action problem: With
the reconversion of manufacturing toward a more open orientation, the capitalist and working classes along with the state elite may benefit in the long run,
for their incomes (profits, wages, and taxes) could be greater. But a switch to
Model 2 inevitably creates losers, even assuming an elaborate industrial policy.
Whereas gains would be diffuse, uncertain, and long term, losses are specific,
definite, and closer in time. The status quo wins.

What distinguishes the industrialized Latin American countries from their new
industrialized countries (NIC)[9] is that the latter switched from Model 1 to Model 2
relatively early in the industrialization process, that is, without "deepening" import
substitution beyond light industries (Amsden, 1985, 1989; Cheng, 1991; Li, 1988;
Ranis, 1991), and before the emergence of powerful rent-seeking distributional
coalitions and the consequent blockage described above. In Latin America, the
change of direction began to occur much later in the process, only after intense
polarization and coercive dictatorships showed the long-term inviability of autarkic
industrialization. In Chile and Uruguay, the switch began under military regimes,
established in the first case after overthrowing a government of the revolutionary
Left, and in the second to fight a strong guerrilla movement. In Argentina, after
hesitant attempts under military rule, it is finally beginning to happen under a

democratic administration, which came to power after a long period of political instability, intense social conflict (which produced a revolutionary situation), and a repressive authoritarian regime.

THE SWITCH TO COMPETITIVE CAPITALISM

The problem consists of the specification of the conditions under which a shift from Model 1 to Model 2 can take place in a society with advanced import substitution, subject to the stagnating inertia and the collective action problem characteristic of that situation. The question is: How can a rent-seeking distributional coalition be dislodged from power and substituted by a developmental one? There are three possibilities, one exogenous and two endogenous.

The exogenous variant would be caused by economic factors, basically a large flow of foreign investment. If the purpose of this capital is to produce manufactures for export, rather than to extract natural resources or to produce for the captive domestic market (in which case it would end up participating in the rent-seeking game), the end result could be an outward reorientation of the industrial sector and eventually a relative loss of economic and political power by the distributional coalitions. A large flow of investment capital with these characteristics could produce this effect in a few cases: for example, small nations with cheap skilled labor or other scarce resources and with other attractive traits, such as location, a history of political stability, and strategic significance for the capital-exporting countries. It would not be surprising if a process of this sort cushions the transition to capitalism and democracy in the smaller and more industrialized nations of Central Europe, but it is unlikely that it will become the central switching device in the autarkic developers of Latin America, which are larger and poorer in human capital, are located far away from major consumer markets, have histories of political instability, and are less significant, from the geopolitical standpoint, for major capital exporters.

Endogenous mechanisms could only be political. The switch could originate either in the state or in civil society via a developmental coalition. What is necessary is a situation that leads the state elite, or central social forces in the society, to the conclusion that "it is not possible to go on like this," that is, that the current position of the country in the world economy is just not viable. (This language, by the way, resembles that of Lenin, who defined revolutionary situations as those in which those on top cannot continue ruling as before, those at the bottom do not want to continue as before, and there is a deep economic crisis.) These are the processes that are taking place in the Southern Cone, but at this point we can only speculate on the conditions that are bringing them about.

For elites to reach the conclusion that the system is not viable, radical import substitution must run its course. It should be clear to the state elite and the central social forces that the stagnation and illegitimacy the society experiences are directly connected to autarkic industrialization and that there is no solution to the economic and political crisis within that development strategy. Two current circumstances that contribute to this realization are the bad long-term prospects for some primary exports and the debt crisis. These circumstances make it impossible to continue subsidizing noncompetitive industrialization as in the past, through the expropriation of the surplus generated by efficient economic activities or through indebtedness.

The first factor affects countries, such as Argentina or Uruguay, that have specialized in export commodities (grains and beef) for which production is likely to outstrip consumption for the rest of the century and that are vulnerable to technological advances (biotechnology) that would reduce their comparative advantages. The debt, which in the beginning of the 1980s affected all the countries in the area, is one of those imperious crises that require action and that cannot be faced with stopgap measures. As was the case with the Depression of the 1930s, the debt crisis makes it obvious that the development of Latin American countries is blocked by their position in the world economy (Canak, 1989; Ffrench-Davis, 1988; Wionczek, 1985; Waisman, 1988). This realization may induce a switch, but, of course, there is no necessary correlation between the intensity of a crisis and the effectiveness of the responses to it.

In any case, what is necessary is a process that frees the state from rentiers' control. The two possibilities are, first, the transformation of an authoritarian regime into an opponent of rentier capitalists, and second, the capture of a democratic state by a coalition of antirentier social forces (in the context of autarkic industrialization, this means segments of labor and the capitalists who would not be wiped out by the reorientation of the economy). These alternatives can be called *authoritarian* and *social democratic.*

The authoritarian response to the crisis may arise within an established military regime, but the perception of the need for a reorientation of this type among elites may by itself provoke a military coup. Blockage and illegitimacy, especially when they lead to the activation of the lower classes, and much more so when they give rise to mass radical movements, may drive the state toward greater autonomy. The intervening variable would be the fear of revolution, which is one of the most important determinants of social change in the modern world, perhaps as important as revolution itself.

State managers, the military in particular, may lead a movement that insulates the state from the predatory interest groups that have colonized it. These state managers could conclude that the only effective way to avert a revolutionary threat is by reconverting the economy, either through trade liberalization or through industrial policy, in order to render economic growth possible. Trade liberalization policies in Argentina, Chile, and Uruguay under authoritarian regimes in the late 1970s were more or less explicitly predicated on this expectation.[10] Under military rule, trade liberalization is more likely than industrial policy, for regimes of this type are less dependent for their survival than are elected ones on the maintenance of a modicum of legitimacy, especially as far as labor is concerned. Chile in the 1980s has been a quite successful example of the implementation of this kind of switch, to the point that it has opened its economy to a level comparable to that of the industrial countries most integrated into world markets.

The social democratic response would not be triggered by national security considerations, but by distributional pressures and by state managers' realization that these demands cannot be satisfied because of the self-limiting nature of Model 1. The coalition supporting the policy switch in a democratic setting would have to include a segment of labor, probably in alliance with the sectors of capital less dependent on subsidies and protection (e.g., agrarian or mining capitalists, forward-linkage manufacturers of natural resources, and actual or potential exporters). Thus labor would be abandoning the traditional populist alliances of the postwar period, which were oriented to the internal market and thus to the promotion of import substitution. The aim of this new coalition would be the reconversion of manufacturing, probably on the basis of a strategy that includes some elements of industrial policy, and there would be an emphasis on the use of welfare state mechanisms to cushion the transfer of labor from declining to rising industries. There are no examples so far of successful coalitions of this type in Latin America, but the current Argentine government is moving in this direction (although its orientation toward industrial policy and welfare mechanisms is still weak), and the Brazilian one may have to follow. It is still too early to assess their chances of success, but they will surely have to contend with the mobilization of rent-seeking capitalists, workers, and those sectors of the state bureaucracy and the middle classes that depend on the status quo. The conditions of liberal democracy facilitate group organization and reduce the costs of mobilization, so the prospects for polarization in these societies are high.

CONCLUSION

I have argued that the degree to which the economy is market oriented mediates the relationship between capitalism and democracy. I have discussed one of the mechanisms that produces social structures resistant to liberal democracy in societies at middle levels of development, namely, the generation, through autarkic industrialization, of a peculiar type of capitalism, in which there is private ownership of the means of production but severe constraints on the operation of the market.

This model of industrialization, which I have labeled Model 1, is less conducive to stable liberal democracy than Model 2, competitive industrialization, for two reasons. First, Model 1 is inherently prone to stagnation in the long run, whereas there are no structural reasons for such an outcome in Model 2. The second reason has to do with the nature of the state and social structure generated by the two models. Model 1 requires a large state that controls every area of economic and social life; nothing of this sort is an inherent trait of Model 2. Finally, the social classes generated by Model 1 are dependent and predatory. In Model 2, both capitalists and workers are more autonomous from the state, and their economic and political environment offers many fewer opportunities for predatory behavior.

In a dialectical fashion, Model 1 produces the conditions for its own demise. This pattern of industrialization, when fully realized, leads to political illegitimacy and ultimately to economic inviability, and thus to a switch to Model 2, and eventually to the generation of a social structure more compatible with liberal democracy. The transformation away from nonmarket capitalism presupposes the growing autonomy of the state, which has formerly been strongly influenced by rent-seeking coalitions. Given that this influence is based on the facts that most capital and labor in the society are committed, in different degrees, to rent-seeking activities and that the state is thoroughly penetrated by these interests, the underlying hypothesis is that increasing state autonomy would be less a consequence of the relation of forces (such as strength or degree of unity of economic elites) than of the viability of the system. The argument that a profound economic and political crisis could trigger state autonomy and lead to policies that assault the central interests of the most powerful social forces contrasts with the prevailing theories of the state, which see autonomy as a product either of equilibrium in the relation of forces (the theory of Bonapartism) or of external pressures determined by interstate competition.[11]

In any case, rentier capitalists and their labor partners in distributional coalitions may be strong and unified, but their political power is nevertheless fragile for two reasons. First, they depend on the state for their very existence. And second, in a context of stagnation, a state elite seeking to enhance state autonomy can fragment and subordinate these coalitions through the rationing of rents and the allocation of welfare benefits.

Thus what Marx wrote of capitalism in general applies more specifically to its autarkic variant: It contains the seeds of its own destruction. The crisis of this type of economic organization can be described by paraphrasing a famous passage of *Capital*: The institutions of autarkic capitalism eventually become fetters over the mode of production, and this institutional integument is burst asunder (Marx, 1967, p. 763). However, the collapse of autarkic industrialization can well give way not to socialism, but to competitive capitalism, and even, perhaps, to liberal democracy.

NOTES

1. As for communist regimes, the endogenous cases (as opposed to the ones produced by Soviet intervention) originated in societies that were, at the aggregate level, at lower stages of industrialization. These regimes lost their mobilizational and "totalitarian" characteristics as their societies industrialized and modernized, and they gradually took on the traits of exclusionary or bureaucratic authoritarianism, as was the case all along in the societies, both semi-industrialized and highly industrialized, in which communism was imposed from the outside.

2. For discussion of major social and political developments in these societies in the postwar period, see O'Donnell (1988), Smith (1989), Waisman (1987), Sigmund (1977), Stallings (1978), Valenzuela and Valenzuela (1986), Gillespie and González (1989), and Weinstein (1988).

3. It would be interesting to explore whether the failure of state socialism was due more to its blockage of the market, much stronger and more comprehensive than in the case of autarkic capitalism, than to the absence of private property as such; if this was the case, the viability of "market socialism," the road many times alluded to but never taken, is still an open question.

4. On rent-seeking capitalists, see Krueger (1974). For a discussion of rents and development, see Reynolds (1982).

5. For descriptions of import-substituting industrialization in the societies of the Southern Cone, see Di Tella and Dornbusch (1989), Waisman (1987), Ffrench-Davis (1973), Stallings (1978), and Finch (1981). The Brazilian social structure is quite different from those of the Southern Cone countries, but the economic institutions were similar. On Brazilian import substitution, see Bresser Pereira (1984) and Leff (1968).

6. These rates are computed on the basis of data provided in reports by the Inter-American Development Bank (1989) and the U.N. Economic Commission for Latin America and the Caribbean (1990).

7. In the 1960s, Argentine enrollments in higher education were higher than in any Western European country except the Netherlands; Uruguayan enrollments were higher than those of Italy, Switzerland, Hungary, and Britain; and rates for Chile were still above those in Hungary or Britain (Taylor & Hudson, 1972). In the late 1970s, Argentina had caught up with the Netherlands, and Chile and Uruguay were not very far from the Western European countries with relatively low enrollments (World Bank, 1980).

8. For an analysis of the interaction between state and society in these contexts, see O'Donnell (1975, 1988).

9. This chapter, which originally appeared in *American Behavioral Scientist, 35* (4-5), correctly identifies the acronym NIC as "new industrialized countries."

10. For a description of these policies, see Foxley (1983).

11. For current analyses of state autonomy, see Badie and Birnbaum (1983), Carnoy (1984), and Skocpol (1979), as well as my discussion in Waisman (1987, pp. 143-149).

REFERENCES

Amsden, A. H. (1985). The state in Taiwan's economic development. In T. Skocpol, P. B. Evans, & D. Rueschemeyer (Eds.), *Bringing the state back in.* New York: Cambridge University Press.

Amsden, A. H. (1989). *Asia's next giant: South Korea and late industrialization.* New York: Oxford University Press.

Badie, B., & Birnbaum, P. (1983). *The sociology of the state.* Chicago: University of Chicago Press.

Baldwin, R. E. (1956). Patterns of development in newly settled regions. *Manchester School, 24,* 161-179.

Block, F. (1987). *Revising state theory.* Philadelphia: Temple University Press.

Bresser Pereira, L. (1984). *Development and crisis in Brazil, 1930-1983.* Boulder, CO: Westview.

Canak, W. L. (Ed.). (1989). *Lost promises: Debt, austerity, and development in Latin America.* Boulder, CO: Westview.

Carnoy, M. (1984). *The state and political theory.* Princeton, NJ: Princeton University Press.

Cheng, T. (1991). Political regimes and development strategies: South Korea and Taiwan. In G. Gereffi & D. L. Wyman (Eds.), *Manufacturing miracles.* Princeton, NJ: Princeton University Press.

Di Tella, G., & Dornbusch, R. (Eds.). (1989). *The political economy of Argentina, 1946-1983.* Pittsburgh: University of Pittsburgh Press.

Ffrench-Davis, R. (1973). *Politicas ecónomicas en Chile, 1952-1970.* Santiago: Nueva Universidad.

Ffrench-Davis, R. (1988). External debt, adjustment, and development in Latin America. In R. Ffrench-Davis, *Development and external debt in Latin America.* Notre Dame, IN: University of Notre Dame Press.

Finch, M. H. J. (1981). *A political economy of Uruguay since 1870.* New York: St. Martin's.

Foxley, A. (1983). *Latin American experiments in neoconservative economics.* Berkeley: University of California Press.

Gillespie, C. G., & González, L. E. (1989). Uruguay: The survival of old and autonomous institutions. In L. Diamond, J. J. Linz, & S. M. Lipset (Eds.), *Democracy in developing countries: Latin America.* Boulder, CO: Lynne Rienner.

Inter-American Development Bank. (1989). *Economic and social progress in Latin America: 1989 report.* Washington, DC: Author.

Krueger, A. (1974). The political economy of the rent-seeking society. *American Economic Review, 64,* 291-303.

Leff, N. H. (1968). *Economic policy-making and development in Brazil, 1947-1964.* New York: John Wiley.

Li, K. (1988). *The evolution of policy behind Taiwan's development.* New Haven, CT: Yale University Press.

Lipset, S. M. (1959). Some social requisites of democracy: Economic development and political legitimacy. *American Political Science Review, 53,* 69-105.

Marx, K. (1967). *Capital* (Vol. 1). New York: International.

O'Donnell, G. A. (1975). *Acerca del "corporativismo" y la cuestion del estado.* Buenos Aires: Cuadernos CEDES.

O'Donnell, G. A. (1988). *Bureaucratic authoritarianism: Argentina 1966-1973 in a comparative perspective.* Berkeley: University of California Press.

Ranis, G. (1991). Toward a model of development. In L. B. Krause & K. Kihwan (Eds.), *Liberalization in the process of economic development.* Berkeley: University of California Press.

Reynolds, C. W. (1982). The new terms of trade problem: Economic rents in international exchange. In C. P. Kindleberger & G. Di Tella (Eds.), *Economics in the long view* (Vol. 1). New York: New York University Press.

Schumpeter, J. A. (1950). *Capitalism, socialism, and democracy.* New York: Harper & Row.

Sigmund, P. E. (1977). *The overthrow of Allende and the politics of Chile, 1964-1976.* Pittsburgh: University of Pittsburgh Press.

Skocpol, T. (1979). *States and social revolutions.* Cambridge: Cambridge University Press.

Smith, W. C. (1989). *Authoritarianism and the crisis of the Argentine political economy.* Stanford, CA: Stanford University Press.

Stallings, B. (1978). *Class conflict and economic development in Chile, 1958-1973.* Stanford, CA: Stanford University Press.

Taylor, C. L., & Hudson, M. C. (1972). *World handbook of social and political indicators* (2nd ed.). New Haven, CT: Yale University Press.

U.N. Economic Commission for Latin America and the Caribbean. (1990). *Preliminary overview of the economy of Latin America and the Caribbean 1990.* Santiago, Chile: United Nations.

Valenzuela, J. S., & Valenzuela, A. (Eds.). (1986). *Military rule in Chile: Dictatorship and opposition.* Baltimore: Johns Hopkins University Press.

Waisman, C. H. (1987). *Reversal of development in Argentina.* Princeton, NJ: Princeton University Press.

Waisman, C. H. (1988). The Argentine debt crisis and the consolidation of democracy. In R. Wesson (Ed.), *Coping with the Latin American debt.* New York: Praeger.

Waisman, C. H. (in press). Latin American studies. In E. F. Borgatta & M. L. Borgatta (Eds.), *Encyclopedia of sociology.* New York: Macmillan.

Weinstein, M. (1988). *Uruguay: Democracy at the crossroads.* Boulder, CO: Westview.

Wionczek, M. S. (1985). *Politics and economics of external debt crisis.* Boulder, CO: Westview.

World Bank. (1980). *Poverty and human development.* New York: Oxford University Press.

8

Interest Systems and the Consolidation of Democracies

Philippe C. Schmitter

TO the neophyte graduate student at the University of California, Berkeley, in the early 1960s, attending Seymour Martin Lipset's course on political sociology (Sociology 290) was a revelation. The big "comparative" questions—development and democracy, class conflict and political change, nation building and state formation, national trajectories and international trends, public opinion and public policy—were there, and they all got a serious hearing. Lipset handled each with awe-inspiring erudition and that heterodoxical blend of behavioral, structural, and cultural factors that is his hallmark. I remember references to incidents of working-class history in obscure towns I had never heard of, to parties, unions, and movements over a century-long span, to scholars—living and dead—from almost every continent, and to books written in Finnish and Swedish, not to mention German, French, and Italian!

As one of the requirements for that course, I wrote a review of an article that Lipset had published only a few years previously: "Party Systems and the Representation of Social Groups" (Lipset, 1960a). This has not proven to be one of his more cited works. Indeed, I wonder if anyone else has been similarly influenced by it.[1] The review I wrote then has long since been lost in one move or another, and I cannot even recall how the author reacted to my effort. What I do remember is that reading and criticizing this particular article not only provided me with several important themes that appeared in my subsequent doctoral dissertation (Schmitter, 1971), but sent me on a lifetime trajectory of research.

The lessons I drew from it at the time may not seem so surprising today, but in the atmosphere of triumphant "behavioralism" and "functionalism" that then prevailed in the social sciences they were decidedly unorthodox:

AUTHOR'S NOTE: I am indebted to Brad Wilcox and Sharon Pressner for research assistance.

- Political processes cannot be reduced to the preferences or behaviors of individuals, but are conditioned by group actions and interactions.
- These groups—their solidarities and their conflicts—make independent contributions to determining political outcomes.
- "Representation" is the key (but not the exclusive) relationship between such groups and the making of authoritative decisions.
- This relationship is increasingly structured through specialized, "legally constituted" organizations with identifiable and reproducible boundaries. Together, they form distinctive subsystems within the polity.
- These representative organizations have a relative autonomy and an operative logic of their own that cannot be reduced either to the preferences of individuals or to the solidarities of groups that compose them. In Lipset's terms, they were neither just "a means for political adjustment" among conflicting social groups nor merely "an instrument of manipulation" by dominant authorities.
- However, the formal institutions of government—their procedures and substantive policies—can have a significant and enduring effect upon groups and the organizations that represent them. In other words, public policy is not a mere epiphenomenon produced by previously formed group interests, even less by independently established individual preferences.

What I disagreed with in the article was its main empirical conclusion, namely, that "parties are by far the most important part of the representative structure in complex democratic societies" (Lipset, 1960a, p. 53). Perhaps my objection was due to the fact that I had come to Berkeley from Switzerland (admittedly, an implausible explanation given my total lack of attention to Swiss politics when I was a student at the University of Geneva). In that country, parties were hardly capable of dominating—certainly not monopolizing—the representation of social groups. Even in the United States, it seemed obvious to me that much of the "action" was bypassing its two-party system and electoral process altogether.

So, I was convinced by Lipset's plea for the importance of social groups and the autonomy of representation processes, but I drew the perverse conclusion that this implied looking elsewhere—not at political parties but at what were then called "pressure" or "interest" groups—on the hunch that this was where the linkage between social groups and public authorities would increasingly be channeled.

After a research trajectory that has taken me to several countries and continents, involving a lengthy effort at refining and adapting the categories used to analyze how interest associations structure the representation of social groups, I am now prepared to return to that initial disagreement with Lipset and to focus it on what may well be the most significant issue for contemporary political science: *How can democracy be consolidated in the aftermath of the transition from autocratic rule?* What are the respective roles of such intermediaries as political parties, interest associations, and social movements in this highly complex (and, in most cases, still undecided) process? To what extent do different ways of structuring and governing the process of representation determine what the outcome will be?

THE CONSOLIDATION OF DEMOCRACY

Intuitively, the notion of consolidating democracy seems rather obvious. After a period of considerable uncertainty and unknown duration during which the previous autocracy "transits" to some other form of political domination, it becomes necessary to transform its improvisations into stable rules and alliances under which actors can compete and cooperate on predictable terms. From a "war of movement" in which many have high expectations (and some have great fears) about the magnitude of change, the democratic struggle should settle into a "war of positions" along established lines of cleavage for mutually agreed-upon advantage (Gramsci, 1971, pp. 108-110, 229-239). *Consolidation could be defined as the process of transforming the accidental arrangements, prudential norms, and contingent solutions that have emerged during the transition into relations of cooperation and competition that are reliably known, regularly practiced, and voluntarily accepted by those persons or collectivities (i.e., politicians and citizens) that participate in democratic governance.* If consolidation sets in, the democratic regime will have institutionalized uncertainty in certain roles and policy areas,[2] but it will also have reassured its citizens that the competition to occupy office and/or to exercise influence will be fair and circumscribed to a predictable range of outcomes. Modern, representative, political democracy rests on this "bounded uncertainty" and the "contingent consent" of actors to respect the outcomes it produces (Schmitter & Karl, 1991).

Leaving aside the difficulties inherent in distinguishing the two stages and in measuring their duration and effect, it should be noted that the insistence upon transition and consolidation that one can find in so much of the contemporary discussion of democratization represents an important, if often implicit, theoretical option (O'Donnell & Schmitter, 1986). It involves a rejection of the previously widespread notion that democracy was a functional requisite or an ethical imperative. Neither the level of economic development, the stage of capitalist accumulation, nor the hegemony of the bourgeoisie can automatically guarantee the advent, much less the persistence, of democracy. Nor is this regime outcome the inevitable product of some previously attained level of "civilization," literacy, educational attainment, or distinctive political culture. This is not to deny that affluence, a relatively equal distribution of wealth, an internationally competitive economy, a well-schooled population, a large middle class, and a willingness to tolerate diversity, to trust adversaries, and to settle conflicts by compromise are not advantageous; it is just that democracy still has to be chosen, implemented, and perpetuated by "agents," real live political actors with their distinctive interests, passions, memories, and—why not?—*fortuna* and *virtù*. No doubt, they will be constrained by the above developmental and cultural factors, but there is still plenty of room for making right or wrong choices. Even the most inauspicious setting can still give rise to an attempt to democratize, vide Haiti, Mongolia, Benin, and Albania—and, who knows, some of them may succeed—vide India, Costa Rica, Bolivia, Portugal, and Papua New Guinea, none of which seemed to stand much of a chance when regime change began.

It is the focus on these strategic interactions that distinguishes much present-day theorizing on democratization from earlier work that stressed functional requisites or cultural imperatives.[3] The ensuing years taught a bitter lesson as many relatively highly developed and "civilized" countries descended into autocracy. Moreover, some of the recent democratizers are simultaneously facing acute problems of adjusting to international economic competition and accommodating to internal cultural diversity—and they have not (yet) regressed to the status quo ante.

Let us not, however, be misled by all this emphasis on choice and voluntaristic action. *The core of the consolidation dilemma lies in coming up with a set of institutions that politicians can agree upon and citizens are willing to support.* Arriving at a stable solution, especially in the climate of exaggerated expectations that tends to characterize the transition, is no easy matter. Not only are the choices *intrinsically conflictual*—with different parties of politicians preferring rules that will ensure their own reelection or eventual access to power and different groups of citizens wanting rules that will ensure the accountability of their professional agents—but they are *extrinsically consequential.* Once they are translated via electoral uncertainty into governments that begin to produce public policies, they will affect rates of economic growth, willingness to invest, competitiveness in foreign markets, distributions of income and wealth, access to education, perceptions of cultural deprivation, racial balance, and even national identity. To a certain extent, these substantive matters are anticipated by actors and incorporated in the compromises they make with regard to procedures, but there is lots of room for error and unintended consequence. In the short run, the consolidation of democracy depends on actors' and citizens' ability to come up with a solution to their intrinsic conflicts over rules; in the long run, it will depend on the extrinsic impact that policies made under these rules will have on social groups. Here is where the "objective realities" of levels of development, positions in the world economy, conflicts over sectoral product and distributions of welfare, and the "subjective preferences" of classes, generations, genders, ethnic types, status groups, and situses reenter the picture with a vengeance. Given the likelihood that some time must elapse before the new rules of cooperation and competition produce observable results, it seems safe to assume that the process of consolidation will be a great deal lengthier than that of transition.

NOTIONS OF PARTIAL REGIMES
AND TYPES OF DEMOCRACY

It may also be a more differentiated and variegated process, for modern democracy is a very complex set of institutions involving multiple channels of representation and sites for authoritative decision making. Citizenship, its most distinctive property, is not confined to voting periodically in elections. It also can be exercised by influencing the selection of candidates, joining associations or movements, petitioning authorities, engaging in "unconventional" protests, and so forth. Nor is the accountability of authorities guaranteed only through the traditional mechanisms of territorial constituency and legislative process. Much of it can circumvent these partisan mechanisms and focus directly through functional channels and bargaining processes on elected or appointed officials within the state apparatus.

If this were not the case, the process of consolidation would be much simpler—and I would readily concede Lipset's point that "parties are by far the most important part of the representative structure." All one would have to do would be to focus on the formation of a party system sufficiently anchored in citizen perceptions, an electoral mechanism reliable (and acceptable) enough to produce winning candidates, and an institutional arrangement for ensuring that decisions binding on the public would be held accountable to its properly elected representatives. Much of the recent literature does exactly this, with considerable confidence and erudition (Pridham, 1990).

My hunch is that this may be inadequate. Either it ignores the very substantial changes that have taken place in the nature and role of parties in well-established Western democracies or it anachronistically presumes that parties in today's neodemocracies will have to go through all the stages and perform all the functions of their predecessors. I believe it is preferable to assume that today's citizens—even in polities that have long suffered under authoritarian rule—have quite different organizational skills, are less likely to identify so closely with partisan symbols or ideologies, and defend a much more variegated set of interests. Moreover, the new regimes are emerging in an international environment virtually saturated with different models of successful collective action. All this may not preclude a hegemonic role for parties in the representation of social groups, but it does suggest that they will be facing more competition from interest associations and social movements than their predecessors and that we should revise our thinking about democratization accordingly.

First, *what if modern democracy were conceptualized not as "a regime," but as a composite of "partial regimes," each of which was institutionalized around distinctive sites for the representation of social groups and the resolution of their ensuing conflicts?* Parties, associations, movements, localities, and various clientele would compete and coalesce through these different channels in efforts to capture office and influence policy. Authorities with different functions and at different levels of aggregation would interact with these representatives and could legitimately claim accountability to different citizen interests (and passions).

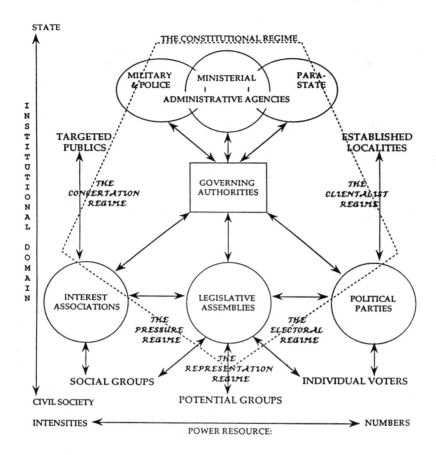

Figure 8.1. Sketch of the Property Space Involved in the Consolidation of Whole and Partial Regimes in Modern Democracies

Constitutions, of course, are an effort to establish a single, overarching set of "metarules" that would render these partial regimes coherent by assigning specific tasks to each and enforcing some hierarchical relation among them, but such formal documents are rarely successful in delineating and controlling all these relations. The process of convoking a constituent assembly, producing an acceptable draft constitution, and ratifying it by vote and/or plebiscite undoubtedly represents a significant moment in democratic consolidation,[4] but many partial regimes will be left undefined, for it is precisely in the interstices between different types of representatives that constitutional norms are most vague and least prescriptive.[5]

Imagine trying to deduce from even the most detailed of constitutions (and they are becoming more detailed) how parties, associations, and movements will interact to influence policies, or trying to discern how capital and labor will bargain over income shares under the new metarules.

If political democracy is not a regime but a composite of regimes, then the appropriate strategy for studying its consolidation would be disaggregation. Not only is this theoretically desirable, it also makes the effort more empirically feasible. In Figure 8.1, I have attempted to sketch out the property space that would be involved and to suggest some of the specific partial regimes that are likely to emerge. On the vertical axis, the space is defined in terms of the institutional domain of action, ranging from authoritatively defined *state agencies* to *self-constituted units of civil society*. Horizontally, the variance concerns the power resources that actors can bring to bear on the emerging political process: *numbers* in the case of those relying primarily on the counting of individual votes; *intensities* for those based on weighing the contribution of particular groups of citizens. Competing theories and models of democracy— liberal versus statist, majoritarian versus consociational, unitary versus federal, presidential versus parliamentary—have long argued the merits of particular locations in Figure 8.1. In my view, all are potentially democratic (provided they respect the overarching principle of citizenship and the procedural minima of civil rights, fair elections, free associability, and so on).

Second, *what if it were not "democracy" but "democracies" that are being consolidated?* Beyond some common threshold of basic procedures that must be respected[6] lies a great deal of divergence in concrete rules and practices. These types of democracy are the result of different (but relatively stable) combinations of what I have already termed partial regimes. No single format or set of institutions embodies modern democracy—even if, at a given moment in time, some particular country may seem to represent "best practice." Instead, there is an array of possible combinations, and the dilemma of those who would consolidate democracy is to pick the one among many that satisfies both the short-term interests of politicians and the longer-run expectations of citizens.

If so, *the challenging issue facing political scientists becomes not whether autocracy will be succeeded by democracy, but by what type of democracy.* It could be argued that in the contemporary period (or at least since April 25, 1974, when the Portuguese "Revolution of the Carnations" launched the current wave) most polities are condemned to be democratic. The absence of a plausible alternative to some form of popularly accountable government means that those autocracies that resist (e.g., Burma, China, Cuba, Vietnam, Indonesia, Kenya, and most of the Middle East) must expend an increasing proportion of their resources in sustaining themselves in power—without much prospect for long-run success.

This "condemnation," however, does not ensure that all those that enter into a transition will succeed in consolidating a democratic regime. Some will regress to autocracy, probably in rather short order, vide Haiti and Burma. More are likely to get stuck in a sort of purgatory. They will persist as "unconsolidated democracies," where the procedural minimum will be respected, but politicians and representatives will prove incapable of agreeing on a viable set of rules for limiting uncertainty and ensuring contingent consent. Argentina and the Philippines are prominent examples of this outcome, and its specter is haunting Eastern Europe.

Third, *what if the outcome of democratization were dependent, not so much on the presence or absence of certain prerequisites or on the virtues or vices of certain persons, but on the sequence with which certain processes occurred?* There are a number of rather concrete tasks to be accomplished during a change in regime: Elections have to be convoked and held; parties, associations, and movements formed or revived; chief executives elected or chosen; ministerial and administrative positions filled or eliminated; collective bargaining arrangements created and institutionalized; constitutions drafted and adopted; legislatures elected and organized; and so forth.[7] My hunch is that the role of different representative organizations and, with it, the type of democracy that will emerge, is determined to a significant degree by the timing and sequence of accomplishing these tasks.[8] A sensible rule of thumb would be that those arrangements that get consolidated first should have a greater and more persistent effect on those coming later. This would normally imply an advantage for political parties, because it is the convocation of so-called founding elections that typically links liberalization to democratization and serves to accelerate the process of transition (O'Donnell & Schmitter, 1986, pp. 57-64).

THE PARADOX OF ASSOCIABILITY

Modern democracies tend to emerge as compromises. Their protagonists (not all of whom are "democrats") prefer very different institutions and practices that, not coincidentally, tend to correspond to the arrangements of power that they believe will best defend their interests or advance their ideals in the future. In the initial uncertainty of the transition, however, no dominant group may emerge that can impose its "format," and what comes out is likely to be a hybrid—a second-best solution—that resembles no one's first preference.[9]

In this competitive process to define future rules and practices, interest associations and social movements are likely to find themselves in a paradoxical situation. Not infrequently, they will have been more tolerated by the *ancien régime* than political parties, especially if they concentrated on the representation of relatively localized or circumscribed interests.[10] The defections of key professional and business groups often serve to challenge the "indispensability" of authoritarian rulers, just as the declarations of human rights movements discredit their legitimacy. Once the transition has begun, these and other organizations are usually swept up in what Guillermo O'Donnell and I have called "the resurgence of civil society" (O'Donnell & Schmitter, 1986, p. 48). This unexpected mobilization can be a crucial factor in driving the authoritarian rulers beyond their hesitant and limited measures of liberalization toward full-scale democratization.

These initial organizational advantages, when combined with a particularly strategic location in the system of production or administration, can be translated into a genuine, if momentary, power advantage. In fact, associations representing important class, sectoral, and professional interests may even be victimized by their capacity to disrupt or nullify actions taken by the new democratic rulers.[11] Not only will this be interpreted as extracting unfair rewards for "some" at a time when the rhetoric focuses on the rewards for "all," but the disruption of social peace their actions inevitably provoke can also be seen as encouraging a coup by hardliners already convinced that the transition has gone too far. The pressure on these "functional" organizations not to make opportunistic use of their power during the transition is likely to be great.

For more loosely organized, topically focused "attitudinal" movements, the difficulties are of another nature. Many of their objectives may have been satisfied by the demise of autocracy itself. Others seem too specialized to provide general guidelines for the design of subsequent institutions. Whatever their role in bringing down the *ancien régime* (and it has varied a great deal), social movements depend on massive amounts of voluntary labor and personal enthusiasm, which are difficult to sustain over time and to focus on the minutiae of consolidation. Sporadic interventions may still be mounted—around the founding elections, the convocation of constituent assemblies, eventual coup attempts, and so on—but the role of these organizations seems inexorably to decline with the definition of stable rules and practices, at least until they are revived by another wave of protest (Tarrow, 1991).

Let us, therefore, concentrate our attention on those permanent associations that specialize in protecting or promoting class, sectoral, or professional interests, and try to discern the conditions under which they might intrude on the putative monopoly of political parties in the representation of social groups. As I have speculated above, they can rarely be expected to play a sustained role during the transition, even if their momentary influence can be quite significant. They may also experience a good deal of difficulty in adapting to the rules of the game that emerge out of the consolidation period.

First, interest associations tend to be displaced from the center of political life and public visibility by political parties once elections have been announced, if their outcome appears to be uncertain and it seems safe to run for office. The former are organized along functional lines and can rarely adapt to compete in territorial constituencies. Moreover, their programs and symbols are too specialized to appeal to wider publics.[12] Despite the fact that they rarely play much of a role in initiating the transition, parties do have access to those symbols and programs of general identification and may even draw resources and personnel away from preexisting (and less persecuted) associations and movements once the prospect of "founding elections" is in sight. The dynamics of electoral competition will compel party strategists to appeal to wider and more heterogeneous publics (especially where districts are relatively large and the electoral system less than perfectly proportional), and they may even have to deny their dependence on the very "special interests" that helped them get started. Territorial constituencies impose a different logic of competition and cooperation from that of functional constituencies. Interest associations will try the best they can to penetrate, even to colonize, these partisan units, but the imperative of assembling numbers and the rhetoric of appealing to the public interest work against their success—at least until longer-run needs for financial resources and specialized information can assert themselves.[13]

Rather, the inverse is more likely to occur during the transition and early consolidation periods. Political parties will seek to penetrate and colonize interest associations. Where they are very successful, the result will be a set of partisan subcultures: *Lager* or *familles spirituelles* in which communities of differing color—"red, black, white, orange"—will confront each other and demand the exclusive affiliation of their members. Where they are only partially successful, they can leave behind a set of interest associations split internally into competing party factions or fragmented into competing units of representation. In either case, the sum total is likely to have fewer members and more limited financial resources than in the more favorable outcome, where class, sectoral, and professional organizations manage to retain their respective unity and hence their monopolistic location in the emergent system of interest politics.

These tendencies toward fragmentation and/or competitiveness may, in some cases, be further exacerbated by emergent difficulties in responding to regionally or locally based challenges. The highly centralized nature of authoritarian regimes typically leaves an accumulated heritage of frustration in peripheral areas—all the more so when these are ethnically, linguistically, or culturally distinctive. Transition toward a new configuration of public offices may bring out simultaneous demands for a new configuration of territorial authority. These tensions are also likely to affect the unity of political parties, but the creation of regional representative bodies with their own party systems may absorb much of their impact. Because the core issues of economic management and social policy that most affect class, sectoral, and professional associations tend to remain firmly in the hands of central authorities, regionalism can bring little more than symbolic satisfaction to these interests. Effective influence requires a capacity to respond and negotiate at the national level, but resurgent peripheral identities may be hard to ignore (and difficult to gauge) in the relative uncertainty of the transition.

Finally, interest associations šeem to face rather special problems of "resource extraction" during the democratization process. The new basis for both joining and contributing to them is (presumably) *voluntarism*. Invariably, the new constitutions enshrine freedom of association among their fundamental rights. Some may even guarantee *Negativekoalitionsfreiheit,* or freedom *from* having to join any specific association. This implies an end to exclusive state recognition and compulsory contributions. Willing individuals from different social classes, economic sectors, and professional categories must come forward to support their respective associations in a situation where many other claims are being made on their time and money. One does not have to be a strict devotee of Mancur Olson's *Logic of Collective Action* (1965) to recognize that once the "uncalculated" enthusiasm of participating in the mobilizational phase of regime change is over, the temptation to free ride on the effort of others is likely to settle in.

One can hypothesize, therefore, that the more the departing autocracy was characterized by extensive state corporatism or monistic control by the governing party, the greater will be the probable difficulty of adjusting to voluntarism and "official" indifference. Admittedly, there exist ample possibilities for granting informally to groups what constitutional freedom of association formally denies them. The complex provisions of a labor code, social security, and labor court systems, and the operation of assorted advisory commissions, not to mention the (often surreptitious) concession of outright subsidies, can help to overcome the limitations of voluntary associability. In some instances, the resource problem may center on the ownership of certain physical assets and the control over certain monopolistic services that associations acquired under authoritarian auspices. Whatever the case, the *patrimoine* from the defunct regime will be a major potential source of group struggle and an important determinant of the resources available to newly "liberated" interest associations. One of the murkiest areas of their operation during the transition and early consolidation is finance. Regardless of the formula that is eventually applied—retention of monopolistic privileges, distribution of the *patrimoine,* subsidization by government in power (or by other *inconfessable* sources, domestic or foreign)—the adjustment to new conditions of membership should weaken the role of organized business, labor, and agriculture during the interim. Once these problems are resolved, however, their respective associations may come to play a role in defining what type of democracy will consolidate itself.

For the reasons sketched above, my hunch is that such class, sectoral, and professional associations will *not* be a major factor in determining whether democracy as a general mode of domination will succeed authoritarian rule and persist for the near future; rather, their (delayed) impact will be significant in determining what *type* of democracy will eventually be consolidated. In the longer run, this will affect the distribution of benefits that is likely to set in, the formula of legitimation that is likely to be employed, and the level of citizen satisfaction that is likely to prevail. Another way of putting it is that the *quality of democracy,* rather than its quantity and duration, will vary with the emergent properties of associability (Schmitter, 1991). Organized class, sectoral, and professional interests can have an impact on the consolidation process, but it is going to take some time before the full extent of this becomes evident.

The strongest case for their long-run significance comes from the literature on societal corporatism or neocorporatism.[14] Liberal thought had long suggested that political order rests on an implicit social contract between individuals and their rulers. "Rational choice Marxists" added the notion that a compromise between classes was necessary if "capitalist democracy" were to survive.[15] Neither (at least initially) paid much attention to the associations that actually aggregated the interests at stake into diverse categories and engaged in the negotiation of explicit agreements—liberals presumably because these organizations were expected to behave no differently from individuals; Marxists because classes *an sich* were supposed to be objectively capable of imposing their logic of conflict over whatever "class fractions" had emerged *für sich.*

The corporatist perspective that flourished during the 1970s and 1980s focused specifically on historical differences in the ways these organizations had emerged and how they continued to affect contemporary economic performance, mainly across the advanced industrial countries. It suggested that formalized and centralized intermediation, primarily (but not exclusively) through associations representing class, sectoral, and professional interests, had become an important characteristic of some (but not all) modern political democracies. Moreover, the social contracts/class compromises negotiated under corporatist auspices seemed not only to have a significant impact on rates of inflation, levels of unemployment, and fiscal equilibria, but to contribute to the "governability" of the polity (Bruno & Sachs, 1985; Cameron, 1984; Paloheimo, 1984; Schmidt, 1982; Schmitter, 1981; Schott, 1985; Wilensky & Turner, 1987).

The reasons for this were to be found not in the normative dilemma of ensuring obligation or in the functional imperatives for reproducing capitalism, but in such contingent factors as the organizational response to previous social conflicts, the impact of war, and, most of all, the development of the modern welfare state, with its Keynesian policy agenda. Once public officials intervened heavily and diversely in the macromanagement of the economy, they found themselves increasingly dependent on organized interests for the information and compliance needed to make their policies work. Associations, meanwhile, sought to shake off the limits of liberal, voluntary collective action by acquiring state recognition, centralized monopoly representation, licensing authority, guaranteed access, and other characteristics that would enhance their membership and resources.

In the well-established democracies of Northern Europe, these developments occurred piecemeal and without explicit ideological justification, even if the predominant Social Democratic parties of the region did stress the generic necessity for reformism and class compromise. Elsewhere, neocorporatist arrangements either survived from precapitalist practices or emerged pragmatically to solve specific postwar crises. In other words, their legitimacy was questionable—and not just because they resembled previous attempts by authoritarian rulers such as Mussolini, Franco, Salazar, Vargas, and Perón to impose such structures from above during the 1930s and 1940s. To this day, the connection between corporatism and democracy remains "essentially contested" (Schmitter, 1983).

It is, therefore, all the more ironic that the theme should emerge so insistently in discussions of the consolidation of neodemocracies. Here we are faced with a case of international diffusion. The Spaniards were clearly inspired by the relative success of such arrangements in northern and central Europe during the 1960s and 1970s. Their *Pacto de Moncloa* and its successors, in turn, encouraged others to attempt to forge an explicit macro-level agreement between peak or sectoral associations representing capital and labor in the aftermath of authoritarian rule. While the record outside of Spain has, so far, not been encouraging, and one can even question whether the various Spanish pacts from 1975 to 1984 really had much of an impact on controlling key economic parameters, the potential political effects can be very significant. The very image of representatives from such a wide diversity of interests signing such an accord—in the Spanish case, with the added blessing of the king—can serve to reduce uncertainty about substantive outcomes and "reciprocally legitimate" both the negotiating organizations and the government officials who brought them together.[16] In this case, neocorporatism will have switched from being a "consumer" of legitimacy already well established in state institutions to being a "producer" of it in democratic institutions that are just emerging. What an irony that just as corporatism seems to be dying (or, better, moribund) in the old democracies (Schmitter, 1989), it should be revived in the new ones!

The corporatist "growth industry" of the past two decades has, however, had some impact on the rapidly evolving discussion of types of democracy. Traditionally, these were delineated according to either formal constitutional/institutional criteria or the nature of their party systems. More recently, analysts have used variation in the structure of interest associations to generate new types (Lange & Meadwell, 1985), or have explored the relationship between the variation in the pluralist-corporatist dimension and the more conventional distinctions (Lijphart & Crepaz, 1991). While it is my conviction that these are steps in the right direction that should improve our understanding of the consolidation of democracy, I would like to enter a dissenting note. One of the reasons for the shifting fate of corporatist arrangements in advanced industrial countries has been the changing nature of their working class and, with it, the changing role of trade unions. To the extent that most of the discussion and virtually all of the measurement of corporatism has focused on certain properties of the union movement—concentration, monopoly, density of membership, hierarchical structures, official recognition, guaranteed access, and so on—this may prove misleading, especially in countries where urban, regularly employed, unionized workers are a small, relatively privileged (and usually diminishing) proportion of the total work force. Granted that they may still be sufficiently well located strategically to bring production to a halt (and they may also be concentrated in sectors of state employment where they are politically well protected from the consequences of their actions), nevertheless, one should not assume that their consent is necessary for corporatism to work. It may be possible to work out "bipartite" deals between capital and the state that could have similar effects or to bring in associations representing the self-employed, professionals, service employees, consumers, housewives, even various marginal groups from the underground economy to give agreements a "popular" component. Admittedly, this will be a lot messier than the classic tripartite formula, but in places such as Latin America, where wages are already at a subsistence level and constitute a small percentage of national income, where overmanning and unemployment exist side by side, and where the policy thrust is toward privatization, it may be a feasible alternative. In

Eastern Europe, "classic" blue-collar workers are a much more significant proportion of the population, but their ranks are rapidly shrinking and their organizations are in disarray. Who is to say that associations representing emergent "political capitalists," shareholders in privatized enterprises, professionals, farmers, and various petit bourgeois interests will not play a more important role than trade unions in whatever social contracting takes place?

With these heretical thoughts in mind, let us now turn to the issue of how to capture these emergent properties during the difficult period of consolidation.

THE EMERGENT PROPERTIES OF ASSOCIATIONS

In response to the opportunities (and threats) of democratization, individual associations are likely to have to change significantly in their internal structures and operative practices. Some will make every effort to retain the organizational advantages they enjoyed under the previous autocracy; others will seize on the chance of establishing a new relationship with their members and inserting themselves independently into the policy process. Here, there is a deep-seated irony, because *those social groups that are in greatest need of collective action (i.e., those with numerous, dispersed, and relatively impoverished individuals as potential members) are the least likely to be successful in attracting these members on a rational and voluntary basis.* The small, concentrated, and privileged groups should have less difficulty in generating resources under democratic conditions. Not only do they need them less (their members may have adequate resources to act individually), but they were usually the privileged interlocutors and beneficiaries of the previous autocracy. Left to its own devices, then, the new "liberal" associability could produce a systematically skewed overrepresentation of dominant class, sectoral, and professional interests. Subordinate groups have, of course, the new resource of voting between competing parties to pursue their general interests, but they may have to rely on the state recognition, licensing, and subsidization characteristic of the *ancien régime* to participate effectively in the democratic game when it comes to advancing their more particular interests. The practical temptations of neocorporatism, in other words, may outweigh the ideological attractions of pluralism.

First, let us turn briefly to some properties of individual, direct membership organizations representing the interests of business, labor, and agriculture that may change with the advent of democracy: number, member density, and representational domain.

Number

Theoretically, this should be unlimited under the newly acquired twin freedoms of association and petition. As James Madison put it so bitterly in the *Federalist Papers* (No. 10): "The most frivolous and fanciful distinctions have been sufficient to kindle their unfriendly passions and excite their most violent conflicts." Indeed, his pluralist formula was designed to increase the potential number by multiplying the levels of authority around which they could form, as well as placing no barriers to their continual fragmentation. Several factors, however, may either raise the threshold of association formation for specific social groups or restrict access to bargaining arenas by those that do manage to get organized. Here is where public policies, either held over from the previous regime or created anew under the new democratic regime, can be expected to play a crucial role. Linked to this basic condition are subsidiary questions of whether the associations are new or merely rebaptized versions of previous ones, whether their formation is spontaneous or sponsored (and, if so, by whom), and whether they tend to emerge early or late in the process of transition.

Member Density

According to liberal democratic theory, the proportion of those eligible to join and contribute to this form of collective action who actually do so is supposed to be determined only by the rational and independent calculation of individual capitalists, workers, and agriculturists. In fact, the usual social and economic "filtering mechanisms" are often supplemented by deliberate public and private actions. This leads to the murky area of outside sponsorship by political parties,[17] statutory obligations by state agencies (vide chamber systems for capitalists and agriculturists, closed shops, and union taxes for workers), and even more subtle forms of fiscal discrimination, licensing, export certification, subsidized services, and outright coercion—all of which can bind various social and economic categories to their respective units of representation in ways they do not freely choose but that have been accepted as compatible with democratic practice.

Representational Domain

According to the usual canons of democracy, interest associations (old or new) should be able to determine by themselves whom they wish to represent. They set the limits on whom they attempt to recruit as members and what they purport to speak for. Rarely, however, is this the case. Under state corporatist auspices—the usual Southern European and Latin American inheritance from authoritarian rule—these domains were specified by law or administrative regulation. Interests had to be organized by economic sector or professional specialization, to have adopted a given territorial format, to have restricted themselves to a certain level of interaction, and to perform a prescribed set of tasks. Conversely, certain domains and activities were proscribed, as were specific political, ideological, or cultural affiliations. These are organizational "habits" that may decay slowly, even when the original measures are revoked.[18]

Whatever the inheritance and the inertia, countries are likely to vary considerably in the ways they define interest domains. Two dimensions seem especially crucial for future democratic practice: the *degree of specialization* into functional (e.g., product, sector, or class), territorial (e.g., local, provincial, or national), and task (e.g., trade versus employer associations, unions oriented toward militant action versus those oriented toward the provision of services) domains, and the *extent of discrimination* according to individual member characteristics, such as size of firm, level of skills, public/private status, religious belief, ethnicity, party affiliation, and so forth.

Summarizing this "bundle" of characteristics relative to individual associations, the two emergent properties that seem to make the most difference for the consolidation of different types of democracy could be called "strategic capacity" (Pizzorno, 1977) and "encompassingness" (Olson, 1965): Are these newly created or recently renovated organizations sufficiently resourceful and autonomous to be able to define and sustain a course of action over the long run that is neither linked exclusively to the immediate preferences of their members nor dependent on the policies of parties and agencies external to their domain? If this is the case, how broad a category of represented interests can be covered by any given organization or coordinated by peak associations through hierarchical arrangements?

Where polities acquire class, sectoral, or professional associations with both strategic capacity and encompassing scope, these associations play a more significant role in the consolidation process than where a great multiplicity of narrowly specialized and overlapping organizations emerge with close dependencies on their members and/or interlocutors. Pluralist associations, in other words, weaken the role of interest intermediaries; corporatist ones strengthen it. This difference also affects the probability of establishing stable partial regimes and, hence, the type of democratic regime. For example, the chance of creating a viable *concertation regime,* the kind of regime that links associations directly with each other and/or to state agencies, seems contingent on the development of strategic capacity and encompassingness. Furthermore, once this linking is initiated, it will tend to encourage "participant associations" to acquire even more autonomy from members and party interlocutors and to extend their scope to bring wider and wider interest domains under their control. At the extreme, the neodemocracy could become populated with a series of "private interest governments" in sensitive policy areas (Streeck & Schmitter, 1984), with profound consequences for political parties, local clienteles, and the legislative process, as well as for the overall governability of the political order (Schmitter, 1981).

THE EMERGENT PROPERTIES OF ASSOCIATIONAL SYSTEMS

The second set of emergent characteristics refers to what one may loosely term the *system of interest intermediation.* The impact of organized interests on the type of democracy cannot be assessed merely by adding together the associations present in a given polity; one must also take into account the properties that emerge from their competitive and cooperative interaction. To keep the discussion focused, let us again concentrate on just the three most salient dimensions.

The first is *coverage*. Which social groups are organized into wider networks of collective action, which operate strictly on their own, and which are completely left out? My decision to privilege class, sectoral, and professional associations already implies a biased assessment that these, among all the varied types of interest groups, are likely to make the most crucial decisions with regard to partial regime consolidation and, eventually, the type of democracy. In the narrow sense, the issue is whether identifiable segments or factions of these interests ("potential groups," in the pluralist jargon) fail to organize— or do so to a degree appreciably less than would appear possible. Is this due to the persistence of repressive measures (e.g., prohibitions on the unionization of civil servants or the organization of shop floor units of worker representation), to a strategic calculation that their interests would be better promoted/defended through other means of collective action (e.g., political parties, informal collusion, or clientelistic connections), or to a structural incapacity to act under the new conditions of voluntarism and competitiveness? Granted, it may be difficult to assess counterfactually the presence of interest categories that "exist but do not act" and to reconstruct the logic that leads conscious and active groups to be satisfied through one mode rather than another of representation, but a comprehensive assessment of the coverage of emergent interest systems requires at least some effort in this direction, if only because of the hypothesis that democracies will face serious problems of legitimacy and governability if they exclude (or simply ignore) such potentially active social groups.

The problem is exacerbated when one shifts from this narrow class and sectoral focus to the much broader question of the coverage of "other" interests (not to mention passions), specifically, those people who are poor, aged, sick, unemployed, illiterate, dwelling in slums, foreigners deprived of decent treatment, natives suffering from ethnic, linguistic, or sexual discrimination, anxious about environmental degradation, concerned about world peace or the rights of animals, *e così via*. Here, there can be no initial presumption that collective action will take the rather limited and specialized form of associability. Their demands may be better addressed via political parties (if they are voters), religious institutions (if they are believers), local governments (if they are spatially concentrated), or state agencies (if they are designated clients). They can also form their own social movements, with both an agenda and a means of action that may not be compatible with the more narrowly constrained scope of interest organizations. No empirical study could possibly cover all forms of actual and potential interest and their corresponding organizations. For Southern Europe, it can be argued that functionally based interest associations will be more significant in the consolidation process than, say, social movements[19] and, subsequently, will contribute more to defining the type of regime that will emerge (Tarrow, 1991). This cannot, however, become a license to ignore completely the role of organizations and institutions representing those "other interests," if only because they will affect to some degree the number, member density, and domains, as well as the coverage, of class, sectoral, and professional associations.

The second emergent property is *monopoly*. The advent of democracy should encourage competition among associations for members, for resources, and for recognition by, as well as access to, authorities. It does not, however, make it imperative or unavoidable. The usual assumption is that the previous authoritarian regime—if it did not suppress associability altogether for specific groups—compelled them to act within a singular, monopolistic, state-recognized (and often state-controlled) organization. Whether this situation persists after that regime has fallen seems to be contingent on political factors that assert themselves during the transition and that can have a lasting effect. By far the most salient, especially with regard to trade unions, is the emergent structure of competition among political parties. Rivalry among communists, socialists, and, occasionally, Christian Democrats over worker affiliation often antedates the demise of authoritarian rule, but it may be only after electoral politics has been restored that it can become sufficiently salient to split more or less unitary workers' movements—as has happened in Italy, Spain, and Portugal. Business associations have historically been less organizationally affected by partisan divisions—even when their members voted for competing parties—but they have sometimes been fragmented by linguistic or religious differences. Far more divisive for them has been the conflict of interests among small, medium, and large enterprises—analogous to the difficulties of containing white- and blue-collar workers within the same peak association or of working out "non-raiding agreements" between unions representing differing skill levels. As mentioned above, regionalism and "micronationalism" have also led to situations of competition for members or access.

Whatever the source, the emergent postauthoritarian system will possess varying degrees of "monopoly power" in the representation of interests—and this will be crucial for the formation of partial regimes. Often, this will prove difficult to assess for the simple reason that associations may appear to have defined their domains in ways that imply competition while in practice coming to less obtrusive arrangements under which they agree not to try to lure away each other's members or to share key resources and even leaders or to engage in a subtle division of labor vis-à-vis potential interlocutors. For example, capitalists in northern and central European countries are organized into separate hierarchies of trade and employer associations that seem to be competing for member allegiance and political access. On closer examination (and despite some past conflicts), this turns out to be a quite stable division of labor that lends considerable flexibility and "redundant capacity" to that class's defense of its interests.

The third system property is *coordination*. Single associations tend to have a limited span of control and capacity for managing interest diversity. The age-old quest for "one big union" has gone unfulfilled for workers, although capitalists and farmers have sometimes come closer to that goal. In order to represent more comprehensive categories, the usual technique has been to create "associations of associations." These peak organizations (*Spitzenverbände* is the incomparable German phrase) may attempt to coordinate the behavior of entities within a single sector (e.g., the entire chemical industry), a whole branch of production (e.g., all of industry), or the class as a whole (all capitalists, workers, or farmers irrespective of branch or sector). They may cover a locality, a province or region, a national state, or even a supranational unit such as the European Community. Their success in effectively incorporating all relevant groups and forging a unity of action among them also varies from very incomplete and loose confederal arrangements, in which members retain their financial and political autonomy and are moved to common action only by exhortation or the personal authority of leaders, to highly centralized and hierarchical bodies with superior resources and even a capacity to discipline all class or sectoral interests that refuse to follow an agreed-upon policy line.

Such a high coordinative capacity is not attained without struggle, or, at least, never without significant threats to the interests at stake. This is obviously easier to do where the scope is purely local and the sector quite narrow, for at these levels the mutual effects of small numbers and close social interaction can be brought to bear. To accomplish such feats on a national and class basis requires much greater effort. Normally, it comes only after the building blocks, the direct membership of local and sectoral associations, have been created,[20] but this tends to make the subsequent subordination of the latter more difficult. Perhaps the heritage of centralization from the immediately preceding state corporatist experience may facilitate such an outcome in Southern Europe. The extraordinary success of the Spanish Confederation of Employers (CEOE) at the peak of Spanish business suggests this (Aguilar, 1983; Perez-Diaz, 1985; Rijen, 1985), but the example of next-door Portugal shows that exactly the contrary can follow. The latter has two competing national industrial associations with little or no power to coordinate the behavior of their members, much less to speak for those (numerous) sectors of business that do not fall within the purview of either.

If strategic capacity and encompassingness were the two composite, emergent properties of individual associations that seemed most relevant, the two that best define the nature of interorganizational systems of interest intermediation are class governance and congruence.

Class governance is the capacity to commit a comprehensive social category (e.g., all owners of productive property, workers in all industries, self-employed in all sectors) to a common and long-term course of action *and* to be able to assure that those bound by such a policy do indeed comply with it. Theoretically, this could be accomplished by a political party, although the logic of continuous electoral competition tends to undermine this for manual workers—and parties have almost never performed this function for capitalists.[21] In practical and contemporary terms, if class governance is to become a property of civil society and the political order, it is a set of interest associations (or even a single peak association) that will have to do the job.

Congruence refers to the extent to which the coverage, monopoly status, and coordinative capacity of one class or sector are similar to others. One could postulate an underlying trend in this direction, especially between clusters of associations that represent conflicting interests. Nevertheless, in historical terms, some may take the lead in experimenting with (and, occasionally, borrowing from abroad) novel forms of self-organization that subsequently diffuse to their opponents or imitators. Given the high uncertainty of the transition period, incongruence would seem a rather normal state, and the question would be whether this tends to diminish during the course of democratic consolidation. Several cases suggest that these differences in timing and structural context may institutionalize initial incongruence across classes and sectors. Japan, for example, has not been an easy case to classify since its location shifts considerably depending on whether it is being scored for its workers (close to the syndicalist pole), its capitalists (close to the societal or neocorporatist position), or its agriculture (close to state corporatism). Switzerland is another—if not so extreme—case of incongruence, with labor much less centrally coordinated and monopolistically organized than capital. Elsewhere, the class and sectoral disparities are less marked, but Austria, Sweden, and Norway stand out as models of congruence. Everywhere—even in such otherwise competitive and uncoordinated (i.e., pluralist) systems as in the United States and Canada—agriculture seems to find a distinctively corporatist way of organizing itself!

Together, class governance and congruence (where they are present) play a major role with respect to the partial regimes outlined in Figure 8.1. "Concertation" (direct-link) arrangements—bilateral or trilateral—are difficult to run without them. Agreements cannot be enforced, and parity in representation becomes illusory. The representation regime—the division of labor among associations, parties, and movements—seems to rest on a particularly close networking between the former two and an exclusion of the latter from effective exchanges. Finally, the pressure regime becomes less relevant, because most of the interaction takes place directly with involved state agencies. Parliament is brought in only when changes in fiscal legislation, welfare measures, and so forth are required in order to seal social contracts drawn up elsewhere. All this is very sketchy, but it should serve to illustrate how these two emergent system properties—as well as those of coverage, monopoly, and coordination that lie behind them—can (but do not necessarily) become significant factors in determining what type of democracy is going to consolidate itself.

A TENTATIVE CONCLUSION

Nothing in this chapter proves that "parties are (no longer) the most important part of the representative structure in complex democratic societies."

Rather, on the contrary, these territorially based, symbolically laden, and electorally oriented organizations seem to have a considerable initial advantage in the process of consolidation. Whether they will succeed in converting it into a permanent hegemony within whatever type of democracy eventually manages to implant itself remains to be seen. Since it was in Southern Europe (Portugal, Greece, and Spain) that the current wave of democratization began in the mid-1970s, and it is there that the processes of consolidation are furthest advanced, these should be the countries that can teach us the most about what (if any) changes have occurred in the respective roles of parties, associations, and movements.

Whatever the evidence should prove, the generic point should remain valid. The label *democracy* hides a continuous evolution in rules and practices and an extraordinary diversity of institutions. Just because the world is being swept on an unprecedented scale by the demise of autocratic regimes (themselves of considerable diversity) does not mean that their successors will necessarily follow the paths taken by the democracies that have gone before them. Not only are these neodemocrats likely to try to "jump stages" in an effort to emulate what they regard as the best practices of their most successful forerunners, but they may even come up with novel arrangements of their own.

It seems highly unlikely that they will be able to do without what has long been the hallmark of modern political democracy, namely, its dependence on the indirect representation, rather than the direct participation, of citizens (Bobbio, 1978). They may, however, be able to produce a different mix of the forms that modern representation can take and, in so doing, consolidate a type of democracy that will be more appropriate to the distinctive cleavages and conflicts of their respective societies. This is not to suggest that "democracy by political parties" is about to be replaced with "democracy by interest associations" or, even less, "democracy by social movements." Those pundits in the past who predicted that function would supplant territory as the basis of representation, or that the legislative process would be gradually displaced by tripartite bargaining among capital, labor, and the state, or that identification with party would wither in comparison to mobilization through social movements, were all proven wrong. If nothing else, they should have learned that representation between social groups and public agencies is not a zero-sum matter. It is a capacious realm in which there is room for movement in several directions, as well as for the simultaneous presence of different forms. Whether the leaders of today's neodemocracies, assailed on all sides by social, economic, and cultural conflicts, will have the imagination and the courage to experiment with these forms and to expand the realm of representation remains to be seen.

NOTES

1. A revised, abbreviated, and presumably more widely circulated version was published as Chapter 9 in *The First New Nation* (Lipset, 1963).

2. For this emphasis on uncertainty as "the" characteristic of democracy, see Przeworski (1986, pp. 57-61).

3. The *locus classicus,* of course, is Seymour Martin Lipset (1959, 1960b). It should be noted that in his recent work the level of economic development is described not as a requisite but as one among several "facilitating and obstructing factors" (Diamond, Linz, & Lipset, 1990, pp. 9-14).

4. However, in some cases this experience can be avoided by pulling off the shelf a venerable constitution from the past, as was the case for Argentina and Uruguay during their recent transitions.

5. For a fascinating argument that it is often the "silences" and "abeyances" of constitutions—their unwritten components—that are most significant, see Foley (1989).

6. The standard list of "minimal procedures" can be found in Dahl (1982). For a revised version, see Schmitter and Karl (1991).

7. There will, of course, be infinitely more to be accomplished if the change in political regime is accompanied by a simultaneous transformation in the distribution of wealth, the institutions of private property, the nature of civil-military relations, or the territorial basis of state authority. Where such "simultaneity" occurs (as in Eastern Europe and the Soviet Union), the potential complexity of timing and sequence increases exponentially.

8. It should be noted that timing and sequence have two distinct points of reference: first, with regard to the accomplishment of these tasks in other polities undergoing regime change in the same "wave of democratization," and second, with regard to when and how these tasks are handled within the country itself. Normally, we would assume the latter to be more significant, because so many functional interdependencies are involved, but under contemporary circumstances, communication across national units has become so frequent that the diffusion effects may be quite powerful. Moreover, there now exist a large number of organizations, national and international, specifically dedicated to spreading lessons about the most appropriate type of institutional response.

9. This was the central insight of a long-forgotten and now frequently cited article by Rustow (1960). I have expanded on this, with a great deal of help from Machiavelli, in Schmitter (1985a, 1985b).

10. The most common scenario is one in which the previous authoritarian regime exercised severe and systematic control over parties and politicians representing working-class constituencies but left trade unions and their leaders relatively free to build their own organizations and defend specific clienteles, often in the shadow of the official corporatist system. Spain fits this pattern during the last decades of the Franco regime more closely than do Greece or Portugal. See Zufieur (1985).

11. This is all the more likely in situations where the previous regime has banned or controlled tightly the activities of so-called peak associations that might be capable of coordinating the broad demands of whole classes. The type of associational behavior that emerges during the transition is, therefore, likely to be fragmented, uneven, and localistic, making it even easier to discredit on grounds of "particularism."

12. The "superiority" of parties in organizing for electoral competition will be all the greater where the duration of authoritarian rule has been brief and the leaders, symbols, and ideologies of former parties can be readily appropriated once the transition begins. Greek parties, according to this line of reasoning, had a considerable advantage over those of Spain, Portugal, and Italy.

13. Juan Linz (1983), speaking of Spain, has put the point well, if cryptically: "Politics takes precedence over interests." In the past when manual workers formed a larger proportion of the potential citizenry, trade unions might have been in a stronger strategic position in the

event of regime change. The British Labour party seems a unique instance when unions took the lead in organizing a party, but that was not a case of change in the type of regime. Indeed, the recent successes of socialist parties in Southern Europe (France, Greece, Spain) have been gained in the absence of, rather than because of, these parties having a strong link with the trade union movement.

14. The literature is enormous and varied. For a guide to its complexities and controversies, see Cawson (1986) or Williamson (1989).

15. See, especially, Przeworski (1980) and Przeworski and Wallerstein (1982). In subsequent work, especially that of Wallerstein, the organizational structure of representation is taken into account, but class actors are always treated dichotomously as "capital" and "labor."

16. The Spanish experience with *pactos economico-sociales* has been examined from a variety of perspectives. See especially Perez-Diaz (1987) and Roca (1987); see also Foweracker (1987), Martinez-Allier and Roca (1987-1988), and Espina (1991). In Latin America, there has been much more discussion than actual experience with these agreements. See Grossi and dos Santos (1982), Pareja (1984-1985), Delich (1985), Lechner (1985), Flisfisch (1986), and dos Santos (1988). For an overview by an outsider, see Cella (1990). The most impressive example, outside of Spain, has been Uruguay. See Rial (1985) and Mieres (1985). The least impressive example has been Argentina (and not for lack of trying); see Cavarozzi, de Riz, and Feldman (1986), Portantiero (1987), and Acuna and Golbert (1988).

17. Compare this to the work of LaPalombara (1964, p. 306), who gives this relationship the label *parentela*.

18. That this "decay" may be very slow and that surviving associations, especially trade unions, may struggle to retain the status (and resources) they were guaranteed under state corporatism is especially well illustrated in Southern Europe by the Greek case after 1974.

19. However, the Basque nationalist movement—and, more particularly, its armed militant component, the ETA—is clearly an exception that proves the rule.

20. To my knowledge, there has been only one case—Norway—in which the formation of comprehensive national class associations of business and labor largely preceded that of their respective, more specialized or localized member associations. Norway retains one of the most centralized and hierarchically structured interest systems in Western Europe.

21. A recent study of the peak association of French business is titled *Le Parti des Patrons: Le CNPF 1946-1986* (Weber, 1986). Its main theme is that precisely because capitalists in France lacked reliable and significant access to political parties, they were compelled to rely heavily on the CNPF for the defense of their class interests.

REFERENCES

Acuna, C., & Golbert, L. (1988). *Los empresarios y sus organizaciones: Actitudes y reacciones en relacion al Plan Austral y su interacción con el mercado de trabajo*. Buenos Aires: CEDES.

Aguilar, S. (1983). El associacionismo empresarial en la transicion postfranquista. *Papers, 24,* 53-85.

Bobbio, N. (1978). Are there alternatives to representative democracy? *Telos, 35,* 17-30.

Bruno, M., & Sachs, J. (1985). *Economics of worldwide stagflation*. Cambridge, MA: Harvard University Press.

Cameron, D. R. (1984). Social democracy, corporatism, labor quiescence and the representation of economic interest in advanced capitalist society. In J. H. Goldthorpe (Ed.), *Order* and conflict in contemporary capitalism policy, power and order: The persistence of economic problems in capitalist states. New Haven, CT: Yale University Press.

Cavarozzi, M., de Riz, L., & Feldman, V. (1986). Concertación, estado y sindicatos en la Argentina contemporanea. Buenos Aires: CEDES.

Cawson, A. (1986). Corporatism and political theory. Oxford: Basil Blackwell.

Cella, G. P. (1990). Debolezze del pluralismo in America Latina: Quali possibilita per la concertazzione sociale. Stato e Mercato, 28, 3-27.

Dahl, R. (1982). Dilemmas of pluralist democracy. New Haven, CT: Yale University Press.

Delich, F. (1985). Pacto corporativo, democracia y clase obrera. In F. Delich, Los limites de la democracia. Buenos Aires: CLACSO.

Diamond, L., Linz, J. J., & Lipset, S. M. (Eds.). (1990). Politics in developing countries: Comparing experiences with democracy. Boulder, CO: Lynne Rienner.

dos Santos, M. R. (1988). Pacts in the crisis: A reflection on the construction of democracy in Latin America. Paper presented at the Conference on the Micro-Foundations of Democracy, University of Chicago.

Espina, A. (Ed.). (1991). Concertación social, neocorporatismo y democracia. Madrid: Ministerio de Trabajo y Seguridad Social.

Flisfisch, A. (1986). Reflexiones algo obicuas sobre el tema de la concertación. Desarrollo Economic, 26, 3-19.

Foley, M. (1989). The silence of constitutions: Gaps, "abeyances" and political temperament in the maintenance of government. London: Routledge.

Foweracker, J. (1987). Corporatist strategies and the transition to democracy in Spain. Comparative Politics, 20, 57-72.

Gramsci, A. (1971). Selections from the prison notebooks (Q. Hoare & G. N. Smith, Eds., Trans.). New York: International.

Grossi, M., & dos Santos, M. R. (1982). La concertación social: Una perspectiva sobre instrumentos de regulacion economico-social en processos de redemocratizacion. Critica y Utopia, 9, 127-147.

Lange, P., & Meadwell, H. (1985). Typologies of democratic systems: From political inputs to political economy. In H. Wiarda (Ed.), New directions in comparative politics. Boulder, CO: Westview.

LaPalombara, J. (1964). Interest groups in Italian politics. Princeton, NJ: Princeton University Press.

Lechner, N. (1985). Pacto social en los processos de democratizacion: La experiencia latino-american. Santiago: FLACSO.

Lijphart, A., & Crepaz, M. L. (1991). Corporatism and consensus democracy in eighteen countries: Conceptual and empirical linkages. British Journal of Political Science, 21, 235-246.

Linz, J. J. (1983). Transition to democracy: A comparative perspective. Paper presented at the Conference on Transition to Democracy, San Jose, Costa Rica.

Lipset, M. S. (1959). Some social requisites of democracy: Economic development and political legitimacy. American Political Science Review, 53, 69-105.

Lipset, M. S. (1960a). Party systems and the representation of social groups. European Journal of Sociology, 1, 50-85.

Lipset, M. S. (1960b). Political man: The social bases of politics. Baltimore: Johns Hopkins University Press.

Lipset, M. S. (1963). The first new nation. New York: Basic Books.

Martinez-Allier, J., & Roca, J. (1987-1988). Spain after Franco: From corporatist ideology to corporatist reality. International Journal of Political Economy, 17.

Mieres, P. (1985). Concertación en Uruguay: Expectativas elevadas y consensos escasos. *Cuadernos del CLAEH, 36*, 29-44.

O'Donnell, G., & Schmitter, P. C. (1986). *Transitions from authoritarian rule: Tentative conclusions about uncertain democracies.* Baltimore: Johns Hopkins University Press.

Olson, M. (1965). *Logic of collective action.* Cambridge, MA: Harvard University Press.

Paloheimo, H. (1984). Distributive struggle, corporatist power structures and economic policy of the 1970s in developed capitalist countries. In H. Paloheimo (Ed.), *Politics in the era of corporatism and planning.* Helsinki: Finnish Political Science Association.

Pareja, C. (1984-1985). Las instancias de concertación: Sus presupuestos, sus modalidades y su articulación con las formas clásicas de democracia representativa. *Cuadernos del CLAEH, 32.*

Perez-Diaz, V. (1985). Los empresários y la clase política. *Papeles de la Economia Española, 22,* 2-37.

Perez-Diaz, V. (1987). Economic policies and social pacts in Spain during the transition. In I. Scholten (Ed.), *Political stability and neo-corporatism.* London: Sage.

Pizzorno, A. (1977). Scambio politico e identità colletiva nel conflitto di classe. In C. Crouch & A. Pizzorno (Eds.). *Conflitti in Europa: Lotte di classe, sindacati e stato dopo il '68.* Milano: Etas Libri.

Portantiero, J. C. (1987). La transición entre la confrontación y el acuerdo. In J. Nun & J. C. Portantiero (Eds.), *Ensayos sobre la transición democrática en 'al Argentina.* Buenos Aires: Puntosur.

Pridham, G. (Ed.). (1990). *Securing democracy: Political parties and democratic consolidation in Southern Europe.* London: Routledge.

Przeworski, A. (1980). Material bases of consent: Economics and politics in a hegemonic system. In M. Zeitlin (Ed.), *Political power and social theory* (Vol. 1). Greenwich, CT: JAI.

Przeworski, A. (1986). Some problems in the study of the transition to democracy. In G. O'Donnell, P. C. Schmitter, & L. Whitehead (Eds.), *Transitions from authoritarian rule.* Baltimore: Johns Hopkins University Press.

Przeworski, A., & Wallerstein, M. (1982). The structure of class conflict in democratic capitalist societies. *American Political Science Review, 76,* 215-238.

Rial, J. (1985). *Concertación y governabilidad, proyecto, acuerdo político y pacto social: La reciente experiencia uruguaya.* Montevideo: Seminario de Síntesis, Subprograma Concertación Social en Processos de Democratización.

Rijen, H. (1985). La CEOE como organización. *Papeles de la Economia Española, 22,* 115-121.

Roca, J. (1987). Neo-corporatism in post-Franco Spain. In I. Scholten (Ed.), *Political stability and neo-corporatism.* London: Sage.

Rustow, D. (1960). Transitions to democracy. *Comparative Politics, 2,* 337-363.

Schmidt, M. (1982). Does corporatism matter? Economic crisis and rates of unemployment in capitalist democracies in the 1970s. In G. Lehmbruch & P. C. Schmitter (Eds.), *Patterns of corporatist policy-making.* Beverly Hills, CA: Sage.

Schmitter, P. C. (1971). *Interest conflict and political change in Brazil.* Stanford, CA: Stanford University Press.

Schmitter, P. C. (1981). Interest intermediation and regime governability in contemporary Western Europe and North America. In S. Berger (Ed.), *Organizing interests in Western Europe.* Cambridge: Cambridge University Press.

Schmitter, P. C. (1983). Democratic theory and neo-corporatist practice. *Social Research, 50,* 885-928.

Schmitter, P. C. (1985a). Speculations about the prospective demise of authoritarian rule and its possible consequences: I. *Revista de Ciencia Politica, 1,* 83-102.

Schmitter, P. C. (1985b). Speculations about the prospective demise of authoritarian rule and its possible consequences: II. *Revista de Ciencia Politica, 1,* 125-144.

Schmitter, P. C. (1989). Corporatism is dead! Long live corporatism! *Government and Opposition, 24,* 54-73.

Schmitter, P. C. (1991). *Public opinion and the quality of democracy in Portugal.* Paper presented at the Coloquio sobre Sociedade Valores Culturais e Desenvolvimento, Fundação Luso-Americana para o Desenvolvimento.

Schmitter, P. C., & Karl, T. (1991). What democracy is . . . and is not. *Journal of Democracy, 2,* 75-88.

Schott, K. (1985). *Policy power and order: The persistence of economic problems in capitalist states.* New Haven, CT: Yale University Press.

Streeck, W., & Schmitter, P. C. (Eds.). (1984). *Private interest government.* London: Sage.

Tarrow, S. (1991). *Transitions to democracy as waves of mobilization with applications to Southern Europe.* Paper presented at the SSRC Subcommittee on Southern Europe, Delphi, Greece.

Weber, H. (1986). *Le parti des patrons: Le CNPF 1946-1986.* Paris: Seuil.

Wilensky, H., & Turner, L. (1987). *Democratic corporatism and policy linkages: The interdependence of industrial, labor market, incomes and social policies in eight countries.* Berkeley, CA: Institute for International Studies.

Williamson, P. J. (1989). *Corporatism in perspective: An introductory guide to corporatist theory.* London: Sage.

Zufieur, J. M. (1985). El sindicalismo Español en la transición y la crisis. *Papeles de la Economia Española, 22,* 286-317.

9

Change and Continuity in the Nature of Contemporary Democracies

Juan J. Linz

THE fact that there is currently no alternative to democracy as a principle of legitimacy, and that so many countries have undergone a transition to democracy, compels us to look more closely at the variety of democracies and the ways they function.[1] This has been one, if not the main, theme of the work of Seymour Lipset, and although I have devoted much time to the problems of the breakdown of democracies, the variety of nondemocratic regimes, and, more recently, transitions to democracy, under his influence I have from early on been interested in how democracies work. That concern initially was largely sociological, the basis of politics in Western democracies (more particularly Germany), the Spanish party system, and the work of Robert Michels, with which Lipset first acquainted me (Linz, 1966). My concern in this chapter is to develop a few themes that deserve research in future years.

THE "NEWNESS" OF THE FUTURE DEMOCRACIES

As Veblen (1915) pointed out in his writings on economic development many decades ago, the latecomers will not reproduce the patterns of the early developers. They will certainly attempt to learn from the experience of those who preceded them, but it is not assured that they will always learn the right lessons from the past, and some critics are likely to judge them by their contrast with the early successful democracies. The new democracies are being born into a different historical, social, cultural, and economic context. Some of their characteristics that might be considered weaknesses result from that different context and should not necessarily be characterized as problems for the functioning of those democracies. In fact, with the passing of time, some of the old democracies might increasingly resemble the new ones in these respects.

On the other hand, the dissatisfaction with the actual working of "real democracies" and the almost inevitable pressure for extending, or deepening, democracy to realms of society other than government will in the stable and advanced democracies lead to innovations that might be diffused to "new" democracies. This might produce the paradox that before political democracy is fully legitimated, effective, and consolidated, the new democracies might experience pressures for further democratization for which they might not be prepared. In fact, it might be argued that those innovations might facilitate the process of creating democratic government, or even some substitute for it. There were those who thought that Yugoslav self-management would be the basis for a successful transition from Tito's authoritarianism to democracy.

There seems to be a broad consensus that to a greater or lesser extent the crisis of communism and even Marxism has led to an age of the end of ideology. Not only the crisis of Marxism but also the previous failures of fascism and of conservative Catholic corporatism mean that outside of the Islamic world there is no comprehensive worldview (*Weltanschauung,* to use the German expression) dominating the minds of people as in the past. In much of the world, there remains the most powerful of nineteenth- and twentieth-century ideologies—nationalism—but about that later.

The end, or at least severe crisis, of ideology as an alternative legitimacy formula to that of Western democracy will contribute to the stability even of democracies performing poorly.[2] The overthrow of democracies will lead to a de facto state of exceptional or even emergency nondemocratic rule, but not to relatively stable nondemocratic regimes. We should not congratulate ourselves too quickly, however. The crisis of ideology also weakens the normal functioning of democracies, as we are accustomed to seeing it. Not only were nondemocratic parties ideological, but some more moderate democratic parties of the left and the right were also linked with different ideological traditions. They offered to their militants and even some of their voters divergent views of the good society. Certainly many people in Europe and elsewhere in the last hundred years got involved in politics, some of them passionately, some much too passionately, to fight for those ideas. Parties have always represented interests, but they have also claimed that those interests represented some broader collective interests. This might have been ideology in the Marxist or Mannheimian sense, but it was real. A variety of interests were aggregated by those more comprehensive worldviews, they were not defended as narrow self-interest, and they made possible broad appeals giving some meaning to major political choices in a wide range of policy areas.

The crisis of such ideological constructs, and their substitution by pragmatic interests, calculations, or rational models of policies, will have consequences for the democratic competitive process to which we should be attentive in the future. One of them is that politics in many societies will become less attractive to those moved by ideas—intellectuals, the clergy, the young, even many professionals. There will be idealistic minorities, but they are more likely than in the past to be mobilized by single issues or by a diffuse hostility to politics, particularly to the way in which democratic politics will have to continue functioning. It also will make it much more difficult for militants to develop strong identification with political parties and for voters to develop relatively stable party identifications. It is an advantage compared to the camp, *Lager,* mentality and the irreconcilable *familles spirituelles* of the politics of the 1920s and 1930s, but it also will affect some of the quality of politics. It will be one among other factors, discussed below, leading to a devaluation of politics and, indirectly, of political leadership. Many organizations other than political parties can serve to represent interests. Experts rather than politicians can solve many problems. Parties in order to win elections will have to rely on something other than symbols linked with ideology.

THE FUTURE OF POLITICAL PARTIES

This brings me to one of my main concerns here: the future of political parties in democracies. Some might argue that the parties to which we are accustomed might be obsolete, but I would surmise that without political parties organizing and structuring to some extent the competition for power at all levels of government (the transnational, the state, the regional, or the local level), democracy, particularly in large urbanized societies, is not possible. Many observers of the new democracies complain about the weakness of political parties, the emergence in some Latin American presidential democracies of nonparty leaders such as Fernando Collor de Mello in Brazil or Alberto Fujimori in Peru, the corruption in parties, the volatility of the electorates.[3] They often attribute this to the failure to develop mass-membership parties, weak member participation in the parties, the lack of internal party democracy, and the like. However, we need to think more about how those parties that we now sometimes idealize were born, and even more about which of their functions have been taken over by other institutions or processes, as well as the changed social context that makes it less likely that mass-membership parties will be formed in the future.

Let us remember how mass parties developed in many established democracies. First, there was an industrial working class whose members shared a style of life, an economic and social condition of powerlessness and exploitation, and who responded by joining trade unions to fight for their interests. These unions sometimes created or supported political parties with ideologies that gave hope for fundamental change. Second, there was in many countries a Catholic community threatened by militant, secularizing bourgeois parties and by antireligious or secularizing working-class movements. This community created a mass organization of laymen—the German Volksverein, Catholic Action, and myriad functional groups and sponsored organizations that at one point or another served as a nursery of political leadership and support for the Christian democratic parties. The same was true to some extent for conservative or peasant parties in the various organizations of the peasantry for the defense of its economic and cultural interests.

These conditions have changed radically. The working class is internally much more differentiated than in the past, and in advanced industrial societies blue-collar workers are becoming a minority. The employees who were once seen as white-collar workers are now a large, complex, and differentiated group. Trade unions, for reasons not easy to explain, have lost some of their appeal and their share of members.

Their representation takes many forms, including elections for plant representatives that do not require, since they are mandatory, the same active involvement in trade unions. The changes in the Catholic church, particularly after Vatican II—which legitimated a pluralism of political ideological options within the Catholic community and new forms of religious expression, and came to terms with growing secularization, at the same time militant atheism, secularism, and anticlericalism had lost their appeal—have led to the crisis and demise of the mass organizations of Catholics and the commitment of the church to Christian democratic parties (Parisi, 1979). This does not mean that the existing Christian democratic parties will disappear, but, as we have seen in Southern Europe and more recently in Latin America, the church has not given its full support to those who wanted to revive or strengthen such parties.

If we look at the functions (mass-membership) parties had, we discover that they have lost many of them. Parties needed militants to do many jobs, from campaigning at the factory gates to putting up posters, to socializing the members in the ideological tenants of the party, to paying dues to maintain the party organization. Many of their activities provided forms of sociability that today have lost their attraction, from the *bierstube* mentioned by Michels, where male party members congregated and paid their dues, to the Spanish *casa del pueblo,* where party members socialized, to the *Festa della Umanita,* which replaced the feast around the village chapel on pilgrimage day. Yet new habits of sociability have emerged. Paid vacations enable people to go to the beach or the mountains. On weekends the whole family can get into the car and go to a park for a picnic. The relationship between the sexes has changed in the nuclear family; the sociability of men alone is dead, and mixing politics with family and kids is not the same. Today the militants and the voters can get the party's message on television directly from the national leadership, or the leader who aspires to become prime minister, and attendance at mass rallies, so important in the interwar period, is less and less important. Dues are less important when there is legal or illegal public financing of parties. In addition, parties believe more and more that their success will depend on appealing to the electorate rather than to the small and decreasing number of party militants. In fact, the militants to some extent have lost their usefulness, and that in turn discourages militancy. Again, these changes are not all negative, but they pose new problems for political parties. One of them, to which we will return later, is how—without a significant number of militants—it will be possible for the parties to select from among their members those they will offer as candidates for office at all levels of government. The absurd situation from the traditional perspective that a party might have more positions to fill in local, provincial, and regional government than subscribed members is no longer unrealistic.

In the late nineteenth century and for much of this century, class lines were rigid. Styles of life were very different. Status considerations, snobbery, kept those who moved upward loyal to their origins. Educational differences were enormous. Social mobility, particularly downward mobility, was low. Even without bitter class conflict and ideological hatred, social class served to structure the choices of the electorate. Today social class position in new democracies seems to be a relatively weak predictor of political identification, of self-positioning on the left-right scale, and of the vote itself (Clark & Lipset, 1991, see especially fig. 1, p. 463). Parties cannot count on the same inviolable class or other electoral base, and the same is true with the old vertical cleavages, the religious *zuilen* of Dutch politics (Andeweg, 1982). People today have a much greater variety of interests than those derived strictly from their positions in the labor market. They have second homes and are concerned about taxes on them; they have some investments and therefore are conscious of the economy not only as employees or consumers. With universal literacy and employment linked with paperwork in multilingual societies, language policies might affect them more than the labor market. The prolongation of life and the extension of youth—with a later entry into the labor market and the lowering of the voting age to 18 (and even 16 in Brazil)—gives a new importance to age-related issues, such as pensions and military service.

With all these changes, it is much more difficult to articulate a party program and appeal around simple, traditional class issues.[4] It is also more difficult than in the past to appeal to specific interests on a local level. With the modern mass media, so different from the traditional party newspapers of the 1920s and 1930s, with television spots or campaign speeches rather than posters in different neighborhoods and campaigns in local settings or at the factory gates, it is much more difficult for parties and their leaders to segment their appeals. The detailed party positions and the very specifically directed appeals that, for example, allowed the Nazis to say very different things in different contexts in the 1930s today are almost impossible except for single-issue parties. The parties that want to aggregate large numbers of votes to govern a country are forced to present a much more diffuse and general appeal. A party that has a long history still can be perceived by some of its militants and voters as the party of the workers, but new generations of voters have to identify with catchall parties.

One consequence of such changes will be that parties will have to focus much more on specific issues that might be changing and probably emphasize more the personality of the party leader, his or her strength and charisma. It is easy to attribute this process of personalization of the party image to television, ignoring those other changes that make it more central to the voter to choose the person who will assume the task of governing the country. In some ways democracy is more than ever in many countries a process of choosing a government, choosing a prime minister, and even more a president. This comes closer than before to the Schumpeterian definition of democracy. Such a person can have an appeal across traditional class and party lines, although in a parliamentary system voters would still have to cast their ballots for his or her party and its candidates to assure him or her a majority in parliament, while in a presidential system voters might split their votes between a party and an individual legislative candidate.

CONSEQUENCES OF CHANGE
IN THE NATURE OF PARTIES

These changes in the nature of parties, their organization and appeal, pose some serious problems for modern democracies. After all, parties are not only organizations to obtain the votes of an electorate, they are also organizations to select and promote leaders into multiple offices, from town counselors to the prime ministership. In fact, with the democratization of many institutions, parties have obtained a role in many nonpolitical bodies as citizens' representatives. Now, if we assume that the pool of people willing to join and be active in party organizations, to spend time attending party meetings, congresses, and conventions, is likely to be smaller, this function of recruitment of political elites will be more difficult to perform. It is also dubious that a party with fewer members will be representative of the larger society, and as a party becomes mainly an instrument to attain office, it is likely that the motivations of those joining might be different from in the past. In modern societies parties cannot count on co-opting traditional local notables—landlords, physicians, pharmacists, or lawyers—educated rentiers devoting part-time to a law practice or the management of their properties, nor can they, like the mass parties, count on the lifetime members who combine party membership with trade union office or leadership in the lay organizations of the church, out of a mix of ideological and social pressures, as in the past. If we add that political office today is less and less an avocation, but increasingly demands full-time attention, the professionalization of politics is likely to grow. People are probably less likely to live for politics but to live off politics; the rewards directly or indirectly linked with office become the central motivation for a dedication to politics.

This change implies also a different relationship to the leadership of the party. To be put on the party list of candidates, to be promoted to higher office, becomes more important, and electoral chances become more dependent on the organization than on the personal appeal of the candidate, particularly in list systems with proportional representation. Moreover, with public funding the central party headquarters gains new leverage over the candidates and representatives. The oligarchic tendencies in parties that Michels observed are reinforced by new and different mechanisms. In some cases the legal incompatibility between certain occupational activities and elective office is likely to eliminate another pool of candidates and reinforce the tendencies toward professionalization of politics.[5] Increasingly, political parties become organizations of officeholders and candidates.

One answer to the dilemmas derived from this transformation is to advocate greater participation, more internal party democracy. Those who emphasize the

importance of membership and its participation assume that politics is important enough to a sufficient number of people to generate involvement (Hirschman, 1982), but we have pointed to some of the social changes likely to reduce
participation, except in certain moments of crisis. Participation in parties may
be a shifting involvement, focused more on single issues than on the normal,
day-by-day life of party organizations. It is a question not only of creating
conditions for greater participation but of finding people ready to devote time
to party affairs on a voluntary, unpaid basis. In some societies patronage
opportunities, clientelistic advantages, opportunity for corruption, and the like
will still move many people to join and get involved in parties, but perhaps not
those the democrat would wish to see involved. There will always be a certain
number of ideologically motivated people, but parties that pursue pragmatic
policies may not be happy with party members who are strongly ideological.[6]
We need to know much more about the motivations for joining and becoming
active in today's political parties. Without such knowledge we will not understand the problems of contemporary democracy.

PARTY COHESION AND DISCIPLINE AND DEMOCRACY

Democracies vary greatly in the cohesiveness of political parties, the degree
of discipline of parliamentary groups, the amount of factionalism, the number
of *correnti,* the frequency with which party representatives change parties, and
more. The ways in which parties and representatives behave in parliamentary
bodies vary enormously; Italy is not Sweden and Brazil is not Southern Europe.
Seen from some countries, the cohesion and discipline of parties, their predictable support of government policies, is an enviable quality. Many American
political scientists regard a more disciplined party system as desirable, while
Europeans often complain about the rigidity and stifling consequences of party
discipline. Certainly, if parties are to produce governments and support them
in the implementation of policies, a certain amount of party cohesion and
discipline is necessary.[7] The idea that the executive has to move each member
of Congress to obtain his or her vote for basic legislation seems wasteful and
helps to explain the importance of patronage, clientelism, and even corruption
in the politics of some countries. Intraparty factionalism makes governing
difficult in some democracies.

On the other hand, one can argue that party discipline in parliament, in the
party caucuses, excessive cohesion, and loyalty to the leadership in party
congresses stifle debate and the internal life of parties, making it less attractive
for independent-minded persons to enter politics. As Carl Schmitt (1926) noted
many years ago in his critique of parliamentarianism, party discipline weakens
the function of parliaments as an arena for debate and decision. In modern
democracies, the outcome of parliamentary votes is practically known for the
whole legislature from the moment that the party composition of the legislature
is known. The speeches are made more for the audience outside of parliament

than to persuade the opposition; in fact, the texts of speeches are often distributed before the session, and sometimes no one refers to what the previous speaker has said. Absence from the debate is only a natural consequence. The logic of the vote of confidence that requires party discipline to assure the stability of government ossifies the parliamentary process. It might be time to separate those issues on which the government and/or the opposition decide whether a government should stay in power from those on which a reasonable debate and free vote by members of parliament should be possible. In the debate about the capital of united Germany, Bonn versus Berlin, the parties decided not to impose discipline because legislators had good reasons to support one or another alternative due to the interests of their districts. It was refreshing to see how interesting, lively, and passionate were the arguments articulated by the parliamentarians. Perhaps a clear distinction between issues on which the life of the government should hinge and those on which there is room for diversity of opinion across party lines could enliven the life of parliamentary bodies and change somewhat the image of politicians.

Democracy is based on two principles that are partly in conflict or at least tension: the idea of representation and the idea that the democratic process has to produce coherent government. The first assures the independence of the legislators—representatives—even when elected on a party ticket by voters who may ignore (and do not need to know) who the candidates are but only the fact that they will support certain policies and leaders. The second principle limits the autonomy of representatives by insisting on party discipline, party cohesion, and loyalty to the leadership. In reality, the U.S. Congress (in its House of "Representatives"), with its loose party structure (in many ways a "survival" of the traditional conceptions), represents one extreme, while the rigid "partycracy" in some European parliaments represents the other. Each generates its own frustrations for the democratic citizen and thus its own attempts at reform. The separation of the study of U.S. and European politics, the absence of comparative studies, has helped to hide this tension.

There is no simple solution, but there might be the need to explore some new approaches, particularly in the way parliamentary business is regulated (an interesting area for comparative study) that would make representative democracy more legitimate without making it less effective. Some of my considerations in this essay try to deal with this problem. It is important to keep in mind that the problems of democracy look different depending upon whether one is viewing them from Capitol Hill or Madrid.

There is also a serious question about how democracy works when a party has the absolute majority. We are trained to believe that democracy is majority rule, but the majority generated by the election results is not a majority on every issue that might be submitted to a legislature. When there is an absolute majority, strict adherence to majority rule combined with party discipline leave the opposition with little opportunity to influence the political process, to control the government, to expose even its corruption effectively. The majority becomes a steamroller. Fortunately, in multiparty democracies, unless there is a plurality system of elections in single-member districts, absolute majorities are unlikely.

We are accustomed to negative assessments of multiparty systems and of coalition governments, particularly when proportional representation assures a certain fragmentation of representation. The critics note the much greater likelihood of cabinet crises and government instability, which the citizens mostly attribute to the ambitions of parties and politicians and irresponsible personal conflicts. This vision is very often encouraged by the way in which the media report such crises, but it may also reflect the fact that different parties represent different points of view on different issues; while they can collaborate in a government on a whole range of issues, on others they might part ways and dissolve the coalition, provoking shifting coalitions or dissolutions of parliament. It could therefore be argued that coalition government provides a much greater opportunity for minorities to present their points of view and influence the policy process, and avoids the implications of strict majoritarianism, which sometimes might mean rule by a small oligarchic leadership group or by a single party leader. In a coalition government, even a powerful party leader will have to pay attention not only to those depending on and loyal to him or her but to leaders of other parties and their representatives. A freer decision-making process might result. The study of democracy should focus not only on the processes of coalition formation or on government stability but on the input that different parties make on policies, their capacity to veto some proposals that might deserve to be vetoed and to force the stronger party to pay attention to minority opinions.

One of the interesting findings of recent studies is that voters prefer highly cohesive and disciplined parties, and are ready to punish any party in which internal debate shows disunity, with articulated factions defending different projects (Linz & Montero, 1986; Noelle-Neumann, 1987/1991, pp. 210-211). This fact is consistent with my assertion that voters today vote for a government, for a prime ministership and the party that can support it, and that they therefore fear and reject parties whose disunity could weaken it.

This would be the ideal democratic voter in the Schumpeterian perspective, but if we think of democracy as an opportunity for contestation, debate, and a process of opinion formation based on argument and open-mindedness, such a negative reaction to contestation and debate within parties certainly can contribute to impoverished political life and discourage independent-minded persons from participating actively in political parties and from seeking office in representative bodies.

The point of equilibrium between discipline and free debate within and between political parties, with the aim of convincing others, is one of the central questions in modern democracies. It will be even more central now that antidemocratic parties will no longer play the role of denouncing parties that converge in competing for a moderate center in the electorate.

DEMOCRACY AS GOVERNMENT PRO TEMPORE

One of the fundamental characteristics of democratic politics is that it is based on the regular holding of elections. The voter is free on election day but loses some freedom after it, yet with the expectation that within a reasonable time he or she will be able to exercise it again. Those who lose can hope to win in a reasonable time if they convince enough fellow citizens. Those who today are in power tomorrow may be in the opposition. It is government pro tempore (Linz, 1986b). This is one of the reasons people are ready to accept the democratic process as a way of deciding who shall govern and to accept policies with which they might disagree.

A number of interesting questions emerge out of this fact. How frequently should elections take place? How long will the mandate of those elected last? Should there be limits on the reelection of officeholders? All these questions differentiate democracies and deserve more systematic and comparative analysis. The ideals of freedom and participation would suggest that elections should be frequent. Some would even go so far as to permit the recall of elected officials at any time. On the other hand, we want efficient democratic government, and this means that those elected should have enough time to become familiar with the challenges they face, to formulate policies and legislation, and to implement those policies so that their performance can reasonably be rewarded or punished by the voters. If elections are too frequent, efficiency might suffer and accountability become difficult.

In an age when the tasks of government are becoming more numerous and complex, the time to govern by those elected might be shortened too much by the democratic process. Even if a government can hold its majority together for the whole legislative period and does not see the need to anticipate elections for one or another reason, the time to govern is in many democracies fairly short. The normal four years are reduced by the time it takes to prepare for the next election. In addition, today's governments are affected not only by the outcome of national elections but by regional elections that directly or indirectly might affect the capacity to govern. The leadership of the government and the parties sometimes must devote inordinate attention to those elections, campaigning for the candidates, evaluating the results, sometimes changing policies as a result of a different balance of power in federal bodies such as the German Bundesrat, whose composition might change as a result of *Länder* (state) elections. Even more important, opinion makers, the media, and even the voters often consider those regional or midterm elections a means to punish the party in power at the national level, and may use the results to question the government's capacity to continue ruling effectively. In Europe we have to add to this timetable of elections the elections to the European parliament in Strasbourg. These supranatorial elections have no immediate consequences for the voters and are very often used to express their grievances against the government they might have elected just two years before. Once again the media interpret those elections as a vote of confidence or nonconfidence by the voters in the government, and party leaders again have to reevaluate their actions in view of those results.

If we subtract all the time devoted to these different levels of elections and the analysis of their implications, we can see that the time for effective government might be reduced appreciably. Fortunately, electorates are not that volatile. In some countries they have given their confidence to the same party and the same leaders over several elections, assuring continuity and probably in that way a certain efficacy to the making and implementation of policies. That advantage is obviously lost when there is a principle of no reelection, as in many presidential systems, particularly in Latin America (Linz & Valenzuela, in press). A successful president might not have a chance to continue policies beyond one term, since the individual cannot be reelected. Some democracies go so far as to exclude the reelection of legislators, something that certainly reduces the accumulation of experience in the political class through continuous work in committees on specific problems over a long period of time.

Although we have empirical data on continuity and change in political elites, cabinets, parliaments, and parties, we have not thought through the implications of these phenomena, much less studied them systematically. The debate moves between indignation about the formation of an oligarchy on the one hand and, on the other, appreciation of a political culture in which personal ties between political leaders facilitate the solving of conflicts, and of the accumulation of experience and knowledge that produces better policies. It is along dimensions such as this that we need to compare much more systematically the wide range of democracies.

IS MORE DEMOCRACY THE ANSWER
TO THE PROBLEMS OF DEMOCRACY?

The almost universal legitimacy of the democratic principle in politics is likely to lead to growing demands for democratization of institutions other than the state. Such a demand has very different implications in the context of different democracies, and different societies and cultures, and our enthusiasm for the democratic method should not leave such demands unanalyzed in their anticipated—and, even more, unanticipated but not unanticipatable—consequences. We should give extensive thought to the nature of different institutions in society and the extent to which decision making in them can and should be subject to democratic procedures.

A national political system is not equivalent to the structures that govern churches, universities, armies, business enterprises, cultural institutions, newspapers, and so on. There are good reasons to question the applicability to those more limited institutions of democratic procedures based on the equality of all members (or of all those affected by the decisions of those institutions). I will

not discuss all those problems, but will instead highlight some of the implications for political democracy and different types of political democracy that
flow from the democratization of a wide range of institutions.

In highly politicized and conflictual societies, especially in moments of deep
political crisis, the democratization of nongovernment institutions is likely to
introduce into previously nonpolitical settings, where criteria of professional
competence or dedication to the task should prevail, the conflicts of the larger
society. A conflict that at the political level might be tolerable (even while creating
interpersonal tensions) could—if translated to all settings, particularly those in
which people are involved every day—contribute to even greater polarization. The
extension of the democratic process to a large variety of settings is likely to produce
a process of *Gleichschaltung,* a Nazi term that describes well the synchronization,
the transforming to the same type of voltage, of all institutions that went with
totalitarianism. In fact, the success of Nazism in its drive to power was facilitated
by the takeover of many functional and voluntary organizations by young Nazi
activists, before the conquest of state power by Hitler.

A political movement in a crisis situation is likely to call on its supporters to
vote, even in institutions in which they previously had little interest, in order to
expand the bases of their movement. A classic example was the process by which
members of the *Glanbensbewegung deutscher Christen* (a pro-Nazi church party)
took over many of the Protestant state churches in the church elections in 1933.
Hitler himself, a Catholic, on the eve of those elections made an appeal in favor of
the pro-Nazi candidates and many people who probably never went to church but
had the right to vote (as baptized Christians) followed his appeal. Only the valiant
resistance of a minority of decided churchmen and the threat of a schism neutralized
this takeover (Meier, 1976; Scholder, 1988). The same would be true with nationalist and ethnic movements in many parts of the world.

In more stable and politically apathetic societies the consequence might not
be as dramatic. However, in the absence of other organized groups one would
expect political parties to present their candidates for such representative
positions in a variety of organizations, and the elected leaderships might very
well reflect the distribution of political preferences in the society rather than
the choice of persons particularly concerned and qualified to run those organizations. Democratization in that case would facilitate the penetration of the
parties into a wide range of institutions, directly or indirectly, thus increasing
the potential for clientelism and patronage in the society.

The problem is relevant to our analysis of pluralism in modern societies.
Pluralism and diversity of opinions among individual citizens is not sufficient
to guarantee a fully pluralistic society. Such a society requires a large number
of very diverse and pluralistic institutions, representing different traditions and
values, not responding to the same climate of opinion in the larger society. Just
as many democratic constitutions provide for only the partial renewal at any
one moment of representative institutions, to prevent sudden shifts of opinion
from engulfing them, we should wonder if the pluralism of intermediate
institutions—with their diverse principles of organization, their distinctive

processes of elite selection, their relative autonomy from the wishes of their members and particularly of temporary majorities among them—is not needed to assure the independence of those organizations from political power, their capacity to resist a potential tyranny of the majority and to sustain values that might be temporarily questioned. The fact that churches have their own principles of legitimacy and rule (e.g., the tie of the Catholic church with the pope) allows them to avoid responding to the pressures of political authorities and even on occasion to stand up to their demands. The same can be said about universities, the boards of autonomous central banks, and even in some cases the military establishment. To politicize all these institutions might in a very stable and nonpolarized democracy involve only modest danger to the social, cultural, and political pluralism, but it could be disastrous in a highly polarized society, helping an antidemocratic force to take control of the state.

It could even be argued that the pluralism of opinions of the citizens is sustained indirectly by the linkages they have with institutions that are not dominated by the same general dominant climate of opinion. The fact that different interests control different newspapers, and that those papers do not necessarily reflect the thinking of the majority of professional journalists, even of their own staff, allows us to know the positions of those who have created and sustained those papers.

The penetration of parties, directly or indirectly, into institutions in a comparatively structured society might favor mediocrity. Rather than choosing one alternative, be it an officer, project, or policy, the application of criteria of proportionality would give each segment a share (at the time or over time). This could disqualify the most outstanding potential leaders (from the "wrong" segments), or exclude any controversial choice or alternative. A foundation might have been ready to support a research project, but once parties were represented on its board it would have to consider partisan objections and would prefer to turn to less "sensitive" proposals.

In addition, it is well known that fewer people are attracted to participation and pursuit of office in voluntary organizations and intermediary institutions than in national electoral politics. There is substantial evidence, and Lipset has contributed much of it, that such organizations are more likely to sustain oligarchic leadership due to the apathy of their members.

Pluralism will be strengthened not by proportional representation in a large number of social institutions, but by the existence of many diverse institutions with their own distinctive values and traditions. It is the pluralism *of* institutions rather than the pluralism *in* institutions that supports a pluralistic society.

ELITES IN DEMOCRATIC SOCIETIES

Another theme intimately related to the internal life of political parties is that of elites in democratic societies. Who are the people who will govern us in the contemporary democracies, and what are the mechanisms for their selection or (often more precisely) their self-presentation for political office? The study of elites has been a central theme of the writings of Pareto, Mosca, Michels, Aron, C. Wright Mills, and many others. However, the field has not been as fruitful for the study of democratic politics as we would have wished. Most of the studies have focused on the representativeness of elites in terms of such social characteristics as class background, sex, regional or ethnic origin, and social mobility, reflecting concern for equality of opportunities. The relative accessibility of biographical information of this kind has contributed to this focus. However, more important perhaps than who the elites are in terms of such characteristics are questions about the quality of those elites, their motivations, and their role in democratic political systems, which cannot be answered with standard biographical data. We need much more careful studies of their values and attitudes, incentives and disincentives for entering politics, the rewards and costs of political activity, the linkages between politicians and the society, the ways in which parties elect and reject people with a political calling, the vertical sequence of positions through which politicians rise in parties, and the horizontal paths through which they enter office. We need to compare democracies on all these dimensions much more systematically, rather than focusing on a few parties. Just think of the amount of work being devoted in recent years to Eurocommunism or the Greens, to leadership of protest movements, compared with the relative paucity of research on ruling parties and governing elites.

We hear complaints about the professionalization of politics, the corruption of politics, the oligarchic character of leadership, but very few questions about politics as a vocation. When we study political elites we discover that very often politicians come from families in which there is a tradition of involvement in politics, sometimes over generations and even in very different regimes. To give one example, among the leaders of the democratic opposition and the democratic parties in Spain, quite a few were related to persons who had been politically active in the Franco regime. The simple, explicit or implicit, reaction is one of dismay, of indignation about oligarchic tendencies, rather than an examination of how some conception of public service might be transmitted in the family. The same is true for the research that uncovers the overlaps among elites, the movement back and forth between business and politics, the over-representation of certain occupations, such as university professor, in the political elites of some democracies, without investigating further what these experiences in other areas of social life bring to the political arena and what valuable understanding of the political process is brought to these other occupations by those who have held political office.

The implicit assumption is that politics in the process always loses its autonomy from society and that the groups from which politicians come and to which they return are the only beneficiaries of the exchange. This certainly is true in many cases; corruption and influence peddling are features of democratic politics that should be exposed and prevented. But one can also ask the question, If we make the holding of political office incompatible with other activities, particularly in our increasingly bureaucratized societies, where will political elites come from? We are concerned about the reentry of women into the professional world after they have spent years as homemakers, but we should also ask ourselves if it might not be desirable that people after years of experience in other professional pursuits should be encouraged to enter politics, as well as encouraging the reentry into the professional world of those who have spent some years in politics. Politics is conceived as a service to the community and is increasingly a full-time occupation, and therefore we should ask how it will be possible for people to leave office unless mechanisms are created to urge and facilitate their return to other activities.

The problem of dispensability of certain occupations and the recruitment of political elites was already on the top of the agenda when Max Weber wrote about politics as a vocation, but since then the problem has become even more acute. Rigid laws about the incompatibility of positions in the larger society and the holding of political office sound very democratic and directed to guarantee the public interest, but they might lead to the other danger noted above, the transformation of politics into a full-time, lifetime occupation, which would make the political elite less representative of the larger society, more isolated from its concerns, and much more dependent on party leadership and less independent-minded. After all, we are impressed by politicians who, when they disagree with the policies of their party leaders, are ready to resign. However, we are at the same time ready to limit the opportunities for exit from politics relying exclusively on voice. We want a vital and open political elite, but we might, by a variety of devices and rules within the political parties, create a ruling stratum for the sake of preventing the existence of a ruling class.

We need to think much more about these problems, and to do so we need more data and therefore more systematic research on political elites at all levels of government, including solid research on political leaders (which might be available only after they leave office). The study of political elites cannot and should not be isolated from the study of other elites, since our assumption is that a democratically representative elite should have close connections with all the sectors of society, so that it can inject into the decision-making process the aspirations and interests of the whole society, or as much of it as possible.

We know very little about how politicians in different societies, parties, and offices straddle the multiple and conflicting demands placed on them by executive office, participation in representative bodies, leadership in party organizations, contact with constituents, the media, campaigning, and some outside professional or personal interests. Just a time log of the life of a democratic politician would illuminate the load involved and the strains among those different roles that sometimes might account for the failures that we perceive in the political class. We should also attempt to understand better to what extent our media-hungry society invades the privacy of politicians' lives, without forgetting the invasion of privacy that is associated with the threat of terrorism in many societies. If we had some adequate description of all these dimensions of politicians' lives, and the impact on their personal and family lives, we might ask ourselves why anyone would go into politics, and we might understand better why there is an apparent crisis in the quality of political leadership. Without bemoaning that past times were better, we should remember that even early in this century many politicians had secure lives derived from their personal wealth and roles as local notables, that public office was only a part-time job, sometimes associated with considerable pleasures derived from sociability, which contributed to a relaxed political atmosphere and was not perceived as a waste by a populist electorate. To make the point by referring to extremes, we might compare the Congress of Vienna or Berlin in the nineteenth century, the meetings of heads of state in the spas of Europe, with contemporary international negotiations such as the Madrid conference or the annual summits of the seven leading industrial powers. Perhaps the root of some of the failings of our politicians in their private lives might lie in the strains derived from the public life to which they are increasingly subject. This is certainly an area in which political scientists, sociologists, and even psychologists should be engaged in collaborative and comparative research.

This problem is not unrelated to the need for much more research on the perception that citizens of democracies have of the role and demands put on politicians. In many democracies we find a growing cynicism and distrust of politicians. This is to a large extent justified, but it is also a result of misperceptions generated by mistaken expectations and by the ways in which politicians are characterized in the media. There is a sharp disjunction between the legitimacy of democratic institutions and the bitter criticism of their performance and of the incumbents—what has been called the confidence gap, the democratic distemper. The more democracy is not a challenged alternative that one has to defend whatever its shortcomings, the more intense those feelings are likely to become and the more likely they are to produce well-intended reforms that might be based on insufficient understanding of how democratic institutions work, with many unanticipated and undesirable consequences. We might have exhausted the intellectual fruitfulness of studying electoral behavior. We might in our research on democracies have to turn to more complex issues, such as the perception of leadership and the functioning of a wide range of democratic institutions, without falling into the trap of believing that criticism of incumbents and the working of the institutions is necessarily a sign of a crisis of democracy.

STATES, NATIONS, AND DEMOCRACY

One of the themes to which Lipset, in collaboration with the late Stein Rokkan (Lipset & Rokkan, 1967), made major contributions has been the study of state and nation building in Western Europe in addition to his pioneering work comparing state and society in the United States, Canada, and other Commonwealth countries. It is therefore most appropriate to highlight the need for much more comparative research on the relationship of democracy to state and nation building in many parts of the world and particularly now in Eastern Europe and the former Soviet Union.[8] Unfortunately, the intellectual discourse has been dominated by the idea of nation building, making it equivalent to state building without analyzing the possibility of building states or assuring the survival of states that would not strictly speaking be nation-states, but rather multinational states (Gellner, 1983).

The relationship between two ideas that presumably were part of the same dynamic process, democratization and self-determination, has largely remained unanalyzed. In the nineteenth century, when some of the new nations of Europe were created out of the disintegration of former imperial or transnational structures, such as the Ottoman empire in the Balkans or the confederation of German states in the remnants of the Holy Germanic Empire, the identification between the national and the democratic ideas seemed plausible. The conflicts between the two goals that would plague the twentieth century— when nationalism in many parts of the world was more important to elites and peoples than democracy—were not yet perceived. The founding of the Italian state on the basis of the building of an Italian nation seemed to open the door to democratization as well, although the two processes were not always synchronic.[9] German unification after 1848 already showed how the building of a German nation and a national state contributed to the failure or delay of the democratization process; certainly some German states would have moved faster toward democratization than Imperial Germany. Nor should we forget the extent to which the "pan" movements—pan-Germanism, pan-Slavism, and so on—contributed to the great disaster of World War I, the rise of fascism and nazism, and the crisis of democracy in the 1920s and 1930s.[10]

In many parts of the world, nationalism and the achievement of national unification, the conquest of irredenta, the imposition of national, cultural, and linguistic homogeneity on minorities became more important than the creation of democratic states in which all the citizens, irrespective of national, cultural, or linguistic identity, could participate freely. Nationalism helped to bring to power authoritarian rulers and to support their rule. It is significant that the concept of freedom was transferred from the freedom of the individual to the freedom of the nation and that one of the Nazi party congresses in Nuremberg would be called the *Reichsparteitag der Freiheit* (Party Congress of Freedom), appealing to the freedom of the nation to justify the lack of freedom of the people. We should never forget that democracy is a way to organize political life in a state; unless people identify with that state, and are ready to participate in it by peacefully electing those who will represent and govern them in that state, democracy becomes impossible.

The simple solution of the sometimes quite naive defenders of the principle of self-determination is that all states should be nation-states, that every group that feels it is a nation should also have the right to statehood.[11] Everything seems easy when the historical, legal borders of the state encompass a "nationally" homogeneous population. This, however, is not the case in most states of the world.

Sir W. Ivor Jennings (1956) formulated the problem when he wrote about the principle of self-determination: "On the surface it seemed reasonable: let the people decide. It was in fact ridiculous because the people cannot decide until somebody decides who are the people" (quoted in Buchheit, 1978, p. 9). This in practice means to define a territory in which "the people," or a majority (50.1%? or perhaps a qualified majority, but of how many?), shall decide. The reality of dispersed populations, of people of potentially different national identification living interspersed in the same area, the different ethnic composition of the cities and the countryside, make the application of a "democratic" method to reach self-determination and nation building inviable or extremely costly. Unless the new "national state" admits that it is also a "multinational state," denying "self-determination" to a number of its citizens but respecting their cultures, the principle can lead to deadly conflicts.

The nationalist in addition ignores that people might have dual "national identities," identifying with both a cultural nation and a state not identical to it, and that identities can change over time.[12] Satisfying the principles of both national self-determination and democratic decision making is far from easy, and could well lead to absurd outcomes or results that would only exacerbate conflicts in the future. Robert Dahl (1986) states the problem very well:

> The fact is that one cannot decide from *within* democratic theory what constitutes a proper unit for the democratic process. Like the majority principle, the democratic process *presupposes* a unit. *The criteria of the democratic process presupposes the rightfulness of the unit itself.* If the unit itself is not a proper or rightful unit then it cannot be made rightful simply by democratic procedures. (p. 122)

In fact, the difficulties had been visible as early as when American idealists tried to apply the principle of self-determination after World War I. R. Lansing, an adviser to President Wilson, wrote that self-determination

> is one of those declarations of principle which sounds true, which in the abstract may be true, and which appeals strongly to man's innate sense of moral right and to his conception of natural justice, but which, when the attempt is made to apply it in every case, becomes a source of political instability and domestic disorder and not infrequently a cause of rebellion. (quoted in Buchheit, 1978, p. 65)

And Wilson himself, in hearings before the U.S. Senate Committee on Foreign Relations, said:

> When I gave utterance to those words ("that all nations had a right to self-determination"), I said them without the knowledge that nationalities

existed, which are coming to us day after day. . . . You do not know and
cannot appreciate the anxieties that I have experienced as the result of many
millions of people having their hopes raised by what I had said. (quoted in
Buchheit, 1978, p. 115)

Perhaps the resistance of many democratic leaders to endorsement of the
principle when facing the breakup of a multinational state such as Yugoslavia
or an empire such as the Soviet Union, or the demands of minorities in India,
reflects that earlier experience and the learning from it. However, it makes it
more imperative than ever to study how democratic states can successfully
manage such problems, be genuinely multinational and multicultural, recognize and protect minorities, and generate loyalties not incompatible with
cultural identities.[13] This might require us to question the ideal of the "nation-
state" and to value consolidating liberal democracy more than "national"
integration.[14]

In view of the hesitation of social scientists to believe in the viability of
multinational democratic states, it is paradoxical that we are considering the
full democratization of transnational organizations such as the European Community, which now is governed by the representatives of the member states.
There is a European parliament in Strasbourg directly elected by the citizens
of the member countries, largely along the party alignments in each of them,
but that until now has enjoyed limited powers and to which the decision makers
in Brussels are not yet accountable. The policies of the EC are not the product
of majorities in the parliament but of negotiations between governments.
Would the alignments in the parliament be the same as today, mostly along the
traditional ideological cleavages in European party systems, when decisions
affecting differently the societies and economies of its members would be made
by the parliamentarians? Once they become directly accountable to the voters
for their decisions, it seems reasonable to assume that new alignments may
emerge and that the present parliamentary groups may be questioned. Is it not
possible that nationalist movements would appear, challenging the parties of
the "European party system," just as nationalist parties in the periphery have
challenged the parties of the statewide party system in multinational states?

CONCLUSION

I have sought here to highlight some of the themes that would deserve more
attention in the comparative study of democracies, old and new. They should
be studied systematically and comparatively, but this requires coordinated
empirical research. Thanks to the work conducted and stimulated by Seymour
Martin Lipset, we know more about the conditions for democracy and particularly its stability, but we still need to know more about the quality of
democratic government. By *quality* I do not mean only efficacy or effectiveness—

performance—but the opportunity for open debate of issues by democratically elected leaders and the relative moral and intellectual quality of leaders. It is these other aspects that might allow democracies facing problems that appear insolvable (by political means) to retain their legitimacy and thus survive crises of efficacy. We should never oversell what democracy can achieve, since ultimately the success of a society depends on its economy, its cultural and scientific achievements, and its values and moral climate. These are attributes that governments can enhance, but that escape their capacity to control directly. Nor should we undersell democracy's possible virtues: freedom and some accountability to the citizens. A realistic analysis of different democracies and their limitations will strengthen a democratic regime by limiting the almost inevitable *desencanto*—disillusion and disappointment—that follows the triumph of democracy over authoritarianism.

This essay will serve its purpose if it stimulates further thinking about the many problems democracies face today in different parts of the world. Although democratic theory is and should be the main stimulus for comparative research on democracies, there is much room for thinking based on the concrete experience of different democracies, their successes and failures, and the responses of their citizens to institutions and processes. Much could be contributed by inductive rather than deductive thinking, leading to cross-national research that includes not only the established democracies of Europe but those in other parts of the world.[15] Lipset helped to launch an extensive comparative project on democracy in developing countries (Diamond, Linz, & Lipset, 1988-1989), bringing together scholars from many countries, but that endeavor will not be realized fully without much more monographic research using comparative research designs and instruments. I hope that he and his students might be able to advance that research agenda in years to come.

NOTES

1. Paradoxically, with all our efforts to distinguish democracies from nondemocracies, to study the conditions for stable democracy, the breakdown of democracies, and the transitions to democracy, the literature comparing democracies is relatively scant. Lipset (1990), with his comparison between the United States and Canada, made an important contribution showing the usefulness of paired comparisons. We have the important study of democratic party systems by Sartori (1976) and of their genesis in Europe by Lipset and Rokkan (1967). But with few exceptions there has been less research on the consequences of different party systems (Dogan, 1988; Katzenstein, 1984; Lane & Ersson, 1987; Powell, 1982).

The most important contribution to the comparative study of democracies (resulting from the challenge of the initial formulation of Gabriel Almond) has been the literature on "consociational" democracies, initiated by the seminal work of Arend Lijphart (1984, 1990), who has done the most to make distinctions among stable democracies. Only recently more attention is being paid to such institutional aspects as presidentialism, parliamentarism, and mixed forms (Linz & Valenzuela, in press). Paradoxically, the unique characteristics of U.S. democracy, the "American exceptionalism" to which Lipset has devoted so much attention, has not led to a comparison between U.S. and European democratic institutions, processes, and behavior (except for an essay on participation by Rokkan, 1970), nor their relation to policy output. This has been in part because "Americanists" have limited themselves to the U.S.-U.K. comparison. Such an important distinction as that between unitary and federal democracies, with the ambiguity of federalism in democratic theory (see Dahl, 1986), has not led to systematic comparisons. Area specializations, which have made such important contributions to comparative politics, implicitly constrained the comparison of democracies across geographic-cultural areas.

Now the transition to democracy and the problems of consolidation of new democracies is generating a renewed interest in the question of what differentiates democracies. The work of Giuseppe Di Palma (1990) is in this respect pathbreaking. The incorporation into our analysis of the new democracies in former communist countries, and of emerging Asian-Confucian democracies, should broaden our horizon. This means that social, cultural, and economic structural factors will become even more salient in our research. There is the risk, however, that theoretical and speculative thinking might exceed our capacity to collect relevant data. Cross-national surveys of political culture, of the understanding people have of democracies, are therefore imperative as a step in the formulation of typologies of democratic political regimes and societies and the interaction between social structures and democratic institutions and processes.

Although there is agreement on the desirability of democracy, there is much room for disagreement on its particular forms, as data from the Institut für Demoskopie for the Länder in the former GDR in April 1991 show. When respondents were asked, "Do you believe that democracy is the best form of government or is there some other that is better?" 70% said yes, 7% said there is some other better form, and 23% were undecided (the figures for the old Federal Republic were 86%, 3%, and 11%, respectively). However, when asked "Do you believe that the democracy that we have in the Federal Republic is the best form of government or that there is a better one?" the answers in the former GDR were 31% yes, 26% there is a better one, and 43% undecided (while in the old GFR the respective figures were 80%, 8%, and 12%) (Institut für Demoskopie, 1991). We should not necessarily assume that in all countries the introduction of democratic institutions and processes will also imply the victory of Western conceptions of freedom, tolerance of behaviors culturally defined by the majority as deviant, "separation of church and state," and the like. The recent Algerian election might not be an exception. Democracy in some countries might serve to challenge the values introduced by Westernized elites that electorally might find themselves in the minority.

2. One of the most striking and encouraging findings of survey research in recent years is that the support for democracy and key institutional dimensions, such as free elections and rejection of single parties and of military rule, is uniformly high in the new democracies of Southern Europe, the Southern Cone countries of Latin America, and Eastern Europe. This is true even in those countries where disenchantment (*desencanto*) with the performance of democracy is high, where many people seriously doubt the efficacy of democracy in solving the problems confronting the nation, and feel that either for the society or for themselves things are not going well. It is also largely true for people who do have a positive or neutral opinion about the preceding regime. I doubt that if there had been comparable data for Weimar Germany and Austria in the interwar years the findings would have been the same.

The broad consensus in Eastern Europe on democracy is reflected in the following data from a survey by Bruszt and Simon (1991). On whether "elections are the best way to choose a government and the authorities of the country," on the desirability of more than one party, and on the perceived opportunity for participation, the Eastern European public responded as follows (numbers in the columns represent percentages):

	Elections Are Not the Best Way (percentage)	Favor One-Party System (percentage)	Now in Our Country Everyone Can Have a Say in Matters of the Country (percentage)
Ukraine	22	24	32
Czechoslovakia	20	9	58
Lithuania	12	16	52
Slovenia	11	15	77
Romania	6	14	31
Hungary	6	13	43
Estonia	4	11	41
Bulgaria	3	3	85
Poland		22	92

SOURCE: Bruszt & Simon, 1991.

3. In the new "fluid" politics citizens are likely to agree on the need for democratic political institutions and processes but to express misgivings about the performance of those institutions and even more about the incumbents of political office. This situation is likely to encourage antisystem "outsider" candidacies based on a populist personal appeal, particularly with weak parties and in presidential systems.

4. One paradox of the declining salience of class politics is that cultural issues are likely to become increasingly important: language, ethnicity, regional interests, feminism, life-style, values—concerns that Inglehart (1977, 1990) calls "postmaterialist." The conflict around such issues might be more complex and sometimes less negotiable then economic issues. Wages and taxes are ultimately divisible, so many dollars more or less, but this is not the case with language in the schools and administration, national symbols, even affirmative action and immigration policies, which involve zero-sum choices. These issues cut across class lines, sometimes appealing to groups that are not those most negatively affected, and therefore lead to complex realignments. Territorially based claims might conflict with nationwide solidarities; demands for local self-government lead to new inequalities.

5. We might remember that in the past priests were not prevented by the Catholic church from running for office. The same was true for serving military officers or professionals in the public sector, who now might have to choose between their jobs and elective office. Even national trade union leaders have been led to resign parliamentary seats to be free to oppose the policies of left parties that often are in conflict with the unions.

6. The functional equivalent to European party militants or members in the United States are the "volunteers," the people who show up at the caucuses and the primaries, who in the Democratic party are left of center, and left of the party's potential electorate (Lipset, 1991). While party discipline and patronage in Europe limit the impact of more left-oriented party members, the absence of strong party organizations and stable party leaderships in the United States gives them a greater influence on the image of the party than their European equivalents.

7. Sartori (1989) has rightly noted how the weakness of parties, particularly in the United States, leads to "localism" in politics, surely reinforced by the single-member-district system

and the practice of reporting roll-call votes. For him the United States is eminently the country where national politics turns out increasingly to be "rainbow aggregation of myriads of village-centered and local-minded pressures and counterpressures." He quotes Luciano Pellicane when he says the United States is a polity "rich in micro-deciders and poor in macro-deciders."

8. The fact that, with the partial exception of Spain, the countries in Southern Europe and Latin America that underwent a transition to democracy were nation-states has led to a lack of attention to "stateness" in the process of democratization. Linz and Stepan (1992) would argue that only a democratic legitimation of the central power, as in Spain in 1977, can allow a constitutional restructuring of the state that might hold it together. If instead democratization starts with the component units confronting a not fully democratically legitimated center, breakup may become inevitable. In this respect, the experience of Yugoslavia and the USSR may hold a lesson for the future democratization of Indonesia.

9. Italian unification is often considered the classic case of "nation building," but it can be and has been argued that it was much more a process of "state building." The much-quoted epigram of Massimo D'Azeglio, a leader of the Risorgimento, "Italy is made; now we must make Italians," drew attention to the fact that the work of fusing its heterogeneous regions and populations had hardly begun.

10. The relation between nationalism and democracy—so important in the crises of democracy in the 1920s and 1930s—has acquired new salience with the breakdown of the communist regimes in Eastern Europe and the former Soviet Union. In some of these countries it would seem that nationalism has and is taking precedence over the institutionalization of democracy. This is surprising for Western Europeans, as the decades since World War II have been characterized by a waning of nationalist sentiments. We should realize, however, that the legacy of totalitarian rule—the "flattened" social landscape, the weakness of the opposition organizations—has led to situations where the sentiment that could be most easily articulated and mobilized by the emerging, and even old, communist elites was nationalism (and sometimes hostility to ethnic or cultural minorities).

Recently, East Europeans were asked: "Your country has many problems to solve. Of those conflicts listed on this card, tell me, please, which do you consider very important, somewhat important, of little importance or not at all important." "Conflicts between nationalists and the rest of the country" were mentioned by 50% in Ukraine, 39% in Czechoslovakia, 29% in Estonia, 27% in Lithuania, more than "between those with money and those without" (36%, 25%, 23%, and 24%, respectively). In Bulgaria, conflict between those with money and those without was mentioned by 57%, where conflict with nationalists was mentioned by 28%, and "between those that speak the language and those who don't" was mentioned by 32% (data from Bruszt & Simon, 1991).

11. On the problem of self-determination and its concomitant secession, see Buchheit (1978) and Buchanan (1991).

12. In different surveys in Spain (Linz, 1985a, 1985b, 1986a), the following question was asked of Catalans (and Basques and Galicians): "Now that one speaks so much of nationalities, would you say that you are Spanish, more Spanish than Catalan [Basque, Galician], as Spanish as Catalan, more Catalan than Spanish, or Catalan?" The responses—by native Catalans (and Basques and Galicians), second-generation immigrants, and immigrants from other parts of Spain—show how complex the problem of identity is, how many people feel a dual identity, and how these answers do not simply coincide with the desire for independence. The pattern of responses proves how misleading the exclusivist conceptions of the extreme nationalists are, and demonstrates how plebiscites might destroy a much more complex social fabric compatible with a nonnational multicultural state. The simplistic "democratic" application of the principle of self-determination might generate conflict where other solutions are possible.

13. An interesting example of how a minority national background is not totally incompatible—in principle—with state building, but probably would be with the building of a culturally homogeneous nation-state, are these survey data from the Baltic countries (Klingemann & Titma, 1990): When asked "How would you wish the future of our republic?" given three main alternatives, the natives and Russians in each of the republics answered as follows:

	Lithuanians	Russian Lithuanians	Estonians	Russian Estonians	Latvians	Russian Latvians
Independent state outside of the Soviet Union	81.3	28.8	87.0	16.1	87.2	29.0
Sovereign republic in the framework of the Soviet Union united by treaties with other republic (Confederation)	15.9	41.2	11.5	36.0	9.0	36.3
Independent republic in the Federation of the USSR	2.0	29.4	.8	44.1	2.6	33.7
Other	.7	.7	.6	3.8	1.2	1.0
	(837)	(163)	(621)	(387)	(449)	(460)

SOURCE: Klingemann & Titma, 1990.

14. While nationalism and its articulation with democracy is a most immediate problem, the relation between religious values/culture and democracy is perhaps the most unexplained problem on our agenda.

15. Ideally, we should have a "world barometer" of democracy (as there is now the Eurobarometer) based on regular surveys in all democratic and democratizing countries, whenever possible using a well-thought-out set of indicators. Such a survey could help us to know what kinds of changes and crises (economic, social, terrorism, common crime, and so on) erode the legitimacy of democratic institutions. The indicators about the support or popularity of governments and leaders on which we have to rely are no substitute for a more sophisticated measurement instrument.

REFERENCES

Andeweg, R. B. (1982). *Dutch voters adrift: On explanations of electoral change (1963-1977)*. Leiden, Netherlands: Leiden University, Department of Political Science.

Buchanan, A. (1991). *The morality of political divorce from Fort Sumter to Lithuania and Quebec*. Boulder, CO: Westview.

Buchheit, L. C. (1978). *Secession: The legitimacy of self-determination*. New Haven, CT: Yale University Press.

Bruszt, L., & Simon, J. (1991). *Political culture: Political and economical orientations in Central and Eastern Europe during the transition to democracy, 1990-1991*. Unpublished preliminary report.

Clark, T. N., & Lipset, S. M. (1991). Are social classes dying? *International Sociology, 8*, 397-410.

Dahl, R. A. (1986). Federalism and the democratic process. In R. A. Dahl, *Democracy, liberty and equality* (pp. 114-126). Oslo: Universitetsforlaget.

Diamond, L., Linz, J. J., & Lipset, S. M. (1988-1989). *Democracy in developing countries: Africa, Asia, and Latin America* (Vols. 2-4). Boulder, CO: Lynne Rienner.

Di Palma, G. (1990). *To craft democracies.* Berkeley: University of California Press.

Dogan, M. (Ed.). (1988). *Comparing pluralistic democracies: Strains on legitimacy.* Boulder, CO: Westview.

Gellner, E. (1983). *Nations and nationalism.* Oxford: Basil Blackwell.

Hirschman, A. O. (1982). *Shifting involvements: Private interest and public action.* Princeton, NJ: Princeton University Press.

Inglehart, R. (1977). *The silent revolution.* Princeton, NJ: Princeton University Press.

Inglehart, R. (1990). *Culture shift in advanced industrial society.* Princeton, NJ: Princeton University Press.

Institut für Demoskopie. (1991). *Die Unterstützung der Demokratie in den neuen Bundesländern.* Allensbach: Author.

Jennings, W. I. (1956). *The approach to self-government.* Cambridge: Cambridge University Press.

Katzenstein, P. (1984). *Corporatism and change: Austria, Switzerland and the politics of industry, London.* Ithaca, NY: Cornell University Press.

Klingemann, H. D., & Titma, M. (1990). *Gesellschaft und Politik im Baltikum: Eine Vergleichende Umfrage in Litauen, Estland und Lettland in Juni-August 1990.* Unpublished manuscript, Berlin.

Lane, J. E., & Ersson, S. O. (1987). *Politics and society in Western Europe.* Newbury Park, CA: Sage.

Lijphart, A. (1984). *Democracies: Patterns of majoritarian and consensus government in twenty-one countries.* New Haven, CT: Yale University Press.

Lijphart, A. (1990). The Southern European examples of democratization: Six lessons for Latin America. *Government and Opposition, 25*(1), 68-84.

Linz, J. J. (1966). Michels e il suo contributo alla sociologia politica. In R. Michels, *La sociologia del partito politico nella democrazia moderna* (pp. vii-cxix). Bologna: Il Mulino.

Linz, J. J. (1985a). De la crisis de un estado unitario al estado de las autonomias. In F. Rodriguez (Ed.), *La España de las autonomias* (pp. 527-572). Madrid: Instituto de Estudios de Administracion Local.

Linz, J. J. (1985b). From primordialism to nationalism. In E. A. Tyriakian & R. Rogowski (Eds.), *New nationalisms in the developed West: Toward explanation* (pp. 203-253). Boston: Allen & Unwin.

Linz, J. J. (1986a). *Conflicto en Euskadi.* Madrid: Espasa Calpe.

Linz, J. J. (1986b). Il fattore tempo nei mutamenti di regime. *Teoria Politica, 2*(1), 3-47.

Linz, J. J., & Montero, J. R. (Eds.). (1986). *Crisis y cambio: Electores y partidos en le España de los años ochenta.* Madrid: Centro de Estudios Constitucionales.

Linz, J. J., & Stepan, A. (in preparation). *Democratic transitions and consolidation: Eastern Europe, Southern Europe, and Latin America.*

Linz, J. J., & Valenzuela, A. (in press). *Presidentialism, parliamentarism: Does it make a difference?* Baltimore: Johns Hopkins University Press.

Lipset, S. M. (1990). *Continental divide: The values and institutions of the United States and Canada.* New York: Routledge.

Lipset, S. M. (1991). No third way: A comparative perspective on the left. In D. Chirot (Ed.), *The crisis of Leninism and the decline of the left* (pp. 183-232). Seattle: University of Washington Press.

Lipset, S. M., & Rokkan, S. (1967). Cleavage structure, party systems and voter alignments. In S. M. Lipset & S. Rokkan (Eds.), *Party systems and voter alignments: Cross-national perspectives* (pp. 1-64). New York: Free Press.

Lipset, S. M., & Schneider, W. (1983). *The confidence gap: Business, labor and government in the public mind.* New York: Free Press.

Meier, K. (1976). *Der evangelische Kirchenkampf: Vol. 1. Der Kampf um die "Reichskirche".* Göttingen, Germany: Vanderhoeck Ruprecht.

Noelle-Neumann, E. (1991). Meinungsklima als neue Dimension der Wahlforschung. In *Public opinion in East and West Germany* (Packet No. 22, Political Science 278/438, pp. 207-213). Chicago: University of Chicago Press. (Original work published 1987)

Parisi, A. (Ed.). (1979). *Democristiani.* Bologna: Il Mulino.

Powell, G. B., Jr. (1982). *Contemporary democracies: Participation, stability and violence.* Cambridge, MA: Harvard University Press.

Rokkan, S. (1970). Citizen participation and political life: Comparison of data for Norway and the United States. In S. Rokkan, *Citizens, elections, parties: Approaches to the comparative study of the processes of development.* Oslo: Universitetsforlaget.

Sartori, G. (1976). *Parties and party systems: A framework for analysis.* Cambridge: Cambridge University Press.

Sartori, G. (1989). Video power. *Government and Opposition,* pp. 39-53.

Schmitt, C. (1926). *Die geistesgeschichtliche Lage des hentigen Parlamentarismus.* Munich.

Scholder, K. (1988). *The churches and the Third Reich: Preliminary history and the time of illusions 1918-1934.* Philadelphia: Fortress.

Schumpeter, J. A. (1947). *Capitalism, socialism and democracy.* New York: Harper & Brothers.

Veblen, T. (1915). *Imperial Germany and the Industrial Revolution.* New York: Macmillan.

10

Two New Nations

ISRAELI AND AMERICAN
FOREIGN POLICIES

Amos Perlmutter

I

SEYMOUR Martin Lipset (1963) described the United States as "the first new nation," explaining that what distinguished it from the old political systems was its dedication to the principles of equality and achievement (p. 2). The commitment to these two principles was in America's revolutionary nature, legitimating its political structures. Two other characteristics that justified calling the United States a new nation, according to Lipset, were the forging of a new national identity and the role of intellectuals in politics. Intellectuals were important in fashioning the Constitution and the structures of federalism and the separation of powers.

Liberals such as Jefferson and Madison and conservatives such as Hamilton and John Adams were intellectuals and political theorists, but they were also pragmatic politicians, businessmen, and landlords. These men wrote the *Federalist Papers,* among the world's last truly great essays in political theory. Their writings are among the most enduring in modern times.

Modern Zionism is rooted in the thinking and writing of a group of prolific and stimulating intellectuals such as socialist Moses Hess, positivist Ahad Ha'am, Marxist Zionist Dov Ber Borochov, and liberal Vladimir Jabotinsky. These theorists left their mark on the Zionist political system that emerged in the twentieth century. The American and Zionist pioneers, with all their differences (see Eisenstadt, 1958), were vital to their respective political systems.

Lipset (1963) sees the postcolonial nations of the United States and Israel as associating revolutionary ideas with their national images. Independence and exceptionalism are elitist values, but so are revolutionary ideas. The concept of republican antimonarchism was an eighteenth-century revolutionary idea that inspired the American founding fathers. Socialism was a twentieth-century revolutionary idea that provided the ideological foundation for Zionism. The United States, as a liberal republic of the nineteenth century, and Israel, as a socialist republic of the twentieth century, were both unique for their time. The United States has become an example of a thriving, liberal, democratic political order, whereas Israel is the Third World's most successful social democratic political system (Dull, 1985; Gilbert, 1961; Huston, 1980; Lang, 1985; Varg, 1963).

Can Israel, small in population and size, be compared with the United States, a continent-size nation with a population of 250 million? Nations' territories, populations, and other quantifiable properties can be compared, as can qualitative properties such as value systems, ideologies, and commitments. However, a comparison of the physical differences between Israel and the United States is not as meaningful as a comparison of the ideologies, governments, and political values of the two countries. Comparison of political systems is the essence of comparative politics.

The evolution and implementation of foreign policies can be compared in a manner similar to the comparison of political cultures. Foreign policy is rooted in the geography and territory, but it is also a manifestation of ideological and political concerns. NATO, for example, is an alliance based on common values, not geography; democratic Israel has little in common with its neighboring Arab states, but is close to the United States; the new Eastern European regimes look to the United States for inspiration; and Western Europe is a political concept as much as a geographic entity.

The similarities between early Israeli and U.S. foreign policies reflect the nature of their ideological and moral commitments. Exalted ideas served in the creation of both Israel and the United States. Both were perceived as havens for persecuted people. Both saw themselves as exceptional political systems.

In America, they would build the land of the free, in Israel the state of the free Jews. These ideas were magnets for people fleeing Europe in search of political freedom. The term *old country* is pejorative in both Israel and the United States. Much of early American isolationism and Israel's exclusivity stems from this feeling toward the "old country," a symbol of oppression to both early Zionists and the Puritans.

Both communities invented new political structures and social cultures. The town-hall political community came from the early American Puritans, and the Zionist collective cooperative came from a combination of Jewish and socialist values embedded in the political culture. Representative government and democracy were outgrowths of the pioneer cooperative-communal orientation of early American and Zionist settlers.

How much did ideology influence foreign policy, and what were the other intervening variables that contributed to both American and Israeli political behavior and foreign policy? I shall restrict myself to discussing what Israeli and U.S. foreign policies have in common and what differentiates the two. We should bear in mind that values and goals are modified by systemic variables and the nature of the challenge each country is facing.

II

Paul Varg (1963), in analyzing the foreign policy of the founding fathers, says that "the colonists gave themselves to two contradictory ideas, loyalty to the mother country and self-government at home" (p. 11). There was a close relationship between their domestic and foreign policies. They viewed the existing international system as "inherently evil." To them, America would be the "leader" of the "new order" (pp. 1-3). They wished to enrich other nations with America's revolutionary message to the world.

The founding fathers had two goals for American foreign policy: territorial expansion and commercial reformation (Tucker & Hendrickson, 1990). The challenge for American security was the European balance of power, particularly the Anglo-French European rivalry that spilled over onto the American continent. The Jeffersonian program was ambitious, rejecting a military system characteristic of Great Britain and Europe while at the same time achieving territorial expansion and conquest without war (Tucker & Hendrickson, 1990).

A pioneering political movement is an ideological entity. What characterizes both the American nationalist and the Zionist nationalist movements is their pragmatism, their ability to fashion a consensus between ideological commitment and political action. The political flexibility of the founders of both movements did not translate into opportunism or dogmatism, the abandonment of basic values, or an unrealistic approach to politics.

The founding fathers' doctrine of neutrality turned out to be unrealistic. In the midst of the imperial world struggle for power between France and England over the North American continent, neutrality could only be achieved through political effort. Support of conservative England had to be reconciled with support for revolutionary France, while staying out of their quarrel. It did not mean a surrender of values but, rather, coming to terms with reality.

To survive amid such pressure, a doctrine of neutrality was proclaimed, one with a major difference. Its crucial aspect was that the territory settled by Americans would be governed by the republican democratic institutional arrangement established in 1789. The American order would eventually spread over the continent, with the colonists rejecting the authoritarian regime for a democratic, republican order.

American foreign policy, tied to its domestic sources, was preoccupied with the contradictory principles of neutrality in international politics and territorial expansion. In fact, neutrality would mean that the Americans had an exclusive right to settle North America. This would push America toward involvement in the "evil" European balance of power, while restricting European territorial advances in America. Neutrality for Americans meant an end to European meddling in American affairs. To Hamilton and Jefferson, it meant that as far as the American realm was concerned, the practice of power politics was legitimate.

The Jay Treaty is representative of the founding fathers' competing ideologies and orientations. The diplomacy that resulted in the treaty demonstrates the consensual action of the founding fathers. The treaty represented a battle over values and the political future of the United States.

According to Combs (1970), a student of the Jay Treaty, "The treaty that John Jay negotiated with England in 1794 was one of the most crucial in United States history" (p. ix). Madison and Jefferson felt it was an "appeasing" settlement with England. "America," they argued, "was powerful enough to have extracted concessions from England" (p. ix). The federalist historians felt differently. Combs is right in saying that "Federalist and Republican alike sought to balance goals with power available" (p. x).

The American response to the European challenge "was determined to a great extent by the actions and attitudes of six men, George Washington, John Adams, John Jay, Alexander Hamilton, Thomas Jefferson and James Madison" (Combs, 1970, p. 15). In spite of the ideological differences that existed among them, their response in the end created consensus. They all felt that British hostility "brought the growth of sentiment in the United States for a stronger central government" (p. 27). Hamilton was confident in the American ascendancy and sought to undertake "a glorious foreign policy" (p. 47). Jefferson and Madison had "a pacific temperament" (p. 65), recognizing the necessity of national power in foreign affairs, while at the same time apprehensive of that power in domestic use.

Neutrality thus meant different things for different men. Hamilton believed that England, with its involvement in a war against France, might jeopardize America if America supported France. But "while Hamilton saw danger in a war between Britain and France, Jefferson saw opportunity" (Combs, 1970, p. 110). For Jefferson, neutrality meant taking advantage of European great power antagonisms. The federalists prepared for war with Great Britain but were ready to negotiate peace if necessary. Both the federalist and republican approaches to the Anglo-American crisis were "direct continuations of the politics formulated by Jefferson, Madison and Hamilton in the period immediately following ratification of the Constitution" (p. 133). The federalist view prevailed.

In practice, neutrality meant defending the principles of the balance of power. "Americans of the revolutionary generation thought of foreign affairs in terms of the balance of power . . . because they genuinely believed that it was a progressive principle in international relations" (Huston, 1980, pp. 9-10). The Jay Treaty demonstrated the consensus on foreign policy among revolutionary Americans, "a consensus formed around the classical European diplomatic concepts of the balance of power and the interests of states" (Huston, 1980, p. 12).

The foreign policy of the American Revolution was not revolutionary. The federalist foreign policy, or the Hamiltonian program, was modern and politically farsighted. It established an American credit by paying the revolutionary debt with British and other European capital to enhance domestic manufacturers, establishing the essence of American commercial and industrial policy.

The Hamiltonian and Jeffersonian ideologies were irreconcilable. According to Tucker and Hendrickson (1990), Jefferson preferred a "diplomacy guided above all by a commitment to peace. War was not absolutely precluded. But it was accepted only in the extreme" (p. 1). "Passivity and determination to avoid war marked the diplomacy of the Jefferson administration during the Louisiana Purchase" (p. 53). The failures of Jefferson's second administration (1804-1808) were connected not merely "to exiguous circumstances. His political vision was central to his failure." He failed to accommodate with Britain for ideological republican reasons, not for "his aversion to war" (p. 54). According to Tucker and Hendrickson, "His moralism . . . not only constituted the central aspect of his diplomatic outlook but is also identifiable as the primary corrupting factor within it" (p. 54).

Whatever the ideological differences among the founding fathers, the formulation and practice of foreign policy was achieved through consensus. Huston (1980) is right in saying that American revolutionary diplomacy was not "idealistic and internationalistic," nor was it influenced by the "philosophers," both French and English. Rather, it was pragmatic and nonrevolutionary, following the traditional diplomacy of Europe. Pragmatism, as personified by territorial expansion, fueled early American diplomacy.

III

The Israeli political system was divided between moderate social democrats and the radical Marxist left (Horowitz & Lissak, 1978; Kimmerling, 1983; Perlmutter, 1957, 1985). The dominant political power in Palestine and later Israel between 1920 and 1977 was the democratic socialist camp. But within its three major institutions—the party, the trade unions (*Histadrut*), and the agricultural cooperative collective (*Hityashvut*)—the ideological divisions ran deep.

The debate, which raged from the second *Aliyah* (immigration) of socialist pioneers of 1904 right through the early 1960s, centered on three themes: the nature and structure of the Jewish society and later state, the method of exploitation of land and labor, and the formulation of foreign policy and alliances.

Mapai advocated the formation of a socialist agricultural workers' union system. The conquest of the land and of labor, the essence of Zionism, saw the nationalization of the land as a Zionist, not a Marxist, idea. Economic institutions must be harnessed for social and later state functions. Although all socialist Zionists advocated an agrarian socialist society, they differed over what institutions should be preeminent. The moderates preferred the party and *Histadrut*; the radicals preferred agricultural collectives, seeing in them the seeds of a Zionist republic of kibbutzim.

The prestate moderates advocated the exploitation of Jewish capital for socialist Zionist purposes. The moderates' David Ben Gurion embraced and advanced the Zionist estatist over the Zionist socialist idea (see Perlmutter, 1985). The radicals were followers and students of the Marxist Zionist doctrines of Dov Borochov, who hoped to combine Marxist collectivist ideology with Zionist nationalist purposes (see Mintz, 1976; Perlmutter, 1968). For this group, the republic of kibbutzim was the essence of the idea of Zionist settlement. They would not be a colonial settlers group dependent on Arab labor. They advocated the blending of Marxism with aggressive settlement of the land, as advocated by the Ahdut Haavoda party, which split from Mapai in 1946 (not to be confused with the early Ahdut Haavoda, which was the parent party of Mapai) (Gorni, 1973).

Even further to the left was Hashomer Hatzair, a movement directly influenced by radical socialist, Leninist-Marxist ideas. Their kibbutzim were not merely farms but fortresses of ideological collectivism, a peculiar form of Leninist Zionism (Margalit, 1971), which meant submitting the kibbutzim movement to rigid, doctrinaire Marxist ideas.

Hashomer Hatzair, formed in the 1920s, joined Ahdut Haavoda, which had split from Mapai in 1946, forming the Mapam Marxist Zionist party. Thus, by 1946, two prestate socialist camps, the majority Mapai and the minority Mapam, were struggling over the nature of Israeli society and foreign policies.

The debate between the two socialist camps resembled the debate in the Hamilton-Jefferson parties. The Jeffersonians were inclined toward revolutionary France, whereas Mapam favored revolutionary Russia. The Hamiltonians sought to buttress federalism in an economic doctrine of manufacturing and a national bank; the Mapai-Ben Gurion school of estatism sought to solidify the state. The former favored England, the latter America.

The idea of the state was the essence of both Hamilton's and Ben Gurion's nationalism. Hamilton sought to make a federal union out of an unsuccessful, unworkable confederation, while Ben Gurion identified with the creation of modern state structure to supersede the Zionist volunteerist, collectivist, and radical socialist institutions. Jefferson's empire of liberty and Hamilton's heroic state were both dedicated to territorial expansion. Ben Gurion sought permanent borders (Shlaim, 1989). He sought to formalize the institutions of the new state, end ideological rancor, and establish secure frontiers, by force when necessary. The achievement of Ben Gurion during the war for Israeli independence was similar to the achievements of the founding fathers during the American Revolutionary War.

The diplomacy of Zionism between 1945 and 1947 was dependent on the support of the two superpowers. Mapai and Ben Gurion opted for alliance with the United States, Mapam preferred the Soviet Union, and Mapai Foreign Minister Moshe Sharett advocated Israeli neutralism, what was called a policy of nonidentification (Bialer, 1990).

At the birth of the state of Israel, the two socialist camps agreed that Israel should choose neutrality, a "nonalignment" policy advocated by the emerging Third World and leaders of the Nehru-Tito generation. Discussion of nonalignment or nonidentification was influenced by ideological considerations of "essentially domestic relevance to the Mapai party itself" (Bialer, 1990, p. 10).

The Zionist diplomatic struggle for independence and recognition, like that of early America, depended on the role of the great powers. The two young nations, each in its time, wanted the support of the superpowers of their time without committing to either camp. Eventually, circumstances and inclination pushed them to seek friendship with one of the powers at the expense of the other of the proclaimed neutrality.

The ideological divisions over the nature and structure of Israel and the United States were tied to different interpretations of international realities. In Israel, Mapai and Sharett said they "would knock on any door" (quoted in Bialer, 1990, p. 10). Ben Gurion said, "The Zionist camp should leave all its options open" (quoted in Bialer, 1990, p. 14). But the radical left Zionists wanted to join the so-called progressive world, led by the Soviet Union and including Eastern Europe and the Third World (when Nasser became a leader in the Third World, the leftist Zionists tempered their enthusiasm).

The socialist Zionists saw the postwar world in terms of the struggle between socialism and capitalism. This was complicated by the ideological visions of Mapai and Mapam. Mapai was a party to the moderate Second International. Mapam, although not a member, was inclined to believe that the communist camp would be the winner in the emerging world order. The Soviet victory over the Nazis, Soviet domination of Eastern Europe, and the role of Jews in Eastern European communist movements influenced Mapam, which went even further to the left after 1946.

The majority Mapai party tended to be more nationalist and less radical, but it could not identify itself with the capitalist states, especially Great Britain. It also abhorred Stalinism. Mapai leaders hoped that the new British Labour government would favor the Zionists, but Foreign Minister Ernest Bevin quickly dashed that hope (Bullock, 1983; Gorni, 1983; Wallach, 1985).

Mapam, especially its Hashomer Hatzair movement, was dedicated to the Soviet Union between 1945 and 1946, falling into Stalin's trap of promoting the idea that communism liberated Europe from Nazism. Soviet propaganda called World War II the war of the great liberation, and this played well to Mapam, especially since key Jewish Communists were now heading Eastern European governments, some of them being early members and followers of Hashomer Hatzair and the leftist Zionist youth movement (Perlmutter, 1985).[1]

Stalin and the Soviet Union were the coming powers, whereas Great Britain was waning. Mapam and Hashomer Hatzair perceived the new partition of Palestine as showing that Soviet support of Zionism would triumph over British imperialism (Roi, 1974).

During the Second World War years, the Yishuv followed with great concern the retreats and advances of the Red Army. Rommel was moving into the Middle East and the Nazi armies could have ended up encircling Iraq, Syria, Palestine, and Egypt, bringing the Jewish tragedy of Europe directly to the Yishuv. The Yishuv leadership had no faith in the British Army, which had absorbed one defeat after another at the hands of Rommel early in the war. To them, the Red Army became a kind of protector. League V (for victory), a pro-Soviet Zionist Yishuv committee, propagated the Father Stalin mythology in Palestine (see Rapaport, 1990; Redlich, 1988). Russian movies extolling the courage of the

Red Army were popular cinematic fare in Tel Aviv and elsewhere in the Yishuv. Russian war songs were popular among members of the socialist youth movements. The left planned a partisan republic on Mount Carmel, similar to Tito's partisan ideas, and contacts between them were frequent and cordial.[2]

Thus ideological influences—for Jeffersonians, the French Revolution; for Mapam, the Russian Revolution—determined much of what influential founders advocated regarding the state and international relations.

The first chapter of Bialer's (1990) section titled "Red Star Over Zion" locates the underpinnings of early Israeli foreign policy: "Let My People Go" (p. 57; see also Krammer, 1974; Roi, 1980). It was in the Eastern European countries where the last remnants of European Jews remained after the Holocaust.[3] Hungary, Romania, and Bulgaria had been nominal allies of the Nazis and were permitted a degree of independence in the conduct of their domestic affairs. As a result, in Bulgaria and Romania the Jewish communities were unharmed, at least until 1944. Virtually all of Bulgaria's Jews escaped the horrors of the death camps (Chary, 1972).

The Zionist leadership prepared to save the Balkan Jewish remnant. This had a particular influence on Israel's concept of nonidentification. Mapam saw immigration from the Balkans as linked to and enhancing its pro-Soviet orientation.

For Ben Gurion and Mapai, saving the Eastern European Jewry was rooted in pragmatic, not ideological, policy. Unlike any other new state in modern times, without Jews there would be no Israel. America was a nation of different immigrants seeking to escape oppression in Europe (Hartz, 1962). Israel's promise was to gather in the Jews of Europe who survived the Holocaust. Immigration from Europe—*Aliyah*—was conducted secretly and organized by Mossad (Bauer, 1970; Hadari, 1991). Ben Gurion saw the Eastern European countries as a reservoir for continued Zionist settlement in Israel. The great dream was to bring in the Soviet Jews, but that dream had to wait until Gorbachev's more liberal immigration policies of the late 1980s and early 1990s.

For Ben Gurion, territorial security was not the "core interest of the state . . . it is Aliyah. . . . Perhaps we could capture the triangle [the northwest part of the West Bank], the Golan, the entire Galilee, but such victories could not bolster our security as much as immigration" (quoted in Bialer, 1990, p. 59).

Israeli policy was divided, as it had initially courted both superpowers. Prestate Zionist diplomacy concentrated on Great Britain until 1945. Between 1945 and 1947, the United States and the Soviet Union became critical targets for Israeli diplomacy. In fact, Israel benefited from both superpowers, because both supported the partition of Palestine in the United Nations. This was a difficult task with the United States, which was reluctant to challenge British policy and Arab regimes (Ganin, 1979; Ilan, 1979, 1980; Snetsinger, 1974; Wilson, 1979).

America's Israeli policy began with President Truman's commitment to the immigration of 100,000 displaced Jews to Palestine and ended with the recognition of Israel, standing against a powerful tide of antipartition forces in the

U.S. bureaucracy (Eilat, 1979-1982; see also Ganin, 1979; Ilan, 1979, 1980). America's position on partition was not clear until the final decision was made.

The Soviets seemed to have no great interest in the Middle East, in spite of Stalin's encouragement of "progressive" Arab regimes (Krammer, 1974, p. 32). Yet the Soviet Union's acceptance of the U.N. resolution on the partition of Palestine in November 1947 amounted to a reversal of Soviet policy.[4] In the end, it was the tacit coalition of the United States and the Soviet Union against Great Britain that brought about the partition of Palestine. This temporary ideological "adjustment" on the part of the Soviets toward Zionism was especially beneficial to Israel at a time when the U.S. delegation and some senior state department officials were trying to derail Truman's support for partition in favor of a trusteeship (Brands, 1991; Clifford, 1991; Eilat, 1979-1982; Wilson, 1979). Soviet Foreign Minister Gromyko's rush to the United Nations to vote for partition strengthened the left's position and the Mapam camp. Even Ben Gurion became sentimental for a moment (see Ben Gurion, 1982, p. 235).

Krammer (1974) explains the Soviet motives in supporting partition: It would provide an opening to the Middle East for the USSR, it would help end British domination in the area, and it would gain support for Soviet policies from the Zionist left (pp. 32-35).

The era of political cooperation between Israel and the Soviet Union was short and ended in bitterness that would not subside until the rise of Gorbachev. While it existed, however, it was beneficial for the fledgling state of Israel. The Soviets played a key role in the strengthening of the IDF, through the Czech-Israeli arms deal of 1947, which helped overcome the U.S.-British embargo on arms. The Soviet vote for partition not only strengthened the Zionist left but bolstered Ben Gurion and Mapai, in spite of their fierce anticommunist stance.

Lissak (1981) notes that 78% of Israel's elites came from Eastern Europe and that the second generation of Israeli leaders were the sons and daughters of those elites. For a time, Zionist leaders hoped that perhaps the anti-Zionist wall had finally been broken. The *Aliyah* from Eastern Europe and the USSR's decisive role in the United Nations "generated a hope—cautious but nevertheless tangible—that policy-makers stood on the verge of a significant turning point in the traditional Soviet attitude toward Israel" (Bialer, 1990, p. 137). The hope was short-lived.

The last years of Stalin (1950-1953) were the worst since 1937-1941. Stalin's paranoia and totalitarian tendencies all combined to begin another round of destruction that might have rivaled the great purges were it not for Stalin's death. He hunted Soviet Jewish doctors and prepared for a great purge of Soviet Jews (see Rapaport, 1990, pp. 55-79). The latest outburst became a struggle against former Marxist Zionist members among the Communist rulers and elites of Czechoslovakia, Hungary, and Romania. These purges were impossible for Stalin's admirers among the leftist Zionists in Israel to comprehend, nor were they understood by Israeli diplomats in Eastern Europe. Golda Meirson (Meir), a senior Mapai leader and Israel's first ambassador to Moscow, spoke before crowds of Jewish supporters on Israel's independence day when Stalinist authorities began muzzling and isolating Israeli diplomats in Moscow. She and her embassy had been acting as Zionist missionaries to Stalin's oppressed Jewry. Stalin retaliated against this "intervention" by purging former Hashomer Hatzair members who had become Communist leaders in Czechoslovakia (see Kaplan, 1990).

In the face of the new Soviet stance, Israel's policy of neutrality could no longer be sustained. After 1951, the foundation for neutrality disappeared as Stalin turned from supporting Jewish sovereignty to slavish support of every radical, praetorian Arab regime, including Nasser and the Syrian military between 1952 and 1955. The era of innocence was over for Israel.

The turnabout in Israel's policy from neutralism to a pro-Western—specifically, a pro-American—stance began over the issue of the Korean War, when Israel voted in the United Nations to support intervention in Korea. Israel hoped that the United States would realize that what was happening in Korea was symptomatic of the same kind of aggression practiced by the Arabs in 1948. In June 1950, Israel's political leaders convened a meeting of the diplomatic corps in order "to re-examine the diplomatic line and to see whether our policy should be adhered to or changed" (Bialer, 1990, p. 218). On July 2, 1950, Israel's cabinet had unanimously supported the American position. Ben Gurion told the diplomats in a lecture called "Israel Between East and West" that Israel needed to both preserve and, more important, modify its nonidentification policy (Bialer, 1990, p. 221). The foreign minister said that "the network of our relations with the United States constitutes the most important of all Israel's external relations" (quoted in Bialer, 1990, p. 221).

The Korean decision was not an enthusiastic one, but it was foisted on Israel when the United States demanded that "the Jewish state stand up and be counted" (Brecher, 1974, p. 113). This was accompanied by opposition, especially from the left, when Mapam joined Maki, Israel's Communist party, in condemning the decision to support U.S. intervention in Korea.

Even the so-called American school among Israel's elite did not advocate complete abandonment of the neutrality policy: "We have never asked to join the Marshall Plan or any regional pacts," said Abba Eban, a leader of the "American camp" (Bialer, 1990, p. 223). Ben Gurion pushed for the creation of a political strategy involving a de facto link with the United States. Even though Ben Gurion was ready to go along with a nonidentification policy temporarily (Bialer, 1990, p. 224), he opposed what he saw as its ideological underpinnings, which were tantamount to a surrogate Soviet policy in the Third World.

Ben Gurion never hid his attitude toward neutrality, or his willingness to do anything to achieve his goals. He said once that he would "refuse to give up his soul, but would give up his pants for absorption of immigration" (Bialer, 1990, p. 224). He correctly saw neutrality as a trick, "a communist political maneuver" (p. 225). Bialer writes that "access to Israeli cabinet protocols is still barred," making it difficult to establish Ben Gurion's position (p. 225). It is possible, however, that Ben Gurion was so absorbed in strengthening the IDF that he could not avoid making the Korean decision that he did, which also bolstered Israel's military position. Ben Gurion's lack of enthusiasm for ideological neutrality was in conformity with his long-standing struggle with the Zionist left in all of its manifestations. Ben Gurion, the estatist, clearly realized the crucial importance of the United States and American Jewry for Israel. With Eastern European immigration dwindling, with the Soviet gates shut, the principal reasons for supporting nonidentification no longer existed and were no longer practical. Ben Gurion sought a military alliance with the United States, as events in the late 1950s and early 1960s demonstrated.

When it came to Arabs, Ben Gurion's view, however complex, was also clear (see Perlmutter, 1985; Teveth, 1985). The Arabs were not willing to accept Zionism or partition, and only a strong Israel, backed by a powerful IDF, would deter Arab military action, if not their goals. The only way to negotiate or come to terms with the Arabs was from a position of strength. Sharett, more optimistic than Ben Gurion, believed in coming to terms with the Arabs and in the need for substantive, serious compromise with them. Sharett was apprehensive about the drift away from the Soviet Union, but Ben Gurion moved strongly toward the United States (Brecher, 1974, p. 253).

The core of Ben Gurion's foreign policy was "the restored state of Israel," and that idea of "restoration" influenced his global politics and thinking, a restoration to the "values of human freedom, freedom of thought and spirit," to an "affinity of values" (quoted in Brecher, 1974, p. 265). This meant a robust pragmatic Hamiltonian vision of international politics, with security and the IDF as the bulwark of the Israeli republic. For Sharett, diplomacy meant negotiation and balanced alliances as the key to a workable foreign policy. He would pursue nonidentification until the outbreak of the Korean War (Brecher, 1974, p. 220). Sharett believed in conflict resolution, reconciliation, and territorial compromise as a way to achieve a stable peace with the Arabs.

IV

What lessons did the two young and idealistic republics learn from their experiences? They were hopeful that their example would serve as a light to other nations. They were not always successful in that goal.

Their experience was often a balancing act that caused debate and division. They needed to reconcile legalism and moralism with the pursuit of international power politics and the balance of power. The dilemma was how to bring to consonance the idea of just war with balance of power theories (Lang, 1985). "Just war champions tended to reduce balance of power advocates to the status of mere power politicians, while balance of power thinkers condemned just war theorists as crusaders or even virtual pacifists" (Lang, 1985, p. 1).

Washington's neutrality and Sharett's nonidentification policy emerged not so much as a result of empirical conditions but as moral policies to suit the pioneers of the new republics. Conducting impartial relations with Great

Britain, France, and Spain for the United States and pursuing nonidentification with the United States and the Soviet Union for Israel were, in the end, policies that were not realizable because of the realities of international politics. Classical political theory that informs international law and relations depends more on "unforeseeable circumstances" than on the moral stature and the wisdom and "discretion of wise and prudent rulers" (Lang, 1985, p. 2).

The balance of power in Europe was an objective condition for the success of the American revolution. The tacit bargaining over partition on the part of the United States and the Soviet Union was a reality from which an independent Israel could emerge.

Thus we come back to James Huston's (1980) provocative monograph on John Adams, in which he concludes that "the foreign policy of the American Revolution was not revolutionary" (p. 1). Diplomacy based on power was an eighteenth-century practice. The fact that Israel became independent as a result of action on the part of the United Nations, a universalist collective security organization, does not deny the fact that it was achieved by virtue of Soviet-American balance of power politics in the Middle East. Soviet motivations may have been colored by postwar foreign policy, and America's purposes in partition were both moral and domestically oriented, but the result amounted to a bargaining transaction for power between the two superpowers of the time, each perceiving its action in its own light.

International politics and "the peace did not sustain the American broad neutralist interpretation of the law of nations" (Lang, 1985, p. 159). The great powers continued their European rivalry into the American continent, just as the U.S.-USSR Cold War rivalry spilled over into the Middle East and changed alliances and alignments and the local and international perception of friend and foe.

It is significant that most of the American Revolution's leaders matured during the French and Indian Wars (Huston, 1980, p. 4). Zionist leaders had as their experience Hitler, the Holocaust, European and Arab anti-Semitism, and Stalinism. With the exception of some marginal Mapam Marxist-Leninist ideologues, none of the early American and Zionist leaders was oblivious to the nature of power in all of its forms. Hamilton and Jefferson, as well as Ben Gurion, were nationalists first and revolutionaries second. Yet their rhetoric on foreign policy was always clothed in universalist, moralist language and, in the case of the Zionists, even apocalyptic and metaphysical language.

Steering between the major powers of their time was the difficult task of the leaders of the new nations. For the Americans, this meant formulating a response to the European balance of power, staying out of European conflicts yet remaining involved. It was not so much a matter of choosing between France and England for the early Americans or between the United States and the Soviet Union for Israel, for neither could afford to antagonize or alienate the contemporary superpowers. Overt and covert diplomacy was always pursued by the two new nations as a way to advance their territorial and security aspirations. Yet "neutrality had been the great desideratum of American foreign policy from the early days of the revolution" (Lang, 1985, p. 93).

American statesmen, including Hamilton and Jefferson, "generally under-stood the best policy to be that of remaining as little entangled as possible in the policies and controversies of the European nations" (Lang, 1985, p. 93). This did not prevent American leaders from taking advantage of breakdowns in the European balance of power. Hamilton, ahead of others, understood the threat posed by the French Revolution to European legitimacy and the balance (Lang, 1985, p. 92). Jefferson was more ambivalent, but he did not miss the opportunity to suspend French treaties in 1793, acting as secretary of state, on "constitutional, legal and prudential grounds" (Lang, 1985, p. 94).

America's inability to conduct war called for pragmatic neutrality. Israel's policy of nonidentification did not stem from regional military weakness but from a desire to take advantage of both camps, expediting Jewish immigration from the Soviet bloc while getting political and economic support from the United States.

Neutrality is not only the result of strength or weakness, but is sometimes spurred by the desire to avoid war. This has not always worked well for Israel. The end of neutrality and the turning away of the Soviets resulted in several Arab-Israeli wars. It is doubtful that the Arab states would have contemplated war without the military and political-diplomatic support they received from the Soviet Union.

Ben Gurion, like Hamilton, was a defender of the national interest, and he understood that the creation of new nations must be forged in war. Hamilton, "as befitting a military man, put a high value on the possession of strategic assets" (Lang, 1985, p. 124). In his advocacy of war with revolutionary France, Hamilton was echoed by Ben Gurion, who foresaw and prepared for a second round of war with the Arabs. He had no faith in negotiations or the armistice.

Jefferson's purchase of the Louisiana territory from the French had its counterpart in Ben Gurion's conquest of the Negev. Both could be achieved only through careful calibration of the balance of power. Borders and territories are key elements for new pioneer societies, which act by colonizing the land and extending frontiers. Their foreign policy, tied to the international balance of power, nevertheless would not tolerate territorial intervention on the part of others. In the American case, this meant exclusively American imperial terri-torial expansion into what were conceived of as "empty spaces." In Israel, it translated into the socialist Zionist concept of the conquest of the land, that is, cultivating land that the native population had not considered cultivatable. Keeping the great powers at bay while forging ahead with settlement and frontier expansion requires great diplomatic skills, skills that distinguished the founding fathers of both the United States and Israel.

The difference between American imperial expansion and Israel's colonization of Palestine was that the Americans tended to covet and dominate the best and most fertile lands, while the Zionists had to reclaim the marshes, the deserts, and the mountains of uncultivatable land. Yet the necessity of aggressive pioneer expan-sion began to erode the very ideals the pioneers had set for themselves and excluded the natives (Indians and Arabs) from their civilization and ideals.

The Jeffersonians distrusted standing armies and executive aggrandization and championed the yeoman farmer as "a bulwark of American liberty" (Lang,

1985, p. 122). The Hamiltonian entrepreneurs favored industrial federalism and a strong executive. The two strains of political thinking never reconciled themselves to each other, even though they would prevail to become the two essential political traditions in the United States.

In Israel, the left lost and the center won, with executive power in the hands of Ben Gurion. A succession of Mapai-Labor governments, headed by Eshkol, Golda Meir, and Rabin, continued the Ben Gurion tradition of nationalism over socialism. The Likud government of Menachem Begin and its coalition successors had no predecessors in Israeli political history. Begin and Shamir always advocated radical nationalist goals. For them, the frontier of Israel remains incomplete. There is still no complete Eretz Israel for the successors to Labor and Mapai.

In spite of differences, the early foreign policies of the United States and Israel were products of environment and needs, even if the guiding principles of a new nation as a model never stopped inspiring subsequent generations of Israelis and Americans.

From 1920 to 1947, socialist Zionist diplomacy managed to achieve without war recognition and support from the world's two superpowers. The American founding fathers shrewdly handled the European balance of power, managing to avoid a ruinous war with either superpower that might have split the United States into several spheres of influence. Labor's current Zionist successors have not managed to bring to reality the Zionist dream of a secure Israel, failing to understand or ignoring Ben Gurion's principle that the in-gathering of Jews is more important than territorial concerns, that human beings, not acreage, form the cement of Israel's security. As a result, Israel is still at the mercy of a vicious Arab-Israeli-Palestinian conflict.

The American dream was fulfilled not only because the distractions of the Napoleonic wars kept European powers away from imperialist adventures on the American continent—at least for a time—but because expansion was achieved through war with Mexico. The restored balance of power in Europe ended the American respite, which had taken speedy and full advantage to consolidate territory, trade, and political freedom, and had thus discouraged European powers from extending their rivalries into the American continent.

The dream was not always achieved in the way that Jefferson had hoped— that is, short of war. There were other, perhaps necessary, ways to win a commonwealth and achieve American security besides the avoidance of war and the belief that commerce was the prevailing instrument for achieving expansion, for building the nation from the Atlantic to the Pacific, from the Great Lakes to the South, where America's great rivers meet at the sea.

NOTES

1. I conducted interviews with old Hashomer Hatzair, Ahdut Haavoda, and Mapam veterans of the 1940s and 1950s during the summers of 1984, 1985, 1986, and 1987.

2. This was related to me by Vladimir Dedijer (winter 1967, Berkeley, California). See also Gelber (1990).

3. The number of European Jews after World War II:

Czechoslovakia	40,000
Romania	350,000
Hungary	200,000
Bulgaria	50,000
Polish Jews in Russia	230,000

4. Until the Soviet foreign ministry documents for 1947-1950 become available, we can only speculate on Soviet motives for support of Zionism.

REFERENCES

Bauer, Y. (1970). *Flight and rescue: Brichah.* New York: Random House.
Ben Gurion, D. (1982). *War diary* (Vol. 1). Tel Aviv: Ministry of Defense.
Bialer, U. (1990). *Between East and West: Israel's foreign policy orientation, 1948-1956.* Cambridge: Cambridge University Press.
Brands, R. W. (1991). *Inside the Cold War: Loy Henderson and the rise of the American empire 1918-1942.* New York: Oxford University Press.
Brecher, M. (1974). *Decision in Israel's foreign policy.* London: Oxford University Press.
Bullock, A. (1983). *Ernest Bevin: Foreign secretary 1945-1951.* London: Heineman.
Chary, F. (1972). *The Bulgarian Jews and the final solution.* Pittsburgh: Pittsburgh University Press.
Clifford, C. (1991). *Counsel to the president.* New York: Random House.
Combs, J. (1970). *Political background of the founding fathers.* Berkeley: University of California Press.
Dull, J. A. (1985). *A diplomatic history of the American Revolution.* New Haven, CT: Yale University Press.
Eilat, E. (1979-1982). *Struggle for statehood, 1945-1948* (3 vols.). Tel Aviv: Am Oved.
Eisenstadt, S. N. (1958). *From generation to generation.* New York: Free Press.
Ganin, Z. (1979). *Truman, American Jewry and Israel, 1945-1948.* New York: Holmes & Meier.
Gelber, Y. (1990). *"Masada": The defense of Palestine during the Second World War.* Jerusalem: Bar Ilan University Press.
Gilbert, F. (1961). *To the farewell address: Ideas of early American foreign policy.* Princeton, NJ: Princeton University Press.
Gorni, J. (1973). *Ahdut Haavoda 1919-1930.* Tel Aviv: Hakibbutz Hameuchad.
Gorni, J. (1983). *The British labour movement and Zionism 1917-1948.* London: Cass.
Hadari, Z. (1991). *Second Exodus: The full story of Jewish illegal immigration to Palestine 1945-1948.* London: Cass.
Hartz, L. (1962). *The liberal tradition in America.* Cambridge, MA: Harvard University Press.
Horowitz, D., & Lissak, M. (1978). *From Yishav to state.* Chicago: University of Chicago Press.
Huston, J. H. (1980). *John Adams and the diplomacy of the American Revolution.* Lexington: University Press of Kentucky.

Ilan, A. (1979). *America, Britain and Palestine*. Jerusalem: Yad Ben Zvi.

Ilan, A. (1980, April). The British decision to evacuate Palestine. *Cathedra,* pp. 140-189.

Kaplan, K. (1990). *Report on the murder of the general secretary*. Columbus: Ohio State University Press.

Kimmerling, B. (1983). *Zionism and territory: The socio-territorial dimension of Zionist politics*. Berkeley: University of California Press.

Krammer, A. (1974). *The forgotten friendship: Israel and the Soviet Bloc, 1947-1953*. Urbana: University of Illinois Press.

Lang, D. (1985). *Foreign policy in the early republic*. Baton Rouge: Louisiana State University Press.

Lipset, S. M. (1963). *The first new nation: The United States in historical and comparative perspective*. New York: Basic Books.

Lissak, M. (1981). *The elite of the Jewish community in Palestine*. Tel Aviv.

Margalit, E. (1971). *"Hashomer Hatzair": From youth community to revolutionary Marxism 1913-1936*. Tel Aviv: Hakibbutz Hameuchad.

Mintz, M. (1976). *Ber Borochov, circa 1900-1906*. Tel Aviv: Hakibbutz Hameuchad.

Perlmutter, A. (1957). *Ideology and organization: Socialist Zionist parties 1897-1957*. Unpublished doctoral dissertation, University of California, Berkeley.

Perlmutter, A. (1968). Dov Ber Borochov. *Middle Eastern Studies, 5,* 32-43.

Perlmutter, A. (1985). *Israel: The partitioned state*. New York: Scribner.

Rapaport, L. (1990). *Stalin's war against the Jews*. New York: Free Press.

Redlich, S. (1988). *The rise and fall of the Jewish Anti-Fascist Committee in the war, 1941-1945*. New York: New York University Press.

Roi, Y. (1974). *From encroachment to involvement: Soviet policy in the Middle East 1945-1973*. New York: John Wiley.

Roi, Y. (1980). *Soviet decision making in practice: The war and Israel 1947-1954*. New Brunswick, NJ: Transaction.

Shlaim, A. (1989). *Collusion across the Jordan*. Oxford: Oxford University Press.

Snetsinger, J. (1974). *Truman, the Jewish vote and the creation of Israel*. Hoover: Stabual.

Teveth, S. (1985). *Ben Gurion and Palestinians*. New York: Oxford University Press.

Teveth, S. (1987). *Ben Gurion: The burning ground 1886-1948*. Boston: Houghton Mifflin.

Tucker, R. W., & Hendrickson, D. (1990). *Empire of liberty: The statecraft of Thomas Jefferson*. New York: Oxford University Press.

Varg, P. A. (1963). *Foreign policy of the founding fathers*. Lansing: Michigan State University Press.

Wallach, Y. (1985). *We were as dreamers* (Vol. 1). Tel Aviv: Massada.

Wilson, E. M. (1979). *Decision on Palestine*. Hoover: Stadyad.

PART III

POLITICS AND SOCIAL CHANGE IN AMERICAN DEMOCRACY

11

State Formation and
Social Policy in the United States

Theda Skocpol

NO living scholar has done more than Seymour Martin Lipset to inspire sociologists and political scientists to examine U.S. politics in comparison to other nations. Throughout his long and distinguished career, Lipset has sensitized us to the specificities of American liberal values, to the distinctive features of U.S. unions and labor politics, and to the impact of U.S. electoral arrangements on various kinds of political movements. As a student of Lipset's, I have absorbed these valuable lessons. Yet I have also pursued the quest to understand the paradoxes of American political development—in what might seem to be a very "un-Lipsetian" fashion!—by focusing on "the state."

"Americans may be defined as that part of the English-speaking world which instinctively revolted against the doctrine of the sovereignty of the State and has . . . striven to maintain that attitude from the time of the Pilgrim Fathers to the present day" (Pollard, 1925, p. 31). Lipset would surely agree with this cogent formulation by Pollard, an insightful observer of the U.S. Constitution. Citizens of the United States view themselves as fortunate not to be subject to any overbearing "state." And observers rightly have trouble identifying elements of concentrated sovereignty in the American political system—except, perhaps, when the United States acts aggressively on the world stage. There are, of course, excellent historical reasons Americans lack a strong or positive sense of the state, many of which have been brilliantly illuminated in Lipset's scholarship. Nevertheless, we can learn a surprising amount about American politics by treating state-society relationships in strictly analytic terms.

To imagine that the United States has been a dynamic society and capitalist economy unencumbered by any state would be an ethnocentric illusion. Instead, the specific organizational forms that state activities have taken in America have profoundly affected the social cleavages that have gained political expression and helped to determine the sorts of public policies that U.S. governments have—and have not—pursued from the nineteenth century to the present day. Drawing on my own current research, I can illustrate this argument by exploring why the historically evolved patterns and phases of U.S. public social provision have differed from those characteristic of European welfare states.

SOCIAL POLICIES IN THE UNITED STATES

Modern "welfare states," as they eventually came to be called, had their start between the 1880s and the 1920s in pension and social insurance programs established for industrial workers and needy citizens in Europe and Australasia. Later, from the 1930s through the 1950s, such programmatic beginnings were elaborated into comprehensive systems of income support and social insurance encompassing entire national populations. In the aftermath of World War II, Great Britain rationalized a whole array of social services and social insurances around an explicit vision of "the welfare state," which would universally ensure a "national minimum" of protection for all citizens against old age, disability and ill health, unemployment, and other causes of insufficient income. During the same period, other nations—especially the Scandinavian democracies—established "full employment welfare states" by deliberately coordinating social policies, first with Keynesian strategies of macroeconomic management and then with targeted interventions in labor markets.

Comparative research on the origins of modern welfare states typically measures the United States against foreign patterns of "welfare state development." America is considered a "welfare state laggard" and an "incomplete welfare state" because it did not establish nationwide social insurance until 1935 and because it never has established fully national or comprehensive social programs along European lines. But this approach overlooks important social policies that were distinctive to the United States in the nineteenth and early twentieth centuries. It also distracts us from analyzing why U.S. social policies since 1935 have been characterized by sharp bifurcations between "social security" and "welfare," as well as by persisting federal diversity in certain policy areas.

Early American "social policy" included state and local support for the most inclusive system of primary and secondary public education in the industrializing world (Heidenheimer, 1981; Rubinson, 1986). It also included generous local, state, and federal benefits for elderly Civil War veterans and their dependents. By 1910, the U.S. federal government was giving old-age and disability pensions to more than a third of all elderly men living in the North and to many widows and orphans (and some elderly men in the South) as well (Skocpol, in press, chap. 2). In terms of the large share of the federal budget spent, the hefty proportion of citizens affected, and the relative generosity of the benefits by contemporary international standards, the United States had become a precocious social spending state!

In the early 1900s, a number of U.S. trade union officials and reformers hoped to transform Civil War pensions into more universal publicly funded benefits for all workingmen and their families. But this was not to be. Many social reforms were enacted into law during the progressive era, but not measures calling for new public social spending on old-age pensions or other kinds of workingmen's social insurance. The United States thus refused to follow other Western nations on the road toward a paternalist welfare state, in which male bureaucrats would administer regulations and social insurance "for the good" of breadwinning industrial workers and their dependents.

Instead, America came close to creating a pioneering maternalist welfare state, with female-dominated public agencies implementing regulations and benefits for the good of women and their children. From 1900 through the 1920s, a broad array of protective labor regulations and social benefits were enacted by state legislatures and the national Congress to help adult American women as mothers or as potential mothers (for full details, see Skocpol, in press, pt. 3). The most important of these "maternalist" social policies were mothers' pensions enacted by 44 states to authorize regular benefits for impoverished widowed mothers, laws enacted by all but 2 states to limit the hours that women wage earners could work, laws enacted by 15 states authorizing minimum wages for women workers, and the federal Sheppard-Towner Infancy and Maternity Protection Act of 1921, which authorized the U.S. Children's Bureau to supervise federal matching payments subsidizing local and state programs for maternal health education. Overall, a remarkable number of policies for women and children were enacted in the United States during a period when proposed regulations and benefits for male industrial workers were defeated.

The Great Depression and the New Deal of the 1930s subsequently opened possibilities for old-age pensions and social insurance. In what has been called a "big bang" of national legislation (Leman, 1977), the Social Security Act of 1935 created a basic framework for U.S. public social provision that is still in place. Public health insurance was omitted from the Social Security Act, and later schemes for universal national health benefits also failed. Yet three major kinds of nation-spanning social provision were included in the 1935 legislation: federally required, state-run unemployment insurance, federally subsidized public assistance, and national contributory old-age insurance.

Unemployment insurance was instituted in 1935 as a federal-state system. All states were induced to establish programs, but each individual state was left free to decide terms of eligibility and benefits for unemployed workers, as well as the taxes to be collected from employers or workers or both. Unemployment benefits and taxation became quite uneven across the states, and it remained difficult to pool risks of economic downturns on a national basis or to coordinate unemployment benefits with Keynesian demand management. Despite efforts in the 1930s and 1940s to nationalize unemployment insurance and join its operations to various measures of public economic planning, no such explicit joining of "social" and "economic" policy developed in the postwar United States.

Public assistance under the Social Security Act was administered through a set of programs already existing in certain states by the early 1930s, for which the federal government would henceforth share costs. Assistance for the elderly poor and for dependent children (previously "mothers' pensions") were the most important programs to receive new federal subsidies. Free to decide whether they would even have particular programs, the states were also accorded great discretion to decide matters of eligibility and benefits and, in practice, methods of administration. Over time, as old-age insurance expanded to cover virtually all retired employees in the United States, federal old-age assistance became proportionately less important than it was originally. Meanwhile, by the 1960s, the Aid to Dependent Children program (now Aid to Families with Dependent Children, or AFDC, providing benefits to caretakers as well as to the children themselves) expanded enormously with a predominantly female adult clientele. Labeled "welfare," AFDC has very uneven standards of eligibility, coverage, and benefits across the states, generally providing the least to the poorest people in the poorest states, and leaving many impoverished men and husband-wife families without any coverage at all.

Since 1935, the one program originally established on a purely national basis, contributory old-age insurance, has usurped the favorable label "social security" that once connoted the whole and has become the centerpiece of U.S. public social provision. Payroll taxes are collected from workers and their employers across the country. Ultimately, retired workers collect benefits roughly gauged to their employment incomes, with some redistribution toward the low-wage contributors to the system. After 1935, additional programs were added under this contributory insurance rubric: for surviving dependents in 1939, for disabled workers in 1956, and for retirees in need of medical care in 1965. Equally important, "social security" grew in coverage and benefits, as more and more employees and categories of employees were incorporated during the 1950s and benefit levels were repeatedly raised by Congress. By the 1970s, the United States, uneven and often inadequate in the help provided to unemployed and dependent people, had nevertheless become reasonably generous in the benefits offered to retired people of the working and middle classes.

"Welfare" became an explicit area of U.S. political controversy and policy innovation only during the 1960s, when the War on Poverty and the effort to create a "Great Society" were declared. For the first time since 1935, major new programs of needs-tested public assistance were established in the form of in-kind aid through Food Stamps and Medicaid. In 1972, moreover, old-age and other assistance programs (originally established as federal programs under Social Security) were nationalized, ensuring more standardized benefits. Still, the much larger AFDC program remained federally decentralized—and standards for other benefits, such as medical care, are often tied to this uneven standardbearer of the American welfare system. In turn, U.S. welfare remains, as always, both institutionally and symbolically separate from national economic management, on the one hand, and from non-means-tested programs benefiting regularly employed citizens, on the other.

EXISTING THEORIES AND THEIR SHORTCOMINGS

Among many of those seeking to understand the development of social policies in the United States, several approaches currently hold sway. Each offers insights but falls short of offering fully satisfactory explanations of the historical phases and policy patterns just reviewed.

One school of thought can be dubbed the *logic of industrialism* approach (e.g., Cutright, 1965; Wilensky, 1975, chap. 2; Wilensky & Lebeaux, 1965) because it posits that all nation-states respond to the growth of cities and industries by creating public measures to help citizens cope with attendant social and economic dislocations. Once families are off the land and dependent on wages and salaries, the argument goes, they cannot easily cope with disabling accidents at work or with major episodes of illness, unemployment, or dependent elderly relatives unable to earn their keep. Social demand for public help grows, and all modern nations must create policies to address these basic issues of social security without forcing respectable citizens to accept aid under the demeaning and disenfranchising rules of traditional poor laws.

Plausible as this sounds, recent cross-national studies on the origins of modern social insurance policies have demonstrated that urbanization and industrialization (whether considered separately or in combination) cannot explain the relative timing of national social insurance legislation from the late nineteenth century to the present (see Collier & Messick, 1975; Flora & Alber, 1981). The United States in particular does not fit well into the logic of industrialism schema. Not incidentally, proponents of this perspective have tended to include data for "the U.S. case" only when doing cross-national analyses of social insurance for the period after 1935. Before the 1930s, the United States is an awkward outlier: This country was one of the world's industrial leaders, yet "lagged" far behind other nations (even much less urban and industrial ones) when it came to instituting public pensions and social insurance. Nor does this perspective help us to understand why the United States prior to 1935 emphasized public social provision first for veteran soldiers and then for mothers, but not for workingmen.

Another school of thought—let's call it the *national values* approach—accepts many underlying dynamics posited by the logic of industrialism argument but introduces a major modification to explain why some nations, such as Bismarck's Imperial Germany in the 1880s, initiated modern social policies at relatively early stages of urbanization and industrialization, whereas others, most notably the United States, delayed behind the pace of policy innovation that would be expected from the tempos of urbanization and industrialization alone. The answer, say proponents of this approach (e.g., Gronbjerg, Street, & Suttles, 1978; Kaim-Caudle, 1973; King, 1973; Rimlinger, 1971), lies in the values and ideologies to which each nation's people adhered as urbanization and industrialization gathered force. Cultural conditions could either facilitate or delay action by a nation-state to promote social security, and cultural factors also influenced the shape and goals of new policies when they emerged. Thus

Gaston Rimlinger (1971), one of the ablest proponents of the national values approach, argues that early German social insurance policies were facilitated by the weakness of liberalism and the strength of "the patriarchal social ideal" and "the Christian social ethic" in nineteenth-century Germany (p. 91). In the United States, however, laissez-faire liberal values were extremely strong and a "commitment to individual achievement and self-help" led to a "tenacious . . . resistance to social protection" (p. 62).

Like the logic of industrialism approach, the national values school fails to notice, let alone explain, U.S. Civil War benefits or social policies for mothers and children. These approaches focus solely on modern social insurance and old-age pensions. Yet even here, general deductions from national values simply cannot give us adequate answers to many crucial questions about timing and programmatic structure.

Laissez-faire liberal values were in many respects more hegemonic and popular in nineteenth-century Britain than they were in the nineteenth-century United States, yet in the years before World War I, Britain enacted a full range of social protective measures, including workers' compensation (1906), old-age pensions (1908), and unemployment and health insurance (1911). These innovations came under the auspices of the British Liberal party, and they were intellectually and politically justified by appeals to "new liberal" values of the sort that were also making progress among educated Americans around the turn of the century. Under modern urban-industrial conditions, the "new liberals" argued, positive governmental means must be used to support individual security, and this could be accomplished without undermining individuals' dignity or making them dependent on the state. If British liberals could use such ideas to justify both state-funded pensions and contributory social insurance this way in the second decade of the twentieth century, why could American progressives not do the same? In both Britain and the United States, sufficient cultural transformation within liberalism had occurred to legitimate fledgling welfare states without resort to either conservative-paternalist or socialist justifications (see Orloff & Skocpol, 1984, for further elaboration of this argument).

Then, too, when American "New Dealers" of the 1930s at last successfully instituted nationwide social protections justified in "new liberal" terms, why did they end up with the specific array of policies embodied in the Social Security Act? Why was health insurance left aside, despite the availability of liberal rationales for it just as good as those put forward for unemployment and old-age insurance? And why did the public assistance programs subsidized under Social Security actually cement the dependence of many individuals on the arbitrary discretion of state and local authorities, rather than furthering individual dignity and the predictable delivery of citizen benefits as a matter of "rights"? A final query is perhaps the most telling: Given the clear value priority that Americans have always placed on individuals getting ahead through work, why did the New Deal as a whole fail to achieve proposed measures to guarantee jobs for everyone willing to work? Arguably, the social security measures that were achieved were less in accord with long-standing American values than governmental commitments to full employment would have been.

Arguments stressing the impact of either industrialism or national values on social policy development tend to downplay political struggles and debates. During the last 15 years, however, many historians and social scientists have analyzed the political contributions of capitalists and industrial workers in shaping patterns of social policy since the 1930s in the capitalist democracies. As part of this trend, two sorts of class politics perspectives have been applied to American social politics: One highlights what is called "welfare capitalism," and the other stresses "political class struggle" between workers and capitalists.

Proponents of the *welfare capitalism* approach (e.g., Berkowitz & McQuaid, 1980; Domhoff, 1970; Ferguson, 1984; Quadagno, 1984) take for granted that corporate capitalists have dominated the U.S. political process in the twentieth century, and they look (in various ways) for economically grounded splits between conservative and progressive capitalists as the way to explain social policy innovations. Early in this century, the argument goes, certain American businesses preceded the public sector in evolving principles of modern organizational management, including policies for stabilizing and planning employment and protecting the social welfare of loyal employees. Prominent "welfare capitalists" then pressed their ideas upon policy intellectuals and public officials, so that public social insurance measures in key states and at the federal level were supposedly designed to meet the needs of progressively managed business corporations.

This perspective has served as a good lens through which to view the complementarities that have sometimes developed between public social policies—once enacted—and the labor-management practices of American corporations. For example, many American corporations accommodated nicely to Social Security's contributory old-age insurance program, meshing it with their own retirement benefits systems, especially after World War II. But business groups originally opposed the passage of the Social Security Act as well as the passage of most earlier and later federal or state-level social and regulatory measures applicable to men or women workers. However adaptable American capitalists have proven to be after the fact, the historical evidence is overwhelming that they have regularly fiercely opposed the establishment of public social policies. Political processes other than the initiatives of capitalists have nearly always been the causes of U.S. social policy innovations.

The other class politics perspective takes for granted that capitalists everywhere tend to oppose the emergence and expansion of the welfare state. This "social democratic" or *political class struggle* approach has predominated in recent cross-national research on the development of social policies in Europe and the United States (see Bjorn, 1979; Castles, 1978, 1982; Esping-Andersen, 1985; Korpi, 1983; Myles, 1984; Shalev, 1983; Stephens, 1979). No attention is paid by these theorists to early U.S. social provision for Civil War veterans, and their worker-centered definitions of modern social provision prevent them from analyzing pioneering U.S. social spending and regulations for mothers and women workers. To explain why American public social provision for workingmen commenced later and has not become as generous as European public social provision, this approach underlines the relative weakness of U.S. industrial unions and points to the complete absence of any labor-based political party in U.S. democracy. Given these weaknesses of working-class organization, proponents of this approach argue that U.S. capitalists have been unusually able to use direct and indirect pressures to prevent governments at all levels from undertaking social welfare efforts that would reshape labor markets or interfere with the prerogatives or profits of private business. Only occasionally—most notably during the New Deal and afterward through the liberal wing of the Democratic party—have American workers or unions been able to muster sufficient strength to facilitate some innovations or expansions of public social provision.

Certainly, this emphasis on political class struggle between workers and capitalists helps to explain why the United States has not developed a comprehensive full-employment welfare state along postwar Scandinavian lines. Nevertheless, if our intention is not merely to contrast the United States to Europe since World War II but to explain the phases and specific patterns of U.S. social policies since the nineteenth century, then the political class struggle approach is insufficient in several ways. Strict attention to political conflicts of interest between capitalists and industrial workers deflects our attention from other socioeconomic forces that have intersected with the U.S. federal state and with decentralized American political parties to shape social policy-making. Until very recently, agricultural interests in the South and the West were crucial arbiters of congressional policy-making. Associations of middle-class women were crucial—and often successful—proponents of social provision for women and children during the early twentieth century. And struggles over social welfare or labor market interventions have often involved regional, ethnic, and racial divisions. We need a mode of analysis that will help us understand why social identities and conflicts grounded in gender, ethnicity, and race have been equally or more telling than industrial class conflicts in the shaping of social provision in the United States.

Political class struggle theories have been argued with certain state and party structures in mind, namely, centralized and bureaucratized states with parliamentary parties dedicated to pursuing policy programs in the name of entire classes or other broad, nation-spanning collectivities. For much of Europe, the existence of such features of political organization has given substance to the presumption that the industrial working class may translate its interests into social policies, whenever "its" party holds the reins of national power over a sustained period. But of course the United States has never had a centralized bureaucratic state or programmatic parliamentary parties. Thus the American case highlights the importance of bringing much more explicitly into our explanations of social policy-making the historical formation of each national state—as well as the effects of that state's institutional structure on the goals, capacities, and alliances of politically active social groups.

U.S. STATE FORMATION AND
PATTERNS OF SOCIAL PROVISION

"State formation" includes constitution making, involvements in wars, electoral democratization, and bureaucratization—large-scale historical processes, in short, whose forms and timing have varied significantly across capitalist industrializing countries. In sharp contrast to many European nations, the United States did not have a premodern polity characterized by monarchical absolutism, a locally entrenched standing army and bureaucracy, or recurrent mobilization for land warfare against equal competitors. Instead, the American colonies forged a federalist constitutional republic, and (after some years of continued sparring with Britain) the fledgling nation found itself relatively geopolitically sheltered and facing toward a huge continent available for conquest from militarily unformidable opponents. Wars have never had the same centralizing effects for the U.S. state as they have had for many European states, in part because America's greatest war was about itself and also because mobilization for the two world wars of the twentieth century relied heavily on the organizational capacities of large business corporations and trade associations (Cuff, 1973; Vatter, 1985). Only after World War II, when the United States took on global imperial functions, did a federal "military-industrial complex" emerge, nourished by the first persistence into peacetime of substantial direct federal taxation.

The American Revolution was a revolt not only against the British Empire but against any European-style notion of concentrated political sovereignty— whether focused in a supreme parliament, as in Britain after the English Revolution, or in an official bureaucracy built up under absolute monarchy, as in much of Continental Europe. After years of political skirmishes between colonists and royal governors, a confederation of 13 colonies separated Americans from Britain; then the founding fathers sought to cement a precarious national unity by designing a new federal government. Under the Constitution adopted in 1788, the powers of the states and the central government were carefully divided and balanced against one another in a "compound" arrangement (Scheiber, 1978) that left many ambiguities for the future, while the new rules for the federal government spread cross-cutting responsibilities among Congress, the president, and a system of courts. In the words of Samuel P. Huntington (1968), "America perpetuated a fusion of functions and a division of power, while Europe developed a differentiation of functions and a centralization of power" (p. 110).

Americans looked to "the Constitution" and "the rule of law" as the loci of fundamental sovereignty. Especially in pre-Civil War America, these functioned as a "roof without walls," in the apt words of John Murrin (1987), as "a substitute for any deeper kind of national identity" because "people knew that without the Constitution there would be no America" (pp. 346-347). Although never-ending rounds of legislation in Congress and the states expressed shifting sets of special interests, the sovereign ideals of constitutionalism and the rule of law could reign impersonally above an economically expansionist and socially diverse country. Only during the Civil War did a Republican-run crusade to save a northern-dominated nation temporarily transfer the locus of sovereignty to an activist federal government. But even the Civil War did not generate an autonomous federal bureaucracy: The forces of localism, divisions of powers, and distrust of government activism never disappeared, even in the North. The U.S. "Tudor polity" (Huntington, 1968) reemerged in full force after the southern states rejoined the union in the 1870s.

It will not do, however, to leave the matter here, stipulating that Europeans had concentrated sovereignties and a sense of "stateness" while Americans had neither. Stephen Skowronek (1982) places the totality of early American political arrangements in a framework that helps to highlight their distinctive features. Skowronek points out that America certainly did have a state, both in the sense of "an organization of coercive power" (p. 19) and in the sense of "stable, valued, and recurring modes of behavior within and among institutions" (p. 24):

> The early American state maintained an integrated legal order on a continental scale; it fought wars, expropriated Indians, secured new territories, carried on relations with other states, and aided economic development. Despite the absence of a sense of the state, the state was essential to social order and social development in nineteenth-century America. (p. 19)

To be sure, this early American state was not a set of locality-penetrating bureaucracies headed by a monarch or a parliament. Rather, in Skowronek's telling phrase, it was a "state of courts and parties" (p. 24). Operating across state and federal levels, courts and parties were the key organizations—and judges and party politicians the crucial "officials in action"—that made up the American state in the nineteenth century: "Party procedures lent operational coherence to the disjointed institutions of the governmental apparatus, [and] court proceedings determined the meaning and the effect of the law itself" (p. 27).

Courts were not very prominent in the original debates over constitutional design, yet as the nineteenth century progressed they carved out a more authoritative role than the founders had envisaged or than British courts enjoyed. "There is hardly a political question in the United States," observed Alexis de Tocqueville (1850/1969, p. 270), "which does not sooner or later turn into a judicial one." To be sure, early American judges and lawyers needed to adjust English common law precedents to U.S. circumstances, and they had to fend off various movements to codify the laws and reduce judicial discretion. Yet these elites and the courts through which they operated also enjoyed important benefits. They could take advantage of their countrymen's regard for the Constitution and legal procedures as common points of reference in a polity wracked with jurisdictional disputes, where fundamental issues regularly required adjudication. And there was no national civil bureaucracy that could compete with the courts by promoting "the national interest" in a more substantive fashion.

Along with courts, political parties and vocationally specialized partisan politicians became the pivots of the nineteenth-century American polity. Ironically, this happened even though the Constitution made no mention of them, given that the founders disapproved "the baneful effects of the spirit of party" (George Washington, as quoted in Wallace, 1968, p. 473). Foreign observers of the actual workings of American government noticed the increasing centrality and distinctiveness of U.S. parties. James Bryce (1895) observed in the 1880s that in "America the great moving forces are the parties. The government counts for less than in Europe, the parties count for more" (p. 5). A description of them is therefore a necessary complement to an account of the Constitution and government, since "their ingenuity, stimulated by incessant rivalry, has turned many provisions of the Constitution to unforeseen uses" (p. 3). "The party organizations in fact form a second body of political machinery existing side by side with that of the legally constituted government" such that "the whole machinery, both of national and of state governments, is worked by the political parties" (Bryce, 1893, p. 6). American parties, Bryce (1893) noted, "have been organized far more elaborately than anywhere else in the world, and have passed more completely under the control of a professional class" (p. 6).

The regular American parties of the nineteenth century managed the complex, never-ending processes of nominations and elections for local, state, and national offices. Party conventions became the typical means of nominating candidates, and the nineteenth century's frequent elections required that party supporters be kept in a high state of enthusiasm and readiness through canvasses and rallies. Crucially, from the Jackson era through the end of the century, parties also controlled the staffing and functioning of public administration in the United States (Shefter, 1978). Administrative staffing through patronage was complementary to the intensified electoral activities of the new political parties. The opportunity to control the allocation of public offices inspired party cadres and allowed national and state party brokers to offer local loyalists influence over appointments allocated from their levels of government. In turn, public officeholders were highly motivated to contribute portions of their salaries and their time to foster the popularity of their party, for only if their party won the next election would their jobs be safe. Otherwise, the opposite party and all of its appointees would claim the "spoils of office."

Once in place by the 1840s, the parties and their managers proved remarkably resilient, dominating U.S. politics and knitting together the branches and levels of the "Tudor polity" throughout the nineteenth century (Keller, 1977; McCormick, 1986). The local roots of the parties sunk deep into particular neighborhoods; yet party efforts simultaneously spanned localities within states and, to a remarkable degree, reached across the nation as a whole. Certainly, the party organizations were not top-down hierarchies; rather, they were ramified networks fueled by complex and shifting exchanges of favors for organizational loyalty. As such, however, they successfully linked local to state politicians and kept state politicians in touch with one another and with whatever national officeholders their party might have.

Not until the twentieth century—decades after electoral democratization and well after capitalist industrialization had created private corporate giants operating on a national scale—did the U.S. federal, state, and local governments make much headway in the bureaucratization and professionalization of their administrative functions (Shefter, 1978; Skowronek, 1982). With the greatest changes coming first at municipal and state levels, bureaucratic-professional transformations happened piecemeal through reform movements spearheaded by the new middle classes. As the various levels of government were thus partially reorganized, the fragmentation of political sovereignty built into U.S. federalism and into the divisions of decision-making authority among executives, legislatures, and courts was reproduced in new ways throughout the twentieth century. American political parties have remained uncoordinated in their basic operations, and in many localities and states the major parties uneasily combine patronage-oriented and interest group-oriented modes of operation (Mayhew, 1986). Within the federal government, Congress, with its strong roots in state and local political establishments, has remained pivotal in national domestic policy-making—even during periods of strong executive initiative such as the New Deal, the two world wars, and the Cold War (Amenta & Skocpol, 1988; Fiorina, 1977; Grodzins, 1960; Huntington, 1973; Patterson, 1967).

The patterns of U.S. state formation just summarized have conditioned social policy-making from the nineteenth century to the present. We can briefly survey some of the most important ways in which this has happened.

Early democratization of the U.S. white male electorate ensured that masses of ordinary Americans could support public schooling as a right of democratic citizenship rather than warily opposing educational institutions imposed from above by officials and upper classes, as happened in Europe (Katznelson & Weir, 1985, chap. 2). In the United States, moreover, no national bureaucracy existed to regulate, finance, or serve as a central magnet for educational development, and no single dominant church served as a prop of a counterweight to the state. Thus local and voluntary forces, including Catholic parishes and a multiplicity of Protestant and Jewish sects, took more initiatives than they did in other nations. In a democratic political context, "participatory localism" encouraged many such groups to support free public schools, while others built and defended private schools. Decentralized federalism allowed local, state-level, and private initiatives to compete with one another—and often to imitate one another as well, in waves of analogous institution building. The result was the world's first system of mass primary and secondary schooling.

In addition, nineteenth-century America's nonbureaucratic and party-centered patronage democracy had a strong proclivity for legislative enactments that would distribute material benefits to many individuals and local communities within the major party coalitions (McCormick, 1979). In the context of close electoral competition between the Republicans and the Democrats between 1877 and 1896, patronage democracy fueled the expansion of de facto disability and old-age benefits for those who could credibly claim to have served the Union forces during the Civil War. The Republican party, especially, enjoyed advantages from expanding access to Civil War pensions (Bensel, 1984, chap. 3; McMurry, 1922; Sanders, 1980). That party could simultaneously promote high tariffs, with benefits finely tuned to reach groups of businesses and workers in various Republican areas of the country, and generous pensions, which spent the "surplus" revenues raised by the tariffs disproportionately on townsmen, farmers, and skilled workers who were also concentrated in Republican-leaning areas of the North. Moreover, during crucial, close-fought elections, the Republicans manipulated the processing of pension applications through the federal Bureau of Pensions in attempts to influence the Republican vote in such tightly competitive states as New York, Ohio, and Indiana.

Once American government began to bureaucratize and professionalize, the surviving structures of patronage democracy and elite perceptions of "corruption" in the Civil War pension system discouraged U.S. progressive liberals from supporting the generalization of veterans' benefits into more universal old-age pensions or workingmen's social insurance. The absence of strong civil service bureaucracies made it impossible for U.S. advocates of contributory social insurance to imitate the strategies of contemporary British social insurance advocates, who devised plans within national ministries and then persuaded parliamentary politicians to enact them. What is more, progressive reformers were preoccupied with building bureaucratic regulatory agencies that could circumvent the control of patronage-oriented political parties, and they feared that any new forms of public social spending directed at masses of voters would only reinforce party patronage (Orloff & Skocpol, 1984; Skocpol, in press, chap. 5). The only way social welfare reforms could be enacted in the United States during the early twentieth century was through waves of similar legislation across many of the state legislatures. But policies that would have entailed new public spending for male voters could not get enthusiastic support from nation-spanning groups active in reformist politics during this period.

Finally, the U.S. state and federal courts also discouraged regulations for workingmen. Prior to the 1930s, most U.S. courts invoked constitutional principles of "free contract" and "due process" for private property holders to overrule protective labor laws covering adult male workers. Frustrated reformers responded by channeling most of their efforts for regulatory reforms toward protective labor laws covering women workers alone (Skocpol & Ritter, 1991, pp. 56-62). From the time of the 1908 "Lochner" decision, American courts allowed many such laws regulating female labor to stand. Judges accepted the arguments put forward by reformers and women's groups that governments possessed legitimate "police power" to protect future "mothers of the race" from overwork.

During the New Deal and in its aftermath, the United States finally launched nationwide public assistance and social insurance measures, including policies for workingmen and the elderly. Nevertheless, the Social Security Act was rooted in prior state-level laws or legislative proposals under active debate in the 1930s, and congressional mediation of contradictory regional interests ensured that national standards could not be established in most programs (Skocpol & Amenta, 1985). Subsequently, American national mobilization for World War II—a mobilization less total and centrally coordinated by the state than the British mobilization for the same war—did not overcome congressional and local resistance against initiatives that might have pushed the United States toward a nationalized full-employment welfare state. Instead, this pivotal war enhanced federal fiscal capacities and created new possibilities for congressionally mediated subsidies and tax expenditures but did not permanently enhance public instrumentalities for labor market intervention or executive capacities for coordinating social spending with macroeconomic management (Amenta & Skocpol, 1988).

Basic structural features of the U.S. state have thus powerfully set overall institutional limits for social provision in the United States. Yet fundamental patterns of state formation are only the starting point for analysis. In addition, political struggles and their policy outcomes have been conditioned by the institutional leverage that various social groups have gained, or failed to gain, within the U.S. polity. By analyzing ways in which America's distinctive state structure has influenced possibilities for collective action and for political alliances among social groups, we can go even further toward explaining the phases and patterns of U.S. public social provision from the nineteenth century to the present.

U.S. INSTITUTIONS AND SOCIAL GROUPS IN POLITICS

America's precociously democratized federal polity has always made it difficult for either capitalists or industrial workers to operate as a unified political force in pursuit of class projects on a national scale. Ira Katznelson (1981, 1985) and Martin Shefter (1986) have spelled out the situation for workers in a series of important publications. Because in the United States white manhood suffrage and competing patronage parties were in place at the very start of capitalist industrialization, American workers learned to separate their political participation as citizens living in ethnically defined localities from their workplace struggles for better wages and employment conditions. No encompassing "working-class politics" emerged, and American trade unions developed no stable ties to a labor-based political party during the period around the turn of the century when European social democratic movements were forged. Nationally, American workers were left without the organizational capacities to push for a social democratic program, including generous and comprehensive social policies. In localities where they did have considerable political clout, American workers tended to gain advantages along ethnic rather than class lines. Only during and after the New Deal was this situation modified, as alliances developed in many places between urban liberal Democrats and industrial unions. Yet the Democrats and the unions never went beyond flexible and ad hoc partnerships. Particular Democratic politicians put together unique constellations of supporters, sometimes including certain unions and some-times not, while unions retained the option of supporting friendly Republicans as well as Democrats.

Whereas political forces claiming to represent the industrial working class had (in cross-national perspective) relatively little presence in U.S. social politics, national and local groups claiming to speak for the collective interests of women as homemakers were able around the turn of the twentieth century to mount ideologically inspired efforts on behalf of maternalist social policies. Patterns of exclusion from—and tempos of incorporation into—electoral pol-itics shaped the possibilities for women's political consciousness just as they influenced possibilities for working-class consciousness. But the results for women were quite different.

In major European countries during the nineteenth and early twentieth centuries, either no one except monarchs, bureaucrats, and aristocrats had the right to participate in national politics or else property ownership, education, and other class-based criteria were used to limit electoral participation by categories of men. Thus European women were not the only ones excluded from the suffrage, and, at least at first, economically privileged women did not have to watch lower-class men exercise electoral rights denied to them. Class-de-fined political cleavages tended to proliferate and persist in Europe, and even politically active women's organizations oriented themselves to class issues. In the United States, by contrast, for almost a century the rights and routines of electoral democracy were open to all men (even to the black ex-slaves for some decades after the Civil War), but were denied to all women (Baker, 1984).

By virtually universal cultural consensus, woman's "separate sphere" in the nineteenth century was the home, the place where she sustained the highest moral values in her roles as wife and (especially) mother. Yet this did not mean that American women stayed out of public life. Through reformist and public-regarding voluntary associations, American upper- and middle-class women, joined by some wives of skilled workers, claimed a mission that they felt only their gender could uniquely perform: extending the moral values and social caring of the home into the larger community. In the process, women's groups took a special interest in social policy issues that they felt touched the well-being of other women. By the progressive era, indeed, women's associations had concluded that women should act as "housekeepers for the nation." Promoting such ideas were huge, nation-span-ning federations of women's clubs organized at local, state, and national levels. These included the Women's Christian Temperance Union, the National Congress of Mothers, and the General Federation of Women's Clubs—the last of which had by 1911 more than a million members in thousands of clubs spread across all states. These women's federations were well placed to press upon legislators and public opinion across the land the "moral necessity" for new social policies designed to protect women workers and mothers and children (for full details, see Skocpol, in press, pt. 3).

Although such "maternalist" ideas about social welfare spread across the industrializing world in the late nineteenth and early twentieth centuries, they loomed largest in the United States for both social and political reasons. Socially, American women gained more and better higher education sooner than any other women in the world. This prepared a crucial minority of them for voluntary or irregularly recompensed public leadership, especially since regular elite career opportunities were limited. Widespread education also set the stage for strong alliances between higher-educated professional women and married housewives scattered across the nation, many of whom were relatively well educated and some of whom in every locality had been to college and worked as schoolteachers before marriage.

Politically, meanwhile, American women reacted sharply against their exclusion from a fully democratized male democracy. Throughout the nineteenth century, no major industrializing country differentiated worlds of politics—understood in the broadest sense as patterns of participation in public affairs—so sharply *on strictly gender lines* as did the United States. Given the absence in the United States of bureaucratic and organized working-class initiatives to build a pioneering paternalist welfare state for industrial workers and their families, there was more space left for maternalism in the shaping of fledgling modern social policies. Thus the policies and new public agencies especially for women and children sponsored by American women's associations loomed especially large on the overall agenda of issues that progressive era legislators took seriously.

Using the same perspective that was just applied to understand the possibilities for working-class and women's political consciousness, we can also gain insights about the political outlooks and capacities of U.S. capitalists. To a greater degree than businesspeople in many other capitalist nations, U.S. capitalists (in the apt phrase of David Vogel, 1978) "distrust their state." This is, of course, somewhat ironic, given that American capitalists have not had to contend with a highly mobilized, nationally politically conscious working class and often get their way in governmental affairs. Yet U.S. business owners have had to operate in a long-democratized polity prone to throwing up periodic moralistic "reform" movements, including farmers' movements and women's movements inclined to challenge business prerogatives. What is more, the distrust that U.S. capitalists feel toward government reflects the frustrations they have recurrently experienced in their dealings with a decentralized and fragmented federal state—a state that gives full play to divisions within business along industrial and geographical lines.

Conflicts within the ranks of U.S. business are readily politicized because losers can always "go to court"—or back to the legislatures or to another level in the federal system or to a new bureaucratic agency—for another round of battle in the interminable struggles that never seem to settle most public policy questions. For U.S. capitalists, the state has seemed neither coherent nor reliable. Indeed, the uneven and inconstant effects of U.S. political structures help to explain why—contrary to the expectations of the "welfare capitalism" school—"progressive" corporate leaders have always found it difficult to inspire broad business support for national social policy initiatives, even those that might benefit the economy as a whole on terms favorable to the dominant sectors of business. With a few individual exceptions, American capitalists have never seen government as a positive means to achieve classwide purposes. For the most part, various industries and smaller as well as larger businesses have concentrated on fighting one another through politics. Different sectors of business have come together only episodically and then usually in efforts to block reformers or popularly appealing social movements that want to extend government regulation or taxation and spending for social welfare purposes.

The U.S. federal state, with its single-member-district legislatures and its nonprogrammatic political parties, allows considerable leverage to interests that can coordinate a policy stance across many legislative districts. What we may call "widespread federated interests" include women's associations such as the General Federation of Women's Clubs, organizations of farmers from the Grange to the American Farm Bureau Federation, business groups such as the Chamber of Commerce, and professional associations such as the National Education Association and the American Medical Association. Such widespread federations of local and state member units are ideal coalition partners for national policy advocacy groups that want to promote, obstruct, or rework social policies—especially as proposals have had to make their way through dozens of state legislatures or through the House of Representatives in Congress.

Occasionally, social groups organized as widespread federations have spurred the enactment of social policies in the United States. Examples of this include support by Union veterans in the Grand Army of the Republic for Civil War benefits during the 1880s and 1890s; support by the General Federation of Women's Clubs and the National Congress of Mothers for mothers' pensions, protective legislation, and Sheppard-Towner programs during the 1910s and 1920s; and support by the Townsend Movement, an association of old people's clubs, for old-age benefits during the 1930s and 1940s. Equally or more often, however, widespread federations of commercial farmers and small business-men have obstructed or gutted proposed social policies. For example, during the early New Deal, from 1933 to 1935, federal agricultural policies had the not fully intended effect of strengthening interest group association among commercial farmers across the disparate crop areas of the South and the Midwest (Finegold & Skocpol, 1984). In turn, this meant that the American Farm Bureau Federation was better able to ally with business organizations, including the Chamber of Commerce, to pressure congressional representatives against one liberal New Deal social welfare proposal after another from 1936 onward.

Pinpointing institutional leverage through Congress also helps us to make sense of the special role of "the South" in modern American social policy-making, a role that certainly rivals that of either capitalists or the industrial working class. To be sure, the South's role cannot be understood without underlining the class structure of southern cotton agriculture as a landlord-dominated sharecropper system from the late nineteenth century through the 1930s (Alston & Ferrie, 1985). Nor could we possibly ignore the explicit racism that ensured minority white dominance over black majorities in all sectors of economic and social life. Yet the South was militarily defeated in the Civil War, and by the

1930s this region was not very weighty in the national economy as a whole, nor were its social mores typical of the nation. Thus socioeconomic factors and generalized references to racism will not alone tell us why southern politicians had so much leverage during and after the New Deal that they could take a leading role in congressional alliances opposed to national welfare standards and any strong federal presence in economic planning.

The influence of southern agricultural interests in the New Deal depended on the insertion of their class power as landlords and their social power as white racial oligarchs into federal political arrangements that from the 1890s to the 1960s allowed an undemocratized single-party South to coexist with competitive two-party democracy in the rest of the national polity (Key, 1949). Above all, southern leverage was registered through a congressionally centered legislative process in Washington that allowed key committee chairmen from "safe" districts to arbitrate precise legislative details and outcomes. From the New Deal onward, the "national" Democratic party used congressional committees to broker the internal divisions between its southern and urban liberal northern wings (Bensel, 1984, chap. 7). This prevented the often contradictory orientations of the two wings from tearing the national party apart, but at the price of allowing the enactment of only those social policies that did not bring the national state into direct confrontation with the South's nondemocratic politics and racially embedded systems of repressive labor control.

The U.S. state structure as it had been formed by the 1930s and 1940s, along with the operations of the New Deal party system, magnified the capacities of southern economic and social elites to affect national policies at the same time that the capacities of other interests, including those sections of organized industrial labor allied with urban Democrats in the North, were simultaneously enhanced by the same U.S. state structure and party patterns. Many features of the New Deal Social Security system—and indeed of the entire disjointed configuration of social and economic policies with which the United States emerged from the political watersheds of the New Deal and World War II—can be understood by pinpointing the social interests and the political alliances that were able to gain or retain enhanced leverage through the long-standing federal and congressional institutions of the U.S. state. The New Deal certainly brought social policy innovators to the fore through the newly active federal executive. It also energized urban liberal forces and created new possibilities for political alliances through the electorally strengthened and partially realigned Democratic party. Nevertheless, in the end, America's federal state and regionally uneven democracy placed severe limits on the political alliances and policies that could prevail as the original foundations were laid for nationwide public social provision in the United States.

Finally, to understand major developments in social policies since the New Deal, it is crucial to remember that the United States was—paradoxically—both the "first" and the "last" to democratize its electorate among the long-standing capitalist democracies. It was the first for white males, who were irreversibly enfranchised by the 1830s, and it became the last for *all* citizens because, except briefly during Reconstruction and its immediate aftermath, most blacks in the United States could not vote until after the migrations from the South following the 1930s and the civil rights upheavals of the 1960s. For all of the twentieth century until the 1960s, the United States was a regionally bifurcated federal polity: a mass two-party democracy in the East, North, and West, coexisting within the same national state with a single-party racial oligarchy in the South. Only since the 1960s, through major transformations that are far from completed, have American blacks been mobilized into national democracy and has two-party electoral competition made headway in the deep South.

The civil rights revolution of the 1960s began the process of mobilizing blacks into the southern electorate and on new terms into the national electorate and the Democratic party. These are processes that have had tumultuous effects both on agendas of debate over social policy and on political alliances concerned with policy alternatives from the Great Society to the present. Yet the incorporation of blacks into the national polity has not been happening in a social policy vacuum; it is taking place in the context of the configuration of social policies inherited from the New Deal. Within this configuration of policies, "social security" for the stably employed majority of citizens had become by the 1960s institutionally and symbolically bifurcated from "welfare" for the barely deserving poor (Skocpol, 1988). For socioeconomic and political reasons alike, working-age blacks were disproportionately clients of the vulnerable welfare components of U.S. social provision.

During the social policy reforms of the 1960s and early 1970s, welfare clients temporarily benefited from the widespread recognition that the New Deal system of social policies had not adequately addressed issues of poverty or responded to the needs of blacks, who could now vote in greater numbers. Liberal Democrats tried to use welfare extensions and new "antipoverty" programs to incorporate blacks into their—otherwise undisturbed—national political coalition. But many social policy reforms of the 1960s and 1970s soon backfired to disturb rather than reinforce Democratic coalitions. National politics underwent a sea change, and since the 1970s conservative forces hostile to enhanced public social provision have found renewed sources of strength within and beyond the Democratic party. This has left impoverished people, including many blacks, increasingly isolated in national politics. And it has left welfare programs more vulnerable than ever to attacks by those who question the U.S. federal government's role in providing support for vulnerable citizens.

CONTINUING AMBIVALENCE
ABOUT THE ROLE OF THE STATE

Currently, Americans remain as ambivalent about concentrated political authority as they were two centuries ago, when the Constitution was framed. They are quick to see the ills that government can inflict and slow to perceive the good things that a responsible national state can do for all citizens. But it would be wrong to suggest that Americans have ever been a people "without a state" either in fact or in fancy. As long as we are prepared to specify the peculiar sets of institutions that have added up to America's distinctive versions of the modern state in different historical periods, we can identify the ways in which political officials have shaped policies and analyze the ways in which state structures have patterned the conflicts and alliances of major social groups.

The nineteenth-century American "state of courts and parties" presided over the widespread distribution of economic and social benefits, including the Civil War pensions that served as de facto disability and old-age pensions for many around the turn of the new century. Women who were excluded from America's early fraternal democracy created federations of voluntary associations to counter and reform the male-dominated system, and during the 1910s and early 1920s these women's associations found themselves in a strong position to promote maternalist social policies across all states and in Congress. During the mid-twentieth century, America's unevenly bureaucratized and democratized federal state hampered social democratic class politics and placed severe limits on comprehensive provision for the poor and unemployed. Yet this same national state has allowed the elaboration of many public benefits for the broad working and middle strata—benefits that these groups have eagerly accepted and politically supported, even when it means paying visible federal taxes, as in the case of social security's contributory retirement insurance. Americans are happy enough to take benefits from government when they are widely distributed and mesh well with private pursuits.

The poor in America have benefited the most from public social provision when they have been included in relatively universal programs along with the middle and working classes (see Skocpol, 1991). When left to themselves, however, impoverished minorities have suffered the most from the divisions encouraged by America's fragmented political institutions and by the continuing ambivalence of most citizens about the proper—or possible—role of concentrated governmental authority in national life. No doubt, the poor and the marginal would have done better in a European-style full-employment welfare state. But U.S. political institutions have never allowed the possibility for any such comprehensive regime of public social provision to emerge here. And the weight of history being what it is, it seems unlikely that they ever will. In the future as in the past, the fate of the American poor will remain tied to possibilities for their inclusion in political coalitions that transcend class and race. Recurrently, U.S. political structures have encouraged and responded to such broad alliances on behalf of inclusive social policies. And there is every reason to hope that this might happen again in the future, even if Americans continue to be ambivalent about "the state."

REFERENCES

Alston, L. J., & Ferrie, J. P. (1985). Labor costs, paternalism, and loyalty in southern agriculture: A constraint on the growth of the welfare state. *Journal of Economic History, 65,* 95-117.

Amenta, E., & Skocpol, T. (1988). Redefining the New Deal: World War II and the develop-
ment of social provision in the United States. In M. Weir, A. S. Orloff, & T. Skocpol
(Eds.), *The politics of social policy in the United States.* Princeton, NJ: Princeton
University Press.
Baker, P. (1984). The domestication of politics: Women and American political society,
1780-1920. *American Historical Review, 89,* 620-647.
Bensel, R. F. (1984). *Sectionalism and American political development, 1880-1980.* Madison:
University of Wisconsin Press.
Berkowitz, E., & McQuaid, K. (1980). *Creating the welfare state.* New York: Praeger.
Bjorn, L. (1979). Labor parties, economic growth, and redistribution in five capitalist
democracies. *Comparative Social Research, 2,* 93-128.
Bryce, J. (1893). *The American commonwealth* (3rd ed., Vol. 1). New York: Macmillan.
Bryce, J. (1895). *The American commonwealth* (3rd ed., Vol. 2). New York: Macmillan.
Castles, F. (1978). *The social democratic image of society.* London: Routledge & Kegan Paul.
Castles, F. (1982). The impact of parties on public expenditures. In F. Castles (Ed.), *The
impact of parties* (pp. 21-96). Beverly Hills, CA: Sage.
Collier, D., & Messick, R. (1975). Prerequisites versus diffusion: Testing alternative expla-
nations of social security adoption. *American Political Science Review, 69,* 1299-1315.
Cuff, R. D. (1973). *The War Industries Board: Business-government relations during World
War I.* Baltimore: Johns Hopkins University Press.
Cutright, P. (1965). Political structure, economic development, and national social security
programs. *American Journal of Sociology, 70,* 537-550.
Domhoff, W. (1970). *The higher circles.* New York: Random House.
Esping-Andersen, G. (1985). *Politics against markets: The social democratic road to power.*
Princeton, NJ: Princeton University Press.
Ferguson, T. (1984). From normalcy to New Deal: Industrial structure, party competition,
and American public policy in the Great Depression. *International Organization, 38,*
41-93.
Finegold, K., & Skocpol, T. (1984). State, party, and industry: From business recovery to the
Wagner Act in America's New Deal. In C. Bright & S. F. Harding (Eds.), *Statemaking
and social movements: Essays in history and theory* (pp. 159-192). Ann Arbor: University
of Michigan Press.
Fiorina, M. P. (1977). *Congress: Keystone of the Washington establishment.* New Haven, CT:
Yale University Press.
Flora, P., & Alber, J. (1981). Modernization, democratization, and the development of welfare
states in Western Europe. In P. J. Flora & A. Heidenheimer (Eds.), *The development of
welfare states in Europe and America* (pp. 37-80). New Brunswick, NJ: Transaction.
Grodzins, M. (1960). American political parties and the American system. *Western Political
Quarterly, 13,* 974-998.
Gronbjerg, K., Street, D., & Suttles, G. D. (1978). *Poverty and social change.* Chicago:
University of Chicago Press.
Heidenheimer, A. J. (1981). Education and social security entitlements in Europe and
America. In P. J. Flora & A. Heidenheimer (Eds.), *The development of welfare states in
Europe and America* (pp. 269-304). New Brunswick, NJ: Transaction.
Huntington, S. P. (1968). *Political order in changing societies.* New Haven, CT: Yale
University Press.
Huntington, S. P. (1973). Congressional responses to the twentieth century. In American
Assembly, *Congress and the American future* (2nd ed., pp. 6-38). Englewood Cliffs, NJ:
Prentice-Hall.

Kaim-Caudle, P. (1973). *Comparative social policy and social security.* London: Martin Robertson.

Katznelson, I. (1981). *City trenches: Urban politics and the patterning of class in the United States.* New York: Pantheon.

Katznelson, I. (1985). Working-class formation and the state: Nineteenth-century England in American perspective. In P. B. Evans, D. Rueschemeyer, & T. Skocpol (Eds.), *Bringing the state back in* (pp. 257-284). Cambridge: Cambridge University Press.

Katznelson, I., & Weir, M. (1985). *Schooling for all: Class, race, and the decline of the democratic ideal.* New York: Basic Books.

Keller, M. (1977). *Affairs of state: Public life in late nineteenth century America.* Cambridge, MA: Harvard University Press.

Key, V. O. (1949). *Southern politics in state and nation.* New York: Alfred A. Knopf.

King, A. (1973). Ideas, institutions and the policies of governments: A comparative analysis, parts I and II. *British Journal of Political Science, 3,* 291-313, 409-423.

Korpi, W. (1983). *The democratic class struggle.* Boston: Routledge & Kegan Paul.

Leman, C. (1977). Patterns of policy development: Social security in the United States and Canada. *Public Policy, 25,* 26-291.

Mayhew, D. R. (1986). *Placing parties in American politics.* Princeton, NJ: Princeton University Press.

McCormick, R. L. (1979). The party period and public policy: An exploratory hypothesis. *Journal of American History, 66,* 279-298.

McCormick, R. L. (1986). *The party period and public policy.* New York: Oxford University Press.

McMurry, D. (1922). The political significance of the pension question, 1885-1897. *Mississippi Valley Historical Review, 9,* 19-36.

Murrin, J. M. (1987). A roof without walls: The dilemmas of American national identity. In R. Beeman, S. Botein, & E. C. Carter II (Eds.), *Beyond confederation: Origins of the Constitution and American national identity* (pp. 333-348). Chapel Hill: University of North Carolina Press.

Myles, J. (1984). *Old age in the welfare state.* Boston: Little, Brown.

Orloff, A. S., & Skocpol, T. (1984). Why not equal protection? Explaining the politics of public social spending in Britain, 1900-1911, and the United States, 1880s-1920. *American Sociological Review, 49,* 726-750.

Patterson, J. T. (1967). *Congressional conservatism and the New Deal.* Lexington: University of Kentucky Press.

Pollard, A. F. (1925). *Factors in American history.* New York: Macmillan.

Quadagno, J. (1984). Welfare capitalism and the Social Security Act of 1935. *American Sociological Review, 49,* 632-647.

Rimlinger, G. (1971). *Welfare policy and industrialization in Europe and America.* New York: John Wiley.

Rubinson, R. (1986). Class formation, politics, and institutions: Schooling in the United States. *American Journal of Sociology, 92,* 519-548.

Sanders, H. T. (1980). Paying for the "bloody shirt": The politics of Civil War pensions. In B. Rundquist (Ed.), *Political benefits* (pp. 137-160). Lexington, MA: Lexington.

Scheiber, H. N. (1978). Federalism and the constitution: The original understanding. In L. M. Friedman & H. M. Scheiber (Eds.), *American law and the constitutional order: Historical perspectives* (pp. 85-98). Cambridge, MA: Harvard University Press.

Shalev, M. (1983). The social democratic model and beyond: Two generations of comparative research on the welfare state. *Comparative Social Research, 6,* 315-351.

Shefter, M. (1978). Party, bureaucracy, and political change in the United States. In L. Maisel & J. Cooper (Eds.), *Political parties: Development and decay* (pp. 211-265). Beverly Hills, CA: Sage.

Shefter, M. (1986). Trade unions and political machines: The organization and disorganization of the American working class in the late nineteenth century. In I. Katznelson & A. Zolberg (Eds.), *Working-class formation: Nineteenth century patterns in Europe and the United States* (pp. 197-276). Princeton, NJ: Princeton University Press.

Skocpol, T. (1988). The limits of the New Deal system and the roots of contemporary welfare dilemmas. In M. Weir, A. S. Orloff, & T. Skocpol (Eds.), *The politics of social policy in the United States* (pp. 293-311). Princeton, NJ: Princeton University Press.

Skocpol, T. (1991). Targeting within universalism: Politically viable policies to combat poverty in the United States. In C. Jencks & P. E. Peterson (Eds.), *The urban underclass* (pp. 411-436). Washington, DC: Brookings Institution.

Skocpol, T. (in press). *Protecting soldiers and mothers: The politics of social provision in the United States, 1870s-1920s.* Cambridge, MA: Harvard University Press.

Skocpol, T., & Amenta, E. (1985). Did capitalists shape social security? *American Sociological Review, 50,* 572-575.

Skocpol, T., & Ritter, G. (1991). Gender and the origins of modern social policies in Britain and the United States. *Studies in American Political Development, 5,* 36-93.

Skowronek, S. (1982). *Building a new American state: The expansion of national administrative capacities, 1877-1920.* Cambridge: Cambridge University Press.

Stephens, J. (1979). *The transition from capitalism to socialism.* London: Macmillan.

Tocqueville, A. de. (1969). *Democracy in America* (13th ed.) (J. P. Mayer, Ed.; G. Lawrence, Trans.). Garden City, NY: Anchor. (Original work published 1850)

Vatter, H. G. (1985). *The U.S. economy in World War II.* New York: Columbia University Press.

Vogel, D. (1978). Why businessmen distrust their state: The political consciousness of American corporate executives. *British Journal of Political Science, 8,* 45-78.

Wallace, M. (1968). Changing concepts of party in the United States: New York, 1815-1828. *American Historical Review, 74,* 453-491.

Wilensky, H. (1975). *The welfare state and equality.* Berkeley: University of California Press.

Wilensky, H., & Lebeaux, C. (1965). *Industrial society and social welfare.* New York: Free Press.

12

The Insurgent Origins
of Union Democracy

Maurice Zeitlin
Judith Stepan-Norris

A pathetic paradigm prevails in the writings on union democracy; in it, undemonstrable "needs"—such as for stability, security, and continuity—are attributed to "organization" and converted into inescapable, tragic realities (Selznick, 1943, p. 49). Thus, within this theoretical world, the "spread of bureaucracy and the decay of democracy in trade unions are not abnormal excesses" (Herberg, 1943, p. 413), but an "immanent necessity" (Michels, 1949, pp. 382, 402). A real democratic union is conceptually transmogrified into a "deviant case"—that is, the union is said to "deviate from the iron law of oligarchy" (Lipset, Trow, & Coleman, 1962, p. 12)—and the "quest" for union democracy becomes "futile" (Magrath, 1959, p. 525), for "all that remains" of the dream of the democratic self-determination of labor "is the inevitable current moving the trade unions toward bureaucratization and oligarchy" (Jacobs, 1963, p. 151).

We reject this cast of thought as a theoretical guide to the analysis of union democracy, because it both mistakes postulation for analysis and rests on a "teleology of bureaucratic imperatives" (Zeitlin, 1989, p. 7; compare Edelstein & Warner, 1975, p. 339). If history often has the retrospective *appearance* of inevitability, the analysis of the concrete circumstances in which labor unions originate reveals that "oligarchy," like democracy, is not the product of "inevitable currents" but of contingent, though determinate, political struggles.

This proposition is consistent, we want to emphasize, with the actual analytical thrust of much of *the* pathbreaking work, *Union Democracy,* despite its Michelsian pathos. In the course of their own substantive analysis of the origins of democracy in the so-called deviant case of the International Typographical

Union, Seymour Martin Lipset, Martin Trow, and James Coleman (1962) draw freely (and often explicitly) on radical democratic and socialist theory (see, e.g., pp. 15-16, 69-76).

INTRACLASS STRUGGLE

The most democratic unions, C. Wright Mills (1948/1971) suggests, "are usually born of a direct struggle, such as the sit-down strikes. . . . Everything has been gained bitterly over long periods of time" (p. 268). Mills's focus is on the political effects of the workers' "direct struggle" against their bosses. But this struggle of "class against class" is simultaneously an *intra*class struggle. It is a fight on two fronts at once. The main front, of course, is the workers' common fight against capital. The second front is the fight among the workers' own factions and parties over their political leadership and, consequently, over the shape of the actual political forms through which they define their common interests, decide on their strategy, and mobilize for "industrial battle." In short, the fights on this second front are not only crucial in determining *who* wins "power and trust" in organized labor (Stepan-Norris & Zeitlin, 1989), but also *how* that power is held and that trust fulfilled.

This analysis focuses on the "international unions" of the Congress of Industrial Organizations during the 1940s, at the height of the CIO's independent existence.[1] Born in 1935, in the midst of an upheaval that "ripped the cloak of civilized decorum from society, leaving exposed naked class conflict" (Bernstein, 1970, p. 217), the CIO organized so many workers so quickly that within less than a decade its affiliated unions represented roughly 80% of the country's industrial workers (Bell, 1960, p. 91). Indeed, by mid-century, unionization was so extensive that organized labor had become "to all intents and purposes the government of the labor community" in the United States (Leiserson, 1959, p. 3).

THE "DIVIDED SOUL"

Any analysis of the sources of democracy necessarily implies a conception of the democratic ideal against which any concrete polity has to be measured. What democracy is, moreover, is not a mere matter of definition, but involves contentious questions in political theory, especially the question of whether the active participation of ordinary men and women in making the decisions that affect them is essential to democracy (see Pateman, 1970) or if it suffices that—instead of "tak[ing] upon themselves collectively" the responsibility for governing—they merely take part, as John Stuart Mill (1963) sardonically remarked long ago, in elections, "a political act, to be done only once in a few years" (p. 229).

Conceptualizing "*union* democracy" and trying to measure it is thus doubly difficult. Even assuming theoretical agreement on the meaning of democracy in a state or other polity, the question remains whether a labor union "ought to" be democratic, and, if so, what that means empirically, for the union's sine qua non is that it is supposed to be a fighting organization of workers in constant readiness to defy the "sway of property" over their daily working lives (Mills, 1948/1971, pp. 4, 8). The union is, minimally, a sort of irregular (if unarmed) workers' "army" engaged in "a guerrilla war against the effects of the existing system" and "the encroachments of capital" (Marx, 1973, pp. 75-76).

So, asking what determines union democracy implies that the labor union not only can but also *should* be both an "army" and a "town meeting": The union's irregulars, its rank and file, should participate fully in making the decisions that affect them (Muste, 1928/1948, p. 187); they should freely argue the issues, decide on a battle plan, elect their officers, and themselves vote on the "declaration of war" (strikes) and on the terms of each truce (contract) (Mills, 1948/1971, p. 4).

But why "should" they? Why should the labor union be torn by a "divided soul," in A. J. Muste's words (1928/1948, pp. 187, 189), and seek to "combine within itself two extremely divergent types of social structure, the army and the democratic town meeting"? Two polar answers have been given: first, that it "should," because democracy is of the union's essence; second, that it "should" not, because democracy is irrelevant or even detrimental to the union's real objective.

"For the union to become an instrument of social transformation," in the first view, its members "must think of it as their creature; they must want to know all about it and want to run it in as much detail as possible." In this way, Mills (1948/1971) argues, their common struggle also makes the workers "humanly and politically alert" (pp. 268, 253). Without internal democracy, without "a sophisticated organized opposition," Lipset et al. (1962) argue, "the members have no way of discovering for themselves what is possible" (pp. 460-461). Nor can the "unions represent their members' interests when the members have little control over policy formation."

In the opposite view, "trade union organization is not based on theoretical concepts prior to it, that is, on some concept of democracy, but on the end it serves. . . . the end of trade union activity is to protect and improve the general living standards of its members and not to provide workers with an exercise in self-government" (Allen, 1954, p. 15). According to C. Peter Magrath (1959), "Successful union activity vis-à-vis modern industry demands businesslike, i.e., *non*democratic, organization. . . . democracy is as inappropriate within the international headquarters of the UAW [United Automobile Workers] as it is in the front office of General Motors" (p. 525; emphasis added).

MEASURING UNION DEMOCRACY

Union democracy is conceived here in terms of the "critical theory of democratic constitutionalism" (Neumann, 1957, pp. 173-176): Certain basic "freedoms"—inscribed in a constitution or common law—are the indispensable (though not sufficient) foundation of the active participation, and self-realization, of men and women in self-governing communities. All CIO unions were governed under a constitution of their own making. So the extent of constitutional democracy varies with the content of the provisions in the union's constitution that specify, and limit or expand, the civil and political rights of its members. The question, of course, is whether constitutional provisions can provide a rough measure of the "real" level of democracy in the unions of the CIO, for "the differences between formal democratic structure and the real exercise of rank and file rights" can be vast (Levenstein, 1981, p. 333). As Jacob Dubinsky, then president of the International Ladies Garment Workers Union (ILGWU), told Victor Reuther at the UAW's tumultuous founding convention, "In my union, we have democracy too—but they know who is boss!" (quoted in Cochran, 1977, p. 339).

Thus any realistic analysis has to recognize that discrepancies necessarily existed between the letter of the law and political actualities in America's unions. But this is not the same as simply assuming that they were not related. In "nominally democratic [trade unions] . . . the *clauses in the constitutions* which set forth the machinery for translating membership interests and sentiments into organizational purpose and action *bear little relationship to the actual political processes*" (Lipset et al., 1962, pp. 2-3; emphasis added).[2] Rather, the critical questions concern how widespread the discrepancies between constitutional provisions and actual political processes were, and what the pattern was, for even if they were discrepant (as they probably were, to some unknown extent), they could have been (and, we argue, probably were) *systematically* related.

If clauses *protecting* basic rights are mere shibboleths (as Lipset et al. imply), should this not also be true (by the same reasoning) of clauses that *restrict* these rights? We doubt that clauses in a union's constitution endowing the executive with extensive power over its members are "little" related to "the actual political processes" in the union. For instance, the constitution of the AFL International Brotherhood of Electrical Workers authorized the president to remove any officer for "non-performance of duty"; to suspend or expel locals; to "suspend the cards and membership of any member who, in his judgment, is working against the welfare of the I.B.E.W. in the interests of any group or organization detrimental to the I.B.E.W.—or for creating dissension among members or among L.U.'s [local unions]"; and to decide all "questions of law and organization disputes" (Taft, 1948, p. 468). The Musicians Union vested the power in its president to "annul and set aside constitution, by-laws, or any portion thereof . . . and substitute therefor other and different provisions of his own making; the power to do so is hereby made absolute [*sic*] in the president" (Shister, 1945, p. 104). Take, for instance, the authority given to the president of the CIO's conservative Steelworkers or the radical Farm Equipment Workers (FE). The USWA president had "the authority to appoint, direct, suspend, or remove, such organizers [and] representatives . . . as he may deem necessary" (USWA, 1948, p. 8). FE's had "the power to suspend local unions for violation of the laws of the Constitution of the International union, or to suspend the officers or Executive Board members of such local unions" (FE, 1949; quoted in Gilpin, 1988, p. 27).

Surely it is not sensible (indeed, it is dangerous) simply to assume that such clauses, which concentrate power in the hands of top union officials, "bear little relationship to their actual political processes." [3] And if such *anti*democratic clauses really matter, then clauses that provide *guarantees* of democratic political rights ought to be taken no less seriously, as meaningful if imperfect measures (and determinants) of the internal political life of America's unions.

Several prior studies have documented the extent to which the constitutions of America's international unions in the 1940s protected internal democracy. Clyde Summers (1946) examined the clauses relating to equality of franchise; Philip Taft (1948) examined the provisions relating to the accountability or "constitutional power of the chief executive." [4] The results of these analyses certainly indicate that, at least during the 1940s, it was probably a "fact [that] . . . entrenched oligarchy and lack of internal opposition . . . character-ize[d] most unions on the national level" (Galenson & Lipset, 1960, p. 203).[5] But, it has to be emphasized, this was not a "fact" about most of the *CIO*'s unions (not, at least, until the mass Cold War purges of dissidents on the Left). Both the relative equality of franchise and the concentration of executive power embodied in the constitutions of the AFL and CIO unions differed sharply.

Among the 87 AFL and 26 independent unions, only a small fraction (ranging—depending on the provision—from 1 in 6 to fewer than 1 in 20) of the constitutions expressly prohibited discrimination on the grounds of race, creed, citizenship, sex, or political beliefs or affiliation. But in the mass industrial unions of the CIO—born in an insurrection against the immobilism and conservatism of the AFL, as "naked class conflict" raged in the nation—three-quarters prohibited discrimination by race or creed; and—give or take a few percentage points—more or less half of the CIO's 38 durable internationals prohibited discrimination against noncitizens or women, or on political grounds. Similarly, though the contrast on this political dimension is not as sharp, some half of the CIO constitutions examined (14 of 29) gave their top officers only "routine" power, but this was so for slightly more than one-sixth of the AFL union constitutions examined (13 of 74) and one-fourth of the 12 independent unions. On the other end of the spectrum of power, one-fifth of the heads of CIO internationals but half or more of the heads of the AFL and independent unions held "considerable power." [6]

So the vast majority of the independent and AFL unions (quite consistent with the latter's autocratic reputation) were not even "nominally democratic" (as measured by these constitutional provisions), but from half to three-fourths (depending on the provision examined) of the CIO unions were at least "nom-inally democratic."

These sharp differences in the pattern of the franchise and executive power embodied in the constitutions of the AFL, independent, and CIO unions suggest that their constitutions were, indeed, relevant to their inner political life—and should be taken seriously as the unions' "enacted rules of the game," for they both reflected and shaped "the nature of parties and of representation" within them (see Lipset, 1963, pp. 292, 313). Surely the constitutions of *states* often have been swept aside or ignored. But labor unions are not states. Nor do they possess a "monopoly of legitimate violence" with which their officials can defy their unions' constitutions and impose their rule on members.[7]

In the United States, in particular, the judiciary has long reinforced the potency and dominion of union constitutions. In "intraunion disputes" concerning members' rights brought before the courts, from the early years of the twentieth century through the CIO era, the source of the court's decisions was "in most instances" the relevant provisions of the unions' constitutions (Shister, 1945, p. 79; Summers, 1955, pp. 604-606; Williams, 1954, p. 829). Indeed, the courts often protected "union members by demanding literal compliance with the [union] constitution" (Summers, 1955, p. 605). In some instances, therefore, they went so far as to uphold the right of a union—in order to defend itself against slander and libel, and as a means of punishing deliberate violations of union rules—to invoke provisions in its constitution forbidding criticism of its officers, printing and distributing leaflets to union members without the consent of its officers, or forming factions within the union. On the other hand, the courts during the era in question (1935-1950) were "prompt to set aside union abuses of these provisions for the purposes of taking revenge upon defeated political opponents [and] suppressing criticism" (Aaron & Komaroff, 1949, p. 657). Evidently, then, the working of our courts at this time tended to assure that the provisions of union constitutions and their "real" internal political processes were systematically if not closely related.

Moreover, the constitutions of the CIO's international unions—whatever might have been the situation in the AFL or in independent unions at the time—were undoubtedly not mere shibboleths, but living political documents. They were written originally during a moment of escalating workers' insurgency and self-organization that transformed the political terrain of labor/capital conflict in the nation. In the aftermath of the CIO's split from the moribund if not reactionary AFL, the constitutions defined the distinctive identity of the new, militant, socially conscious, industrial unions. They embodied the decisions of the unions' founders about the unions' future structure, defined and channelized their aims, and established the organizational forms of the unions' internal political life (see Neumann, 1944/1966, pp. 8-9). From the constitutions' original formulation, not "by constitutional lawyers, but working men" (Taft, 1962, p. 125), at the unions' founding conventions (which often involved heated, lengthy, and detailed debates and political infighting among contending union factions over each crucial provision) through their repeated amendment and revision in the midst of serious political struggles over the years, a close reading of union history suggests that the constitutions of the CIO unions roughly reflected their real inner political dynamics.

The regular convention of the CIO international union was simultaneously a legislature, a supreme court, and a constitutional assembly (Leiserson, 1959, p. 122). It was at these conventions that the major political battles of the internationals were fought to a conclusion, compacts made, officers elected, and, as a result, their constitutions often amended or revised. So, under these circumstances, "the constitution itself paints a very vivid picture of the actual operation of the union" (Shister, 1945, p. 78) and, especially, of the union's "dominant political machine . . . in action" (Seidman, 1953, p. 227).

Decisive political shifts, especially in the balance of power among the unions' rival factions, were usually sealed at their conventions by new constitutional provisions affecting their members' civil and political rights, local autonomy, executive authority, "rank-and-file" power, and even their formal aims or official union political philosophy.[8] So if gaps existed between the provisions of CIO international constitutions and their inner political realities, these were nonetheless "effective forces"—as men on opposing sides agreed—in the often "bitter factional struggle" within them (Herberg, 1943, p. 408). "Correct constitutional laws . . . are vital," said the sometime Wobbly, syndicalist, and then Red unionist William Z. Foster in 1937, "as they place in the hands of the rank and file effective democratic weapons, if they will but use them" (1937/1952b, p. 258).[9] In sum, the constitutions of the CIO international unions were palpable reflections and embodiments of their actual political life, and they can, therefore, provide us with meaningful measures of their "real" level of internal democracy.

If a political system claims to be a democracy, it must implement specific, minimal basic civil and political rights: Equal franchise and equal access to all public offices, and equality of treatment, without regard to class or calling, are the most basic political rights, without which open participation in political life is impossible. The actual import of equality of the franchise, of course, depends on the accountability of political officals. And these political rights in turn presuppose basic civil rights (or "liberties"), both "personal"—freedom of the person—and "societal"—freedom of association (or organization)—without which equal suffrage is a sham and political representation an illusion. Any abrogation of civil rights necessarily vitiates political rights—though not vice versa (Neumann, 1957, pp. 173-176).

A comprehensive measure of the level of constitutional democracy would be based on the extent to which a union's constitution guaranteed these same or equivalent civil (both personal and societal) and political rights.[10] Here, however, we focus only on basic political rights, namely, equality of the franchise and executive accountability; and we use measures based on the information provided on CIO union constitutions as of the mid- to late-1940s in the studies mentioned earlier (Taft, 1948; Summers, 1946). As a measure of equality of the franchise, we utilize the information provided by Summers on whether or not a constitution expressly prohibits discrimination on the grounds of race, creed, citizenship, sex, or political beliefs or affiliation; he provides this information on all 38 of the CIO's durable internationals. On this basis, we constructed a simple additive scale of the number of these five grounds on which a constitution explicitly prohibits discrimination. For convenience of exposition, we define a score of 4-5 points on this scale as a "high" level of equality of the franchise, and a score of 0 (i.e., the constitution has none of these nondiscrimination provisions) as a "low" level. As a measure of the level of accountability of the union's executive (or, conversely, the concentration of executive power), we have borrowed Taft's classification of the "constitu-

tional power" of the union's "chief executive"; his article provides this classification for 24 of the 38 durable CIO international unions.

FACTIONALISM

The entire bundle of personal, civil, and political rights is meant, above all,
to guarantee the freedom of political opposition, that is, the freedom to oppose
the existing regime and its policies, alone or in association with others; to form,
join, and participate actively in organized opposition groups, factions, or
parties. "Liberty is to faction what air is to fire, an ailment without which it
instantly expires," James Madison wrote during the debate over the provisions
of the U.S. Constitution (Beloff, 1987, p. 42).

Union "liberty" also "nourishes faction"—and is nourished by it. "Faction
is the life blood of [union] democracy," if not its very definition (Martin, 1968,
p. 207; see also Lipset et al., 1962, pp. 7-11, 13; Magrath, 1959, p. 505;
McConnell, 1958b, p. 604). The "theoretical freedom [to voice opposition to
leaders and policies] is made instrumental," Bert Cochran (1977) argues, "only
by the corollary right to organize opposition factions" (p. 340). In other words,
the "decisive proof of democracy," as Irving Howe and B. J. Widdick (1949)
put it well, is "the right to organize freely into 'parties' [or factions] . . . and
function freely [and] the equally important right of the membership to express
its attitude toward them. . . . The alternative is dictatorship" (pp. 262-263).

Even when a constitution enshrines basic rights, organized opposition—and
an active minority anxious to guard its own freedoms—is essential to enforce
them, and to preserve and enliven democracy (McConnell, 1958a, p. 639;
1958b, p. 604).

If most of the international unions of the AFL were probably "characterized
internally by the rule of a one-party oligarchy" (Lipset et al., 1962, p. 1), many
if not most of the internationals in the CIO probably were relatively democratic,
for their established leadership often faced serious organized internal opposition: Organized "caucuses," "blocs," or "factions"—which were recognized
parties in all but name—regularly contended for power within them. (In fact,
Lipset et al. concede elsewhere that "many international unions have had
competing political groups within them" [pp. 75-76]. But they ignore the
analytical implications of this—which allows them to treat the ITU as a unique
deviant rather than as merely an extreme variant of the pattern of durable
internal factionalism characteristic of many other—but especially CIO—unions.)

Many if not most CIO internationals were characterized (in words as apt for
them as for the major British unions so described) by a "fluid and fragmented
'multi-party' political system," whose government involved "an uneven and
uneasy coalition between representatives of different ideological tendencies."
The dynamic of such intraunion coalitions, "like the dynamic of government
formation in the French Fourth Republic," was determined by the relative
strength of the contending factions (Martin, 1971, p. 244). In short, the

government in CIO unions often was a form of "polyarchy," in which "multiple minorities" having their own independent political bases competed for power (Dahl, 1956).

So, if both pluralist and critical theories (see Neumann, 1944/1966, pp. 10, 11, 79, 477) would predict a close relationship between the level of constitutional democracy in CIO unions and the presence of internal political factions, the same is suggested by the available historical evidence. As we have already stressed, intraunion fights among rival factions often involved attempts to amend and revise the union's constitution.

A couple of examples are instructive. In 1941, a fight in UE over the issue of "local autonomy" led to "an open split" between its left and right. UE's president, James Carey, responding to an inquiry from a union local, answered that UE's constitution allowed a local to bar Communists and fascists from positions of "responsibility and trust." Other UE officers objected that such a prohibition would be unconstitutional. *UE News* carried letters for months afterwards taking sides on the issue. A newly organized caucus for "progressive trade unionism" openly denounced UE's leadership for "following the Communist line." At the convention that year, the delegates voted overwhelmingly against amending the constitution, but reaffirmed the right of local unions to set qualifications for office as long these would not deprive any "good standing member of the Union" of rights guaranteed by UE's constitution. At the Oil Workers 1940 convention, in contrast, an insurgent "workers' control" group, which had been active since the union's founding four years earlier, won the union's leadership, and then carried its program into effect by passing a complex of constitutional amendments that aimed to limit the executive power of the union's top officers. These amendments provided that all members, rather than convention delegates alone, could vote on the election of officers and the executive council; and they excluded full-time officers from the executive council (Galenson, 1960, pp. 262-264, 417, 423).

Whether or not the presence of factions was associated with constitutional democracy in CIO international unions is not an easy question to answer empirically, for the available information on factionalism provided in historical works, while occasionally detailed, is mainly spotty and sparse. Much has been written about the same few major unions and little or nothing about most. Even in the few works that do give information on the extent of organized opposition in certain unions, it tends to be quite sketchy. Using such information, it was possible to classify 23 of the 38 durable CIO unions on the presence of factionalism, that is, whether they had enduring or "organized" factions, periodic or "sporadic" factions, or no factions.

Remarkably, even these crude data on a truncated universe, with small numbers in the cells compared, reveal a rough, if not close, relationship between the levels of factionalism and of both executive accountability and equality of the franchise in CIO unions during the 1940s. (Not incidentally, this finding thereby also tends to confirm the validity of these measures of political rights, for it shows that the CIO unions' written constitutions tended to reflect their actual inner political life.) Information on the "constitutional power" of the union's "chief executive" was missing from Taft (1948) on six of the 23 unions we were able to classify on the level of factionalism. Among these 17 unions: of the six with organized factions, three endowed their executive with only "regular" power, one with "moderate," and two with "considerable" power; of the seven unions with sporadic factions, the distribution in these categories was four, two, and one; and of the four unions with no factions, all granted their executive "considerable" power. Summers (1946) has information on the equality of the franchise for all 23 of the unions we classified on the level of factionalism. Of the 10 with organized factions, six had a high level of equality (i.e., 4-5 points) and none a low level (i.e., 0 points). Of the eight with sporadic factions, four had a high level and two a low level. Of the five with no factions, two had a high level and two a low level. In short, a close association existed between the levels of factionalism and of equality of the franchise in these unions.

INSURGENCY AND DEMOCRACY

No "factional system" is born full blown; nor is it somehow self-induced. Rather, it is the product of both earlier and continuing struggles over the nature of the common interest—in the CIO's case, of intraunion struggles over the nature of the common *class* interest of workers.

The CIO itself was born as an organized faction of the American Federation of Labor. When the Committee for Industrial Organization was formed on November 9, 1935, by the heads of eight AFL unions, this was merely the formal culmination of a long-raging factional struggle within the AFL. Their split with "reactionary AFL leaders" over the issue of "organizing the unorganized" in mass-production industries (CIO, c. 1949, p. 3) was no solitary act. Rather, it came in the immediate wake of battles for industrial unionism that thousands of workers had been waging since the early 1920s, both within and outside the AFL.

Thus the CIO was born as an amalgam of disparate, often hostile, elements: Involved in organizing the CIO unions were new, young, and inexperienced organizers and battle-hardened survivors, ex-AFL officials, "pure-and-simple" unionists, Catholic activists, liberals, Communists, and radicals of all stripes— and they were all determined to take charge, to lead their unions, and thus their class, in accordance with their own conceptions of its interests.

The critical question, then, is whether the struggles among contending working-class factions and parties, and their organizing strategy and actual political practices—whatever the "objective conditions" (or "structure") of the industry in which the union is located—mattered in determining the union's internal political relations and, consequently, its form of government, democratic or authoritarian.

These intraclass struggles and their resultant political relations can be seen as constituting and being constituted by four bundles of historical events involved in the drive to organize the unorganized into the new CIO unions:

(a) whether or not earlier Red organizing had taken place in an industry; (b) whether the union seceded from the AFL "from below," in a workers' insurgency, or "from above," in a revolt of its top officers; (c) whether the union was originally organized independently or under the aegis of a CIO "organizing committee"; and (d) whether the union was formed as an amalgamated or as a unitary organization. These bundles, we want to emphasize, represent both crucial types of political practices and constellations of internal relationships among contending political forces. The immediate empirical question, then, concerns how and to what extent these different political practices and relations were involved in the consolidation of basic democratic political rights in the international unions of the CIO.

Red Unionism

For many years before the CIO took up the call, the cause of *industrial* unionism and of "revolutionary" or "Red" unionism had been all but synonymous. In the early days of the CIO's split with the AFL, "the Communists looked upon the CIO as a rival that was capitalizing on some of its issues, particularly that of industrial unionism" (Saposs, 1959/1976, p. 123). From 1920 through late 1935, two successive Red "trade union leagues" under Communist leadership had been trying to organize some of the same industries and plants that the CIO later targeted for organizing. By the time of the CIO's birth, tens of thousands of workers had been involved in mass strikes and unionizing drives under Red leadership, most recently through the Trade Union Unity League (TUUL).[11]

Communist union organizers led some heroic, fiercely fought, and bloodily suppressed strikes. "All unions were fought bitterly in those days. But the most brutal terror was reserved for the Communist unions" (Draper, 1972, p. 392). Some of the "brutal terror" reserved for them came, however, not from employers but from hostile AFL unionists, who collaborated with employers in heading off radical unionism and in quashing the rival Red unions. "The American Federation of Labor had no qualms when it came to breaking I.W.W. and T.U.U.L. strikes" (Galenson, 1940, pp. 40-41). Characteristic, for instance, were the clashes between Red unionists and AFL adherents: in the "garment industry wars of the 1920s" (Levenstein, 1981, p. 108); in the anthracite coal fields, where "one of the bloodiest fratricidal wars in the history of trade unionism" was waged during the late 1920s and early 1930s (Galenson, 1940, pp. 12-13); and among furriers, sailors, longshoremen, and many other rival unionists on the East Coast during the same years (Levenstein, 1981, p. 107). Some of the ablest and toughest opponents of the Red unionists were themselves other radicals, especially elements of the Socialist party and ex-Reds who had quit or been expelled from the Communist party (CP) after the late 1920s. Some ex-Red unionists even found themselves battling former comrades with whom they had suffered through earlier Red organizing struggles (Saposs, 1959/1976, pp. 136-141, 150). In the clashes in the early 1930s between rival unionists in the auto industry, for example, elements of the CPUSA-Opposition (led by Jay Lovestone), whose members had been expelled from the Communist party in 1929, were the bitterest enemies of the Red unionists (and of such Red "tools" as the Reuther brothers!) (Levenstein, 1981, pp. 107-108).

To this motley and explosive political mix were added, from the late 1930s on, Catholic activists organized in the Association of Catholic Trade Unionists (ACTU), who saw their mission as fighting against Communist unionists, even—if not mainly—within Red union strongholds. ACTU's earliest rank-and-file caucus activity was often a direct response to earlier Red organizing (Levenstein, 1981, pp. 110-120; Seaton, 1981, pp. 144, 153-159).

So the CIO unions organized in industries that had been penetrated by earlier Red unionism inherited not only nuclei of experienced Red organizers and effective leaders, but a variety of rival political activists and alert leaders, ready, willing, and able to engage in battle with each other over the destiny of the union, no matter which grouping had won its immediate leadership.

Some of the rival groupings were especially active in seeking constitutional guarantees of basic civil and political rights, out of both principle and self-interest, given their own vulnerable, minority political situation.[12] This applies, in particular, to the Red unionists, who bore the brunt of repression, as well as expulsion, in their battles to form "revolutionary oppositions" inside AFL unions or to amalgamate existing AFL "trade" unions, and organize the unorganized, into industrial unions.

So, like other opposition groups, Red unionists also tended to "develop . . . a democratic ideology, an insistence on specific minority rights, as a means of legitimating their own right to exist" (Lipset et al., 1962, p. 16); they insisted that "the fight for industrial unionism [went] hand-in-hand . . . with the need for genuine trade union democracy" (Foster, 1936/1952a, p. 208; also see 1927, pp. 286, 296-297, 299).

We find, in fact, that among the unions in industries penetrated by earlier Red unionism (N = 15), 53% granted only "routine power" to their executive but this was so for only 11% of the unions in the other industries (N = 9). Yet their percentages of oligarchical unions scarcely differed (and were even a bit the reverse of expectations): 27% of the former versus 22% of the latter gave "considerable power" to their executive. Similarly, 57% of the unions in industries with earlier Red unionism (N = 21) had a high level of equality of franchise compared with 35% of the others (N = 17). But again, the percentages of unions with a low level of franchise equality were not much different: 19% of the former as compared with 23% of the latter. We suggest a crucial reason for this below, in discussing how the odds of union democracy were indirectly affected by earlier Red unionism.

AFL Secession: "From Above" or "From Below"

In the fall of 1936, the AFL "suspended" 10 unions affiliated with the CIO (then still the *Committee* on Industrial Organization) on charges of "dual unionism." The 10 unions immediately started making their per capita payments to the now independent CIO (Bernstein, 1970, pp. 422-423).[13] These founding unions of the CIO, and a few others that soon followed them, came into the new industrial union movement as the result of a revolt "from above." Their top officers broke away from the AFL and joined the CIO with their staff and organizational hierarchy—and much of their union jurisdiction—intact. As a result, there was continuity of leadership, and little if any internal dissension or crystallized—let alone organized—opposition factions; for the same reasons, probably only minimal changes were made in the relatively autocratic constitutions they inherited from the AFL.

In contrast, most other CIO unions grew out of local and district battles between craft and industrial unionists over the control of their AFL precursors. Such workers' insurgencies "from below" split many AFL unions. The workers in these AFL locals and districts then joined the CIO to form the core of new international unions, and brought their leading organizers into the new unions with them. This happened, for instance, in the AFL's Upholsterers International Union in 1937, where a number of locals defected from the AFL and combined with some other independent craft unions and a few CIO locals to form the CIO United Furniture Workers (Peterson, 1944, p. 135). Other struggles "from below" took place in the newly chartered AFL "federal labor unions," that is, the newly organized locals given a temporary AFL charter to "store workers" until they could be "parcelled out" to AFL craft affiliates (Bernstein, 1970, p. 355). Some seceded from the AFL to become the locals of a new CIO union rather than be parcelled out and subordinated to craft control.

Of course, radicals and Communists abounded among the original insurgent leaders, but these rebellions also probably resulted in a "colossal overproduction of organizers" (in Nikolai Bukharin's apt phrase) and of experienced and skilled rank-and-file leaders at all levels of these new unions. Thus such insurgent origins must have endowed these unions with an ample pool of skilled activists—with their own personal ambitions and differing political commitments and conceptions of workers' interests—that would "nullify the *stability*" of the union's officials and form the basis of an organized opposition to them (Bukharin, 1925, pp. 310, 311; see also Lipset et al., 1962, p. 455).

At their founding conventions, one of the first political acts of the unions that arose out of workers' insurgencies often was to throw out their old AFL constitutions, which had concentrated power in a handful of top officials, and write new ones that broadened rank-and-file representation in the unions' executive bodies and provided guarantees against the kinds of organizational abuse suffered by their insurgent organizers when they had been dissidents or radicals in the AFL. The members of the new ILGWU, for instance, abolished the notoriously dictatorial ILA constitution and replaced it with one that was more open to rank-and-file control (Kimeldorf, 1988, pp. 10-11).

In fact, the levels of democracy in the unions in these categories differ sharply: 70% of the unions that arose through workers' rebellions ($N = 10$) granted their executive only routine power compared with 14% of those whose top officers broke with the AFL and took their union into the CIO (N = 14); and 10% of the former but 36% of the latter endowed their executive with considerable power. Similarly, 56% of the unions born from below (N = 18) but 40% of those born from above (*N* = 20) had a high level of equality of the franchise; and 11% and 30%, respectively, had none of the provisions protecting equal franchise.

Independent Organizing

Most of the CIO unions were organized by independent rank-and-file committees, made up of both workers who organized clandestinely "on the inside" and their comrades on the outside. They decided for themselves on their overall organizing strategy and on the detailed tactics of the struggle: They wrote and then distributed their own leaflets at the factory gates or in the workers' neighborhoods, decided what demands to make, and when and how to make them, and whether to call strikes.

Top CIO officials, such as UMW's John L. Lewis and the Amalgamated Clothing Workers' Sidney Hillman, often had little alternative but to let independent rank-and-file organizers alone, for without their hard work, courage, commitment, and sacrifice to organize the unorganized, the CIO could well have been stillborn. Radicals of all kinds were found among the organizers. Some were experienced, battle-hardened old hands, "the flotsam and jetsam of years of sinking radical dreams"—Wobblies, homegrown and immigrant class-conscious Socialist unionists, and Reds—who had been baptized in earlier organizing battles (Levenstein, 1981, p. 63). But many others were young radicals who came of age in the Great Depression and were drawn to the cause of industrial unionism by the mass misery and the open class war then being waged in the United States. Although CIO officials had to give "some leeway" to the ready but recalcitrant, even politically dangerous, radical organizers who usually took the lead in organizing the new unions, they also did what they could to keep "firm control" in their own hands.

Whenever they could, CIO officials set up "organizing committees" instead of independent international unions, put their own men in charge, and tightly controlled the organizers (Bernstein, 1970, p. 616; Taft, 1964). For example, Lewis put Philip Murray, his own union's vice president, in charge of the Steel Workers' Organizing Committee (SWOC), and Van Bittner, another United Mine Workers Union official, at the head of the Packinghouse Workers' Organizing Committee. CIO organizing committees were also set up in shoes, textiles, oil, and other industries. These committees were not autonomous; only Lewis and Hillman and their closest associates made the organizing decisions.

If a CIO organizing committee's members, whatever their political coloration, but especially if they were radicals of any hue, began to gain an independent following among the local workers, or became "too dangerous a threat, they were discharged" (Saposs, 1959/1976, p. 122). The SWOC was archetypal in this regard (Levenstein, 1981, p. 51; Taft, 1964, p. 57). Set up in 1937, it was under the tight control of Lewis and his then lieutenant Phil Murray. They did not allow the establishment of the union itself, United Steel Workers of America, until 1942 (and then this was possible only because Lewis resigned and took his UMW out of the CIO). At its first constitutional convention that year, the USWA was born without enduring the sharp "birth pangs" characteristic of the independently organized unions. Its foundation was accompanied by "nothing that could be called factional strife" (Leiserson, 1959, p. 159). When a couple of delegates tried to get time to study the 24-page printed draft of the constitution submitted by a committee (because, as one delegate said, "I think this constitution paper we have here is going to build our rights for years to come, and we have got to establish them"), Murray told them they would have "plenty of time" to study it while it was being read from the podium. He told the delegates that he was not trying to push a "single solitary line in this constitution . . . down your throat," but wanted the "bickering and . . . noise making, . . . and all that stuff" stopped. After less than 10 hours of discussion, at a convention attended by 1,700 delegates from 1,100 locals, "every clause of the constitution was adopted by the delegate body without changing a word in the printed draft. . . . Each of the national officers was elected by unanimous ballot"—the previous heads of SWOC (Leiserson, 1959, pp. 159-163).

In auto, in contrast, a host of contending radical, Communist, Socialist, Coughlinite Catholic, and other factions competed to organize the unorganized and to win power in the new CIO union. The UAW financed many of its own organizing drives by collecting dues from the workers. Although the CIO also contributed money and organizers to the Ford drive, top CIO officials had little direct influence on the conduct of the campaigns against the big auto companies. As a result, "even at the height of CIO influence in the internal affairs of the UAW," the CIO was unable to impose "outside leadership" (Galenson, 1960, p. 133). Also, the major auto companies bitterly resisted unionization. GM, for instance, agreed to bargain with the CIO union only after a tenacious and often violent struggle with the workers. In these battles, and in some of the decisive sit-down strikes—for example, in Flint, "the first great victory" for the UAW "and one of the epic confrontations in American labor history" (Zieger, 1986, pp. 46-47)—all sorts of radicals (from anti-Communist Socialists such as the Reuther brothers and Emil Mazey, Trotskyists such as John Anderson, "anti-anti-Communists" such as George Addes and Richard Leonard, to Communists such as Nat Ganley, Bob Travis, and Wyndham Mortimer)—earned reputations as superb organizers and combative and courageous leaders. Consequently, these groups were able to create strong rank-and-file bases in the auto industry (Galenson, 1960, p. 150). No wonder, then, that shortly after its founding in 1937, the union split, and had to be refounded again as a CIO affiliate at a special convention two years later. Whatever their differences, the various UAW factions, which held regular meetings and had recognized delegates, sought in one way or another to enhance rank-and-file power, protect dissent, decentralize authority, and, especially, limit the authority of the president and other international executive officers (Galenson, 1960, pp. 171-172; Leiserson, 1959, pp. 154-159). The founding conventions of other unions that were organized independently may have "lacked the exaggerated conflicts and spectacularism of the UAW-CIO," but otherwise they were quite similar (Leiserson, 1959, p. 158).

These were the circumstances, we suggest, in which the chances were highest that various factions of a union could build their own political bases and continue to contest if not win union leadership over the years. Where, however, the organizing was done under the aegis (and thumb) of an official CIO organizing committee (as in SWOC), this tended to prevent the organizers from putting down roots from which an independent opposition might grow, and whose activities in the union would be reflected in a more democratic constitution. If this reasoning is correct, then the unions built by independent organizers should be more likely to be democratic than those built by CIO organizing committees.

That is, indeed, what we find. Half of the unions that were organized independently (N = 16) but only 12% of those built by a CIO committee (N = 8) endowed their executive with only routine power; and, on the other end of the spectrum, half of the latter but only 12% of the former gave their executive considerable power. Similarly, 54% of the independently organized unions (N = 26) compared with 33% of those built by a CIO committee (N = 12) had a high level of equality of the franchise, though the proportions with no provisions protecting equal franchise were nearly identical: 23% of the former versus 25% of the latter.

Amalgamation

Whether they were born "from above" or "from below," independently or under the aegis of a CIO organizing committee, the formation of CIO unions tended to follow roughly either a "unitary" or a "federated" (or "amalgamated") path. Unitary (i.e., centralized) organizations tend, as they grow, to incorporate new members and locals into their existing (usually hierarchical) structure, "with the new subordinate officials and groups deriving their authority from the summits of the organization." In contrast, an amalgamated organization grows through the lateral merger or combination of a number of existing unions, locals, or groups of leaders (Lipset et al., 1962, p. 442).[14]

Some unions amalgamated because their "jurisdictions," whatever their CIO charter said, were still mixed and shifting. Sometimes several unions were organizing in different branches of the same "industry." Sometimes a single union branched out and organized locals in several closely related "industries." To amalgamate or not to amalgamate was thus always a political question, as well as a specific issue in the organizing strategy of the unions and locals involved. Whether such coalitions should be permitted or not was also a crucial political question for top CIO officials. For example, the CIO's head office ordered the UE, which soon was to become known as the CIO's "Red fortress," to relinquish the utility worker locals UE had been organizing for more than a year. CIO officials created a new jurisdiction and established a separate, conservatively led, Utility Workers Union (Galenson, 1960, p. 253).

Two of the CIO's "Big Three," UAW and UE, arose through amalgamation; but the USWA, as we know, was a thoroughly unitary structure, "built from the top down, with power firmly concentrated at the top. Indeed, despite its enormous growth, . . . the union's top officers [retained] total administrative power . . . [in the] still highly centralized union" (Levenstein, 1981, p. 51). It became the very model of a unitary organization, with little if any local or district autonomy, and "no serious factional disputes [giving] . . . the members the right to choose among rival candidates for office. Any local center of disturbance was eliminated by [Philip] Murray" (Lipset et al., 1962, p. 443).

Was the USWA's authoritarian regime a "functional requirement" of the industry's (large-scale, highly concentrated) structure itself? As plausible as such a suggestion is, it does not square, for instance, with what happened in auto—that is, in another industry with a similar scale of production and level of concentration.

During the 1920s, a number of rival unions had been involved in trying to organize auto workers, among them the TUUL's Auto Workers Union; in 1937, their battered remnants, revivified by the decade's mass struggles, amalgamated to form the UAW. In turn, they formed the basis for the UAW's internal factions, most of whose leaders had been deeply involved in the earlier years of organizing. These factions consisted largely of "coalitions of the groups headed by these different leaders jointly resisting efforts to subordinate them to the national administration." So, despite the unfavorable "structural conditions . . . for internal democracy and large-scale rank-and-file participation" in a huge union in a mass production industry such as auto, it remained a relatively democratic union throughout most of the CIO era (and, as Lipset et al. wrote in the mid-1950s, "it has taken close to two decades to approach a one-party structure and the process is still not completed"; p. 443).

So the formation of a union through amalgamation, as the example of the UAW suggests, in bringing the leaders, members, and finances of the merged unions into a single organization, results in the redistribution of rank, authority, and power within the new union. Some officials of the previously separate unions are reduced, at best, to secondary officers of the new international or even to officers of a local, while others emerge as top officers of the international. But whatever the outcome for individuals, amalgamation ordinarily also tends to preserve autonomous centers of power in the new union and to improve their leaders' chances to retain political bases within it, from which they can try to extend their influence and contend for the international's leadership. In a sense, then, such amalgamated unions tend to "have internal opposition groups . . . built into them" (Lipset et al., 1962, p. 465). Unitary unions, in contrast, do not tend to have such internal political heterogeneity built into them; and this in turn, probably, would lessen their chances of being democratic.

Consistent with this reasoning, the executives of 71% of the amalgamated unions (N = 7) but only 23% of the unitary unions (N = 17) held only routine power; and *none* of the amalgamated unions gave their executive considerable power, although 35% of the unitary unions did so. Similarly, 66% of the amalgamated (N = 12) but only 38% of the unitary unions (N = 26) had a high level of equality of the franchise; and 8% of the former but 27% of the latter had a low level.

INDEPENDENT EFFECTS OF THE
FOUR INSURGENT POLITICAL PRACTICES

Among the four "insurgent political practices," that is, earlier Red unionism, workers' insurgency, independent organizing, and amalgamation, only Red unionism did not have a measurable independent effect in determining the odds in favor of the consolidation of either set of democratic political rights in the unions. This is revealed by a logit model constructed to measure the independent effects of these insurgent practices.[15] The odds that the top executive of a union was relatively accountable (that is, held only routing or moderate power, rather than considerable power) were about even for unions in industries penetrated by earlier Red unionism and unions in other industries. But, in contrast, the odds were four to one that independently organized unions as compared with those built by a CIO committee were relatively accountable. The odds were five to one for amalgamated as compared with unitary unions. And the odds were nearly six to one for unions born from below rather than from above. As to the equality of the franchise, only independent organizing and amalgamation had measurable independent effects in its favor: The odds were nearly three to one that independently organized unions as compared with those built by a CIO committee had a high level of equality of the franchise; and the odds were five to one that amalgamated as compared with unitary unions had a high level.

Why did earlier Red organizing not have a direct effect in enhancing the odds of democratic political rights? This was so, we suggest, because CIO officials emplaced tightly controlled organizing committees in these Red-organized industries to forestall Communist penetration and leadership of the new CIO unions there. (Many *more* of the CIO unions that arose in these Red-penetrated industries than in the remaining industries were actually the product of a CIO organizing committee [38% of the former, N = 21, versus 23% of the latter, N = 17; Stepan-Norris & Zeitlin, 1989, p. 516].) Thus, perhaps unwittingly, they also prevented deep-rooted opposition factions and internal democracy from emerging there. As a result, the effects of earlier Red unionism on the odds of union democracy were really contradictory (i.e., both positive and negative simultaneously), for earlier Red unionism contributed *in*directly to the process that enhanced democratic rights.

Radical industrial unionists—from Eugene Victor Debs to William Z. Foster—had fought to make "amalgamation" a "burning issue" long before the formation of the CIO. They advocated the "concentration of the forces of organized labor [through] amalgamation of the six score craft unions into a few industrial unions," and saw amalgamation as a "life necessity of trade unionism" (Foster, 1927, pp. 32, 22). For both practical and principled reasons, the organizers and other workers (especially the radicals among them) who had been involved in, or at least influenced by, these earlier organizing battles probably tried to amalgamate the new CIO unions they were building; in this way they could "concentrate their forces" against capital. For these reasons, the CIO unions organized in industries penetrated by earlier Red unionism tended to originate through amalgamation. In addition, since the AFL long had opposed industrial unionism, in principle, and had "made so little effort to organize the unorganized" (Draper, 1972, p. 374), the major industrial unions probably arose, with rare exceptions, only where radicals, and Red unionists particularly, had been active in the pre-CIO era. Perhaps most of the TUUL unions had become "moribund" or had "faded away" by the time of the CIO upsurge (Klehr, 1984, pp. 47, 133). But some of them or their remnants had survived with enough independence and cohesion to be able, once the CIO drive began, to amalgamate with other such remnants, AFL federal locals, or independent unions. So, for instance, UE grew out of the amalgamation of the locals of the TUUL's Steel and Metal Workers Industrial Union led by James Matles; several independent electrical worker locals organized by skilled immigrant English Socialist unionists, who elevated Julius Emspak to their leadership; and the Radio and Allied Trade Union Workers led by James Carey (who only a few years earlier, in 1933, had been clashing with Red unionists in Philadelphia) (Levenstein, 1981, p. 60).

This reasoning about the effect of earlier Red unionism on the chances that unions in the industry would amalgamate is supported by the findings of this study: Of the unions in industries that saw earlier Red organizing ($N = 21$), 52% were formed through amalgamation; but of the unions in industries without significant earlier Red organizing ($N = 17$), 94% were formed as unitary organizations. In turn, of course, amalgamation was to be crucial in establishing democratic rights in the union.

Similarly, to the extent that earlier Red unionism radicalized the workers involved or created local Red bases within AFL unions, this made insurrections against their officials and secession to join the CIO more likely. As many as 635 AFL union locals had radical or Red nuclei organized within them by the time the CIO was born (Klehr, 1984, p. 225). These nuclei were decisive, we suggest (as AFL officials themselves charged) in "fomenting insurrection" against the AFL, and in leading their fellow workers into the burgeoning CIO unions. Again, this reasoning is consistent with our findings: Of the unions in industries with earlier Red unionism ($N = 21$), 62% were born of workers' insurgencies; but 71% of the unions in industries untouched by earlier Red unionism ($N = 17$) came into the CIO in a revolt of their top (AFL) officers. In turn, as we know, establishment of a CIO union through a workers' revolt rather than through a revolt of top officers favored the establishment of executive accountability. Thus, earlier Red unionism increased the chances of both union amalgamation and workers' insurgency and so indirectly contributed to the consolidation of democratic rights.

CONCLUSION

Contrary to the theory that oligarchy in labor unions is an "immanent necessity" of "organization," this analysis has revealed that oligarchy is no more immanent or necessary than democracy. Rather, the two are alternative possible paths of union development. Which of these paths is taken by unions is not determined by any "iron law," but by concrete, relatively contingent political struggles among contending workers' factions and parties and thus by their (the unions') resultant pattern of internal political relations. The unions that were organized through insurgent political practices tended, as a result, to have political diversity built into them and thus to inscribe basic democratic political rights in their constitutions. In a phrase, insurgency and democracy in America's industrial unions were inseparable. Or, as Alvin W. Gouldner (1955) put it metaphorically, "If oligarchical waves repeatedly wash away the bridges of democracy, this eternal recurrence can happen only because men doggedly rebuild them after each inundation" (p. 506).

NOTES

1. "International" because these unions organized workers not only in the United States but also in U.S. territories and Canada.

2. *Union Democracy* "began to take shape" during the late 1940s, at the tail end of the CIO era, and was published in 1956, a year after the CIO-AFL merger. Which "clauses" its authors have in mind here, they do not tell us. They provide no systematic evidence (or even cite the "studies of social scientists") that, they say, would "tend to confirm" this "generalization" that union constitutional clauses and actual union internal political life "bear little relationship" to each other. (They do, however, provide *one* salient, and important, *example* of the discrepancy between formal constitutional provisions and actual practice in a union: Although the International Typographical Union had an institutionalized two-party system, its constitution explicitly prohibited ITU members from joining a "combination composed wholly or partly" of ITU members "with the intent or purpose to . . . influence or control the legislation of this union.") Yet, by the end of the book, Lipset et al. (1962) formulate a hypothesis that contradicts their rejection at the book's outset of the importance of constitutional rights: "The greater the protection for the rights of political opposition included in a union's code of law, the greater the chances for democracy" (p. 468). This hypothesis is indeed the underlying assumption of the measures of constitutional rights used here, and is consistent with a close reading of the history of the CIO unions, as we discuss below.

3. In fact, despite their blanket denial of the relevance of constitutional clauses, Lipset et al. (1962) themselves specifically point to such authoritarian clauses as evidence of "the power of top officials": "Most unions have given their executive boards the right to suspend local officials for violating policies of the central bodies" and thereby increase "their monopolization of internal power." They specifically refer to constitutional provisions that forbid "slandering union officers," distributing circulars to union members, or forming internal factions, cliques, or parties as restrictions on union democracy (pp. 8, 271-272, 290).

4. Neither author tells us the exact year of the constitutions they examined. Summers (1950) also studied the disciplinary powers codified in 154 union constitutions. He found that "two

thirds of the unions have clauses [in their constitutions] which expressly restrict internal political action" (p. 513). Unfortunately, in this article—unlike in his 1946 article on the franchise, discussed below—Summers does not provide systematic information on each clause for each union constitution examined, so a secondary analysis of his data was not possible.

5. Mills's (1948/1971) appraisal, therefore, is not correct insofar as it applies to the AFL: "Almost always *on paper*, . . . the American labor unions are democratic societies" (p. 5; emphasis added).

6. The data were compiled and these relationships calculated on the basis of information in Taft (1948, pp. 459-466) and Summers (1946, table 3); unions on Summers's list that had fewer than 2,000 members or for which membership was not given are omitted.

7. Of course, some union officials, always in collusion with employers, have had a hand in the control of *illegitimate* means of violence (e.g., in the racket-ridden East Coast International Longshoremen) (Kimeldorf, 1988) or the UMW's "benevolent satrapy" under John L. Lewis during the 1920s (Foster, 1927, pp. 132-137; Taft, 1948, pp. 469-471).

8. For some important instances, in the unions in steel (USWA), auto (UAW), electrical (UE), rubber (URW), textiles (TWU), wood (IWA), oil (OWIU), and the newspaper industry (ANG), see Galenson (1960, pp. 114, 171, 263-265, 273, 347, 396-397, 405-406, 417, 423, 562-563); in East Coast maritime (NMU), see Levenstein (1981, p. 257) and Saposs (1959/1976, p. 141); in West Coast longshore (ILWU), see Kimeldorf (1988, pp. 10-11); in transport (TWU), USWA, and UE, see Preis (1964, pp. 372, 327, 339, 401).

9. Foster (who later became a leading figure in the Communist party) led the organizing of Chicago's packinghouse workers, under the aegis of the AFL after World War I, and the "great steel strike" of 1919; in 1920, he organized and led the "Red" Trade Union Educational League (TUEL) (on which, see below) (Cochran, 1977, pp. 92-93).

10. We have carried out a preliminary replication of the present analysis using a comprehensive "Index of the Level of Constitutional Democracy" (Stepan-Norris & Zeitlin, 1991), and the findings of both of these analyses are similar.

11. The first phase of Red union organizing, from 1920 through late 1929, was under the direction of the TUEL. The second phase, through late 1935, was under its successor, the TUUL.

12. This was surely not true, however, of many ex-Communists and Socialists or, especially, of their allies in ACTU, which consistently "endorsed increased restrictions on the civil liberties of left-wing CIO members and demanded government intervention within the CIO should the CIO unions prove unwilling to 'clean house' " (Seaton, 1981, p. 192).

13. The CIO officially transformed itself into the Congress of Industrial Organizations at its constitutional convention in November 1938.

14. *Amalgamation* refers here to the merger in the 1930s of several independent units to form one CIO union. Thus unions are not classified as amalgamated if they were formed out of the merger of AFL federal locals alone; in general, these federal locals had little if any prior independent organizational existence. Only if the merger of an established AFL union led to a substantial reorganization of its administrative or political structure when it joined the CIO is the emergent union classified as amalgamated.

15. Logit modeling provides coefficients interpretable as precise measures of independent effect. We have reported only the odds multipliers, in "everyday language," that is, as the comparative odds of alternative political outcomes.

REFERENCES

Aaron, B., & Komaroff, M. I. (1949). Statutory regulation of internal union affairs—II. *Illinois Law Review, 44,* 631-674.

Allen, V. L. (1954). *Power in trade unions.* London: Longmans, Green.

American Civil Liberties Union. (1948). A "bill of rights" for union members. In E. W. Bakke & C. Kerr (Eds.), *Unions, management and the public* (pp. 191-192). New York: Harcourt, Brace.

Bell, D. (1960). Union growth and structural cycles. In W. Galenson & S. M. Lipset (Eds.), *Labor and trade unionism* (pp. 89-93). New York: John Wiley.

Beloff, M. (Ed.). (1987). *The Federalist: or, the New Constitution, by Alexander Hamilton, James Madison, and John Jay.* Oxford: Basil Blackwell.

Bernstein, I. (1970). *Turbulent years: A history of the American worker 1933-1941.* Boston: Houghton Mifflin.

Bukharin, N. (1925). *Historical materialism.* New York: International.

CIO. (c. 1949). *The CIO: What it is and what it does.* Washington, DC: Author.

Cochran, B. (1977). *Labor and communism: The conflict that shaped American unions.* Princeton, NJ: Princeton University Press.

Dahl, R. A. (1956). *A preface to democratic theory.* Chicago: University of Chicago Press.

Draper, T. (1972, Spring). The communists and the miners. *Dissent,* pp. 371-392.

Edelstein, J. D., & Warner, M. (1975). *Comparative union democracy.* London: George Allen & Unwin.

FE (United Farm Equipment and Metal Workers of America). (1949). *International Harvester double talk.* Leaflet.

Foster, W. Z. (1927). *Misleaders of labor.* Chicago: Trade Union Educational League.

Foster, W. Z. (1952a). Labor and politics. In W. Z. Foster, *American trade unionism: Principles and organization, strategy and tactics: Selected writings* (pp. 136-143). New York: International. (Original work published 1936)

Foster, W. Z. (1952b). Organizational problems of industrial unionism. In W. Z. Foster, *American trade unionism* (pp. 244-260). New York: International. (Original work published 1937)

Galenson, W. (1940). *Rival unionism in the United States.* New York: American Council on Public Affairs.

Galenson, W. (1960). *The CIO challenge to the AFL.* Cambridge, MA: Harvard University Press.

Galenson, W., & Lipset, S. M. (1960). Democracy and bureaucracy in trade union government. In W. Galenson & S. M. Lipset (Eds.), *Labor and trade unionism* (pp. 203-205). New York: John Wiley.

Gilpin, T. (1988). *The FE-UAW conflict: The ideological content of collective bargaining in postwar America.* Paper presented at the North American Labor History Conference, Detroit, MI.

Gouldner, A. W. (1955). Metaphysical pathos and the theory of bureaucracy. *American Political Science Review, 49,* 496-507.

Herberg, W. (1943). Bureaucracy and democracy in labor unions. *Antioch Review, 3,* 405-417.

Howe, I., & Widdick, B. J. (1949). *The U.A.W. and Walter Reuther.* New York: Random House.

Jacobs, P. (1963). *The state of the unions.* New York: Atheneum.

Kimeldorf, H. (1988). *Reds or rackets? The making of radical and conservative unions on the waterfront.* Berkeley: University of California Press.

Klehr, H. (1984). *The heyday of American communism.* New York: Basic Books.

Leiserson, W. M. (1959). *American trade union democracy.* New York: Columbia University Press.

Levenstein, H. A. (1981). *Communism, anticommunism, and the CIO.* Westport, CT: Greenwood.

Lipset, S. M. (1963). *The first new nation: The United States in historical and comparative perspective.* New York: Basic Books.

Lipset, S. M., Trow, M. A., & Coleman, J. S. (1962). *Union democracy: The internal politics of the International Typographical Union.* Garden City, NY: Anchor.

Magrath, C. P. (1959). Democracy in overalls: The futile quest for union democracy. *Industrial and Labor Relations Review, 12,* 503-525.

Martin, R. (1968). Union democracy: An explanatory framework. *Sociology, 2,* 205-220.

Martin, R. (1971). Edelstein, Warner, and Cooke on "Union Democracy." *Sociology, 5,* 242-244.

Marx, K. (1973). Wages, price and profit. In *Karl Marx and Frederick Engels: Selected works in three volumes* (Vol. 2, pp. 31-76). Moscow: Progress.

McConnell, G. (1958a). Factionalism and union democracy. *Labor Law Journal, 9,* 635-640.

McConnell, G. (1958b). Historical traits and union democracy. *Monthly Labor Review, 81,* 603-605.

Michels, R. (1949). *Political parties.* New York: Free Press.

Mill, J. S. (1963). *Essays on politics and culture* (G. Himmelfarb, Ed.). Garden City, NY: Anchor.

Mills, C. W. (1971). *The new men of power: America's labor leaders.* New York: Kelley. (Original work published 1948)

Muste, A. J. (1948). Army and town meeting. In E. W. Bakke & C. Kerr (Eds.), *Unions, management and the public* (pp. 187-192). New York: Harcourt, Brace. (Original work published 1928)

Neumann, F. (1966). *Behemoth: The structure and practice of national socialism, 1933-1944.* New York: Harper & Row. (Original work published 1944)

Neumann, F. (1957). The concept of political freedom. In H. Marcuse (Ed.), *The democratic and authoritarian state: Essays in political and legal theory* (pp. 160-200). New York: Free Press.

Pateman, C. (1970). *Participation and democratic theory.* Cambridge: Cambridge University Press.

Peterson, F. (1944). *Handbook of labor unions.* Washington, DC: Fraternity.

Preis, A. (1964). *Labor's giant step.* New York: Pathfinder.

Saposs, D. J. (1976). *Communism in American unions.* Westport, CT: Greenwood. (Original work published 1959)

Seaton, D. (1981). *Catholics and radicals.* London: Associated University Presses.

Seidman, J. (1953). Democracy in labor unions. *Journal of Political Economy, 61,* 221-232.

Selznick, P. (1943). An approach to a theory of bureaucracy. *American Sociological Review, 8,* 47-54.

Shister, J. (1945). Trade-union government: A formal analysis. *Quarterly Journal of Economics, 60,* 78-112.

Stepan-Norris, J., & Zeitlin, M. (1989). "Who gets the bird?" or, How the communists won power and trust in America's unions: The relative autonomy of intraclass political struggles. *American Sociological Review, 54,* 503-523.

Stepan-Norris, J., & Zeitlin, M. (1991). Insurgency, radicalism, and democracy in America's industrial unions. *Working Paper Series,* no. 215. University of California, Los Angeles: Institute of Industrial Relations.

Summers, C. (1946). Admission policies of labor unions. *Quarterly Journal of Economics,*
  61, 66-107.
Summers, C. (1950). Disciplinary powers of unions. *Industrial and Labor Relations Review,*
  3, 483-513.
Summers, C. (1955). The political liberties of labor union members: A comment. *Texas Law*
  Review, 33, 603-619.
Taft, P. (1948). The constitutional power of the chief officer in American labor unions.
  Quarterly Journal of Economics, 62, 459-471.
Taft, P. (1962). *The structure and government of trade unions.* Cambridge, MA: Harvard
  University Press.
Taft, P. (1964). *Organized labor in American history.* New York: Harper & Row.
USWA (United Steel Workers of America). (1948). *Constitution of the International Union,*
  United Steel Workers of America, CIO. Boston: Author.
Williams, J. S. (1954). The political liberties of labor union members. *Texas Law Review, 32,*
  826-838.
Zeitlin, M. (1989). *The large corporation and contemporary classes.* Cambridge: Polity.
Zieger, R. H. (1986). *American workers, American unions, 1920-85.* Baltimore: Johns
  Hopkins University Press.

13

Class, Race, and Higher Education in America

Martin Trow

SOCIAL CLASS AND HIGHER EDUCATION

MASS higher education in the United States, with universal access in many places, shares many functions with similar institutions around the world. However, it has one function that is perhaps unique to us: It is the central instrument for the legitimation of a society around the principle of broad (and, in principle, equal) opportunities open to all individuals, opportunities to improve themselves and to make their careers and lives better through their own efforts and talents. Our 3,500 accredited colleges and universities, offering course work at every level of difficulty to an enormously diverse student body, serve a wide variety of functions for the students and for the society at large. While most of them offer some liberal and general studies, they serve as the chief avenue of entry to middle-class occupations—even to quite modest lower-middle-class occupations, which in most countries would not require or reward exposure to postsecondary education. These institutions, without the kinds of educational ceilings common in European nonuniversity forms of postsecondary schooling, encourage students to raise their aspirations through further study, full- or part-time, and provide the possibility of transfer to advanced studies elsewhere if they do not have such provisions themselves.

AUTHOR'S NOTE: This chapter is a revised version of a paper prepared for a seminar on the report *Review of Higher Education Policy in California,* delivered to the Organization for Economic Cooperation and Development by a committee chaired by A. H. Halsey, 1989. The seminar was sponsored by the Center for Studies in Higher Education, University of California, Berkeley, June 1990. Quoted material in this chapter from *The Grapes of Wrath,* by John Steinbeck, copyright © 1939, renewed © 1967 by John Steinbeck, are used by permission of Viking Penguin, a division of Penguin Books USA Inc.

They thus reflect and reinforce the radical individualism of American values, a set of values deeply opposed to socialist principles, which center on cooperative efforts at group advancement and on the common effort to create a society whose members all profit (more or less equally) from the common effort. American higher education, as a system, both serves and celebrates the American Dream of individual careers open to talents, a dream given much of its institutional reality in the contemporary world precisely by America's system of mass higher education offering a clear alternative to socialist principles of class identification and horizontal loyalty. The contrast between these competitive visions is captured in the stirring appeal of Eugene Debs, the last socialist leader in the United States with any significant following (he gained nearly a million votes for president on the Socialist ticket in 1920), when he called on his followers, most of them in the working class, to "rise with your class, not out of it."

Mass higher education in the United States (and to some extent elsewhere as well)[1] is deeply opposed to this vision of society, to which it offers the alternative exhortation, "Rise out of your class, not with it." That unexpressed call (unexpressed precisely because it is understood beyond need for explication by all Americans) touches a fundamental chord in American society, not least among its workers and immigrants. It is a long-standing cliché of American life that parents say with fervor of their children, "I want them to have a better life than I have had," a better life seen as achievable not through collective or political action but through more and better education, and, in recent decades, through college education. In 1825, George Ticknor, then a professor at Harvard, expressed an American truism when he observed, "There is, at this moment, hardly a father in our country, who does not count among his chief anxieties, and most earnest hopes, the desire to give his children a better education than he has been able to obtain for himself" (quoted in Rudolph, 1962, p. 216). In the same year, the president of the University of Nashville, then near the frontier, declared that "every individual, who wishes to rise above the level of a mere labourer at task-work, ought to endeavor to obtain a liberal education" (quoted in Rudolph, 1962, p. 214). Already 160 years ago, "every individual," not just gentlemen, as in most of Europe, was being exhorted to rise out of the ranks of the "mere labourer" through education. Even though higher education in the United States would not be providing the means of social mobility for large numbers for a century or more, and not for the whole society until after World War II, the sense of the possibilities for achievement through education was evident very early indeed. And these were the expressions not of radical leaders but of members of the solid professional middle class, who believed they were voicing perfectly ordinary middle-class sentiments, not those of political radicalism.

The idea of higher education as an instrument of mobility for poor young men "making their way" was present in the United States throughout the eighteenth century, but it required the enormous growth in the numbers of colleges after 1800, the fierce competition among them, and the effect this competition had on the costs of college attendance to bring large numbers of penurious students to college. Allmendinger (1975), a historian of this period, notes that

> poor young men, sometimes described as "needy" or "indigent" or even "paupers" gathered in large numbers in the colleges of New England during the years between 1800 and 1860. They came down from the hill towns, where opportunities were few, to the small colleges at Hanover or Williamstown or Brunswick. Even before New York State and Ohio drew many of their kind to the West, they began to infiltrate—almost imperceptibly at first—the student population. They did not want new farm lands, nor would they try to find places at home as hired workers in an agricultural proletariat; they joined, instead, a rural intelligentsia of students and teachers aspiring to the middle-class professions. (p. 8)[2]

The proliferation of colleges in the United States in the first half of the nineteenth century resulted chiefly from the weakening of political constraints on their establishment. In the Colonies, as in most countries to this day, governments (in America, the colonial governments) controlled the establishment of colleges and universities through their control over the awarding of charters that would allow institutions to award degrees. Governments almost everywhere have had political and religious reasons for limiting the numbers of institutions of higher education; moreover, new universities have been subsidized by the state or been given guarantees of their continued survival. The Revolution in America greatly weakened central state power over higher education, as over almost everything else. The Constitution took education (including higher education) completely out of the authority of the federal government; it took both federal and state governments out of the direct administration of the new independent colleges springing up everywhere after the Revolution, and it also removed any firm commitment by government of public funds for their support. The hundreds of new colleges that opened in the period between the Revolution and the Civil War, many sponsored by the competitive Protestant denominations, had few academic or social pretensions, and in their need they were open and available to poor students. It did not take the democratic revolutions of the post-World War II era to create the possibility of a college education for poor youths; America had its democratic revolution in the first half of the nineteenth century. The nineteenth century, and especially the freeing of higher education from the control of the state, created the potential for the expansion of access to mass higher education in the United States, but that potential was fulfilled only after the Second World War (Rothblatt & Trow, in press; Trow, 1991).

This spirit of individual aspiration, opportunity, and achievement, present throughout our history but taking special force during and after the Revolution, is at marked variance with socialist principles of collective aspiration, opportunity, and achievement. It is at odds also with the instruments of that collective spirit, notably trade unions and the European socialist (or social democratic) parties of the past century, along with the cultural institutions that were created in many European nations around those institutions. Those institutions— schools, newspapers, sports clubs, cooperatives, and others—together consti- tuted not just a political/economic movement but an alternative subculture, the achievement of socialism in everyday life even before the triumph of socialism nationally.[3] But this subculture tied individual workers firmly to their class; it did not encourage mobility out of it. Even the adult education it provided was aimed at raising the moral and cultural level of workers, not at providing them an avenue of mobility into the middle class: These institutions characteristi- cally offered "humanistic" studies designed to raise the cultural level of the working-class members of the subculture, not vocational courses designed to equip members for mobility up and out of their class. For example, the studies provided the British workingman in his leisure hours by the Mechanics Insti- tutes and, later, by the Workers' Education Association pivoted around litera- ture and "pure" science, not professional engineering.[4]

Mass higher education is the enemy of a class-oriented society and of class-ori- ented institutions such as trade unions. In the United States it has always been so, but dramatically so since enrollments have broadened and grown to include large numbers who would formerly have joined the labor force directly from high school. The turning point was World War II, when the wartime effort created a quasi-so- cialist society for a few years without affecting the underlying individualistic ethos of the society (with the partial exception of its academic and intellectual elites). At the end of the war, American trade unions enrolled nearly 40% of the nonagricul- tural labor force, the highest level it ever achieved. It reached this level largely on the strength of wartime government requirements that firms having contracts with the government allow trade union organization of the labor force, a policy that in part reflected the close connections between organized labor and the northern wing of the Democratic party and in part came about because of the usefulness of the unions in organizing a wartime labor force and supporting the war. When the wartime rules were rescinded, along with the direct role of the government in the economy and a little later the decline of the industries in which unions were heavily represented (e.g., steel and mining), the proportion of the labor force in unions declined precipitously. During the years since World War II, while enrollments in higher education grew from 1.5 million to over 14 million and the proportion of the age grade enrolled in colleges and universities increased from 15% to about 50%, the proportion of the nonfarm labor force in trade unions fell from roughly 40% just after World War II to about 19% in 1988, and in the private sector to 14%.[5]

I am not suggesting a simple direct causal relationship between these fig- ures—for example, that all those who did not join the unions were going to college instead. Both sets of figures point to and reflect even more fundamental changes in the economy and society, changes that also occurred in other societies but that in the United States took on characteristically individualistic forms. As traditional heavy industry and the big manual occupations, such as mining and cargo handling, which everywhere have been the heart of the trade union movement, declined, other occupations grew that required (or came to be seen as requiring) a postsecondary education. In the United States, this meant a massive growth of enrollment in the same institutions that had educated the older social and professional elite groups and in the reinforcement of the individualistic ethos of opportunity and social mobility. All horizontal bondings that might inhibit or discourage individual mobility were avoided or weakened—not only trade union membership but church membership, as well as neighborhood and friendship ties. At the very least, they were modified and made instruments of individual mobility, as, for example, family ties. The family, for most people (outside of a small social elite that could pass on substantial wealth across generations), became not the source of an individual's inherited social status but a launching pad for an individual career, with the advantages of money and higher social status translated into opportunities for more and better formal education and thus of better life chances for individual achievement and mobility. Indeed, the very idea of a "career," the planned sequence of upward steps in a chosen occupation, as against a series of jobs gained and changed in the course of working life, is in the United States now largely a function of some experience of higher education; it is hard to have a career without having been to college. And a "career" is inherently the property of the individual, not that of an organization or class.

Institutions have survived in America by adapting to the conditions of a society marked by easy social and geographic mobility. Already in the eighteenth and nineteenth centuries, as George Homans shows, New England farmers (not peasants) were alert to the main chance; only 1 farm in 5 was passed on from father to son, and thus only 1 farm in 25 stayed in the same family over three generations. New England farmers' sons left for better land in the West or for better opportunities in other callings, as Americans have always done. Those who remained farmers showed less attachment to the land than to the idea of individual betterment, a betterment that in many cases included attendance at a state land-grant university, with its school of agriculture, and use of the university's agricultural research and demonstration units.

After World War II, the trade union movement survived least well because it could not adapt to social mobility: Unions are intrinsically instruments of horizontal bonding and are hence the enemy of individual achievement and mobility, except for the tiny number who could make the unions a career. (Many union leaders were and are college educated; they came to the unions out of ideological commitment rather than as a reflection of common class membership.) The absence in the United States of a solidly based socialist party and its related institutions narrowed further the possible reconciliation of class-linked organizations with some possibilities for individual mobility and achievement within the labor movement, as, for example, has been possible in Sweden and Great Britain, until recently.

The radically individualistic spirit of America is also opposed to a more conservative concept of social organizations that envisions society as organized around status groups and strata or corporate guilds, the careers (or, echoing

Weber, the life fates) of whose members are closely tied to those larger social entities. That spirit is embedded in most Western European societies, whether governed by social democratic or more conservative parties. And while market forces (the economic reflections of an individualistic ethos) have been gaining ascendancy everywhere over more corporativist modes of economic organization, they are still resisted by most European systems of higher education or are adapted within close constraints on access. Such constraints, tying access to universities to highly selective upper secondary schools, minimize the power of the consumer and thus limit (or at least postpone) the emergence of a system of higher education at the service of the society rather than of the state or of specific elite strata that will serve the state.

Throughout its history, U.S. society has, for many reasons, provided an unfriendly environment for socialist ideas and institutions. The absence of a feudal past, early extension of the vote to all white men, the frontier, relative affluence, ethnic heterogeneity, religious roots, and social mobility have all been cited as explanations of why the United States has been and continues to be the only industrialized society in the world without a significant socialist movement or party.[6] Mass higher education has been an important element in this "unfriendly environment," especially over the last half century. And it works in a variety of ways. For example, mass higher education, especially since the great expansion following World War II, has drained off from the working and lower middle classes many of their brightest and ablest young men and women—not only the most intelligent but those with the most energy and initiative—making for a kind of brain drain out of the working class and weakening its organizations.

Ironically, the strong cultural emphasis on social mobility, on "getting ahead" in life, may have accounted equally for the leaders who governed and ran the unions, the businessmen they bargained with, and the mob bosses with whom they all too often were allied. Strong aspirations for personal achievement, for getting ahead, drive Americans of all kinds to seek avenues of mobility of all kinds, both legitimate and illegitimate. The chief legitimate avenues have been through speculation in land, entrepreneurship, and education. The latter two have historically been alternative routes up for different groups in different generations. The chief illegitimate channel of mobility, of course, is crime, both blue- and white-collar, of which we have a fair amount. And white-collar crime increasingly requires an MBA, or at least the opportunities and access gained through higher education, both its skills and its connections. These channels have all been in competition with one another throughout American history, a competition that has provided the story for much of our literature and even more of our movies. Since World War II, they have become complementary. One can still start a small grocery store in an ethnic neighborhood without a college degree, but you need a college education to be a consultant about anything or to provide the sophisticated services of modern urban life.

But all of this—the multiple channels of mobility open to ordinary people and the ambitions behind them—is strongly corrosive of all institutions that depend on horizontal solidarity and collective improvement, not least the labor unions.[7] The brain drain through education out of the unions of their best and brightest young members is part, but only part, of that corrosion; it is one of the mechanisms of that corrosion.

We can see this also when we look at the last great period of union growth in the United States—the creation of the big industrial unions—the steelworkers, the automobile workers, the electrical workers, and then the CIO—during the Great Depression of the 1930s. This period preceded the great expansion of American higher education, for although our system in the 1930s was large by European standards, it was still exceptional then for poor or working-class youths to go to a college or university (Trow, 1961). For the ordinary industrial worker, something closer to the classic conditions of class struggle between labor and capital seemed to prevail. The new industrial unions—led to some considerable extent by socialists such as Walter Reuther and his brother in the United Auto Workers—had broader dreams and hopes for what a labor movement could do to reshape the politics, the economics, and indeed the basic character of American society. Such unions could evoke the deep loyalties of their members and could also be a real alternative to "getting ahead" as the guiding principle of life. It was perhaps not a fair test for the unions, because during most of that decade there was not much chance for anybody to get ahead in America. Still, perhaps for the first and last time in the United States, large numbers of people could envision building a working-class movement, one with real weight and influence on one of the two major political parties. The Roosevelt Democratic coalition provided an opening, with the more radical or visionary union leaders seeing perhaps a labor party of their own in the future.

Indeed, there seemed to be some historical warrant for such hopes; had not the democratic socialist and labor parties of Western Europe emerged out of just such coalitions with liberal bourgeois parties 30 to 50 years earlier? Could the United States replicate that history? Some, in any event, believed so.

Yet another element contributed to the building of working-class institutions during those Depression years, and that was the production, really for the first time, of a sizable group of unemployed college and university graduates, many of whom had themselves come from working- or lower-middle-class backgrounds. Many had grown up in homes with socialist ties or sympathies—"red diaper babies," as they were called—and had early taken advantage of relatively open access to higher education, particularly to free urban public universities such as New York's City College and Temple University in Philadelphia. Moreover, many of these young men were themselves socialists—of both the democratic and communist varieties. For these young men, job prospects in the 1930s were poor. Some, trained as economists or sociologists, could find work in the expanding welfare agencies of the New Deal and could believe themselves contributing in that way to a nascent socialism in America. Others threw in their lot with the new unions, sometimes serving apprenticeships on the shop floor and then getting elected to union office. Some went directly into union management by appointment to a staff position, as aides and advisers to the new, more politically minded, socialist-minded leaders. Sometimes the young men who went from college into the unions were members of the Communist party, and occasionally they were members of the Socialist Party of America. But for a short while, union leadership offered the prospect of a real ideologically oriented career for a small number of college-educated youths.[8]

But the dream of a politically relevant mass labor movement, one that would evolve into an independent Labor party embodying socialist principles, died with World War II.[9] It more obviously collapsed with the election of Truman in 1948, because that kept the labor movement inside the Democratic party. The pent-up wartime demand fueled an immediate boom; moreover, the government economists had learned something from the New Deal and the war about how central government interventions could avoid deep depressions as well as shorten and mitigate recessions. The growing economy, together with the GI Bill, encouraged and supported literally millions of veterans to go back to college, and the subtle permeation of democratic sentiments and higher aspirations throughout the society created a burst of demand for access to postsecondary education. The educational system thus grew to meet the demand. There were similar tendencies in all Western European countries; the difference was that in the United States, demand for education at every level drove supply. At the level of higher education, it was not constrained by either resources or academic standards. In 1950, a comprehensive secondary system was already bringing 50% of the young to high school graduation; that figure by 1990 was about 75%. During those postwar decades, the United States built and opened hundreds and hundreds of colleges of every kind, in some years nearly one every day, under an implicit, sometimes explicit, doctrine: "Something is better than nothing; let the future worry about standards. Right now, let us provide as good an education as possible for as many as possible."

And so between 1940 and 1970, nationwide enrollments rose from about 1.5 million to about 8.5 million. By 1991, enrollment in all U.S. colleges and universities stood at about 14 million. Roughly two-thirds of high school graduates get some exposure to postsecondary education in the seven years directly after high school graduation, comprising roughly half of the age cohort. And some 44% of the whole labor force, including of course older people, have now had some exposure to postsecondary education.

The enormous expansion of the postwar years changed the perceptions of higher education among broad strata who had never before seen it as a realistic possibility for people like themselves. Higher education thus became for many the vehicle for social mobility that high school graduation had been for the half century between 1890 and 1940. Those 50 years had seen the growth of a broad system of state-supported secondary education all over the country. Thus, while higher education had actually served as a vehicle of mobility for many before 1945, especially for youths from farms preparing themselves for teaching, and for such educationally precocious ethnic groups as Jews and Armenians, it was not seen as available for career making and mobility by broad segments of the population until after World War II.

The significance of the war as a watershed of values and attitudes ushering in the mass higher education that followed is suggested by *The Grapes of Wrath*. John Steinbeck's powerful novel, which was published in 1939, is about the mid-1930s in America, the Great Depression, and the migration of thousands of impoverished farmers from Oklahoma and Arkansas (the "Okies" of American history) to California. This great internal migration can best be compared to the post-World War II mass immigrations to California by people from other countries: Mexicans, Chinese from Hong Kong and Singapore, Vietnamese, Koreans, and Filipinos. Like the Okies, these more recent immigrants from around the Pacific Rim are predominantly poor people, and they in turn resemble the earlier European immigrants of the decades from 1860 to 1925. But the extent to which (and the ways in which) these different groups have used education in their strategies of acculturation have differed. *The Grapes of Wrath,* like so much of Depression-era literature, is a story infused with socialist values, marked by anger at the exploitation of workers by employers and the condemnation of injustice and inequality. It is a story of the class struggle, even if in the nonideological form in which that struggle was experienced and expressed by the migrant workers created by the Depression and fleeing to California from the Dust Bowl.

At the end of the novel, Casey, an itinerant preacher turned union organizer, is clubbed to death by some goons, thugs hired by a big farm company (or agrobusiness) to break a strike of migrant workers. In the melee, Tom Joad is injured, but he in turn kills the company thug, thus becoming a fugitive. He hides out in a field for a few days near his family, whose members are picking cotton for starvation wages. Ma Joad comes out to give him some food and to tell him he must go away to avoid arrest. He agrees, and in a final stirring speech tells her that he is going to take up Casey's work and become a union organizer, allied with poor people like himself against the rich and the exploitive. Ma asks where she will be able to find him, and his answer to her still moves us, more than half a century later.

> Well, maybe like Casey says, a fella ain't got a soul of his own, but on'y a piece of a big one—an' . . . then it don' matter. Then I'll be all aroun' in the dark. I'll be ever'where—wherever you look. Wherever they's a fight so hungry people can eat, I'll be there. Wherever they's a cop beatin' up a guy, I'll be there. . . . I'll be in the way guys yell when they're mad. . . . An' when our folks eat the stuff they raise an' live in the houses they build—why, I'll be there.

Tom goes out to fight for his people, the ordinary poor people pushed around by big corporations and their cops and thugs—a man committing his life to the struggle to rise with his class, not out of it: "Like Casey says, a fella ain't got a soul of his own, but on'y a piece of a big one."

What Tom Joad does *not* say to his Ma, in that hole in the ground where he's hiding near the boxcars in which she and the rest of his family are living and starving along with the other cotton pickers in prewar California, is

Ma, I've got to go and make it on my own. This is my chance to find out who
I am and what I'm made of. So, Ma, I'm going to Fresno State College down
the road. If *they* don't take me in, I'll go to one of these community colleges
springin' up all over the place, and I'll work my way through school and get
my bachelor's degree and then get my state license and mebbe an MBA and
buy and sell real estate. Maybe I'll start up my own little consulting firm and
make a pile of money and build a big house for you and Pa and Rose a' Sharon
and the kids, with four bathrooms and a swimming pool.

Tom doesn't say that, but he might have done so in a different novel out of
a different but equally authentic American tradition. What Tom did not say is
essentially what migrants both to and within America have said since our
beginning and certainly what most of Tom's successors have said in the great
migrations to California since World War II. These new immigrants, and the
children and grandchildren of the Okies, too—the descendants of the Joads and
their friends from Oklahoma—have flooded into California's colleges and
universities, which have expanded enormously in number and size to meet that
demand. Since World War II, very little has been heard in California of "rising
with your class," and a great deal about the need to create more truly equal
opportunities for individual advancement for all, rich and poor, black, brown,
and white, through education—and especially through higher education.

There is in American history and popular culture a heroic saga to compete
with the socialist saga: the story of the self-made man rising through his own
talents and industry. The saga is also often about the loneliness of that climb
and the pain that accompanies the breaking of strong ties to family, class, ethnic
group, and friends—a different kind of sacrifice in a different kind of struggle.
We hear it in the stories of the frontiersmen and in the saga of Swedish
emigration to America in Moberg's great epic. It is a sacrifice not *for* social
ties, ties of class and ethnicity, but *of* ties, and that can be an equally wrenching
sacrifice. We see and hear it endlessly in the films and stories of men and women
rising out of the urban slums and neighborhoods of the big Eastern melting-pot
cities, and it often has a bitter and sardonic twist of failed ambition and thwarted
aspiration. But after World War II, that saga usually includes attendance at a
college or university, as that becomes the alternative to failure or crime.

Today, we are not hearing many heroic sagas about young men and women
struggling out of the barrios (the Mexican-American slums of Los Angeles) up
to UCLA and law school and on to a partnership in a big law firm or elected
office. We are not hearing many black sagas of the rise out of the "projects"—
the public housing units that have become slums—up to the University of
California at Berkeley and beyond. These sagas are waiting to be told; it may
be that we haven't heard many yet because they don't seem heroic to those who
experience them. Or maybe the tellers are too busy just now making it up the
ladder to write about it.

RACE, ETHNICITY, AND HIGHER EDUCATION

A culture is defined, in part, by what it feels guilty about. Western European nations, on the whole, feel guilty about their working classes, about the sacrifices they made during the rapid industrialization of the nineteenth and early twentieth centuries, about their substantial exclusion from opportunities to get good health care, recreation and leisure, good education, economic security and security in old age, and to share in the high culture of their society. Much of public policy in European countries over the last 100 years, and more rapidly over the last 50 years, has been aimed at ameliorating and reducing those disadvantages linked to class.

Americans, in contrast, are remarkably free of guilt toward working-class people, individually or collectively. There is, of course, an enormous body of legislation on the books that aims at helping people who are, as we used to put it, "down on their luck," or, as we would now say, "disadvantaged." Some of it is federal law; much is state law.

The United States has more social legislation on the books than Europeans give us credit for and less, probably, than we need. But it has not been put there, for the most part, out of a sense of class guilt. If we have any national policy regarding social or economic class, it is an educational policy designed not to strengthen the working class or ameliorate its conditions but to abolish it. The American Dream, I believe, is that eventually everyone will be either self-employed or a salaried professional, and higher education is the instrument for the achievement of both.

If Americans do not feel especially guilty about the "working class"—even if they accept that there is such a thing—we as a nation still feel intensely guilty about our history of race relations, and especially about our history of black slavery and the elaborate social and legal machinery (much of it at the state level) for the subordination of blacks from the end of Reconstruction after the Civil War all the way to the burst of U.S. Supreme Court decisions and legislation that marked the racial revolution of the 1950s and 1960s. There is, of course, still plenty of racist sentiment in the society, although the polls show less all the time. But at the level of public policy, policies that are put in place by legislatures elected for the most part by white voters, the commitment to what can only be called a prominority policy is strong and persistent. The general term for prominority policies, policies aimed at benefiting particular racial or ethnic groups, is *affirmative action*. Affirmative action is pervasive throughout American society—in the hiring policies of private business, in public housing, in federal employment and its policies for contracting in the private sector for goods and services, in the military—but nowhere can its presence be seen more clearly than in the policies of higher education. It is apparent not only in public institutions, in response to legislative or government pressure, but in private institutions, in response chiefly to the powerful dictates of a collective conscience—a force that *also* operates in publicly supported institutions, where its effects are mixed up with those of expedience and institutional responsiveness to external pressures from government and interest groups.

"Affirmative action" as a concept and a set of institutional policies is the subject of intense debate and controversy, chiefly centering on whether government intervention in favor of racial or ethnic groups should be aimed at *equalizing* the *opportunities* for achievement and advancement of members of that group, or whether those efforts should continue in ways that will ensure instead the *equality of achievement itself* for that group, compared with the more advantaged groups in the society. The differences between these conceptions—of equality of opportunity and of achievement—are large, and the issue is still in doubt; all such issues in America end up in the Supreme Court, where the constitutional rights of the groups and individuals involved are determined.

Although sharp differences exist about the proper scope of affirmative action in American higher education and the appropriate degree of governmental or institutional intervention against the free play of competitive meritocracy, there is near unanimity in our colleges and universities that some kind and degree of affirmative action is appropriate and necessary.

Affirmative action makes the contrast sharp between our policies regarding class and our policies regarding race. Perhaps I can capture the difference in the realm of higher education by observing that I cannot remember ever hearing a California legislator demand that a university increase access to it for the sons and daughters of working-class families. Moreover, a recent report of the Organization for Economic Cooperation and Development (OECD) (1989) on California higher education could not say what proportion of the students at Berkeley are of working-class origins; our statistics are simply not collected that way. Chapter 2 of that OECD report, "Planning and Market in Higher Education," addresses "education and stratification" and "education and social selection," familiar categories when analyzing European education systems. But the report's authors are unable to discuss specifically Californian issues within these categories; the necessary statistics are not available, and the discussions carried on in California are rarely couched in these terms. It is the only chapter that rests completely on European perspectives and theories; its distance from Californian realities is apparent by contrast with the rest of the report.

The failure of traditional models of social stratification and social mobility to illuminate California's society helps clarify American exceptionalism. Elsewhere in advanced societies, education is seen as a vehicle or instrument for social mobility, both between generations and within a single lifetime. Social class is ordinarily defined by the physical nature of one's job or occupation, the income it commands, the status it enjoys, the sense of horizontal identity it engenders, or some combination of these dimensions of class position. In California at the end of the twentieth century, education is not so much a vehicle or channel to higher social status as it is itself the defining feature of one's social status. To "place" a person in the social world, one ordinarily asks where he or she went to "school" (i.e., college or university) and perhaps whether the individual finished and took a degree and what he or she studied. In 1987, less than 20% of Californians 25 years and older had not graduated from high school; nearly half had attended college, and the proportions were much higher among younger cohorts (Fay & Fay, 1990, p. 65). It is less important how one happens to be employed at any given moment, as people change jobs and occupations frequently, and what they do or appear to do correlates poorly with their education. Education predicts life-styles, attitudes, and loyalties much better than it does whether people are "manual" workers or self-employed, or their standing in one of the other ordinary categories of social stratification.

Ethnicity is the other great defining feature of Californians: If one knows a person's ethnicity and formal education, one knows a great deal about him or her. In contrast to the paucity of data on the class positions of Californians, the official statistics are rich in ethnic and racial data. The legislature is constantly affirming the importance of special efforts to recruit, retain, graduate, and sponsor members of disadvantaged minority groups. (In California, this includes blacks and Hispanics but now excludes almost all those of Asian origin. They are too successful to qualify for the special benefits and attention of affirmative action policies.) Many university policies pivot around racial issues, enormous amounts of statistics are collected within racial and ethnic categories, and discussions of affirmative action (mostly how to strengthen it and make it more effective in the university) are central themes in academia, from the department level on up.

In California, as elsewhere in the United States, student admissions are heavily influenced by affirmative action policies. As just one example of these policies, the proportion of blacks and Hispanics in the entering freshman class at UC Berkeley rose from about 11% in 1983 to about 29% in 1990, more than double. The proportion of Asians entering classes remained roughly constant at 29%, while the proportion of white enrollees fell from 58% to about 37%.[10] This was accomplished by applying quite different criteria for admissions to students in these different racial and ethnic groups. Similar policies are in place in almost every American college and university; the numbers in many are not as dramatic as at Berkeley only because they have fewer minority applicants.

Two questions might be asked: How can we explain these quite dramatic policies? Why has there not been a vigorous backlash by the now discriminated-against white students? Part of the answer to both questions is surely the sense of guilt among white Americans concerning certain minority groups, especially blacks and Native Americans, that I mentioned earlier. But the other related reason arises out of a national commitment to achieving a genuinely multiracial society, one in which blacks and other minorities are represented in numbers roughly similar to their proportions within the population at large and are represented proportionally in the leadership of all the institutions of the society—in its political, economic, military, and educational institutions. To attain leadership in almost all of these social institutions, experience of, if not a degree from, an institution of higher education is a necessity. That, in a word, is the driving force behind these affirmative action policies in higher education—policies keyed to the mobility of individuals through competitive performance.

Blacks and Hispanics in the United States have made conspicuous progress in some areas of national life, but less in others. My focus here is mainly on blacks; the situation of recent immigrants from Mexico is similar in some respects, but different in others.

Blacks are very well represented in all ranks of our armed forces; General Colin Powell, chairman of the Joint Chiefs of Staff, our highest ranking military officer during the war with Iraq, is only the most prominent. Blacks have also done well in politics: Thousands have been elected to local and municipal office, many are in Congress, the mayor of almost every big city in the country is black, and a black man was recently elected governor of Virginia.

Blacks as a whole have done much less well economically or in the leadership of economic institutions or in academic life. A few figures can stand for all: In 1988, 625 Americans nationwide received Ph.D.s in mathematics or computer science. Of those, only 2 were black. Of the roughly 500 doctorates awarded that year in the United States in marine, atmospheric, and earth sciences, again only 2 were awarded to blacks. The problems are not confined to the physical or natural sciences; in that same year, only 5 American-born blacks gained Ph.D.s in anthropology; 11 were granted doctorates in economics, 7 in political science, and 14 in sociology (National Science Foundation, 1990, p. 151, table 47)—this in a country with 3,500 colleges and universities, most of which require a Ph.D. for a regular tenure-track appointment.

The indicators of educational handicaps for blacks in America are many and striking, and go all the way back to performance in grade school on up to scores on national tests of scholastic aptitude. Blacks do not enter colleges or universities in proportions that reflect their proportions in the general population. A university such as Berkeley can attract and admit blacks at higher rates than their proportion in the California population, but nationally, despite many academic and financial support efforts on the part of these colleges, only about 7% of college and university enrollments are black, compared with their 12% proportion of the population. This represents a huge improvement over the terribly low numbers before the racial revolution of the 1960s, but, sad to say, that figure of 7% has not changed much in the last 15 years and indeed has declined somewhat for young black males. Moreover, blacks are far more likely to drop out of college before graduation, and those who do graduate are much less likely to go on to graduate school than their white counterparts.

All of this may help explain something of the near-desperate efforts American colleges and research universities have been making to enroll black undergraduates, hoping that some will do well and gain entry to graduate studies, and that perhaps some growing fraction of those will opt for careers in science or scholarship while others will enter both old and new professions, thus providing leadership not only for these institutions but for the black community at large.

American universities, and not least those in California, have been making great efforts to identify talented minority youngsters at the secondary and even primary levels and have encouraged and sponsored those individuals for university entry. In these and related ways, American higher education has become a part, indeed a central part, of a national effort to transform American blacks from a racial caste into a "normal" American ethnic group. A caste, of course, is a social category in which membership defines an individual's life fate permanently, even more rigidly than that of class, whereas membership in an ethnic group in the American context says something about an individual's origins but in principle does not define or limit present or future prospects. The nature and strength of an individual's connections with an ethnic group are, in principle, voluntary; one may use them as an aid to individual advancement, but those ties need not be a hindrance to personal achievement. The reality behind these norms, of course, varies. It is great for most "old" ethnic groups, but more problematic for, say, recent Mexican immigrants, and most troublesome for blacks. To be treated as an ethnic rather than a racial group has become an increasing reality for most people of Asian origins, both recent immigrants and the children of earlier immigrants. There is remarkably little racial prejudice today against Asian Americans of any kind. Racial identity is still a handicap for blacks, although less so for middle-class, well-educated blacks than for the less well educated. Thus education is still the quickest road to ethnic status for blacks.

The nation's preference for ethnic rather than racial identities and relations is clear historically. The United States, on the whole, has not had an enviable record in race relations. On the other hand, it has had a comparatively good record on ethnic relations, starting with the assimilation and integration of peoples from all over the world to a common, overriding identity as Americans. Scholars still argue whether the metaphor of the "melting pot" is the best way to describe this process, or whether some other term is necessary to describe the nature and mechanisms of this process. Whatever they decide, in the United States, Protestants and Catholics of Irish origin live peacefully side by side, as do Jews and Arabs and Maronite Christians, Turks and Armenians, and so on. A multiethnic society is our model of a good society; it encompasses the possibility of individuals' continuing strong *voluntary* cultural ties to their ethnic origins. And the historical images of the mobility of whole ethnic groups reflect the parallel mobility of their *individual* members. We have watched these mobility patterns over two, three, four, and more generations, with the first poor immigrants from an ethnic group coming in at the bottom of the social and economic ladder, living usually in ethnic enclaves (sometimes miscalled ghettos), speaking the mother tongue, and striving to advance their children's opportunities. The next generation tends to get more education, and then to move out of those neighborhoods into whatever suburbia of American life the individual's ambition, talent, and achievement will allow. The ethnic ties may remain strong into the third and even fourth generation, but usually only when these ties aid rather than hinder individual mobility.

This is, of course, a greatly oversimplified model of reality, but it is not too far from popular image and sentiment. In some sense, for Americans, this is the way things are supposed to be. To some important extent, the racial revolution

of the 1960s, the enormous changes in law, and the parallel changes in sentiment and institutional behavior have brought American blacks into this model.
The 1960s also gave to blacks the political and social freedom (and, to some
extent, the economic affluence) of a rising ethnic group rather than that of a
low and despised caste. Up to half or two-thirds have moved into the main-
stream of American life. Perhaps a third live middle-class lives (i.e., have
careers as opposed to jobs), and perhaps half are in reasonably stable working-
class occupations. But somewhere between 15% and 25% of blacks (2-3% of
the whole American population) compose an underclass, living mostly in the
central cities, caught in a morass of problems: crime, alcoholism, drugs, the
collapse of family ties and responsibility, child and spouse abuse, and welfare
dependency. These are the things that constitute the greatest problem facing
American society; thus far we have been conspicuously unsuccessful in our
approaches to it and to them.

For the rest of the black population, movement is visible and appreciable, if
too slow. It may be reasonably fast by the standards, say, of the Irish in America
in the 1860s, or the Italians in the 1920s. But that rate of change is not
acceptable by or for blacks in the 1990s, both because of our special guilt
regarding blacks in the United States and because of our heightened standards
regarding the rights and opportunities due all citizens. Moreover, blacks also
point out that they are not new immigrants but have been in America as a group
longer than most white ethnic groups and all Asians, though some proportion
of the black population seems always to fill the niche left by the most recent
immigrant group at the bottom of the social and economic ladder.

Nevertheless, affirmative action throughout American life, but most especially in higher education, is a conscious effort to accelerate the transformation
of blacks as a whole from a racial into an ethnic group and accelerate their
mobility as a group by accelerating their mobility as individuals upward
through American society. Looked at another way, it is an effort to accomplish
for blacks in one generation what may have taken two generations for Irish or
Swedish Americans and perhaps three for Italian and Polish Americans. It is,
in short, a set of policies designed to improve the opportunities for individual
members of racial and ethnic groups toward whom we as a society feel
especially guilty. These efforts are made by many social institutions, and not
just the government, to improve life chances and to enable blacks to rise in the
society, with a common goal being for some significant proportion of blacks
to take their places in leadership positions in all the social institutions.

The final irony is that policies designed to improve and thus equalize life chances
for disadvantaged individuals may, by the very character of the enormous advantages they carry for designated ethnic and racial groups, be creating status groups
whose members, and especially whose leaders, have more to gain through emphasizing their group memberships than by asserting their independence of group ties.
These patterns, and their associated ideological claims and assertions, point to a
new kind of permanent, racially based group identity that differs from the old in
being voluntary and privileged rather than involuntary and disadvantaged.

These new claims to racial identity and cultural autonomy involve stronger horizontal bondings than do most class-based institutions, such as trade unions or socialist parties. Unlike working-class identification, "race consciousness" does not inhibit or discourage college attendance, but is brought onto the campuses by the next generation of minority groups themselves. It is clear that the assertion of the primacy of racial identity for most blacks and Hispanics arises out of shared life experience, but it is not so clear that it anticipates a shared life fate. That poses a special challenge to minority group leadership, which has to struggle against the corrosive effect on the primacy of racial identity posed by an institution that in principle is indifferent to it and that prepares people for life in a competitive world that is also, and increasingly, indifferent to racial identity. The intense efforts currently being made to rationalize and reinforce the primacy of racial identity in the colleges and universities, where the future leadership of racial groups is being educated and prepared—through "multiculturalism" in the curriculum and social segregation outside the classroom—attests to the sharp tensions created by these new forms of horizontal bonding in institutions that have led society in throwing them off. The danger is that the new conceptions of permanent and self-conscious racial groups may be no more assimilable to the classic models of an ethnically diverse society of individual careers and achievement than the old caste groups. This raises many more questions for higher education, but at the least suggests that public policies often have perverse and unintended effects. Sometimes they generate new problems as great as the ones they overcome. But higher education in America has already had some experience with those ironies of history and public policy.

NOTES

1. In Western European countries, fewer youths of modest social origins have taken advantage of the call to mobility inherent in mass higher education, in part because of tight restraints on access to higher education, restraints chiefly through a class-linked stratification of the secondary school system, and of related requirements and standards for entry to higher education. But institutions of higher education everywhere serve to weaken working-class ties and affiliations.

2. Allmendinger (1975) did his research on poor students in the emerging colleges of New England, but I believe that the patterns he describes were also to be found in the much larger number of small, modest, largely denominational colleges springing up along the Western frontier. Indeed, then as now, "one clear sign of the presence of the poor was the increasing maturity of the student population. . . . Men in their middle twenties now enrolled in large numbers, along with boys in their early teens. . . . Many had started trades, and then having changed their minds, had continued in their work to get money for education. This brought about a mixing of the social classes, as well as ages" (p. 9). It was crucial that these new, mostly "private" colleges were cheap, not too far away, provided charity (i.e., student aid), and were not too particular about their students' academic preparation. The students' education was also substantially subsidized—indeed, made possible—by the tiny salaries

paid to the teaching staff, who themselves did not have the dignity of the guilds of learned men in the old countries.

3. On the concept of an "occupational community" in the American context facilitating the development of class-based institutions, see Lipset, Trow, and Coleman (1956).

4. Writing in the 1920s, Lillian Herstein observed that "the differentiation between adult and workers' education . . . has been stated and can be accepted. The responsibility of providing schooling for those who are seeking a way out of industry by means of education can be placed on the public schools. Workers' education should concern itself, let us grant, with those who are willing to be the apostles of a new order. 'Labor education,' says Mr. Horace Kallen, 'should become conversant with control rather than escape' " (quoted in Hardman, 1928, pp. 378-379).

5. See U.S. Bureau of the Census (1990, p. 419, table 689). The figures for California show the same pattern: The proportion of union members as a percentage of nonfarm wage and salary workers in 1951 was 41%; in 1987, it was 19% (Fay & Fay, 1990, p. 235).

6. The literature on the problem is very large. See, for example, Laslett and Lipset (1974).

7. This applies also to research universities, which try (with only partial success) to harness the individual ambitions of scholars and scientists to the welfare of the institution.

8. At the end of World War II, when C. Wright Mills (1948) did the study reported in *New Men of Power,* his sample of American labor leaders was distinctly better educated than the American adult population. Already a quarter of AFL and a third of the CIO leaders had been to college, compared with only 10% of adult Americans as a whole.

9. I remember going to a meeting of a democratic socialist group in 1946. It was addressed by a young Irving Howe, later to become a distinguished literary critic, professor, and editor of a small socialist journal. He gave a gloomy speech, anticipating a major economic collapse in America, an event that, in his view, would give socialists an opportunity to create a mass party. (It was perhaps always a handicap for socialists in America that they had to seem to hope for, and not just predict, depression and misery, before they came to the cheerier part.) I was a bit skeptical of the imminence of a depression in America, and afterwards asked the speaker how the socialist movement would respond if there were no depression. His answer, with its hard realism, surprised and impressed me. "If capitalism can buy the workers off with low unemployment and good wages," he said, "it deserves to win." Howe was betting his life that it could not meet those tests. It could, and it did.

10. Figures provided by the Office of Student Research, University of California at Berkeley.

REFERENCES

Allmendinger, D. F., Jr. (1975). *Paupers and scholars: The transformation of student life in nineteenth-century New England.* New York: St. Martin's.
Fay, J. S., & Fay, S. W. (Eds.). (1990). *California almanac* (4th ed.). Santa Barbara, CA: Pacific Data Resources.
Hardman, J. B. S. (1928). *American labor dynamics in the light of post-war developments.* New York: Harcourt, Brace.
Laslett, J. H. M., & Lipset, S. M. (Eds.). (1974). *Failure of a dream? Essays in the history of American socialism.* Garden City, NY: Anchor.
Lipset, S. M., Trow, M., & Coleman, J. (1956). *Union democracy.* Glencoe, IL: Free Press.
Mills, C. W. (1948). *New men of power.* New York: Harcourt, Brace.

National Science Foundation. (1990). *Women and minorities in science and engineering.* Washington, DC: Author.

Organization for Economic Cooperation and Development. (1989). *Review of higher education policy in California.* Paris: Author.

Rothblatt, S., & Trow, M. (in press). Government policies and higher education: A comparison of Britain and the United States, 1630-1860. In C. Crouch & A. Heath (Eds.), *The sociology of social reform.* Oxford: Oxford University Press.

Rudolph, F. (1962). *The American college and university.* New York: Alfred A. Knopf.

Trow, M. (1961). The second transformation of American secondary education. *International Journal of Comparative Sociology, 2,* 144-166.

Trow, M. (1991). American higher education: "Exceptional" or just different? In B. Shafer (Ed.), *Is America different? A new look at American exceptionalism.* Oxford: Clarendon.

U.S. Bureau of the Census. (1990). *Statistical abstracts of the United States.* Washington, DC: Government Printing Office.

14

Inequality and American Culture
THE PERSISTENCE OF VOLUNTARISM

Ann Swidler

T is part of the common wisdom among those who study the United States that America is "different." One of the most important ways it is different is cultural. Americans are distinctively individualist; their collective culture is "voluntarist." Seymour Martin Lipset, among contemporary social scientists, formulated this perspective most clearly in his classic *The First New Nation* (1963). There, using the Parsonian pattern variables for systematic comparison among English settler societies, Lipset analyzed the content of this enduring American distinctiveness. Americans, he argued, are distinctively committed to values of equality and achievement.

In both *The First New Nation* (1963) and *Continental Divide* (1990), Lipset attributes America's distinctive values primarily to the country's historical experience as a national community. Forging a nation through a democratic revolution fostered sharper egalitarianism than in England or in the colonies that did not rebel. America's Puritan heritage and its early and sustained economic growth reinforced values of individual achievement. During the American Revolution, conservative elites who remained loyal to England fled to Canada, weakening the Canadian commitment to equality, and leaving the emerging American nation more committed to egalitarianism.

In Lipset's analysis, those distinctive American value emphases have remained remarkably continuous over two centuries, despite massive economic and technological change. But national differences in character and culture raise difficulties for sociological analysis concerning both the nature of such differences and why they persist. Are we to think of national differences as rooted in *individual-level* character, personality, and values, reproduced from generation to generation by socialization, primarily in the family? This was the

AUTHOR'S NOTE: My thanks to Ron Jepperson, who suggested many of the ideas in this essay, and to Claude Fischer, who helped me think them through.

294

Parsonian model of how value differences are transmitted, and it appears periodically in *The First New Nation* (e.g., p. 103). But such an individual-level argument for the stability of American values is problematic, if only because, in a country subject to repeated waves of immigration, there has been very little continuity in the family contexts through which such transmission of values might occur.

A second level of explanation suggests that values are reproduced not by socialization in individual families, but through such obviously socializing institutions as schools and churches. Of course, even this (more or less Gramscian) explanation simply pushes the problem back a step, as one would have to ask what keeps those who control socializing institutions committed to dominant values. This is particularly problematic in the American case, where there is no state church and no centralized educational system. Because American religious bodies, without state support, compete for members by adapting to popular values rather than imposing a unified set of values on their members (see Finke & Stark, 1989; also Iannaccone, 1991), they are unlikely candidates to explain continuity in American values. Much the same argument applies to American schools. While schools have sought to "Americanize" immigrants, American public schools have been locally controlled and financed, so that we still require some explanation of the values they have taught. Indeed, all explanations that attribute continuity in American values to the influence of what Althusser (1972) calls the "ideological apparatuses of the state" face the difficulty that, as Lipset points out, there have been vast changes in the economic interests and social composition of American elites.

A third set of explanations attributes continuity in American national character or values to persisting structural conditions—to the absence of an established aristocracy and peasantry, the presence of the frontier, and the repeated experience of immigrants searching for economic opportunity. These factors, the argument runs, have continually re-created commitments to values of equality and achievement.

These recurrent-experience explanations are plausible, and they have the great virtue of accounting for the continual reproduction of American values rather than describing their origin and simply assuming their continuity. Yet, in addition to experiences that reinforce values of equality and achievement, Americans have had many experiences that could counteract or dramatically redirect values if values really derived directly from experience. For example, many of the Americans who immigrated in hopes of a better life found no greater social opportunity or mobility than their European forebears. The frontier was open until almost the end of the nineteenth century, but it has been closed for most of the twentieth century, during which the American population has increased from approximately 75 million to more than 250 million. The frontier is unlikely to have directly influenced many contemporary Americans, even through family history or traditions. Americans have also experienced massive collective and individual catastrophes, such as the Civil War, the influenza epidemic of the early twentieth century, and the Great Depression, that could easily have stimulated quite different sets of values.

ALTERNATIVES

I would like to explore several additional explanations for continuities in American culture. The hope is that by laying out in an orderly way several causal models that might account for the kinds of continuities Lipset's work has explored, we could begin actually to test, challenge, and recast some of these arguments.

Earlier attempts to explain national differences failed to explore genuinely collective-level, rather than individual-level, arguments. Although sociologists rest their disciplinary claims on their ability to analyze collectivities, much of our causal thinking remains relentlessly individual-level, despite our condemnations of "reductionism." The problems of individual-level causal imagery are discussed in Abbott (1988) and Lieberson (1985).[1]

If collectivities have different "constitutive rules" (Swanson, 1971), we cannot simply organize those into a typology and then assume them as explanations. If such theories are to be persuasive, it is necessary to show what the constitutive rules consist of, where they are located, and how they are formed, perpetuated, and altered.

Identity/Selection in a World System

As an example of how one might take collective properties seriously while still providing micro-level causal linkages (see Collins, 1981), I want to start with an argument that American distinctiveness is perpetuated through identity and self-selection in a world system. For this argument, nation-states rather than "societies" are the proper units of analysis. National identities derive less from languages, traditions, and institutions than from how nations are seen and how their elites come to define their distinctiveness in a larger international system of nations.

Earlier theories conceptualized nation-states as parts of a larger nation-state system (Skocpol, 1979; Tilly, 1975). Wuthnow (1987), for example, argues that seventeenth- and eighteenth-century science received major stimulus from competition among European states for prestige and power. Studies of national identity stress that identity is oriented toward defining the nation in the eyes of the outside world (Anderson, 1983; Spillman, 1991). Finally, John Meyer and his associates have shown how modern nation-states define themselves and their institutions in world-system terms (Thomas, Meyer, Ramirez, & Boli, 1987).

If national differences in culture are perpetuated by accounts national elites (and patriotic publics) give of their nations' distinctiveness, then we can be clearer about how historical experiences described in *The First New Nation* and *Continental Divide* actually explain continuities in national values. The historical events of a nation's founding are important because, in their initial dramatization by national mythmakers (see Schama, 1989; Schwartz, 1987), they define how the national community is distinctive. That identity is perpetuated by a public culture that retells a particular version of the nation's history, celebrates its distinctive traditions, and defines its particular identity in a world context (see Bellah, 1968).

Such an explanation ascribes distinctive national values to public culture, ritual, and myth without necessarily assuming that individual members of the national community affirm them as personal values. National values shape individual belief and action primarily through public debates over the proper form of national institutions, from political institutions to schools to economic organizations. Arguments that monopoly is un-American or that American schools ought to promote equal opportunity are examples of such public debate.

In the American case, one could argue, the nation's distinctive identity has also continued to shape national values through self-selection. Immigrants, drawn to the new land by its distinctive reputation, may bring powerful commitments to values that the wider international community regards as "American." Such a process is suggested, for example, in Herbert Gutman's (1977) analyses of nineteenth-century American workers' resistance to capitalism. While workers frequently drew on Old Country forms of solidarity, they saw America as a new land where men could be "their own rulers" and "no one could or should become their masters" (p. 52). Thus America's distinctive image may perpetuate American values by differentially attracting immigrants to whom such values appeal and by shaping their understandings of the land to which they have come.

If a nation's identity in an international system explains cultural continuities, we are in a better position to understand America's distinctive commitment to equality and mobility, even if its citizens are no more socially mobile than their European counterparts (Erikson & Goldthorpe, 1987; Lipset & Bendix, 1959). This theory also explains distinctive American values in public life without assuming that those values are dominant for individuals. This is consistent with Sarah Corse's (1990) examination of literary evidence of Canadian/U.S. differences. She finds that prize-winning novels and "canonical" novels (those taught in college courses on Canadian and American literature) reflect elite attempts to define and redefine each nation's distinctive heritage (including, at this moment, special attention to cultural diversity within each nation), whereas the best-sellers in the two countries are nearly identical.

There are other implications of a national-identity theory of national values. One is that national values should have become more distinctive, and more salient, with the growth of a world system of nation-states. Second, some nations—those with high international visibility, or particularly problematic relations with their neighbors—may be more committed to an idea of their own distinctiveness than are other nations. A third implication of this theory is that distinctive national values ought to be salient for various subgroups in a nation, even when those groups differ significantly in their own cultural traditions.

Finally, in this model, changes in national identity and values should reflect changes in the international context—the identity of competitors for prestige and power, the specific others with which a nation-state compares itself (e.g., the

American preoccupation with Britain in the nineteenth century and with the Soviet Union after World War II), and dominant measures of prestige in the world system.

This way of thinking about what is distinctive about American (and other national) values does not point to some deep, essential source of national character, but it has the great advantage of suggesting mechanisms that might perpetuate distinctive national values despite massive changes in social structure, population, and national history.

Institutions and Individual Experience

The argument that distinctive features of American life have continually re-created American values is an appealing one. I have emphasized that if it is to be persuasive, such an argument must identify American historical or institutional experiences that really are distinctive, that have recurred frequently enough to account for the persistence of American values over time, and that are not themselves simply reflections of distinctive American values.

I remain skeptical about many "recurrent experience" explanations— repeated waves of immigration, the frontier, geographic isolation. In part, this skepticism is grounded in my sense of how experiences actually shape individual perceptions and values. Even profound historical traumas sometimes fail to shape national consciousness, and, as I document more fully below, individuals rarely base their public perceptions on such matters as whether they personally have been upwardly mobile, have faced unemployment, or have experienced government corruption. In my view, the usual candidates for such recurrent experiences are not pervasive, recurrent, and powerful enough to account for the reproduction of distinctively American values.

There is, however, one good candidate for an institutional explanation of the reproduction of American values, and that is an absence rather than a presence. The absence in America of centralized institutions of elite education and influence that shape individual opportunities and provide a unified image of dominant values seems enormously important. In addition to educational institutions, American religious, political, and government institutions are decentralized as well.

The perfect contrast is with France. When Michel Foucault (1979) insists that we live in a "carceral society" or Pierre Bourdieu (1984) says that unequal access to "cultural capital" reproduces class differences, I am continually struck by how different French experience is from that in America.[2]

In France, as in many modern industrial societies, a unitary, centrally administered examination determines who can stay in school and who must leave, who can be admitted to a university, and so forth. Such institutions help unify elites, but they also serve to create an image of an objective hierarchy of knowledge, prestige, and value. American institutions, in contrast, lack centralized mechanisms for shaping and sorting elites. Furthermore, the American educational system, because it is so decentralized, continually re-creates the experience of "opportunity" (even when the actual opportunity structure is no more open than elsewhere). As Burton Clark (1960) notes for junior colleges, many entry points and the absence of clear barriers to advancement make people believe that they themselves have shaped their fate through their effort and ability (or lack of them). Without central institutions that authoritatively rank and sort people, it also remains experientially believable that everyone is equal—equal in civil status and in basic worth, if not in income or achievement. This is the difference Ralph Turner (1960) identifies as "sponsored versus contest mobility," and the distinction remains important for describing experiential authoritativeness versus invisibility of societal constraints.

While it is hard to explain a presence by an absence, a reasonable case can be made that the absence of authoritative national institutions—an aristocracy, a state church, a national university or educational system— profoundly affects American life. It not only creates an experiential sense of "openness," it also means that status-group competition is not unified and hierarchical, but multiplex and open. Tom Wolfe suggested in *The Kandy-Kolored Tangerine-Flake Streamline Baby* (1965) and *The Pump House Gang* (1967) that Americans were entering a phase (which he associated with the affluent 1950s) in which unitary status hierarchies were giving way to "status spheres"—leisure-based groups with their own ideas about value and status. But this absence of a central source of cultural authority and a hierarchy of prestige may be a general feature of American life. Tocqueville's (1969) observation that Americans rely on their own judgment and refuse to defer to the opinions of others, regarding themselves as fundamentally equal in value, certainly fits this picture of an institutionally decentered society.

Explaining continuities in values by suggesting that recurrent institutional experiences re-create those values is an appealing strategy. The implication of such a theoretical approach is that were America to develop institutions that more effectively establish a unified hierarchy of evaluation, with effective rewards and sanctions behind it, fundamental American values would change. It might also suggest that, during the colonial period, the "core" American values of equality and achievement should have been stronger in the highly pluralistic Middle-Atlantic colonies such as Pennsylvania (see Zuckerman, 1982) than in more institutionally centralized Puritan New England.

Despite its appeal, a theoretical approach emphasizing recurrent experience as a source of continuity in values still seems insufficient. First, one needs to explain why American institutions have maintained their highly decentralized form. Second, the theory still relies on the notion that individual values are derived directly from personal experience of institutional constraints. Even though such arguments may seem persuasive, in my view they do not adequately conceptualize the collective nature of common values.

Capacities for Collective Action

A third account of the distinctiveness of American values would focus not on values as products of individual experience, but on the ways public values encode capacities for collective action. Such an approach would attempt, in good Durkheimian fashion, to take collective realities seriously.

Whatever the distinctiveness of American public values, there is also disagreement about them. Americans differ in their political and social attitudes, and individuals take very different stances depending on the issues and how they are posed. One set of clues for understanding what is distinctive about American political culture comes from examining the divergences and contradictions within it.

In political culture, as in other realms, mythic ideals often persist even when people claim not to believe them.[3] Much of our public culture is dominated by what we half cynically call "The American Dream"—an image that remains powerful even though we do not quite believe it. Images of America as a land of opportunity, where people get ahead by their own efforts, and as a nation of equals, which provides liberty and justice for all, are parts of this American Dream.

To understand collective culture, we first have to examine the quality of sacredness that inhabits collective symbols and myths. Sacred objects, Emile Durkheim (1915/1965) argues, are those things human beings set apart from the ordinary, profane world and treat with special awe, reverence, and respect. Sacredness inheres not in the things themselves—the ordinary rocks from which the aborigines make their *churingas,* the flour and water that make communion wafers, or the dyed fabrics of a flag—but in the symbolic meanings with which people invest them. Such objects are sacred, Durkheim argues, because they embody the symbolic identity of the group itself. Thus the sacred derives its power from the life of the group. Human beings set apart sacred things from profane ones because they set apart the meanings that give the group its life as a group from the ordinary things that sustain the lives of the group's individual members.

This collective dimension is central to our intuitions about how culture works. When we say that the English are deferential, Americans individualistic, or the French hostile to authority, we refer to what seem to be enduring ways societies organize their collective lives. But must we assume that members of those societies individually hold such views, making collective traits matters of shared individual psychology? Instead, a collective-culture argument would suggest that societies, like individuals, maintain cultural repertoires that support collective strategies of action.[4] Cultural patterns persist because they effectively organize forms of collective action, independent of whether or not they appeal to individuals as plausible descriptions of everyday realities.

American social mythology—its description of opportunity, equality, freedom—persists because it describes and reinforces distinctive ways of organizing collective action. It is therefore resistant to change, even when the social reality it purportedly describes changes.

American Ideals

Many scholars have puzzled over the ambiguities and ambivalences in Americans' attitudes toward equality and opportunity. Americans value equality, yet reject it in the economic sphere (Lane, 1962; Rainwater, 1974). Americans often support liberal social programs to redistribute income or protect the environment, but reject the general principles that would justify such programs (McCloskey & Zaller, 1984). Robert Lane (1962) characterizes this ambivalence as a "fear of equality"—a psychological defense against the self-blame that would ensue from believing that real equality is possible. Lipset (1963) describes a continuing tension between the sometimes incompatible values of equality and achievement. McCloskey and Zaller (1984) analyze the tension between commitment to equality and belief in capitalism.

Much of what seems to be ambivalence about competing values, however, reflects instead the ideological incoherence (Free & Cantril, 1967) between abstract and concrete social understandings.[5] Michael Mann (1970) summarizes similar results from a variety of studies in both England and the United States: In the abstract, Americans and Britons endorse dominant beliefs that "success comes to those whose energies and abilities deserve it, failures have only themselves to blame" (p. 427). No matter how the question is worded, "almost all respondents endorse the key cues of 'ability' and 'hard work' while much smaller numbers endorse 'luck,' 'pull' and 'too hard for a man [with ambition to get ahead]' " when accounting for success in general (p. 427). Asked about their *own* working lives, however, people are much more likely to express cynicism about the opportunity structure they face.

Mann and other researchers also report that it is on the specifics of equality and opportunity that the poor and the working class break with higher-status respondents to express skepticism about the American Dream. Only concrete cases evoke the "class consciousness" investigators expect to find. Rich and poor differently evaluate the circumstances of their own lives and the opportunities open to people like themselves, but both groups subscribe to a general picture of their society as an open one.

Joan Huber and William Form (1973) addressed precisely this gap between general and concrete attitudes in a study of income and ideology. Asked whether there is "not much opportunity in America today" or "plenty of opportunity and anyone who works hard can go as far as he wants," most white respondents— rich, poor, and middle class—saw "plenty of opportunity." But asked whether "a boy whose father is poor and a boy whose father is rich" have the same opportunity if they work equally hard, the interviewees were substantially less optimistic, with belief in equal opportunity dropping from 90% to 37% among poor respondents, from 80% to 49% among middle-class respondents, and from 93% to 57% among rich respondents (pp. 90-91). Thus the more concrete, "income-linked" version of the question shows poor respondents less wedded to the image of America as a land of opportunity than are wealthier respondents, even though all groups endorse this image of America in the abstract. Other questions about opportunity for rich and poor to go to college and about whether American society offers rich and poor "equal and fair treatment from the law" produced similar responses: In the abstract, substantial majorities subscribed to the belief that American society is equal and fair; faced with the concrete corollary of the general question, they more readily acknowledged inequality (pp. 92-94).

The same general pattern of results has emerged in other surveys of public opinion. Herbert McCloskey and John Zaller (1984) report in *The American Ethos* that "discrepancies between abstract statements and particular applications" appear on issues of racial equality (pp. 84-85), property rights (pp. 142-143), civil liberties (p. 85), and public policies that promote equality (p. 184). Kluegel and Smith (1986) note that "the prevalence and stability of belief in the dominant ideology, in the face of enduring objective features of the stratification system . . . produces the inconsistency, fluctuation and seeming contradiction" in American attitudes toward inequality (p. 6).

One might first hypothesize that Americans are simply hypocrites, favoring equality in principle but refusing to implement it. But that interpretation does not fit the evidence. On many issues, in fact, the American public supports conservative principles but liberal solutions for concrete problems. Thus, for example, a majority agree that "the way property is used should mainly be decided by the individuals who own it," but they also "endorse many of the specific measures that property owners perceive as violating traditional property rights" (McCloskey & Zaller, 1984, pp. 142-143). Most Americans reject the idea of government intervention in the economy, yet support particular programs that would redistribute wealth or assure equal opportunity. Based on this sort of evidence, Americans have been called ideological conservatives but pragmatic liberals.

There is a "disjunction between general abstract values and concrete experience" (Mann, 1970, p. 429)—experience that makes Americans both more cynical about the realities of their society and more amenable to concrete programs to remedy its faults than their principles dictate. This disjunction between experience and belief appears with startling clarity in Schlozman and Verba's (1979) study of responses to unemployment. They find a "barrier" between people's evaluations of their own experiences and their images of the society in general: "There is virtually no relationship between beliefs about opportunities in general and evaluation of personal opportunities" (pp. 150-151), even though there *are* reasonably strong relationships between one general belief and another (e.g., between class consciousness and the belief that opportunity for advancement is slight). Schlozman and Verba find very weak associations between people's general beliefs about the economy and their own experiences—between beliefs about the "fairness of opportunities in America" and belief in the fairness of their own wages, for example (pp. 154-155; see the very similar findings in Kluegel & Smith, 1986, pp. 85-86). Most striking is that being unemployed has virtually no influence either on general views of the fairness and openness of the American class system or on images of whether individual effort is more important than social constraints in determining individual success.[6] The authors conclude: "Beliefs about social reality—about either opportunities for advancement or the class structure—seem relatively impermeable to the effects of personal experience"—even the highly disruptive experience of unemployment (p. 156).

Voluntarism and Action

The barriers between people's evaluations of their own experience and their evaluations of wider social and economic realities suggest that the two ways of thinking are in fact "about" two different kinds of things. General images of the American Dream are not generalizations based on averaging (or analyzing) day-to-day experience. Despite their apparent reference to the "facts" of ordinary experience, these images come from, and make sense of, another domain of action. Personal experiences of unemployment do not change general evaluations of opportunity in America because these ideas pertain to different realms of experience. People can endorse ideal images of the American Way of Life without believing in their concrete corollaries because the two views emerge out of and sustain different kinds of activity.

To analyze the different kinds of experience that ground these apparently incompatible understandings, let us look first at how people try to reconcile apparently contradictory elements in their thinking about equality. The classic study of this problem is Robert Lane's (1962) *Political Ideology*, based on interviews done in the 1950s with 15 working-class men. Lane was interested in how the men evaluated the social order and their position in it. He found a widely shared belief that America is a land of opportunity, and that opportunity is equally enough distributed that people must accept responsibility for their own status (p. 61). Lane analyzed what he saw as the psychological defenses the men used to evade the painful implications of their own, relatively limited, life achievements. They minimized the importance of class position, arguing that the working class is really happier or better than the upper class, or stressing moral or spiritual equality across classes (pp. 63-67).

Lane found that the working-class men he interviewed defended the existing social order and its distribution of rewards as fundamentally just. This is not simply passive resignation, but active support—even for a worldview that implicitly makes these men responsible for what they themselves often regarded as limited life accomplishments. Indeed, Lane argues, these working-class men felt that they and others like them deserved their status, just as the rich deserve to be rich (pp. 68-69).

It is not, of course, that these men had a uniformly optimistic or complacent view of their society. Indeed, Lane reports many comments reflecting a cynical and sometimes even embittered view. But even the occasional recognition that American society does not give everyone an equal chance did not make these men seek an equal society. The crucial argument, for all 15 men, was that "equality of income would deprive men of their incentive to work, achieve, and develop their skills." As one man, a railroad guard, put it, "I think it would be a dull thing, because life would be accepted—or it would—rather we'd go stale. There would be no initiative to be a little different, or go ahead" (p. 78). In Lane's terms, an equal society would be "a world running down, a chaotic and disorganized place to live" (p. 78). The struggle for unequal rewards keeps the world organized.

A similar resistance to equality emerges in Lee Rainwater's (1974) research in the Boston area. In this study, men and women from a variety of backgrounds found the idea of economic equality, or of a "classless society," fundamentally unappealing. Their words echo those of Lane's "common men": A 28-year-old lower-class woman said, "It's communism—everybody is the same and they all share. I wouldn't want it. If I work harder than somebody else, why should I share, or if I work harder why shouldn't I be able to get more and live better than somebody else?" (p. 168). Others saw equality as "a very dull existence" (p. 169) or "one big blur and you're not an individual" (p. 169).

The paradoxical nature of people's attitudes about equality is well illustrated by one of Rainwater's respondents, a 30-year-old lower-middle-class woman:

> I don't really think I want a classless society. People being equal in what they earn and what they own. I don't think it would give anyone anything to work for or look forward to. I think it would be a very dull existence. I would like to eliminate the class with not enough to eat or a proper house. But as far as the rest goes, I wouldn't want that. (p. 169)

This woman makes clear that her resistance to equality does not come from a lack of sympathy for the poor; she would like to eliminate dire poverty. But full equality would cause the social world to grind to a halt, deprived of the personal and social energies inequality engenders.

Mary and Robert Jackman (1983) report a parallel contradiction in American views of opportunity. When asked to explain class differences among Americans, a substantial majority of their sample attributed inequalities to differences in the opportunities society provides (a view especially strongly held among blacks of all class levels and among whites who identified themselves as poor). Despite this, Jackman and Jackman note "the singular lack of support for income equality in any class" (p. 207). This resistance to equality is based, in turn, on "the pervasive acceptance of the norm of achievement-based rewards. About two-thirds of each class justify inequality in terms of achievement. An additional 17 percent of whites justify inequality in terms of both achievement and ability. Thus, about 85 percent in all mention achievement-related factors as grounds for inequality" (p. 209). Thus the contradiction between structural understanding of the sources of inequality and the simultaneous attachment to the ideal of achievement-based inequality is pervasive, even among those who do not benefit from such inequalities.

Sacred Myths

What accounts for the persistence of mythic views of America as a land of equality and opportunity, despite skepticism about whether in practical terms America lives up to its promises? What accounts for the tension between the aspiration for greater equality and the fear of an equal society? And, finally, why do even direct experiences with economic "realities" (such as unemployment) fail to dislodge people's commitment to the dominant ideology?

A clue to the underlying pattern behind these ideological disjunctures comes from a critical exception to the patterns of support for America's dominant ideology—the anomalous political attitudes of African Americans. Although support for the dominant ideology is high among white Americans, including those who are disadvantaged by the current system, blacks show nearly the opposite pattern. They are critical of the dominant consensus and are ready to believe that America is not an equal society, even when they themselves have been relatively successful within it. In survey after survey, race shapes attitudes much more strongly than does income. For example, in *Income and Ideology,* Huber and Form (1973) report that when asked about opportunity to get ahead and to go to college, respondents affirmed (as we have come to expect) general statements that opportunity was equal rather than specific, income-linked statements (p. 91). But even more striking were differences by race. Middle-class blacks were substantially more critical of the dominant society than were even poor whites. This pattern repeated itself for virtually every issue Huber and Form examined. Schlozman and Verba (1979) also consistently report such findings, as do Jackman and Jackman (1983) and Kluegel and Smith (1986).

Where does the radicalism of African Americans come from? Why don't they buy the American Dream? They value the same things that whites do: a good income, stable family, education, home ownership. But they less often endorse the dominant ideology. It is not simply that individual blacks have fared less well under the American system. They have, but a critical perception of the society is widespread even among those who have done well economically. Their collective history of oppression and discrimination has radicalized African Americans, but not simply because it has put them at a massive economic disadvantage. If, as we have seen above, even devastating experiences of unemployment do not seem to radicalize whites, why are middle-class blacks more radical than poor whites?

Perhaps the entire attempt to derive the political radicalism of blacks and the complacency of whites from their economic situations is misguided. We need to consider the possibility that ideologies develop not around what has happened to people—good or bad—but instead around the ways people organize their own patterns of action, individual *and collective.* American blacks are more radical than whites because for them channels of collective political action provide an alternative frame for organizing and mobilizing action. The history of discrimination is important not only for its economic impact but for forcing blacks to think of themselves as a group who must pursue their interests through collective strategies. These collective strategies of action then sustain alternative views of politics.

The greater radicalism of black compared with white Americans consists of a greater willingness to see existing social and economic arrangements as unjust (Huber & Form, 1973) and much higher levels of identification with the lower and working classes (Jackman & Jackman, 1983). Indeed, Jackman and Jackman (1983) report that even blacks who *identify themselves* as middle-class nonetheless feel closer to members of the poor and working classes than to members of their own class (p. 48).

I would argue that African Americans subscribe less to the American Dream than do other Americans because they organize their patterns of political action differently. White Americans apparently believe in individual opportunity, even if they personally have little opportunity (or, as for the unemployed, have experienced a drastic constriction of their own opportunities). At the same time, blacks less often believe in individual opportunity, even if they themselves have succeeded. These views are not the result of personal experiences; rather, they result from the ways the two groups organize political and social action.

In American history, African Americans have been a striking exception to the rule of voluntarist political strategies. Since the Freedmen's Bureau after the Civil War, and especially after the civil rights and equal opportunity legislation of the 1960s, blacks have been encouraged to make political claims on the basis of group membership. Treated as a distinct group, often legally segregated and denied opportunity, blacks mobilized politically as a group. This form of political mobilization has produced a critical perspective on the dominant American ideology because blacks' incorporation into the American polity has been less complete and less exclusively voluntarist and individualist than that of whites.[7]

Collective Strategies of Action

If the distinctive social views of blacks are rooted in the patterns of collective action through which they participate in the wider political system, problems of collective action may also account for the peculiar inconsistencies in white attitudes about equality, opportunity, liberty, and justice.

A society's way of organizing the sacred provides a paradigm for the organization of collective action. In *Islam Observed,* Clifford Geertz (1968) describes this link between collective action and sacredness in two very different Islamic societies—Morocco and Indonesia. He describes Moroccan history as dominated by the image of individual holy men, or *marabouts,* who possess a sacred charisma, *baraka,* that makes them worthy to lead others. Indonesian culture instead has portrayed society as unified around an "exemplary center" from which the harmony and well-being of the society flow. Both *baraka* and the exemplary center are "conception[s] of the mode in which the divine reaches into the world" (p. 44). Moroccan *baraka* embodies the proposition that "the sacred appears most directly in the world as an endowment—a talent and a capacity, a special ability—of particular individuals . . . personal presence, force of character, moral vividness" (p. 44). This conception of the sacred embodies a model of collective action organized around the leadership of such extraordinary men. As Geertz (1968) notes: "The cult that all this belief and legend supports consists of mobilizing the baraka embodied in the saint, in his tomb, and in his descendants . . . for purposes ranging from the most petty to the most high" (p. 50).

If, as Durkheim asserts, the sacred is a symbolic crystallization of the power of collective life, then a cultural image of how the sacred enters the world may be thought of as a description of where collective energies can be found or mobilized. Returning, then, to the problems of American voluntarism, we can understand the contradictions in American ideals about opportunity, equality, and justice as deriving from the ways American culture encodes the possibilities of collective action.

In American culture, sacredness is fundamentally located in individuals.[8] Individuals are empowered as agents of collective action. American voluntarism is the assumption that the self and its free choices constitute society, and thus that collective action derives from the voluntary action of individuals united for a common purpose (Bellah, Madsen, Sullivan, Swidler, & Tipton, 1985; Varenne, 1977). The success of collective strategies of action seems to depend on the qualities and the commitments individuals devote to them. In this American understanding, changing collective life requires reenergizing, reforming, or transforming individuals.

This sense that individuals, as repositories of the sacred, must exercise the initiative that keeps collective life going accounts for the puzzling contradictions in the ways Americans think about opportunity, equality, and justice. Americans support policies to ameliorate the worst sorts of poverty (Rainwater, 1974) because poverty undermines the capacities of individuals to be autonomous initiators of action. But at the level of general ideology, government programs to promote equality seem to threaten the individual initiative that is the source of power and energy in social life.

In concrete cases, Americans can easily recognize that particular individuals face constricted life opportunities, need remedial help, or must depend on the help of others. Like the fabric out of which a flag can be sewn, the flour with which a communion wafer is made, or the stone an aborigine might turn into a *churinga,* the actual, profane person is understood quite differently from the abstract image of the Individual. However vulnerable real individuals are, the (sacred) Individual must be autonomous and self-reliant.

This contrast—between the ways Americans think about individuals as concrete persons and as embodiments of the capacity for collective action—also helps account for the contradictions in American views of equality. Americans believe intensely in the fundamental equality of individual persons, an equality of dignity, rights, moral importance—indeed, of sacredness. This passion for equality rests on the belief that individuals are equal in their fundamental significance as sources of collective action. But the other kind of equality—equality of economic condition—implies some limit to the initiative each actor can take, the power he or she can embody. Thus most Americans, even those who would benefit most from equalization of income, reject economic equality, for equality would constrain individuals.

If Americans' reliance on voluntarism as the dominant strategy for collective action accounts for their inconsistent views of poverty, equality, and opportunity, why has that voluntarism persisted? After all, we would not say that

American society, with a powerful state, bureaucratic institutions great and small, and a constraining market, is actually organized primarily through voluntary collective action.

As I have tried to argue, certain features of a society's culture—American voluntarism, Moroccan understandings of charismatic leadership, Indonesian orientation toward an exemplary center—are remarkably persistent, independent of their persuasiveness as descriptions of social reality. This is because the images do not directly describe social reality; rather, they describe channels for collective action.[9]

Such understandings of collective life may persist through vast changes in actual social institutions and ways of life. This is because capacities for mobilizing collective action, invested in symbols of sacredness, operate outside institutional structures. The same capacity for collective action can also be mobilized to achieve a variety of different ends. Thus social reform in nineteenth-century urban America (Boyer, 1978), several waves of religious revival (McLoughlin, 1978), the abolition campaign before the Civil War, the nineteenth-century movement to expand public schooling (Meyer, Tyack, Nagel, & Gordon, 1979), and the contemporary civil rights movement have all taken the same fundamental form as movements of moral reform, seeking to produce broad social transformation by awakening and reforming the consciences of individuals.[10]

Late twentieth-century America is hardly a voluntarist society. Large bureaucratic organizations provide public services, regulate market activities, and conduct much economic activity. Local, state, and federal governments penetrate nearly every sphere of life. Assuring equal rights, eliminating poverty, or reenergizing the American economy requires state action to these ends. Nonetheless, I would argue, American collective strategies of action have remained voluntarist. Americans continue to respond to difficulties by attempting to reform or change the individuals who are conceived to form any given social community.

These collective strategies remain voluntarist in the face of increasingly large, bureaucratic institutions because collective strategies of action do not mirror social structure but mobilize collective action in relation to it. Thus, in some sense, collective strategies of action provide an alternative or a complement to the institutionalized forms of power and authority societies have available. In the American case, voluntarist reform campaigns, revivals, and social movements arise to deal with problems outside established institutional frameworks. In other societies, noninstitutionalized collective action might involve mobilization around a charismatic leader or creation of public disorder to force the state to act as an agent of change (see Reddy, 1984).

For groups, as for individuals, a strategy of action is a readiness or a capacity to organize action in a particular way. Like individuals, collectivities depend on culturally learned patterns in order to organize and carry out strategies of action; and like individuals, collectivities develop new strategies of action only with difficulty, formulating them using chunks of previously established cultural patterns (see Swidler, 1986).[11]

Returning briefly to Geertz's (1968) treatment of Moroccan and Indonesian cultures, we can examine the persistence of collective strategies of action. Geertz describes Moroccan society as making sacred an originally tribal principle of *baraka,* the fierce charisma of individual leaders; Indonesian society as enshrining the ideal of the harmonious "exemplary center." Both these patterns, like American voluntarism, have been enormously resilient, surviving in the Indonesian case through mass conversion to Islam as well as through changes in regime and form of government. I would argue that, as in the American case, Moroccan *baraka* and the Indonesian exemplary center are not the major institutional forms that dominate life in their respective societies (as Geertz fully acknowledges in *Negara,* 1980). Indeed, these patterns are much more persistent than the actual institutional forms of power in their respective societies. But in Moroccan history, the problem of responding to crises has been met by searching for a new leader who has the right kind of personal charisma and following him. In Indonesia, collective crises are met by asking the exemplary center to reestablish harmony. Both patterns describe not how the whole society actually runs, but how collective energies can be mobilized.

Such strategies of action are necessarily collective and public. That is, when people seek collective solutions to problems, they draw upon cultural patterns that they expect others around them to share. This accounts, in part, for the persistence of such collective approaches to the organization of action. When a form of collective action has become established, it is difficult for individuals or subgroups to change it; its idiom is the only one that will be effective with their fellows. Thus such forms of collective mobilization are likely to be more enduring than either the problems they are used to solve or even the particular institutions that actually organize most of a society's collective life.

Because such capacities for the collective mobilization of action complement rather than reflect institutions, they do not necessarily change with changes in institutional realities. Thus the Moroccan pattern of charismatic leadership developed among tribal groups who rallied around tribal leaders to resist central authority. Yet even as modern nation-states have become established throughout the Islamic Middle East, much of political mobilization—revolutions to overthrow governments, mobilization for war, or demands for reformation—take the form of mobilization around the powers of charismatic individuals. This is not a matter of conscious cultural allegiance or of some mysterious "national character," but rather of the persistence of collectively established ways of organizing action.

CONCLUSION

This essay has offered three alternative approaches to explaining the persistence of national differences in values. It has attempted to make problematic the assumption that such differences are located at the individual level, pointing out that, for such a theory to be persuasive, it must at a minimum specify what continuing experiences would re-create or reproduce those values in succeeding generations.

To make such a claim for a more collective level of explanation, however, one should be able to explain the origin and transformation, as well as the persistence, of collective values. For the first two explanations—the persistence of collective values due to differentiated national identities in a world system and the continuity of national values through the persistence of distinctive institutional patterns affecting individual opportunity structures—I have suggested, at least in principle, what the theory would say about conditions that would weaken or change national values.

For the third, the collective action model, one can also suggest at least what changes in collective values might look like. First, such changes should be produced by dramatic, symbolically powerful events that simultaneously show a great many people new ways of acting collectively (see Sewell, 1990). Second, such new forms of action should be linked to the creation of powerful new understandings of the sacred. We may think of Mohammed's proposal of a new source of the sacred in Allah, in the Koran, and in his own person as foci for establishing a new, less fragmented form of social order in seventh-century Arabia (Rodinson, 1971) or the profound influence of Protestantism in creating new sacred symbols of individual conscience and individual moral choice that could ground new, more voluntarist forms of collective action.

Third, such new understandings of collective action should come into being when new ways of organizing action become possible institutionally. David Laitin (1986) argues that the imposition of British colonial patterns in Nigeria had enduring effects on the way political action is organized in Nigeria, institutionalizing identities linked to "home village" as central to collective action, even though these are relatively unimportant social-structurally.

In the contemporary period, we may be going through a modest expansion in our repertoire of collective action, which will have a relatively large effect on traditional understandings of the American Dream. Increasingly, both public debate and public policy recognize group-based "identities" as crucial facts for public life. This has led to a proliferation of such identities and a focus on these identities as public facts. The peculiarly American quality of such identities, from those of feminists, gays, and the disabled to those of Latinos, African Americans, and Asian Americans is that, on the whole, they are understood to be assumed voluntarily. Nevertheless, if in the next generation group identity really does become the major vocabulary through which important aspects of public life are negotiated, and thus an important focus for collective action, then other groups besides African Americans may well come to accept a less idealized image of the American Dream.[12]

NOTES

1. The problem of the relationship of "micro" and "macro" analysis has received renewed attention (see Alexander, Giessen, Munch, & Smelser, 1987; Collins, 1981; Knorr-Cetina &

Cicourel, 1981). The Parsonian tradition, which recognized more genuinely collective-level realities, solved the causal problem largely by ignoring it, treating collectivities as if they were individuals writ large. Sociologists interested in collectivities (Meyer & Scott, 1983; Swanson, 1971) have made substantial progress in recent years, but they have, like the Parsonians, been insufficiently interested in providing "micro-translations" (Collins, 1988) of their collective-level arguments.

2. Comparative research by Michelle Lamont (1989) documents these differences. In *Literary France,* Priscilla Clark (1987) shows how much French literary life matters in France and how themes from the literary hierarchy pervade even popular culture. This is not surprising, given the actual power of French intellectual institutions to shape individual lives through a centralized, hierarchical educational system and uniform national examinations.

3. In *Talk of Love: How Americans Use Their Culture* (Swidler, in press), I develop a detailed argument about why Americans retain contradictory—indeed, what at first appear irreconcilable—understandings of love.

4. See Swidler (1986), who develops the concept of a "strategy of action." I argue that a strategy of action is a persistent way in which an individual organizes action, which may be applied to achieving varied ends or solving different problems. Thus one person may use a strategy of action that involves cultivating a large network of friends on whom she can rely for help, support, and favors, and another person may rely on a strategy of maximizing her individual achievement and personal rewards. Both might be trying to maximize job success, to find a satisfactory mate, or to settle into a respected place in a new community, but their different strategies (and the different cultural skills required to sustain those strategies) would lead them to go about these tasks very differently.

5. This gap between abstract images and the understanding of concrete cases is not only an American phenomenon (see Mann, 1970), but in other societies, where collective strategies of action are different, abstract images of the social world should differ as well.

6. Unemployment *did* affect workers' views about issues directly relevant to their circumstances, increasing the likelihood that they would agree that "the government should provide for those in need," that "the government should end unemployment," and that it should "end unemployment even if the government has to hire the jobless" (Schlozman & Verba, 1979, p. 204). But on questions suggesting more drastic changes to end unemployment, or those indicating disenchantment with the American system as a whole, the unemployed differed hardly at all from their employed counterparts (pp. 203-209). The unemployed were no more likely than employed workers to want the government to assign jobs or to tax the rich to redistribute wealth, nor were they more likely to advocate such drastic measures as ending capitalism (p. 208).

7. The contrast between the patterns of political incorporation of blacks and whites in America is not absolute, but rather a matter of degree. The persistence of Democratic voting among Jews and among American Catholics until the 1960s may also have been due to their integration into community structures that provided alternative channels for pursuing political grievances—urban machines for Catholics and Jewish community organizations for Jews.

8. Durkheim argues that individuals became sacred in all modern societies as a highly developed division of labor made each individual's uniqueness the source of his or her contribution to the wider social community. But I understand the sacred somewhat differently. Sacredness, according to my argument above, embodies the capacity for collective action.

9. In many struggles within societies, the battle is not over the fundamental structural location of the sacred (e.g., in a legitimate king), but over who in particular possesses those sacred qualities. Thus opposition to Russian czars by oppressed peasants often took the form not of opposition to czarist rule but of claiming that the current czar was an impostor and not

the true czar (Bendix, 1974, 1978). Similarly, Geertz (1968) points out that Moroccan Islam has been divided over whether *baraka* is a hereditary power or always a purely personal achievement.

10. Joseph Gusfield (1981) notes that the same emphasis on the moral transformation of individuals persists in the American approach to "public problems" such as drunk driving (and, of course, in the "just say no" approach to drug abuse).

11. Repertoires of capacities for collective action do change. Charles Tilly has developed an argument about the changing repertoire of capacities for collective action in France (see Tilly, 1972, 1976, 1978, 1985; Tilly, Tilly, & Tilly, 1975). William Sewell, Jr. (1990) offers a different, more culturally grounded account. Both theorists focus almost exclusively on social movements and therefore have less to say about how the cultural repertoires that structure violent protests are linked to more general understandings of the nature of membership and participation in collectivities.

12. This analysis may also help to explain the findings of Verba and Orren (1985) showing blacks and feminists to be the most egalitarian of American leadership groups. Women, like blacks, have in recent years mobilized to claim group benefits.

REFERENCES

Abbott, A. (1988). Transcending general linear reality. *Sociological Theory, 6,* 169-186.

Alexander, J. C., Giessen, B., Munch, R., & Smelser, N. J. (Eds.). (1987). *The micro-macro link.* Berkeley: University of California Press.

Althusser, L. (1972). Ideology and ideological state apparatuses. In B. R. Cosin (Ed.), *Education: Structure and society* (pp. 242-280). Harmondsworth, Middlesex: Penguin.

Anderson, B. (1983). *Imagined communities: Reflections on the origin and spread of nationalism.* London: Verso.

Bellah, R. N. (1968). Civil religion in America. In W. G. McLoughlin & R. N. Bellah (Eds.), *Religion in America.* Boston: Houghton Mifflin.

Bellah, R. N., Madsen, R., Sullivan, W. M., Swidler, A., & Tipton, S. M. (1985). *Habits of the heart: Individualism and commitment in American life.* Berkeley: University of California Press.

Bendix, R. (1974). *Work and authority in industry: Ideologies of management in the course of industrialization.* Berkeley: University of California Press.

Bendix, R. (1978). *Kings or people: Power and the mandate to rule.* Berkeley: University of California Press.

Bourdieu, P. (1984). *Distinction: A social critique of the judgment of taste* (R. Nice, Trans.). Cambridge, MA: Harvard University Press.

Boyer, P. (1978). *Urban masses and moral order in America, 1820-1920.* Cambridge, MA: Harvard University Press.

Clark, B. R. (1960). The "cooling-out" function in higher education. *American Journal of Sociology, 65,* 569-576.

Clark, P. P. (1987). *Literary France: The making of a culture.* Berkeley: University of California Press.

Collins, R. (1981). On the microfoundations of macrosociology. *American Journal of Sociology, 86,* 984-1014.

Collins, R. (1988). The micro contribution to macro sociology. *Sociological Theory, 6,* 242-253.

Corse, S. M. (1990). *The mirror cracked: The politics of national identity and national literatures.* Unpublished doctoral dissertation, Stanford University, Department of Sociology.

Durkheim, E. (1965). *The elementary forms of the religious life* (J. W. Swain, Trans.). New York: Free Press. (Original work published 1915)

Erikson, R., & Goldthorpe, J. (1987). Commonality and variation in social fluidity in industrial nations. *European Sociological Review, 3,* 54-166.

Finke, R., & Stark, R. (1989). How the upstart sects won America: 1776-1850. *Journal for the Scientific Study of Religion, 28,* 27-44.

Foucault, M. (1979). *Discipline and punish: The birth of the prison.* New York: Random House.

Free, L. A., & Cantril, H. (1967). *The political beliefs of Americans.* New Brunswick, NJ: Rutgers University Press.

Geertz, C. (1968). *Islam observed.* New Haven, CT: Yale University Press.

Geertz, C. (1980). *Negara: The theatre state in nineteenth-century Bali.* Princeton, NJ: Princeton University Press.

Gusfield, J. R. (1981). *The culture of public problems: Drinking, driving, and the symbolic order.* Chicago: University of Chicago Press.

Gutman, H. G. (1977). *Work, culture, and society in industrializing America.* New York: Random House.

Huber, J., & Form, W. H. (1973). *Income and ideology.* New York: Free Press.

Iannaccone, L. R. (1991). The consequence of religious market structure. *Rationality and Society, 3,* 156-177.

Jackman, M. R., & Jackman, R. W. (1983). *Class awareness in the United States.* Berkeley: University of California Press.

Kluegel, J. R., & Smith, E. R. (1986). *Beliefs about inequality: Americans' views of what is and what ought to be.* New York: Aldine de Gruyter.

Knorr-Cetina, K., & Cicourel, A. V. (Eds.). (1981). *Advances in social theory and methodology: Toward an integration of micro and macro sociologies.* Boston: Routledge & Kegan Paul.

Laitin, D. D. (1986). *Hegemony and culture: Politics and religious change among the Yoruba.* Chicago: University of Chicago Press.

Lamont, M. (1989). The power-culture link in comparative perspective. In C. Calhoun (Ed.), *Comparative social research* (Vol. 11, pp. 131-150). Greenwich, CT: JAI.

Lane, R. E. (1962). *Political ideology: Why the American common man believes what he does.* New York: Free Press.

Lieberson, S. (1985). *Making it count.* Berkeley: University of California Press.

Lipset, S. M. (1963). *The first new nation: The United States in historical and comparative perspective.* New York: Basic Books.

Lipset, S. M. (1990). *Continental divide: The values and institutions of the United States and Canada.* New York: Routledge.

Lipset, S. M., & Bendix, R. (1959). *Social mobility in industrial society.* Berkeley: University of California Press.

McCloskey, H., & Zaller, J. (1984). *The American ethos: Public attitudes toward capitalism and democracy.* Cambridge, MA: Harvard University Press.

McLoughlin, W. G. (1978). *Revivals, awakenings, and reform: An essay on religion and social change in America, 1607-1977.* Chicago: University of Chicago Press.

Mann, M. (1970). The social cohesion of liberal democracy. *American Sociological Review, 35,* 423-439.

Meyer, J. W., & Scott, W. R. (Eds.). (1983). *Organizational environments.* Beverly Hills, CA: Sage.

Meyer, J. W., Tyack, D., Nagel, J., & Gordon, A. (1979). Public education as nation-building in America: Enrollments and bureaucratization, 1870-1930. *American Journal of Sociology, 85,* 591-613.

Rainwater, L. (1974). *What money buys: Inequality and the social meanings of income.* New York: Basic Books.

Reddy, W., Jr. (1984). *The rise of market culture: The textile trade and French society, 1750-1900.* Cambridge: Cambridge University Press.

Rodinson, M. (1971). *Mohammed* (A. Carter, Trans.). New York: Pantheon.

Schama, S. (1989). *Citizens: A chronicle of the French revolution.* New York: Alfred A. Knopf.

Schlozman, K. L., & Verba, S. (1979). *Injury to insult: Unemployment, class, and political response.* Cambridge, MA: Harvard University Press.

Schwartz, B. (1987). *George Washington: The making of an American symbol.* New York: Free Press.

Sewell, W. H., Jr. (1990). Collective violence and collective loyalties in France: Why the French revolution made a difference. *Politics and Society, 18,* 527-552.

Skocpol, T. (1979). *States and social revolutions.* Cambridge: Cambridge University Press.

Spillman, L. P. (1991). *The culture of national identities: Constitutional conventions, centennials, and bicentennials in the United States and Australia.* Unpublished doctoral dissertation, University of California, Berkeley, Department of Sociology.

Swanson, G. E. (1971). An organizational analysis of collectivities. *American Sociological Review, 36,* 607-623.

Swidler, A. (1986). Culture in action: Symbols and strategies. *American Sociological Review, 51,* 273-286.

Swidler, A. (in press). *Talk of love: How Americans use their culture.* Chicago: University of Chicago Press.

Thomas, G. M., Meyer, J. W., Ramirez, F. O., & Boli, J. (1987). *Institutional structure: Constituting state, society, and the individual.* Newbury Park, CA: Sage.

Tilly, C. (1972). How protest modernized in France. In W. Aydelotte, A. Bogue, & R. Fogel (Eds.), *The dimensions of quantitative research in history* (pp. 192-255). Princeton, NJ: Princeton University Press.

Tilly, C. (Ed.). (1975). *The formation of national states in western Europe.* Princeton, NJ: Princeton University Press.

Tilly, C. (1976). Major forms of collective action in western Europe, 1500-1975. *Theory and Society, 3,* 365-375.

Tilly, C. (1978). *From mobilization to revolution.* Reading, MA: Addison-Wesley.

Tilly, C. (1985). Models and realities of popular collective action. *Social Research, 52,* 717-747.

Tilly, C., Tilly, L., & Tilly, R. (1975). *The rebellious century, 1830-1930.* Cambridge, MA: Harvard University Press.

Tocqueville, A. de. (1969). *Democracy in America* (J. P. Mayer, Ed.; G. Lawrence, Trans.). Garden City, NY: Doubleday.

Turner, R. (1960). Sponsored and contest mobility and the school system. *American Sociological Review, 25,* 855-867.

Varenne, H. (1977). *Americans together: Structured diversity in a midwestern town.* New York: Teacher's College Press.

Verba, S., & Orren, G. R. (1985). *Equality in America: The view from the top.* Cambridge, MA: Harvard University Press.

Wolfe, T. (1965). *The kandy-kolored tangerine-flake streamline baby.* New York: Farrar, Straus & Giroux.

Wolfe, T. (1968). *The pump house gang.* New York: Farrar, Straus & Giroux.

Wuthnow, R. (1987). *Meaning and moral order: Explorations in cultural analysis.* Berkeley: University of California Press.

Zuckerman, M. (Ed.). (1982). *Friends and neighbors: Group life in America's first plural society.* Philadelphia: Temple University Press.

15

"Off With Their Heads"

THE CONFIDENCE GAP AND THE
REVOLT AGAINST PROFESSIONALISM
IN AMERICAN POLITICS

William Schneider

W HEN Seymour Martin Lipset and I published *The Confidence Gap* in 1983, our purpose was to explain the decline of confidence in American institutions that had begun in the mid-1960s and persisted through the 1970s. The decline was general. Every institution in American life suffered a diminished reputation during this period—not just government, business, and labor, the institutions of particular concern in our book, but also religion, medicine, science, education, the military, and the press. Even specific industries and companies did not escape the prevailing negativism of the era.

In another sense, however, the decline of confidence was highly specific. People lost confidence in the leaders of the nation's major institutions. But they did not lose confidence in the system. Democracy, free enterprise, the constitutional order, and the system of collective bargaining were always positively valued and showed little evidence of being tainted by the dominant mood of public cynicism. The system was fine. But there was something fundamentally wrong with the way our institutions were being run. Who was at fault? The people in charge. Get better leadership and they would work just fine.

What sustained confidence in the system was not simply ideology but also the phenomenon we identified as "the confidence gap." People's optimism about their own personal lives was strong and resilient, even as their cynicism about institutions mounted. The data showed a sharp discontinuity between the private and public spheres. "My own life is fine," people told poll takers, "and I am confident about my personal future. But there is something wrong 'out there.' The people in charge of things aren't doing their jobs, and the future of the country is in doubt."

We attributed the confidence gap to the bad news Americans were getting about the country's problems and the absence of any consensus about how to solve them. But it was not the fault of the press. The problems were real, and the press was doing its job in reporting them. The country's problems were usually the result of conflicts, corruption, and incompetence that went beyond most Americans' personal sphere of experience. What would it take to reverse the confidence gap? We suggested it would take a sustained period of good news about the way things were going in the country. That, in turn, meant an extended period of responsible leadership and successful problem solving.

When we published the revised edition of *The Confidence Gap* in 1987, we found some evidence of improvement. Ronald Reagan's leadership gave the country a new sense of direction, and 1983 marked the beginning of a record seven-year economic recovery. Americans wanted to believe that Reagan's antitax, antigovernment formulas would provide the answers to the nation's problems. The evidence of improvement can be seen in Figure 15.1.

Antigovernment and antibusiness attitudes have moved in tandem since the 1950s. Note that attitudes toward business and government are measured by different polling organizations in different years. Yet the trend lines are strikingly similar. The Reagan recovery shows up, for both business and government, in the mid-1980s. However, as we noted in the epilogue to the revised edition of *The Confidence Gap*, the positive developments of the mid-1980s did not seem strong enough or persistent enough to reverse the negative trends of the preceding 20 years. As it turned out, they were not.

The federal budget deficit, the Iran-Contra scandal, the stock market crash, the 1990 budget imbroglio, and the recession of 1990-1992 once again dragged confidence levels down. The antigovernment and antibusiness trend lines in Figure 15.1 started moving upward in the late 1980s, reaching peak or near-peak levels in 1990 and 1991. Even the nation's splendid military victory in the Persian Gulf had no lasting impact, as will be shown below.

In January 1992, a Gallup poll taken for Cable News Network and *USA Today* found only 24% of Americans expressing satisfaction with the way things were going in the country, but a resilient 73% said they were satisfied with the way things were going in their own lives. The conclusion we reached in the last sentence of the 1987 edition seems to have been essentially correct: "The confidence gap has been renewed."

Among the consequences of the confidence gap, we identified the tax revolt of the late 1970s and the antigovernment "Reagan revolution" of the 1980s. We argued that the confidence gap did not produce a full-scale legitimacy crisis. Americans never doubted the essential legitimacy of the country's institutional order. What it produced was a populist insurgency against people with power. Leaders in both public and private spheres became the targets of popular antipathy as they were exposed as corrupt, irresponsible, or inept.

This essay discusses the latest manifestation of the confidence gap, one that became increasingly apparent during the 1980s and burst upon the political scene in the 1990 and 1991 elections: a revolt against professionalism in

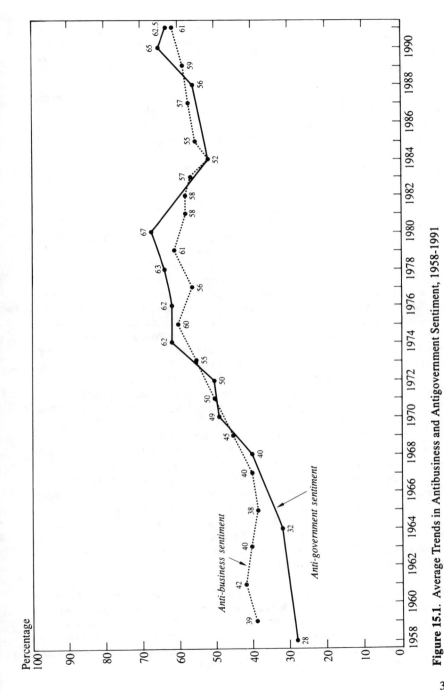

Figure 15.1. Average Trends in Antibusiness and Antigovernment Sentiment, 1958-1991

SOURCE: Antibusiness sentiment: mean, six items (Opinion Research Corporation). Antigovernment sentiment: mean, four items (University of Michigan Center for Political Studies and the Washington Post Poll).

317

American politics. In our 1987 edition, we surmised that "the anti-government revolution may have run its course." The recession of the early 1990s certainly soured Americans on Reaganomics. (In the January 1992 CNN-*USA Today* poll mentioned above, slightly more Americans called President Reagan's economic policies a failure than called them a success.) But the antipolitical sentiment that contributed to the tax revolt and the Reagan revolution is far from spent. The various state and federal budget crises, the savings-and-loan bailout, the congressional pay raise, influence-peddling scandals, and the inability of Congress and the Bush administration to manage the nation's economy contributed to a powerful new sense of resentment against politics and politicians.

ANTIPOLITICS, 1990-1992

American voters perceive themselves to be governed by a class of professional politicians, and they have come to resent it. This resentment was most recently apparent in the 1991 election results. The message of that election was that the voters were dissatisfied with the status quo. They voted for change. Beyond that, nothing was particularly clear. Did the voters move to the left or to the right? Yes, they did. Was it a victory for the Democrats or the Republicans? Yes, it was.

Democrat Harris Wofford got elected to the U.S. Senate in Pennsylvania on a platform of liberal economic populism. He accused President Bush of indifference to the recession and called for national health insurance and extended unemployment benefits. Just across the Delaware River, New Jersey voters roundly repudiated Governor Jim Florio's program of liberal economic populism—tax hikes for the rich and a redistribution of resources from rich to poor school districts. What Pennsylvania showed is that voters were concerned that the Bush administration did not have a domestic agenda. What New Jersey showed is that they were concerned that the Democrats did.

The Pennsylvania vote was what the British call a by-election. In by-elections, people can vote against the government without actually voting for the opposition. It's a way of sending the government a message. The message was that the people wanted change. The left did not have a monopoly on change. Candidates running on right-wing social populist themes—antiquota, antiwelfare, antitaxes—did well in Louisiana, where David Duke got into the runoff, and Mississippi, where the first Republican governor since Reconstruction was elected. In the state of Washington, a high turnout of conservative religious voters helped to defeat a right-to-die measure and turned the vote on an abortion rights initiative into a dead heat.

The Democrats were punished for raising taxes in New Jersey. They were not punished for raising taxes in Kentucky or Pennsylvania, where concern over congressional check bouncing and health insurance displaced concern over taxes. In Mississippi and Virginia, Democratic governors who refused to raise taxes were punished anyway. The voters in those states were unhappy with spending cuts and with the curtailment of state services.

So in the end, was the 1991 election good news for the Republicans or good news for the Democrats? No, it was not.

The voters were certainly angry in states where taxes went up. The record state tax increases of 1991 equaled the federal tax increase of 1990. The voters were also angry because the economy was in recession and nobody seemed to be able to do anything about it. We are supposed to know how to get out of recessions. We've done it before: Cut taxes, increase public spending, or both. But because of the 1990 federal budget deal, neither Congress nor the president was able to do either.

Finally, the voters were angry because they were being governed by politicians who demanded that they be treated like highly skilled professionals. But, unlike true professionals, they could not get their jobs done. In 1990 and 1991, measures to impose term limits passed everywhere they were on the ballot, with the exception of the state of Washington. In 1991, 145 bills were introduced in 45 states to impose term limits on elected officials. Efforts were under way in 1992 to put the issue on the ballot in 18 states.

To many voters, the 1990 budget fiasco symbolized everything wrong with American politics, and they took it out on Congress in the midterm elections that year. That was the only year on record in which House incumbents of both political parties, on the average, saw their margins go down. The usual pattern in congressional elections is that incumbents of one party do better and incumbents of the other party do worse. The 1990 election was the only one in recent decades in which both Republicans and Democrats, on the average, lost support.

We have seen this antipolitical mood before, notably after Watergate in the 1970s, when antipoliticians such as Jimmy Carter were in vogue. What was different about the antipolitical mood of the early 1990s was that voter anger was directed less at the president than at Congress. First Congress raised taxes. Then it raised its own pay. Then the country had to endure the spectacle of the Clarence Thomas hearings, along with revelations of check bouncing and free lunches for legislators. The reputation of Congress has rarely been as negative as it was in 1990 and 1991.

Politicians of both political parties sensed an opportunity. Everyone wanted to run against Washington, the Establishment, the insiders, and most of all, Congress. The signals from the White House were that President Bush intended to take credit for the state of the world in 1992 and blame Congress for the state of the nation. "It's morning in the world," the president seemed prepared to say, "but it won't be morning in America unless the American people give me a Congress I can work with."

Democrats also got into the act. They attacked not only Washington and Congress, but also the leadership of their own party. Former California Governor Jerry Brown was the most extreme. When he entered the presidential race, he wrote a letter to his supporters saying that he was considering running because no other Democrat seemed willing "to take on not only George Bush, but the entire corrupt system, including those entrenched Democratic politicians who have turned our party from a voice of opposition into a party of complicity."

THE PERSONALIZATION OF AMERICAN POLITICS

This voter anger is the culmination of two long-term trends in our public life: Politics has become less substantive, and government has lost credibility. These trends are not unrelated. The nation's political life became less substantive as it became more personalized. Starting with the election of John Kennedy in 1960, politics has been less and less about issues and more and more about personalities.

The widely accepted explanation for this is the rise of television. Television, everyone knows, cannot deal with issues. It can deal only with personalities. That explanation may be plausible, but it is wrong. What actually happened is that politicians made a deliberate decision to personalize their appeal in order to survive.

The 1960s and 1970s saw the decline of political parties and the rise of new, aggressive ideologies on the right and left. Politicians could not survive on party loyalty—there wasn't enough of it anymore. Ideological politics was too controversial and risky. Politicians did not want to end up like Barry Goldwater or George McGovern. So most of the successful ones became independent political entrepreneurs. They went into business for themselves. They applied the techniques of mass marketing to sell the one thing they had confidence in—themselves. Television did not use them; rather, they used television to develop their own personal bases of support, independent of issues, parties, and ideology.

Now we are living with the consequences, among them, rampant careerism, the need for huge amounts of money to market the image, and the increasing power of special interests. Moreover, those who live by personal appeal can die by personal appeal. If you cannot defeat politicians on the issues—and for incumbent members of Congress, it is awfully hard to do that—the only way to defeat them is to discredit them personally. The result has been negative campaigning and the emergence of the press as the principal adversarial force in American politics.

The politicians who can best survive these kinds of attacks are those whose appeal is not purely personal, those who stand for a set of ideas and convictions. Jesse Jackson survived charges of anti-Semitism. Barney Frank survived a homosexual scandal. Ronald Reagan survived Iran-Contra, the worst mistake a president has made since the Vietnam War. Edward Kennedy survived the Chappaquiddick tragedy. Each of those politicians had a base of supporters who stood by him because he stood for something larger than himself.

Conviction politicians are becoming rarer and rarer, however. Could George Bush survive an Iran-Contra scandal as easily as Ronald Reagan did? Reagan was in far less political trouble in the 1982 recession than Bush was in 1992. When Reagan said "Stay the course" in 1982, millions of Americans stood by him. He had a conservative base who believed in him because they knew what he stood for. They had confidence in Reagan's course, even though Reaganomics had never worked. If Bush were to ask people to "stay the course," their response would be, "What course?" The only course Bush ever had was "no new taxes," and he abandoned it after a year in office.

As a result, the voters have become more cynical. They feel betrayed. Their worst suspicions about politicians have been confirmed. They often take out their anger not on the politicians themselves, but on government. In 1990, angry California voters passed Proposition 140, an initiative that set term limits for state officials and slashed the legislature's budget. It was one of the most vicious acts of political retribution in recent American history. California had the most professional state legislature in the country. What the people of California did in 1990 was vote to deprofessionalize it.

Since politicians are now in business for themselves, they survive by creating their own personal followings. Their principal loyalties are to their own careers. One reason this has happened is that political parties have lost the ability to organize and control our political life. As Alan Ehrenhalt writes in *The United States of Ambition* (1991):

> Politics is a profession now. Political careers are open to ambition in a way that has not been true in America for most of this century. Those with the desire for office and the ability to manipulate the instruments of the system— fundraising, personal campaigning, the opportunities to express themselves in public—confront very few limits on their ability to reach the top.

In his book, Ehrenhalt observes politicians at all levels of government, including state legislatures and local city councils. He concludes that what used to be a close-knit group of people who lived and worked and socialized with one another has become a core of individualist professionals focused on their own careers and goals. So we end up with a government of leaderless individualists, prone to petty rivalries and endless bickering. The bitter dispute between Senator Charles Robb and Governor L. Douglas Wilder in Virginia is a perfect example of what happens when two ambitious politicians end up getting in each other's way.

Imagine trying to run a business corporation without any hierarchy of authority based on knowledge or experience. All the executives would try to sell each other out. Nothing would get done. This is exactly what is happening in government, and that is why the voters have become so angry and frustrated.

THE ATTACK ON PROFESSIONALISM

Professionalism and politics don't mix. In fact, Americans see the two as antithetical. The very notion of a professional politician strikes voters as an oxymoron. Professionalism is the art of problem solving, the art of the right. You go to a professional because you want the right answer. Politics is the art of balancing interests, the art of the possible. The politician finds workable answers by balancing public opinion, organized interests, and the interests of his or her own career.

Mark Petracca (1991) of the University of California at Irvine writes:

> During the last forty years, the institution of Congress has been redesigned
> to facilitate and accommodate the career aspirations of its members at the
> expense of its representational and legislative responsibilities. Instead of
> acting as dutiful representatives, dedicated to solving local and national
> problems, Members of Congress achieve career security by serving constit-
> uents as ombudsmen vis-à-vis the federal bureaucracy. (p. 5)

They serve their constituents' interests, they maintain a favorable image, and
they stay elected.

Professionalism creates the perception of a governing class, of elected
officials who treat themselves as privileged experts. It also makes it more
difficult for institutions to solve policy problems. Take, for example, the
legislative modernization movement that got under way in state government in
the mid-1960s. Most legislatures at the time were "sometime governments" that
played weak policy-making roles. The traditional model was a legislature of
citizen politicians—amateurs rather than professionals, people who were close
to the voters in interests and sympathy but who claimed no particular knowledge or expertise in governing. Legislatures met infrequently, usually every
other year for two months. They experienced high rates of turnover. They
depended on lobbyists and bureaucrats for information and expertise. In most
states, the governor ran the show. That is still the case in a number of states
that adhere to the old citizen-legislator model.

The legislative modernization movement aimed to make legislatures more
professional. Reformers demanded more time in legislative sessions. They
called for better staff support. They worked to increase legislative salaries.
They improved budget procedures to allow for greater legislative oversight. To
a considerable extent, these reforms succeeded. According to Rich Jones (1990)
of the National Conference of State Legislatures, state legislatures are stronger
now than they were 20 years ago:

> In 1988, there were over 33,000 staffers working in state legislatures, 40
> percent of them full-time professionals. In 1990, all but seven legislatures
> met in annual sessions. Legislative compensation has been increased in most
> states . . . and legislators in 42 states are eligible for retirement benefits and
> in 46 states receive various insurance benefits such as health and hospital-
> ization. The turnover in state legislatures has declined from almost 40 percent
> in statehouses during the 1950s to 28 percent in the early 1980s. In 1988
> almost one out of every five legislators viewed the legislature as a career.
> (pp. 23-24)

There's only one problem. The voters hate it. They hate the idea that people
go into the legislature as a career. And they hate the fact that state legislatures

are becoming more and more like Congress—full-time professional bodies where members have become independent entrepreneurs requiring elaborate fund-raising activities to mount expensive campaigns.

Many observers see important virtues in amateur legislatures. Amateur legislatures are more representative of the general population. They bring real-world experience to legislative procedures and a pragmatic perspective on the issues. Citizen legislators could be said to take more risks because they are less dependent on their legislative careers. They have something to fall back on. Congress is the most professional legislature in the country, but it still cannot govern. It is unable to form a consensus on tough issues such as the deficit or campaign reform. Political action committees have pervasive influence. Staffs have mushroomed beyond all control. We have a Congress dominated by entrenched incumbents who actually have to make an effort to be defeated, usually by disgracing themselves.

Members of Congress are professionals at getting and staying elected. But the very things that a career legislator must do to stay elected make it more difficult for the collective body to solve problems. Members will not take risky positions. They will not compromise for fear of looking weak and vulnerable against their opponents. They are independent of party leaders and follow no one's advice. They have ways of protecting themselves from the unpopularity of the institution.

In most states, the trend has been toward legislative professionalization, despite a strong emotional and philosophical commitment to citizen-legislatures. This process went furthest in California, whose legislature was a widely acknowledged model of professionalism. On the other hand, the California legislature was no less dominated by special interests than, say, the far less professionalized Texas legislature. Nor was it more efficient as a policy-making body. The reason is that professional legislators need to raise a lot of money from political action committees and special interests in order to keep themselves in office.

In state legislatures as well as in Congress, constituency service takes precedence over problem solving. While constituency service is a good way to stay elected, it is a poor way to make policy. That is why people tell pollsters, "I like my representative, but I hate the legislature." That is a perfectly rational sentiment, given the current legislative environment. Representatives spend a great deal of time making sure they do what their constituents want. They spend less time working collectively to make good public policy. Because representatives concentrate so completely on making sure the voters know them and like them, the institution cannot make tough choices. And unless it makes tough choices, it cannot govern effectively.

A professional may be defined as someone who knows more than you do. You go to a professional doctor or lawyer or accountant because he or she knows more than you do about solving your problem. The relationship works as long as the professional actually solves the problem. Legislators, on the other hand, try to keep their constituents happy, but they do not often solve the problems they were sent to Washington or Boston or Sacramento to solve.

In choosing a doctor, most people do not choose the practitioner they like best. They look for the doctor who can do the best job. Voters, however, usually elect politicians toward whom they feel the most favorably disposed. Then they become frustrated because the legislature is not very effective in getting the job done. The central irony of American politics is that politicians are ineffective because they have to work so hard at being popular.

THE DILEMMA OF TERM LIMITS

The movement for term limits is a direct behavioral consequence of this revolt against professionalism. Many observers were surprised by the defeat of the term limits initiative in the state of Washington in 1991. The measure would have thrown Washington's entire congressional delegation out of office in 1994. According to a *Seattle Times* poll, Washington voters were afraid the state would lose influence in Congress, particularly to California, if the measure passed.

Washington sees California in much the same way Poland sees Russia—as a huge, looming threat. California wants to take Washington's water, and one thing that protects the smaller state is the power and seniority of its congressional delegation. To most Washington voters, the term limits initiative sounded like unilateral disarmament. They did not want to pass term limits for members of Congress unless other states, particularly California, did the same. But Washington is the exception. The movement for term limits is far from dead, and the prospects for a nationwide movement in the 1990s look good.

Term limits are actually an odd remedy. The voters have always had the ability to reject incumbents who are not doing their jobs. Now they want to give up the ability to keep incumbents who are doing a good job. Nevertheless, the movement is perfectly expressive of the voters' mood. Voters don't want to fire their legislator—it's not his or her fault. They want to fire the legislature. That's where the problem is.

The message of the term limits movement is "Stop us before we reelect again." When times are bad and people are angry about the economy, they have always been inclined to vote the ins out and the outs in. But there is something different going on now. It first became evident in 1990, when, as noted earlier, most House incumbents of both parties did worse. People were losing confidence in both the ins and the outs. According to a 1991 survey by the Times Mirror Corporation, cynicism toward the political system is growing rapidly. The public increasingly associates Republicans with wealth and greed and Democrats with fecklessness and incompetence.

The voters are responding to the arrogance and corruption they perceive among politicians. It probably started with the 1989 congressional pay raise. In 1992, according to the Gallup Poll, 70% of Americans still said they would be less likely to vote for any member of Congress who supported the pay raise. The savings-and-loan scandal did its part to convince most voters that politicians were on the take. Finally, there is the widespread perception that politicians are simply not doing their jobs. In a November 1991 Gallup poll, people agreed by two to one that no one in Washington was making any effort to get the country out of recession.

There are reasons politicians cannot do their jobs. One is that there are not many resources available. The antitax, antigovernment movement of the last 12 years has squeezed the public sector and created a huge federal budget deficit. The recession and the savings-and-loan bailout have only made the problem worse. Now the public mood has turned. People seem to be looking to government again to solve problems such as drug abuse, educational decline, and environmental protection. But they resolutely refuse to pay more for government. Politicians are stuck with increasing demands and diminishing public resources. Whose fault is that?

The other reason nothing gets done is the political stalemate that prevails in Washington and in many state capitals. President Bush knows that he cannot get what he wants out of a Democratic Congress. So he has to govern by veto, which he used successfully 24 times in his first 34 months in office. Congress knows that it cannot override a presidential veto. So there is a lot of irresponsible posturing on both sides. The people elect legislatures and executives from different political parties and then they get angry when they don't get along. Whose fault is that?

No politician is going to get very far by blaming the voters, however. We know that term limits are going to have all kinds of unintended consequences, including the loss of legislative experience and expertise. There are very few other jobs where high turnover is considered desirable. Perhaps temporary legislators will take riskier stands, but do the voters really want politicians who are less accountable to public opinion? Term limits are supposed to curb the influence of special interests, but the legislatures will be filled with lame ducks. Lame ducks spend a lot of time feathering their own nests. They worry about what they are going to do when they leave office and do whatever is necessary to protect their careers.

The fundamental problem is uncompetitive elections. Incumbents have far too many advantages, particularly over challengers who remain invisible to most voters. The answer to the problem is campaign reforms aimed at creating a more level playing field between incumbents and challengers. But how do you persuade incumbents to vote for campaign reforms that help challengers? The answer is, you have to threaten them. What can you threaten them with? Well, for this purpose, term limits are a good weapon: "Either you pass serious campaign reforms to make elections more competitive, or the voters will toss you out." Term limits may not make much sense as a remedy, but they are an effective threat.

ANTI-ESTABLISHMENT POPULISM IN 1992

The revolt against professionalism broke out into the open in the 1992 campaign. Anti-Establishment protest candidates ran for president from the right (Patrick Buchanan and David Duke in the Republican Party), the left (Jerry Brown on the Democratic side), and the center (Independent candidate Ross Perot). Nor was anti-Establishment protest limited to the presidential campaign. Congressional incumbents faced a wave of public indignation over abuse of privilege, pay raises, and the legislative gridlock in Washington. A record number of Members decided to give up their seats rather than face an angry electorate.

To be sure, Buchanan, Duke, and Brown did not do particularly well. Voters rejected them as too divisive, but their anti-Establishment protest message did get through. Exit polls found that strong majorities of Republicans felt President Bush should pay attention to the things Pat Buchanan was saying, even though most did not vote for him. On the Democratic side, equally strong majorities—70% in the New York primary—said they agreed with Jerry Brown's criticisms of the political system. They just didn't like Brown.

The voters seemed to be in a surly mood in 1992. Exactly how surly can be documented with reference to two of the questions used to construct the antigovernment index shown in Figure 15.1 (p. 317). Since 1964, the University of Michigan has been asking, "Would you say the government is pretty much run by a few big interests looking out for themselves or that it is run for the benefit of all the people?"

In 1964, 29% of Americans said the government was run for the benefit of a few big interests. By 1974, the year of Watergate, the percentage had reached 66%. In 1980, the year of malaise, it was up to 70%. And in 1992? 80% felt the government was being run for a few big interests, according to a CNN-*USA Today*-Gallup poll taken in April. That's the highest it has ever been.

Another Michigan question asks respondents whether they think "quite a few of the people running the government" are crooked. The number who thought so went from 24% in 1958 to 45% in 1974 and 49% in 1990. It never quite reached a majority—until 1992. In April, 1992, 65% of Americans said they thought quite a few public officials were crooks.

The voters did not think much of the 1992 primary campaign either. In the same CNN-*USA Today*-Gallup poll, 43% said the candidates were not talking about issues voters really cared about; 44% said there was no candidate running who would make a good president—even though one of them *was* president. A majority said the 1992 campaign did not make them feel proud to be an American. Almost 60% said that none of the presidential candidates had come up with good ideas for solving the country's problems.

The voters were clearly angry. But what were they going to do?

Let us define "angry voters" as those who gave negative answers to at least three of the four CNN-*USA Today*-Gallup questions just cited. They comprised almost two voters out of five. When compared with the rest of the electorate, angry voters said they were less likely to vote for Republican candidates. They also said they were less likely to vote for Democratic candidates. They liked Bush less. And they liked Clinton much less.

Angry voters said they were less likely to vote to re-elect incumbents. They were less likely to feel that most Members of Congress deserved to be re-elected. And they were less likely to feel that their own Representative in Congress deserved to be re-elected.

In other words, angry voters were out to make trouble. That is why 1992 is different from other election years. In 1992, voter anger has been more diffuse and nonpartisan. It is not like 1974, the Watergate year, when angry voters turned on the Republicans. Or 1980, the malaise year, when the Democrats got it in the neck. In 1992, voter anger was targeted, not at Republicans or Democrats, but at all politicians.

Is there anybody angry voters did like? Yes. They were more favorable to Ross Perot and more likely to support him for president. Perot's appeal was that of the ultimate outsider and antipolitician. Political professionals claimed Perot was unqualified, inexperienced, naive, and simplistic. All true. His answer to them was, look at all the qualified, experienced, and sophisticated politicians who have been running the country. Could he do any worse?

Perot expressed contempt for professional politicians. He promised to get things done without politics. That is impossible of course, but it sounded pretty good in a year when people were sick to death of politics. Americans who loved politics hated Perot. Americans who hated politics loved Perot. It was a perfect relationship. Especially for Perot, because Americans who hate politics out-number those who love politics by about a thousand to one.

Ultimately, what happened to Perot would depend on the polls. Suppose Clinton started running *third* in the polls. That would have the effect of transforming the 1992 race. A vote for Clinton, not Perot, would look like a wasted vote. Perot would start picking up support at Clinton's expense.

Of course, if Perot started to run second, the press, the interest groups, and the voters would begin to take him more seriously. Perot's wealth, inexperience, authoritarian style, and radical anti-Establishment positions did him no harm as long as he was a protest candidate. But they would create problems for him if he ever became a serious contender.

It is unlikely an Independent like Perot could ever get elected. But he could cause a lot of mischief. In fact, Ross Perot seemed to be in a position to cause more mischief in 1992 than any independent presidential candidate in the last 80 years—not because he was stronger, but because both likely major-party nominees were so much weaker. According to the Gallup Organization, Clinton was rated more negatively in April 1992 than any presidential challenger at that stage of the campaign since Barry Goldwater. Bush got higher negative ratings than any incumbent president since World War II.

Turnout appeared to be the critical factor in the 1992 election. There were two possibilities. One was an election marked by sullen resentment and low turnout. That's what incumbents were praying for. The other was an election marked by angry indignation and high turnout. That always spells trouble. The line between those two outcomes is exceedingly fine.

In the 1990 midterm, voters were angry over the budget deal between the president and Congress and the resulting tax increase. But sullen resentment, not angry indignation, was the rule that year. Turnout was down. House candidates of both parties saw their margins of victory diminish. But very few of them lost their seats.

In the 1992 primaries, angry voters again stayed home. According to the CNN-*USA Today*-Gallup poll, angry voters said they would be *less* likely to vote than the rest of the electorate in 1992. The typical response is, "Why bother? They're all a bunch of bums, and it won't make any difference anyway."

Professional politicians depend on that response. It means that all those angry voters are going to stay home and not give them any trouble. On the other hand, it would not take much to drive voters across the line into angry indignation and high turnout. Racial polarization could do it. So could an attractive Independent candidate like Perot. That is why professional politicians were terrified that the voters would wreak a horrible revenge on them come Election Day, 1992.

WHY THE CONFIDENCE GAP PERSISTS

In *The Confidence Gap,* Lipset and I tried to explain the negative view that most Americans have of politicians. We found that politicians, along with business leaders and labor leaders, were usually at the bottom of the list when people were asked to rank occupations they had the most confidence in and respect for. Scientists, educators, and military and religious leaders were usually near the top of the list. Doctors and lawyers were in the middle. But those involved in government, labor, and business were consistently ranked low.

We identified a widespread public perception that people go into business, government, or labor out of self-interest, not because they want to serve the public good. People describe business, government, and labor leaders as "in it for themselves," whereas they see such professions as religion, military service, and medicine as more altruistic.

The public makes a distinction between the functions performed by institutions and the behavior that makes them work. Our government is an open and competitive democracy. Our economic system is based on open and competitive free enterprise. Both are widely applauded and appreciated by the American public. But the public does not applaud or appreciate the behavior that is implied by an open and competitive system, namely, the relentless pursuit of self-interest.

Competition and self-interest are indispensable for both democratic politics and a free enterprise economy. But the public does not feel constrained, out of devotion to democracy and free enterprise, to admire the self-interested pursuit of power and wealth. This discrepancy might be illogical, but it is deeply embedded in American values. It also implies that our institutions are valued for reasons unrelated to the kind of behavior that makes them work. Our political and economic systems are approved because they result in freedom and prosperity. Profit seeking and power grasping are tolerated as the price that must be paid to attain these objectives. The problem we face today is that the institutions are not working properly. We don't have prosperity, and political institutions are being challenged to reform themselves so that they are closer to the voters' sentiments.

In *The Confidence Gap,* Lipset and I traced the history of public confidence in the leaders of 10 major institutions from 1966 through 1986. They included business ("major companies"), organized labor, organized religion, medicine, education, the press, and various branches of government (Congress, the executive branch, the Supreme Court, and the military).

The story was one of sharp and sudden decline in the late 1960s, followed by a further gradual decline in the 1970s. The Reagan recovery (1983-1986) produced signs of a slight improvement, but there was evidence of slippage after the Iran-Contra scandal broke in November 1986. At the end of 1986, the average level of confidence in leaders of the 10 institutions, at 23%, was about half of what it had been in the mid-1960s.

Polls taken by the National Opinion Research Center (NORC) and the Harris Survey revealed no improvement between 1987 and 1990. This was the period bracketed by the stock market crash of October 1987 and the unpopular federal budget deal of October 1990. Average confidence levels remained stuck in the 22-25% range.

In early 1991, the polling data showed a sudden burst of confidence in institutions immediately following the Persian Gulf war. In the March 1991 NORC poll, for example, leaders of every institution got a lift—even institutions as far removed from the war as organized labor, medicine, and religion. The average level of confidence jumped from 24% to 38%, the highest figure reported since 1966. The United States won a quick and decisive war victory. Americans were feeling good.

It did not last long, however. A July 1991 Harris poll tested confidence in 7 of the 10 institutions, and 6 of them fell sharply, by an average of 20 points (the executive branch dropped 16 points, Congress 25). The only institution to show a steady confidence level was the military.

Even the military didn't hold up much longer, however. The Gallup Poll's time series on confidence in institutions, shown in Table 15.1, reveals a high level of confidence in the military immediately after the war, but a decline to prewar levels by October 1991. In fact, the late 1991 Gallup figures showed the lowest average level of confidence in 18 years. As the Gallup News Service (1991a) reported recently, "Fewer Americans today than at any time in the last two decades say they have a great deal or quite a lot of confidence in these institutions which, along with the presidency, help form the foundation for American political life." Indeed, the 18% figure for Congress was the lowest rating any institution had ever received in the Gallup Poll.

Why did the goodwill engendered by the war vanish so quickly? The easy answer is the recession, which continued unabated. But there is a more complex answer, namely, the public's sharp sense of discontinuity between the nation's success in war and its failure in politics.

Consider what the lessons of the Gulf war were to the American public. Americans concluded that if we just let the military fight the war, they can get

Table 15.1 Confidence in Institutions, 1975-1991

"I am going to read you a list of institutions in American society. Would you tell me how much confidence you, yourself, have in each one—a great deal, quite a lot, some, or very little?"

Institutions	1975	1977	1979	1980	1981	1983	1984	1985	1986	1987	1988	1989	1990	1991 Mar.	1991 Oct.
	Percentage Saying "A Great Deal" or "Quite a Lot"														
The church, or organized religion	68	64	65	66	57	62	54	66	57	61	59	52	56	59	56
The public schools	56	54	53	51	40	39	47	48	49	50	49	43	45	44	35
The Supreme Court	49	46	45	47	52	42	51	56	53	52	56	46	47	48	39
Congress	40	40	34	34	35	28	29	39	41	—	35	32	24	30	18
Organized labor	38	39	36	35	28	26	30	28	29	26	26	—	27	25	22
Big business	34	33	32	29	37	28	29	31	28	—	25	—	25	26	22
The military	58	57	54	52	53	53	58	61	63	61	58	63	68	85	69
Average of seven institutions	49	48	45	45	43	40	43	47	46	—	44	—	41	46	37

SOURCE: Gallup Poll.

the job done. Military leaders thanked the president and the National Security Council for not interfering with them—essentially, for leaving the job of winning the war to military professionals.

Vietnam was a political war. Politicians placed strict limits on what could be done. The Gulf war was a military war. The military was given a mandate to win a victory as quickly and efficiently as possible. That is exactly what they did. What we learned in Vietnam is that the United States does not fight limited wars for political advantage. We fight total wars for total victory. The Persian Gulf experience did not contradict that lesson. It confirmed it.

At the end of the Gulf war, General Norman Schwarzkopf criticized President Bush's decision to stop fighting after 100 hours. Schwarzkopf described it as "one of those decisions that historians are going to second-guess forever." Why didn't we continue the war when we had the enemy routed? The answer was "politics." The White House was eager to pull American troops out as quickly as possible in order to protect the president's political standing, even if our military mission was dangerously incomplete. The administration did not want to get involved in a civil war in Iraq because it was afraid of creating another Vietnam.

After the war, the Democrats tried to apply the new spirit of public purpose and national self-confidence to the domestic agenda. They sensed the public's growing frustration over the gap between foreign and domestic policy. They said, "Why can't we do the same thing in education, infrastructure, and health care—set a goal, mobilize people and resources, just as we did in the Persian Gulf?" The answer, again, was "politics." After the Gulf war, some 85% of Americans said they had confidence in the military. Only 30% expressed confidence in Congress (see Table 15.1).

The war did not increase confidence in the political process. It created confidence in how much we as a country could achieve outside the political process. All the voters had to do was compare the experience of winning the war in February 1991 with the experience of passing a federal budget the preceding October. The war was a triumph of military professionalism. The budget process exposed the failures of political professionalism. Once again, the confidence gap has been renewed.

REFERENCES

Ehrenhalt, A. (1991). *The United States of ambition.* New York: Times Books.
Gallup News Service. (1991a, October 15). Confidence in major U.S. institutions at an all-time low. *Los Angeles Times.*
Gallup News Service. (1991b, November 13). Duke unpopular across country, but his issues strike home. *Los Angeles Times.*
Jones, R. (1990, July). The legislature 2010: Which direction? *State Legislatures.*
Lipset, S. M., & Schneider, W. (1983). *The confidence gap: Business, labor and government in the public mind.* New York: Free Press.
Lipset, S. M., & Schneider, W. (1987). *The confidence gap: Business, labor and government in the public mind* (rev. ed.). Baltimore: Johns Hopkins University Press.
Petracca, M. (1991). The poison of professional politics. *Policy Analysis, 151.*

Appendix

PUBLICATIONS OF
SEYMOUR MARTIN LIPSET

Books and Monographs (in chronological order)

1950   *Agrarian Socialism.* Berkeley: University of California Press. Rev. ed., Garden City, NY: Doubleday-Anchor, 1968. Rev. and expanded ed., Berkeley: University of California Press, 1971. Foreign editions in Britain and Egypt.

1956   (With Martin Trow and James S. Coleman), *Union Democracy.* Glencoe, IL: Free Press, 1953. 2nd ed., Garden City, NY: Anchor, 1962. Paperback ed., New York: Free Press, 1977. Foreign editions in Argentina and Italy.

1959   (With Reinhard Bendix), *Social Mobility in Industrial Society.* Berkeley: University of California Press (paperback, 1961). Expanded ed., New Brunswick, NJ: Transaction Books, 1991. Foreign editions in Britain, Argentina, Poland, Japan, and Italy.

1959   (With Earl Raab), *Prejudice and Society.* New York: Anti-Defamation League.

1960   *Political Man: The Social Bases of Politics.* Garden City, NY: Doubleday (2nd ed., 1963). Expanded, updated ed., Baltimore: Johns Hopkins University Press, 1981. Foreign editions in Britain, France, Italy, Turkey, Argentina, Germany, Sweden, Japan, Brazil, Norway, India, Yugoslavia, Bangladesh, Lebanon, Israel, and Vietnam.

1963   *The First New Nation: The United States in Historical and Comparative Perspective.* New York: Basic Books. 2nd ed., Garden City, NY: Doubleday, 1967. Expanded ed., New York: Norton Library, 1979. Foreign editions in Britain, France, Colombia, Japan, and England.

1965   *Estudiantes universitarios y politica en el tercer mundo.* Montevideo:
        Editorial Alfa.

1968   *Revolution and Counterrevolution: Change and Persistence in Social
        Structures.* New York: Basic Books. Rev. ed., Garden City, NY: Anchor,
        1970. Rev. ed., New Brunswick, NJ: Transaction, 1988. Foreign editions
        in Britain and Japan.

1970   (With Earl Raab), *The Politics of Unreason: Right-Wing Extremism in
        America 1790-1970.* New York: Harper & Row. Rev. ed. (*1790-1977*),
        Chicago: University of Chicago Press, Phoenix, 1978. Foreign editions
        in Britain, Italy, and Mexico.

1972   *Group Life in America.* New York: American Jewish Committee.

1972   *Rebellion in the University.* Boston: Little, Brown. Expanded ed., Chi-
        cago: University of Chicago Press, Phoenix, 1976. Foreign editions in
        Britain and Brazil.

1973   (With Everett C. Ladd), *Professors, Unions and American Higher Edu-
        cation.* Berkeley, CA: Carnegie Commission on Higher Education.

1973   (With Everett C. Ladd), *Academics, Politics, and the 1972 Election.* Wash-
        ington, DC: American Enterprise Institute for Public Policy Research.

1975   (With Everett C. Ladd), *The Divided Academy: Professors and Politics.*
        New York: McGraw-Hill. Paperback ed., New York: Norton Library,
        1976. Foreign edition in Japan.

1975   (With David Riesman), *Education and Politics at Harvard.* New York:
        McGraw-Hill.

1978   (With Irving Louis Horowitz), *Dialogues on American Politics.* New
        York: Oxford University Press.

1983   (With William Schneider), *The Confidence Gap: Business, Labor and
        Government in the Public Mind.* New York: Free Press. Expanded,
        updated ed., Baltimore: Johns Hopkins University Press, 1987.

1985   *Consensus and Conflict: Essays in Political Sociology.* New Brunswick,
        NJ: Transaction. Foreign edition in Portugal.

1989   *Continental Divide: Values and Institutions of the United States and
        Canada.* Toronto: C. D. Howe Institute. New York: Routledge, 1990.

1990   *Distinctive Cultures: Canada and the United States.* Bozeman: Montana
        State University, Borderlands Project.

in press   *Adversary Cultures.* New Brunswick, NJ: Transaction.

Edited Books (in chronological order)

1960   (With Walter Galenson), *Labor and Trade Unionism.* New York: John
        Wiley. Foreign edition in Argentina.

1961   (With Neil Smelser), *Sociology: The Progress of a Decade.* Englewood
        Cliffs, NJ: Prentice-Hall.

1961   (With Leo Lowenthal), *Culture and Social Character.* New York: Free
        Press.

1962   (Abridged modern edition of Harriet Martineau), *Society in America.* Garden City, NY: Doubleday.

1964   (Abridged modern edition of M. Ostrogorski), *Democracy and the Organization of Political Parties* (Vols. 1-2). Garden City, NY: Doubleday.

1965   (With Sheldon Wolin), *The Berkeley Student Revolt.* Garden City, NY: Doubleday.

1966   (With Reinhard Bendix), *Class, Status and Power: Social Stratification in Comparative Perspective.* New York: Free Press. Foreign editions in Italy and Spain.

1966   (With Neil Smelser), *Social Structure, Mobility and Development.* Chicago: Aldine.

1967   (With Aldo Solari), *Elites in Latin America.* New York: Oxford University Press. Foreign edition in Argentina.

1967   (With Stein Rokkan), *Party Systems and Voter Alignments.* New York: Free Press.

1967   *Student Politics.* New York: Basic Books. Foreign editions in Italy and Japan.

1968   (With Richard Hofstadter), *Turner and the Sociology of the Frontier.* New York: Basic Books.

1968   (With Richard Hofstadter), *Sociology and History: Methods.* New York: Basic Books.

1969   *Politics and the Social Sciences.* New York: Oxford University Press.

1969   (With Philip Altbach), *Students in Revolt.* Boston: Houghton Mifflin. Paperback ed., Boston: Beacon, 1970.

1970   (With David Bell and Karl Deutsch), *Issues in Politics and Government.* Boston: Houghton Mifflin.

1974   (With John Laslett), *Failure of a Dream? Essays in the History of American Socialism.* Garden City, NY: Doubleday.

1978   *Emerging Coalitions in American Politics.* San Francisco: Institute for Contemporary Studies.

1979   *The Third Century: America as a Post-Industrial Society.* Stanford, CA: Hoover Institution Press. Phoenix ed., Chicago: University of Chicago Press, 1980.

1981   *Party Coalitions in the 1980s.* San Francisco: Institute for Contemporary Studies.

1986   *Unions in Transition: Entering the Second Century.* San Francisco: Institute for Contemporary Studies.

1988   (With Larry Diamond and Juan Linz), *Democracy in Developing Countries: Vol. 2. Africa.* Boulder, CO: Lynne Rienner.

1989   (With Larry Diamond and Juan Linz), *Democracy in Developing Countries: Vol. 3. Asia.* Boulder, CO: Lynne Rienner.

1989   (With Larry Diamond and Juan Linz), *Democracy in Developing Countries: Vol. 4. Latin America.* Boulder, CO: Lynne Rienner.

1990   *American Pluralism and the Jewish Community.* New Brunswick, NJ: Transaction.

Articles (in chronological order)

1947.1   "The Rural Community and Political Leadership in Saskatchewan." *Canadian Journal of Economics and Political Science* (August), pp. 410-428.

1948.1   "Political Participation and the Organization of the Cooperative Commonwealth Federation in Saskatchewan." *Canadian Journal of Economics and Political Science* (May), pp. 191-208.

1949.1   "Bureaucracy and Social Reform." Proceedings of the Pacific Coast Sociology Society, State College of Washington. *Research Studies, 17,* pp. 11-17.

1949.2   "Polling and Science." *Canadian Journal of Economics and Political Science* (May), pp. 237-240.

1950.1   "Leadership and New Social Movements." In Alvin W. Gouldner (Ed.), *Studies in Leadership* (pp. 342-362). New York: Harper & Brothers.

1950.2   "Changing Social Status and Prejudice." *Commentary* (May), pp. 475-479.

1950.3   "Polling and Science II." *Canadian Journal of Economics and Political Science* (August), pp. 426-429.

1950.4   "The Two Party System in the I.T.U." *Labor and Nation* (Fall), pp. 33-45.

1950.5   "An Aging Population in an Industrial Society: Sociological Aspects." In Harold E. Jones (Ed.), *Research on Aging* (Pacific Coast Committee on Old Age Research, Social Science Research Council) (Fall), pp. 63-66.

1951.1   (With Reinhard Bendix), "Social Status and Social Structure: A Reexamination of the Data and Interpretation I." *British Journal of Sociology* (June), pp. 150-168.

1952.1   (With Reinhard Bendix), "Social Status and Social Structure: A Reexamination of the Data and Interpretation II." *British Journal of Sociology* (September), pp. 230-254.

1952.2   (With Reinhard Bendix), "Social Mobility and Occupational Career Patterns: I. Stability of Job Holdings." *American Journal of Sociology* (January), pp. 366-374.

1952.3   (With Reinhard Bendix), "Social Mobility and Occupational Career Patterns: II. Social Mobility." *American Journal of Sociology* (March), pp. 494-503.

1952.4   "Democracy in Private Government." *British Journal of Sociology* (March), pp. 47-63.

1953.1   (With Reinhard Bendix), "Karl Marx' Theory of Social Classes." In R. Bendix & S. M. Lipset (Eds.), *Class, Status and Power: Social Stratification in Comparative Perspective* (pp. 26-45). New York: Free Press, 1966.

1953.2   (With Joan Gordon), "Mobility and Trade Union Membership." In R. Bendix & S. M. Lipset (Eds.), *Class, Status and Power: Social Stratification in Comparative Perspective* (pp. 491-500). New York: Free Press, 1966.

1953.3   (With Daniel Bell), "Trade Unions and Minority Problems." In D. Bell & S.
          M. Lipset (Eds.), *Journal of Social Issues, 9*(1) (special issue), pp. 2-3, 61.
1953.4   "Opinion Formation in a Crisis Situation." *Public Opinion Quarterly*
          (Spring), pp. 20-46.
1954.1   (With Reinhard Bendix and F. Theodore Malm), "Social Origins and
          Occupational Career Patterns." *Industrial and Labor Relations Review*
          (January), pp. 246-261.
1954.2   (With Paul Lazarsfeld, Allen Barton, and Juan Linz), "The Psychology of
          Voting: An Analysis of Political Behavior." In Gardner Lindzey (Ed.), *Hand-
          book of Social Psychology* (pp. 1124-2275). Cambridge: Addison-Wesley.
1954.3   "The Political Process in Trade Unions: A Theoretical Statement." In
          Monroe Berger et al. (Eds.), *Freedom and Control in Modern Society* (pp.
          82-124). New York: D. Van Nostrand.
1954.4   (With Reinhard Bendix), "Ideological Equalitarianism and Social Mobil-
          ity in the United States." In *Transactions of the Second World Congress
          of Sociology* (Vol. 11, pp. 34-54). London: International Sociological
          Association.
1954.5   "Democracy in Alberta." *Canadian Forum* (November/December), pp.
          175-177, 196-198.
1954.6   (With Natalie Rogoff), "Class and Opportunity in Europe and the U.S."
          Commentary (December), pp. 562-568. (In German: "Klassengesell-
          schaft und soziale Mobilitat. Ein Verleich zwissen Europa und den
          Vereinigten Staten." In Erwin Scheuch & Rolf Meyersohn [Eds.], *Soziologie
          der Freizeit* [Neue Wissenschaftliche Bibliothek], pp. 291-302. C. Mus-
          sel & G. Wallenstein, Trans.)
1955.1   (With Reinhard Bendix and F. Theodore Malm), "Job Plans and Entry
          Into the Labor Market." *Social Forces* (March), pp. 224-233.
1955.2   (With F. Theodore Malm), "First Jobs and Career Patterns." *American
          Journal of Economics and Sociology* (April), pp. 247-261.
1955.3   "The Radical Right." *British Journal of Sociology* (June), pp. 179-209.
1955.4   "Comments on 'The Impact of Income Security upon Individual Freedom'
          by Barbara Wootton." In James E. Russell (Ed.), *National Policies for
          Education, Health and Social Services* (pp. 398-404). Garden City, NY:
          Doubleday.
1955.5   (With Nathan Glazer), "The Polls on Communism and Conformity." In
          Daniel Bell (Ed.), *The New American Right* (pp. 141-165). New York:
          Criterion.
1955.6   "The Sources of the 'Radical Right.' " In Daniel Bell (Ed.), *The New
          American Right* (pp. 166-234). New York: Criterion.
1955.7   "Jewish Sociologists and Sociologists of the Jews." *Jewish Social Stud-
          ies* (July), pp. 177-178.
1955.8   "The Department of Sociology." In R. Gordon Hoxie et al., *History of
          the Faculty of Political Science, Columbia University* (pp. 284-303).
          New York: Columbia University Press.

1955.9   "Social Mobility and Urbanization." *Rural Sociology* (September/December), pp. 220-228.

1955.10 "European Traditions and American Sociology." *Commentary* (December), pp. 568-570.

1956.1   "The American Voter." *Encounter* (August), pp. 55-62. (In Spanish: "La Incognita del Elector Norteamericano." *Cuadernos* [November/December], pp. 85-90.)

1956.2   "Political Sociology 1945-1955." In Hans Zetterberg (Ed.), *Sociology in the U.S.A.* (pp. 55-62). Paris: UNESCO.

1956.3   (With Hans Zetterberg), "A Theory of Social Mobility." *Transactions of the Third World Congress of Sociology* (Vol. 3, pp. 155-177). London: International Sociological Association. (In German: "Eine Theorie der Sozialen Mobilitat." *Klassenbildung und Sozialschichtung* [Wissenschaftliche Buchgesellschaft Darmstadt, 1968], pp. 330-366.)

1956.4   "Democracy in the International Typographical Union." *Yearbook of the American Philosophical Society, 1955* (pp. 211-218). Philadelphia: American Philosophical Society.

1956.5   (With Martin Trow and James S. Coleman), "Trade Union Democracy and Secondary Organization." In William Peterson (Ed.), *American Social Patterns: Five Studies* (pp. 211-218). Garden City, NY: Anchor.

1957.1   (With Martin Trow), "Reference Group Theory and Trade Union Wage Policy." In Mirra Komarovsky & Paul Lazarsfeld (Eds.), *Common Frontiers in Social Sciences* (pp. 391-411). Glencoe, IL: Free Press.

1957.2   "The Fuss About the Eggheads." *Encounter* (April), pp. 17-21.

1957.3   (With Reinhard Bendix), "Political Sociology: A Trend Report and Bibliography." *Current Sociology, 6*, pp. 79-169.

1957.4   "The Egghead Looks at Himself." *New York Times Magazine* (November 17), pp. 104-107.

1958.1   "A Sociologist Looks at History." *Pacific Sociological Review* (Spring), pp. 13-17.

1958.2   (With Hans Zetterberg), "A Comparative Study of Social Mobility: Its Causes and Consequences." *PROD (Political Research: Organization Design)* (September), pp. 13-17.

1958.3   "Socialism: Left and Right—East and West." *Confluence* (Summer), pp. 173-192.

1958.4   "The Surprising Effect of McCarthyism on 'The Academic Mind.' " *Columbia University Forum* (Fall), pp. 25-29.

1958.5   "Aristocracy in America." *Commentary* (December), pp. 534-537.

1959.1   "Political Sociology." In Robert K. Merton et al. (Eds.), *Sociology Today* (pp. 81-114). New York: Basic Books.

1959.2   "Some Social Requisites of Democracy." *American Political Science Review* (March), pp. 69-105.

1959.3   "American Intellectuals: Their Politics and Status." *Daedalus* (Summer), pp. 460-486.

1959.4   "Democracy and Working-Class Authoritarianism." *American Sociological Review, 24,* pp. 482-502.

1959.5   "Stability in the Midst of Change." In *The Social Welfare Forum Official Proceedings, 1959* (pp. 14-38). New York: Columbia University Press.

1959.6   "Social Stratification and Right-Wing Extremism." *British Journal of Sociology, 10,* pp. 346-382.

1959.7   "The Political Animal: Genus Americanus." *Public Opinion Quarterly, 23,* pp. 554-562.

1959.8   "Must We Conform to Succeed?" *California Monthly* (November), pp. 8-11.

1960.1   "Trends in American Society." In Lyman Bryson (Ed.), *An Outline of Man's Knowledge of the Modern* (pp. 389-417). New York: McGraw-Hill.

1960.2   "Party Systems and the Representation of Social Groups." *European Journal of Sociology, 1,* pp. 50-85. (In German: "Partiensysteme und Reprasentation sozialer Gruppen." *Beitrage zue allgemeinen Parteienlehre* [Wissenschaftliche Buchgesellschaft Darmstadt, 1969], pp. 431-476. L. Brock, Trans.)

1960.3   "Some Statistics on Bigotry in Voting." *Commentary, 3,* pp. 286-290.

1960.4   "The British Voter I." *New Leader* (November 7), pp.10-14.

1960.5   "The British Voter II." *New Leader* (November 21), pp. 15-20.

1960.6   "Must Tories Always Triumph?" *Socialist Commentary* (November), pp. 10-14.

1960.7   "Equal or Better in America." *Columbia University Forum* (Spring), pp. 17-21.

1960.8   "A Conflict of American Ideals." *Listener* (November 10), pp. 821-823.

1961.1   "The British Voter III." *New Leader* (February 6).

1961.2   "Any Hope for the Liberals?" *Socialist Commentary* (March), pp. 4-7.

1961.3   " 'Working-class Authoritarianism': A Reply to Miller and Riessman." *British Journal of Sociology* (September), pp. 277-281.

1961.4   "The Law and Trade Union Democracy." *Virginia Law Review, 47,* pp. 1-50.

1961.5   (With Neil Smelser), "Change and Controversy in Recent American Sociology." *British Journal of Sociology* (March), pp. 41-51.

1961.6   "Estratificacao e politica nos estados unidos." *Revista de direito publicae ciencia politica, 4,* pp. 83-104.

1961.7   "A Changing American Character?" In S. M. Lipset & Leo Lowenthal (Eds.), *Culture and Social Character* (pp. 136-171). New York: Free Press.

1961.8   "Le syndicalisme americain et les valeurs de la societe americaine." *Sociologie du Travail, 2-3,* pp. 161-181, 268-286.

1961.9   "Trade Unions and Social Structure: A Comparative Analysis, I." *Industrial Relations* (October), pp. 75-89. (In Spanish: "Sindicatos y Estructura Social: Analisis Comparativo." *Revista de Estudios Politicos,* pp. 3-54.)

1962.1   "Trade Unions and Social Structure: A Comparative Analysis, II." *Industrial Relations* (February), pp. 89-110.

1962.2   "The Alienated Americans: Some Notes on Coughlin, McCarthy and Birch." *Columbia University Forum* (Summer), pp. 19-24.

1962.3   "Michels' Theory of Political Parties." In Robert Michels, *Political Parties* (pp. 15-39). New York: Free Press.

1962.4   "Harriet Martineau's America: An Introductory Essay." In Harriet Martineau, *Society in America* (S. M. Lipset, Ed.) (pp. 5-42). Garden City, NY: Doubleday.

1962.5   "Rotten Boroughs—Twentieth Century Style." *Union Review, 1,* pp. 72-75.

1962.6   "Ideology and Political Bias: A Reply to Peck." *American Catholic Sociological Review, 23,* pp. 207-223.

1962.7   "California: Politics and Growth." *New Society* (October 25), pp. 26-29.

1962.8   "My View from Our Left." *Columbia University Forum* (Fall), pp. 31-37.

1963.1   "Three Decades of the Radical Right: Coughlinites, McCarthyites and Birchers." In Daniel Bell (Ed.), *The Radical Right* (pp. 313-377). Garden City, NY: Doubleday.

1963.2   "Egaliser les chances." *Esprit, 31,* pp. 54-66.

1963.3   "The Value Patterns of Democracy: A Case Study in Comparative Analysis." *American Sociological Review* (August), pp. 515-531.

1963.4   "The Sociology of Marxism." *Dissent* (Winter), pp. 59-69.

1963.5   "Social Stratification and the Analysis of American Society." In Bernard Berelson (Ed.), *The Behavioral Sciences Today* (pp. 188-203). New York: Basic Books.

1963.6   "The Study of Jewish Communities in a Comparative Context." *Jewish Journal of Sociology, 5,* pp. 157-166.

1963.7   (With Edward Shils), "Social Class." *Encyclopedia Britannica* (Vol. 5), pp. 873-875.

1964.1   "Introduction." In T. H. Marshall, *Citizenship and Social Development* (pp. v-xx). Garden City, NY: Doubleday.

1964.2   "Democracy and the Social System." In Harry Eckstein & Klaus Knorr (Eds.), *Internal War* (pp. 267-333). New York: Free Press.

1964.3   "Religion and Politics in American Past and Present." In Robert Lee (Ed.), *Religion and Social Conflict* (pp. 69-126). New York: Oxford University Press.

1964.4   "The United States: The First New Nation." In *Transactions of the Fifth World Congress of Sociology* (pp. 307-361). Louvain: International Sociological Association.

1964.5   "Approaches to Reducing the Costs of Comparative Survey Research." *Social Sciences Information* (December), pp. 33-38.

1964.6   "Research Problems in the Comparative Analysis of Mobility and Development." *International Social Science Journal, 16,* pp. 35-48. (In French: "Problems poses par les recherches comparatives sur la mobilite et le developpement." *Revue Internationale des Sciences Sociales, 16,* pp. 40-54.)

1964.7 "Ostrogorski and the Analytical Approach to the Comparative Study of Political Parties." In M. Ostrogorski, *Democracy and the Organization of Political Parties* (pp. ix-xv). Garden City, NY: Doubleday.

1964.8 "A Private Opinion on the Polls." *New York Times Magazine* (August 30), pp. 62-65.

1964.9 "Changes, Values, and Social Problems in American Society." In *Proceedings of the Asilomar Conference* (October 21-23, 1964) (pp. 6-18). San Francisco: San Francisco State College.

1964.10 "How Big Is the Bloc Vote?" *New York Times Magazine* (October 25), pp. 32-33, 124-127.

1964.11 "Blocs and Groups in America's Election." *New Society* (October 29), pp. 14-17.

1964.12 "University Students and Politics in Underdeveloped Countries." *Minerva* (Autumn), pp. 15-56.

1964.13 "Beyond the Backlash." *Encounter* (November), pp. 11-24.

1964.14 "Goldwaterites: What Now?" *New Society* (November 26), pp. 6-7.

1964.15 "Waiting for the Pendulum." *New Leader* (December 7), pp. 5-8.

1964.16 "Sociology and Political Science: A Bibliographic Note." *American Sociological Review, 16,* pp. 730-734.

1964.17 "Political Cleavages in 'Developed' and 'Emerging' Politics.'" In Erik Allardt & Yrjo Littunen (Eds.), *Cleavages, Ideologies and Party Systems* (pp. 21-25). Helsinki: Westermarck Society.

1964.18 "Canada and the United States: A Comparative View." *Canadian Review of Sociology and Anthropology, 1,* pp. 173-185. (In German: "Kanada und die Vereinigten Staaten: Eine Verleichende Betrachtung." *Kolner Zeitschrift für Soziologie und Sozial-Psychologie, 17* [1965], pp. 659-674.)

1964.19 "The Biography of a Research Project: Union Democracy." In Philip Hammon (Ed.), *Sociologists at Work* (pp. 96-120). New York: Basic Books.

1964.20 "The Changing Class Structure and Contemporary European Politics." *Daedalus* (Winter), pp. 271-303.

1965.1 "The Political Behavior of University Students in Developing Countries." *Social and Economic Studies, 14,* pp. 35-75.

1965.2 "American Sociology Today." *Amerika* (January), pp. 8-11 (in Russian). (In Polish: December 1964.)

1965.3 (With Paul Seabury), "The Lesson of Berkeley." *Reporter* (January 28), pp. 36-40.

1965.4 "Las Elites, la educacion y el dessarrollo economico." *Revista paraquaya de sociologia* (May/August), pp. 5-21.

1965.5 "Revolution and Counterrevolution: The United States and Canada." In Thomas Ford (Ed.), *The Revolutionary Theme in Contemporary America* (pp. 21-64). Lexington: University of Kentucky Press.

1965.6 "An Anatomy of the Klan." *Commentary* (October), pp. 74-83.

1965.7 (With Irving Horowitz), "The Birth and Meaning of America: A Discussion of *The First New Nation.*" *Sociological Inquiry* (Winter), pp. 3-20.

1966.1 "Some Further Comments on the 'End of Ideology.' " *American Political Science Review* (March), pp. 17-18.

1966.2 "Student Opposition in the U.S." *Government and Opposition* (April), pp. 351-374.

1966.3 (With Philip Altbach), "Student Politics and Higher Education." *Comparative Education Review* (June), pp. 320-349.

1966.4 (With Philip Altbach), "American Student Protest." *New Society* (September 1), pp. 328-332.

1966.5 "Doves, Hawks and Polls." *Encounter* (October), pp. 38-45.

1966.6 "The U.S. Backlash at the Polls." *New Society* (November 3), pp. 690-694.

1966.7 (With Mildred Schwartz), "The Politics of Professionals." In Howard Vollmer & Donald Mills (Eds.), *Professionalization* (pp. 299-310). Englewood Cliffs, NJ: Prentice-Hall. (In German: "Das politische Verhalten professioneller Experten." *Berufussoziologie,* Neue Wissenschaftliche Bibliothek 55.)

1966.8 (With Neil Smelser), "Social Structure, Mobility and Development." In Neil Smelser & S. M. Lipset (Eds.), *Social Structure, Mobility and Development* (pp. 1-50). Chicago: Aldine.

1967.1 "Fallas de la Educacion en Latino America." *LIFE en Español* (November 6), pp. 24-26.

1967.2 "Values, Education and Entrepreneurship." In S. M. Lipset & Aldo Solari (Eds.), *Elites in Latin America* (pp. 3-60). New York: Oxford University Press.

1967.3 "Political Sociology." In Neil Smelser (Ed.), *Sociology* (pp. 435-499). New York: John Wiley.

1967.4 (With Philip Altbach), "Student Politics and Higher Education in the United States." In S. M. Lipset (Ed.), *Student Politics* (pp. 199-252). New York: Basic Books.

1967.5 (With Stein Rokkan), "Cleavage Structure, Party Systems and Voter Alignments." In S. M. Lipset & S. Rokkan (Eds.), *Party Systems and Voter Alignments* (pp. 1-64). New York: Free Press.

1967.6 "White Collar Workers and Professionals: Their Attitudes and Behavior Toward Unions." In William A. Faunce (Ed.), *Readings in Industrial Sociology* (pp. 525-548). New York: Meredith.

1967.7 "Foreword." In Mildred Schwartz, *Public Opinion and Canadian Identity* (pp. v-viii). Berkeley: University of California Press.

1968.1 "Cambio, Problemas Sociales y Tensiones Politicas en la Sociedad Americana." *Revista Española de la Opinion Publica* (April/June), pp. 9-30.

1968.2 "Politics of Conscience: Driving Force of Change." *Los Angeles Times* (April 28), pp. G1-G2.

1968.3 "La exposion del poder estudiantil." *LIFE en Español* (June 3), pp. 8-16.

1968.4 "Student Activism." *Current Affairs Bulletin* (July 15), pp. 50-64.

1968.5 "On the Politics of Conscience and Extreme Commitment." *Encounter* (August), pp. 66-71.

1968.6 "George Wallace and the U.S. New Right." *New Society* (October 3), pp. 477-483.

1968.7 "Rebellion on Campus." *American Education* (October), pp. 28-31.

1968.8 "The Possible Political Effects of Student Activism." From ISSC-sponsored Round Table on Student Unrest, Paris, December 6-9; published in Reprint Series, Center for International Affairs, Harvard University, December. (In Italian: "Riflessi Politici Dell'Attivismo Studentesco." Estratto dai *Quaderni di Sociologia, 18* [1969], pp. 95-123.)

1968.9 "The Activists: A Profile." *Public Interest* (Fall), pp. 38-50.

1968.10 "Students and Politics in Comparative Perspective." *Daedalus* (Winter), pp. 1-20.

1968.11 "Anglo-American Society." In David Sills (Ed.), *International Encyclopedia of the Social Sciences* (Vol. 1, pp. 289-302). New York: Macmillan.

1968.12 "Social Class." In David Sills (Ed.), *International Encyclopedia of the Social Sciences* (Vol. 15, pp. 196-316). New York: Macmillan.

1968.13 "The Turner Thesis in Comparative Perspective: An Introduction." In S. M. Lipset & Richard Hofstadter (Eds.), *Turner and the Sociology of the Frontier* (pp. 9-14). New York: Basic Books.

1968.14 "History and Sociology: Some Methodological Considerations." In S. M. Lipset & Richard Hofstadter (Eds.), *Sociology and History: Methods* (pp. 20-58). New York: Basic Books.

1968.15 "Political Sociology." In Talcott Parsons (Ed.), *American Sociology* (pp. 156-170). New York: Basic Books.

1968.16 "The 'Newness' of the New Nation." In C. Vann Woodward (Ed.), *The Comparative Approach to American History* (pp. 62-74). New York: Basic Books.

1968.17 "Voting Behavior." In *Encyclopedia Britannica* (Vol. "Vortex to Voss," pp. 126-128). Chicago: William Benton.

1969.1 "The Political Thrust Motivating Campus Turmoil." *Saturday Review* (March 1), p. 24.

1969.2 "The Politics of the Police." *New Society* (March 6), pp. 355-358.

1969.3 "Why Cops Hate Liberals—and Vice Versa." *Atlantic* (March), pp. 76-83.

1969.4 "Student Activists: A Profile." *Dialogue, 2*(2), pp. 3-12. (In Spanish: "Los Estudiantes Activitas: Una Semblanza." *Facetas, 2,* pp. 3-14.)

1969.5 "Comparing the Crises: Harvard and Berkeley." *Mosaic* (Spring), pp. 6-23.

1969.6 "The Possible Effects of Student Activism in International Politics." *Quest* (April/June), pp. 37-53.

1969.7 "The Possible Effects of Student Activism on International Relations." *Foreign Service Journal* (September), pp. 26-58.

1969.8 (With Earl Raab), "The Wallace Whitelash." *Trans-Action* (December), pp. 23-32, 34-35.

1969.9 "The 'Socialism of Fools': The Left, the Jews and Israel." *Encounter* (December), pp. 24-35.

1969.10 "Socialism and Sociology." In I. L. Horowitz (Ed.), *Sociological Self-Images* (pp. 145-176). Beverly Hills, CA: Sage.

1969.11 "Prejudice and Politics in the American Past and Present." In Charles Y. Glock & Ellen Siegelman (Eds.), *Prejudice U.S.A.* (pp. 17-69). New York: Praeger.

1969.12 "Students and Politics in Comparative Perspective." In S. M. Lipset & Philip Altbach (Eds.), *Students in Revolt* (pp. xv-xxxiv). Boston: Houghton Mifflin.

1969.13 "Foreword." In Philip Altbach (Ed.), *Turmoil and Transition: Higher Education and Student Politics in India* (pp. v-vi). New York: Basic Books.

1970.1 "The Left, the Jews and Israel." *Jewish Spectator* (April), pp. 12-20.

1970.2 "The Banality of Revolt." *Saturday Review* (July 18), pp. 23-26.

1970.3 (With Earl Raab), "The Non-Generation Gap." *Commentary* (August), pp. 35-39.

1970.4 "Cyclical Trends and Futurology." *At Issue* (September/October), p. 7.

1970.5 (With Everett Ladd), ". . . And What Professors Think." *Psychology Today* (November), pp. 49-51.

1970.6 "Cycles and Activism." *Harvard Crimson* (November 24), p. 3.

1970.7 "Faculty and Students: Allied and in Conflict." *Quod Novum: Blad voor de Rotterdamse Academische Gemeenschap* (Rotterdam) (November 27), pp. 8-13.

1970.8 "The Politics of Academia." In David C. Nichols (Ed.), *Perspectives on Campus Tensions* (pp. 85-118). Washington, DC: American Council on Education.

1970.9 "The Problems of Urban Ghettos and the Issues of Public Order." In Anthony H. Pascal (Ed.), *Thinking About Cities* (pp. 140-152). Belmont: Dickenson.

1970.10 "The Ideology of Local Control." In C. A. Bowers et al. (Eds.), *Education and Social Policy: Local Control of Education* (pp. 21-42). New York: Random House.

1970.11 "Political Cleavages in 'Developed' and 'Emerging' Polities." In Erik Allardt & Stein Rokkan (Eds.), *Mass Politics: Studies in Political Sociology* (pp. 23-44). New York: Free Press.

1971.1 "The Socialism of Fools." *New York Times Magazine* (January 3), pp. 6, 7, 26, 27, 34. (In Portuguese: *O Socialisma de Tolos.* [Sao Paulo: B'nai B'rith], pp. 3-14.)

1971.2 "Anti-Semitism: From the Left." *Los Angeles Times* (January 3), pp. H1-H2.

1971.3 [Review of Paul Lendavi, *Anti-Semitism Without Jews: Communist Eastern Europe.*] *Saturday Review* (February 13), pp. 30, 48.

1971.4 "New Perspectives on the Counter-Culture." *Saturday Review* (March 20), pp. 25-28.

1971.5 (With Everett Ladd), "The Politics of American Political Scientists." *PS* (Spring), pp. 135-149.

1971.6 (With Everett Ladd), "American Social Scientists and the Growth of Campus Political Activism in the 1960's." *Social Science Information* (April), pp. 105-134.

1971.7   "Polls and Protest." *Foreign Affairs* (April), pp. 548-555.
1971.8   (With Everett Ladd), "The Divided Professoriate." *Change* (May/June), pp. 54-60.
1971.9   (With Everett Ladd), "College Generations: From the 1930s to the 1960s." *Public Interest* (Fall), pp. 99-113.
1971.10 "Student Activism: An International Perspective." *International Education* (Fall), pp. 47-61.
1971.11 "Perspectives on Student Protests." *Teaching and Learning,* pp. 25-30.
1971.12 "Youth and Politics." In Robert K. Merton & Robert Nisbet (Eds.), *Contemporary Social Problems* (3rd ed., pp. 743-789). New York: Harcourt Brace Jovanovich. (In Spanish: "Juventud y Politica." *Revista Espanola de la Opinion Publica* [July/September 1972], pp. 3-58. M. Leon, Trans.)
1971.13 "Critiques of the Effect of Technology on Society." In James F. Smith (Ed.), *Technology and Human Values* (pp. 22-34). Springfield, MO: Drury College.
1971.14 (With Carl Sheingold), "Values and Political Structures: An Interpretation of the Sources of Extremism and Violence in American Society." In W. J. Crotty (Ed.), *Assassinations and Political Order* (pp. 388-414). New York: Harper & Row.
1971.15 (With Everett Ladd), "Jewish Academics in the United States: Their Achievements, Culture and Politics." In *The American Jewish Year Book, 1971* (pp. 89-128). New York: American Jewish Committee.
1971.16 "Foreword." In Joseph A. Raffaele, *The Economic Development of Nations* (pp. vii-x). New York: Random House.
1971.17 (With Everett Ladd), "College Generations and Their Politics." *New Society* (October 7), pp. 654-657.
1972.1   "Marx Is in the Eye of the Beholder." *Saturday Review* (June 3), pp. 52-58.
1972.2   (With Everett Ladd), "The Politics of American Sociologists." *American Journal of Sociology* (July), pp. 67-104.
1972.3   (With Richard Dobson), "The Intellectual as Critic and Rebel: With Special Reference to the United States and the Soviet Union." *Daedalus* (Summer), pp. 137-198.
1972.4   "The Chosen Party." *New York* (August 14), pp. 30-31.
1972.5   "Social Mobility and Equal Opportunity." *Public Interest* (Fall), pp. 90-108.
1972.6   "How Education Affects the Youth Vote." *Saturday Review of Education* (October 14), pp. 68-70.
1972.7   (With Everett Ladd), "Poisoned Ivy: McGovern's Campus Support." *New York* (October 16), pp. 43-36. (Reprinted as *Contours of Academic Politics: 1972* [Reprint 6]. Washington DC: American Enterprise Institute.)
1972.8   "La Mobilite sociale et les objectifs socialistes." *Sociologie et societes* (November), pp. 193-224.
1972.9   "Ideology and No End." *Encounter* (December), pp. 12-22.

1972.10 "Academia and Politics in America." In T. J. Nossiter (Ed.), *Imagination and Precision in the Social Sciences* (pp. 211-289). London: Faber.
1972.11 "Introduction." In Arthur Liebman et al., *Latin American University Students: A Six Nation Study* (pp. xvii-xxvi). Cambridge, MA: Harvard University Press.
1972.12 "The Return of Anti-Semitism as a Political Force." In Irving Howe & Carl Gershman (Eds.), *Israel, the Arabs and the Middle East* (pp. 390-427). New York: Quadrangle.
1972.13 "Preface." In H. W. Van der Merwe & D. Walsh (Eds.), *Student Perspectives on South Africa* (pp. 1-8). Claremont, S. Africa: David Philip.
1972.14 "Third Parties and Social Movements." *Dialogue, 5*(2), pp. 3-11.
1972.15 "Ideology and Mythology." *Sociological Inquiry, 42*(3-4), pp. 233-265.
1972.16 (With Everett Ladd), "The Political Future of Activist Generations." In P. G. Altbach & R. S. Laufer (Eds.), *The New Pilgrims: Youth Protest in Transition* (pp. 63-84). New York: David McKay.
1972.17 "Discussion on Technology and the Counterculture." In Charles A. Thrall & Jerold M. Starr (Eds.), *Technology, Power, and Social Change* (pp. 83-90). Lexington, MA: D. C. Heath.
1973.1 (With Earl Raab), "The Election and the National Mood." *Commentary* (January), pp. 43-50.
1973.2 "Education and Social Goals." In *Improving School Effectiveness* (pp. 62-71). San Francisco: Educational Testing Service.
1973.3 (With Everett Ladd), "Politics of Academic Natural Scientists and Engineers." *Science* (June 9), pp. 1091-1100.
1973.4 (With Everett Ladd), "Unionizing the Professoriate." *Change* (Summer), pp. 38-44.
1973.5 (With Richard Dobson), "Social Stratification and Sociology in the Soviet Union." *Survey* (Summer), pp. 114-185.
1973.6 (With Earl Raab), "An Appointment With Watergate." *Commentary* (September), pp. 35-43.
1973.7 "Future Political Scientists Still Face 'Old' Issues." *Detroit News* (November 18), pp. 1E-2E.
1973.8 (With Earl Raab), "Watergate: The Vacillation of the President." *Psychology Today* (November), pp. 77-84.
1973.9 "Tom Marshall: Man of Wisdom." *British Journal of Sociology* (December), pp. 412-417.
1973.10 (With William Schneider), "Political Sociology." In Neil Smelser (Ed.), *Sociology* (pp. 399-491). New York: John Wiley.
1973.11 "Konflikt und Wandel in der amerikanischen Gesellschaft." In Willy Hochkeppel (Ed.), *Wie Krank ist Amerika?* (pp. 46-72). Hamburg: Hoffman und Campe.
1973.12 "Foreword." In David Horton Smith, *Latin American Student Activism* (pp. xv-xviii). Lexington, MA: Lexington.
1973.13 "Commentary: Social Stratification Research and Soviet Scholarship." In M. Yanowitch & W. A. Fisher (Eds.), *Social Stratification and Mobility*

in the USSR (pp. 355-391). White Plains: International Arts and Sciences Press.

1974.1   "Education and Equality: Israel and the United States Compared." *Society* (March/April), pp. 56-66.

1974.2   (With Everett Ladd), "The Myth of the Conservative Professor." *Sociology of Education* (Spring), pp. 203-213.

1974.3   (With Everett Ladd), "Portrait of a Discipline: The American Political Science Community, Part I." *Teaching Political Science* (October), pp. 3-39.

1974.4   "Reply to Gus Tyler on 'The Labor Movement and American Values.' " In J. Laslett & S. M. Lipset (Eds.), *Failure of a Dream? Essays in the History of American Socialism* (pp. 581-592). Garden City, NY: Doubleday.

1974.5   "Comment on 'Socialism and Social Mobility' by Thernstrom." In J. Laslett & S. M. Lipset (Eds.), *Failure of a Dream? Essays in the History of American Socialism* (pp. 528-546). Garden City, NY: Doubleday.

1974.6   (With John Laslett), "Social Scientists View the Problem." In J. Laslett & S. M. Lipset (Eds.), *Failure of a Dream? Essays in the History of American Socialism* (pp. 25-82). Garden City, NY: Doubleday.

1974.7   "Who Is the Enemy?" In Sidney Hook et al. (Eds.), *The Idea of a Modern University* (pp. 243-246). Buffalo, NY: Prometheus.

1974.8   "Foreword." In Raymond Boudon, *Education, Opportunity and Social Inequality* (pp. v-vii). New York: John Wiley.

1974.9   "Introduction." In National Association of Secondary School Principals, *The Mood of American Youth* (pp. 7-10). Reston, VA: National Association of Secondary School Principals.

1974.10   "Introduction." In Gareth Williams et al., *The Academic Labour Market* (pp. 1-6). Amsterdam: Elsevier.

1975.1   (With Everett Ladd), "Portrait of a Discipline: The American Political Science Community, Part II." *Teaching Political Science* (January), pp. 144-171.

1975.2   "The People v. the Elites? A Reply to Henry Fairlie." *Encounter* (February), pp. 93-94.

1975.3   "Faculty Unions and Collegiality." *Change* (March), pp. 39-41.

1975.4   "Are Rationality and Reason Dead?" *Humanist* (March/April), pp. 8-10.

1975.5   "The Storm Over Ideology: Harvard's Economics Department." *Change* (April), pp. 22-24.

1975.6   "America Now: A Failure of Nerve?" *Commentary* (July), pp. 58-60.

1975.7   "The Paradox of American Politics." *Public Interest* (Fall), pp. 142-165.

1975.8   "Opportunity and Welfare in the First New Nation." In Irving Kristol et al., *America's Continuing Revolution* (pp. 333-359). Washington, DC: American Enterprise Institute.

1975.9   "Foreword." In F. M. Stern, *Life and Liberty* (pp. v-ix). New York: Thomas Y. Crowell.

1975.10   (With Asoke Basu), "Intellectual Types and Political Roles." In Lewis Coser (Ed.), *The Idea of Social Structure* (pp. 433-470). New York: Harcourt, Brace. (In French: "Des types d'intellectuels et de leurs roles politiques." *Sociologie et Societes, 7*[1], pp. 52-90. F. Peraldi, Trans.)

1975.11   "Social Structure and Social Change." In Peter Blau (Ed.), *Approaches to the Study of Social Structure* (pp. 172-209). New York: Free Press.

1975.12   "Foreword." In William Hanna (Ed.), *University Students and African Politics* (pp. v-vii). New York: Africana.

1975.13   "The American University: 1964-1974: From Activism to Austerity." In Paul Seabury (Ed.), *Universities in the Western World* (pp. 143-156). New York: Free Press.

1975.14   "Trends in American Sociology." *Dialogue,* 8(3-4), pp. 3-15.

1976.1   "Recession and Liberty." *Patterns of Prejudice* (January/February), pp. 1-5, 13.

1976.2   "The Wavering Polls." *Public Interest* (Spring), pp. 70-89.

1976.3   "Those Ubiquitous Polls: Can You Believe What They Are Saying?" *American Views* (August 16), pp. 1-3.

1976.4   "Carter and the Polls: The Trouble With Big Leads." *New York* (August 23), pp. 12-15.

1976.5   "Is Ford Another Truman?" *New Society* (August 26), pp. 433-444.

1976.6   "Student Politics in the Quiet Seventies." *Alternative* (August/September), pp. 11-14.

1976.7   "Israel on the Campus." *Bamakom* (Fall), pp. 3-7.

1976.8   "The Election Is Now a Real Contest." *Washington Post* (September 5), p. B7.

1976.9   "The 1976 Election Is Now a Real Contest." *New York* (September 20), pp. 10, 12, 17.

1976.10   "Is Carter Sure to Win?" *Society* (September/October), pp. 12-15.

1976.11   "The Catholic Defection." *New Republic* (October 2), pp. 10-11.

1976.12   "The Twice Lost Campaign." *Detroit News* (October 22).

1976.13   "The Bewildering Polls: Why Do They Differ So Greatly?" *New York* (October 25).

1976.14   (With Everett Ladd), "How Faculty Members Expect to Vote." *Chronicle of Higher Education* (November 1), pp. 4-6.

1976.15   "Equity and Equality in Public Wage Policy." In A. Lawrence Chickering (Ed.), *Public Employee Unions: A Study of the Crisis in Public Sector Labor Relations* (pp. 109-130). San Francisco: Institute for Contemporary Studies.

1976.16   "Equality and Inequality." In Robert Merton & Robert Nisbet (Eds.), *Contemporary Social Problems* (pp. 305-353). New York: Macmillan.

1976.17   "Introduction" (to the Phoenix ed.). In S. M. Lipset, *Rebellion in the University* (pp. xxii-l). Chicago: University of Chicago Press.

1976.18   "Youth Revolt: An Overview." In S. G. Shoham (Ed.), *Youth Unrest* (pp. 311-318). Jerusalem: Jerusalem Academic Press.

1976.19   "Academics and Collective Bargaining." In Thomas Mannix (Ed.), *Collective Bargaining in Higher Education* (pp. 21-27). New York: National Center for the Study of Collective Bargaining in Higher Education, Baruch College-CUNY.

1976.20   "Radicalism in North America: A Comparative View of the Party Systems in Canada and the United States." *Transactions of the Royal Society of Canada,* 4(14), pp. 19-55.

1976.21 (With Everett Ladd), "The Ladd-Lipset Survey." *Chronicle of Higher Education* (Special series, 35 articles; September 15, 1975-May 24, 1976).

1977.1 "Socialism in America." *Trends* (January) (in Japanese).

1977.2 (With William Schneider), "Pitfalls of Presidential Polls." *Washington Post* (June 19), pp. B1, B5.

1977.3 (With William Schneider), "America's Schizophrenia on Achieving Equality." *Los Angeles Times* (July 31), pp. IV1, IV6.

1977.4 "The Rising Influence of Public Interest Groups." *Openness* (a National Forum on Emerging Issues, Washington, DC) (September 14-16), pp. 66-93.

1977.5 (With Everett Ladd), "The Faculty Mood." *Chronicle of Higher Education* (October 3), pp. 1-2.

1977.6 (With William Schneider), "An Emerging National Consensus." *New Republic* (October 15), pp. 8-9.

1977.7 "5000 Years of Racism." *The Alternative* (October), pp. 5-9.

1977.8 (With William Schneider), "Polls for the White House and the Rest of Us." *Encounter* (November), pp. 24-34.

1977.9 (With William Schneider), "Carter Versus Israel: What the Polls Reveal." *Commentary* (November), pp. 21-29.

1977.10 "American Exceptionalism in North American Perspective: Why the United States Has Withstood the Worldwide Socialist Movement." In E. M. Adams (Ed.), *The Idea of America* (pp. 107-161). Cambridge, MA: Ballinger.

1977.11 "Introduction." In G. R. Urban, *Hazards of Learning* (pp. xi-xix). LaSalle: Open Court.

1977.12 " 'American Exceptionalism' in North American Perspective." In *America's World Role for the Next Twenty-Five Years* (Proceedings of the Second Tamkang American Studies Conference, 1976) (pp. 293-332). Taipei: Tamkang College.

1977.13 " 'The End of Ideology' and the Ideology of the Intellectuals." In Joseph Ben David & Terry Clark (Eds.), *Culture and Its Creators* (pp. 15-42). Chicago: University of Chicago Press.

1977.14 "Observations on Economic Equality and Social Class." In Irving L. Horowitz (Ed.), *Equity, Income, and Policy* (pp. 278-286). New York: Praeger.

1977.15 "Why No Socialism in the United States?" In S. Bialer & S. Sluzar (Eds.), *Sources of Contemporary Radicalism* (pp. 31-149, 346-363). Boulder, CO: Westview.

1977.16 "A Survey of the History and Current Outlook of Philanthropy as a Source of Capital for the Needs of the Health Care Field." In G. McLeod & Mark Perlman (Eds.), *Health Care Capital: Competition and Control* (pp. 455-469). Pittsburgh: University of Pittsburgh, Graduate School of Public Health.

1977.17 (With William Schneider), "Polls, Public Opinion, and the President." *Stanford Magazine* (Fall/Winter), pp. 28-31.

1978.1   "Growth, Affluence, and the Limits of Futurology." In Kenneth Boulding
          et al., *From Abundance to Scarcity: Implications for the American Tradition*
          (pp. 65-108). Columbus: Ohio University Press.
1978.2   (With William Schneider), "The Bakke Case: How Would It Be Decided
          at the Bar of Public Opinion?" *Public Opinion* (March/April), pp. 38-44.
1978.3   "Socialism in America." *Dialogue, 10*(4), pp. 3-12.
1978.4   "Marx, Engels, and America's Political Parties." *Wilson Quarterly* (Win-
          ter), pp. 90-104.
1978.5   "American Populism and Egalitarianism." *Asian Student* (April 8), p. S-3.
1978.6   (With William Schneider), "Racial Equality in America." *New Society*
          (April 20), pp. 128-131.
1978.7   "Foreword." In John Low-Beer, *Protest and Participation: The New Working
          Class in Italy* (pp. xi-xiii). New York: Cambridge University Press.
1978.8   "Epilogue: The 1970's." In S. M. Lipset & Earl Raab, *The Politics of
          Unreason: Right Wing Extremism in the United States, 1790-1977* (2nd
          ed., pp. 517-549). Chicago: University of Chicago Press.
1978.9   "Roots of Prejudice and Racism." *Jewish Digest* (April), pp. 23-33.
1978.10   "Presidential Greatness in the Age of Carter." *American Spectator* (June/July),
          pp. 7-10.
1978.11   "Coalition Politics: Causes and Consequences." In S. M. Lipset (Ed.),
          Emerging Coalitions in American Politics (pp. 437-463). San Francisco:
          Institute for Contemporary Studies.
1978.12   "It Takes Experience." *U.S. News & World Report* (June 26), p. 30.
1978.13   "Racial and Ethnic Tensions in the Third World." In W. Scott Thompson
          (Ed.), *The Third World: Premises of U.S. Policy* (pp. 123-148). San
          Francisco: Institute for Contemporary Studies.
1978.14   (With William Schneider), "How's Business: What the Public Thinks."
          Public Opinion (July/August), pp. 41-47.
1978.15   (With Earl Raab), "The Message of Proposition 13." *Commentary* (Sep-
          tember), pp. 42-46.
1978.16   "How the Jews Stand With America: What the Polls Say." *Israel Horizons*
          (September), pp. 10-13.
1978.17   "The Polls on the Middle East." *Middle East Review* (Fall), pp. 24-30.
1978.18   "How Labor Lost." *Israel Horizons* (November), pp. 17-20.
1978.19   (With William Schneider), "New Politics Pose New Challenge." *Enter-
          prise Magazine* (December), p. 13.
1979.1   "The Great Calm on the American Campus." *Asahi Journal* (January 19),
          pp. 10-17. (Trans. into Japanese.)
1979.2   "The New Class and the Professoriate." In B. Bruce-Briggs (Ed.), *The
          New Class?* (pp. 67-87). New Brunswick, NJ: Transaction. (Also pub-
          lished in *Society* [January/February], pp. 31-38.)
1979.3   (With William Schneider), "The Public View of Regulation." *Public
          Opinion* (January/February), pp. 6-13.
1979.4   "The Public Pulse: What Americans Really Think About Inflation."
          Taxing and Spending (April), pp. 32-33.

1979.5   "American Exceptionalism." In Michael Novak (Ed.), *Capitalism and Socialism: A Theological Inquiry* (pp. 34-60). Washington, DC: American Enterprise Institute.

1979.6   "Religion in American Politics." In Michael Novak (Ed.), *Capitalism and Socialism: A Theological Inquiry* (pp. 61-80). Washington, DC: American Enterprise Institute.

1979.7   "Policy and Equity." In Irving L. Horowitz (Ed.), *Constructing Policy* (pp. 44-62). New York: Praeger.

1979.8   "Summer, 1979: The Jewish Circumstance." *Moment* (June), pp. 20-15.

1979.9   "Political Change in Israel." *Contemporary Sociology* (May), pp. 381-384.

1979.10   (With Everett Ladd), "The Changing Social Origins of American Academics." In Robert K. Merton et al., *Qualitative and Quantitative Social Research* (pp. 319-338). New York: Free Press.

1979.11   "Revolution and Counterrevolution: Some Concluding Comments at a Conference Analyzing the Bicentennial of a Celebrated North American Divorce." In Richard A. Preston (Ed.), *Perspectives on Revolution and Evolution* (pp. 22-45). Durham: Duke University Press.

1979.12   "Predicting the Future of Post-Industrial Society: Can We Do It?" In S. M. Lipset (Ed.), *The Third Century: America as a Post-Industrial Society* (pp. 1-35). Stanford, CA: Hoover Institution Press.

1979.13   "Introduction to the Norton Edition." In S. M. Lipset, *The First New Nation: The United States in Historical and Comparative Perspective* (rev. ed., pp. v-xl). New York: W. W. Norton.

1979.14   "Whither the First New Nation." *Tocqueville Review* (Fall), pp. 64-99.

1979.15   (With Drora Kass), "Israelis in Exile." *Commentary* (November), pp. 68-72.

1979.16   "The Crisis in Confidence." *Taxing and Spending* (Fall), pp. 91-94.

1979.17   "The Myth of a New Jewish Conservatism." *Israel Horizons* (May), pp. 7-11.

1980.1   (With Everett Ladd), "Anatomy of a Decade." *Public Opinion* (December/January), pp. 2-9.

1980.2   (With others), "Liberalism and the Jews: A Symposium." *Commentary* (January), pp. 53-54.

1980.3   "Americans: 'Negative About Nation, Positive About Themselves' " (interview). *U.S. News & World Report* (December/January), pp. 85-86.

1980.4   "Jewish Living in California." *Jewish Living* (March/April), pp. 44-45.

1980.5   (With Everett Ladd), "Public Opinion and Public Policy." In P. Duignan & A. Rabushka (Eds.), *The United States in the 1980s* (pp. 49-84). Stanford, CA: Hoover Institution Press.

1980.6   (With William Schneider), "Stagflation and the Fading American Dream." *Public Opinion* (April/May), pp. 42-45.

1980.7   "Lipset: i vecchi progressisti e i nuovi." *Rinacita* (9 Maggio), pp. 24-26.

1980.8   (With William Schneider), "Is the Tax Revolt Over?" *Taxing and Spending* (Summer), pp. 73-81.

1980.9   "Some Implications of Middle East Peace for Relations Between Israel and the Diaspora." In Raphael Jospe & Samuel Z. Fishman (Eds.), *Go and Study* (pp. 191-207). Washington, DC: Hillel Foundations.

1980.10 "Different Polls, Different Results in 1980 Politics." *Public Opinion*
(August/September), pp. 19-20, 60.

1981.1 (With Earl Raab), "The Election and the Evangelicals." *Commentary*
(March), pp. 25-31.

1981.2 "Whatever Happened to the Proletariat?" *Encounter* (June), pp. 18-31.
(In Spanish: "¿Que ha occurrido con el proletariado?" *Cuenta y Razon*
[June], pp. 187-205.)

1981.3 (With William Schneider), "Lower Taxes and More Welfare: A Reply to
Arthur Seldon." *Journal of Contemporary Studies* (Spring), pp. 95-102.

1981.4 (With William Schneider), "Organized Labor and the Public: A Troubled
Union." *Public Opinion* (August/September), pp. 52-56.

1981.5 "Industrial Proletariat in Comparative Perspective." In Jan F. Triska &
Charles Gati (Eds.), *Labour in Socialist Societies: Blue Collar Workers
in Eastern Europe* (pp. 1-28). London: Allen & Unwin.

1981.6 "The Revolt Against Modernity." In Per Torsvik (Ed.), *Mobilization,
Center-Periphery Structures and National Building* (pp. 451-500). Bergen,
Norway: Universitetsforlaget.

1981.7 "Party Coalitions and the 1980 Election." In S. M. Lipset (Ed.), *Party
Coalitions in the 1980s* (pp. 15-46). San Francisco: Institute for Contemporary Studies.

1981.8 "American Party System: Concluding Observations." In S. M. Lipset
(Ed.), *Party Coalitions in the 1980s* (pp. 423-440). San Francisco: Institute
for Contemporary Studies.

1981.9 (With Everett Ladd), "A Reply to Lang." In Serge Lang, *The File* (pp.
18-30). New York: Springer-Verlag.

1981.10 "Foreword." In Elisabeth Noelle-Neumann & Wolfgang J. Kuschnick,
The Germans: Public Opinion Polls, 1967-1980 (pp. vii-ix). Westport,
CT: Greenwood.

1981.11 "France's Warning to the Reagan Administration." *Journal of Contemporary Studies* (Fall), pp. 35-38.

1981.12 "The Limits of Social Science." *Public Opinion* (October/November), pp.
2-9. (Reprinted in Robert B. Smith [Ed.], *A Handbook of Social Science
Methods* [Vol. 1, pp. 149-168]. Cambridge, MA: Ballinger, 1983.)

1981.13 "The 'Jewish Lobby' and the National Interest." *New Leader* (November
16), pp. 8-10.

1981.14 "The Shifting Bases of American Politics." In H. Baier, H. M. Kepplin-
ger, & K. Reumann (Eds.), *Offentliche Meinung und sozialer Wandel*
(Festschrift for Elisabeth Noelle-Neumann) (pp. 413-428). Wiesbaden:
Westdeutscher Verlag.

1981.15 (With others), "Human Rights and American Foreign Policy" (symposium). *Commentary* (November), pp. 47-49.

1982.1 (With others), "How Critical Is Our Condition?" (symposium). *Dissent*
(Winter), pp. 107-110.

1982.2 (With William Schneider), "Reply: Evidence of No Change." *Journal of
Contemporary Studies* (Winter), pp. 83-88.

1982.3   "U.S. Political Conservatism: Meanings and Origins." In *The Americana Annual 1982, Yearbook of the Encyclopedia Americana* (pp. 34-41). Danbury, CT: Grolier.

1982.4   (With Drora Kass), "Jewish Immigration to the United States from 1967 to the Present: Israelis and Others." In Marshall Sklare (Ed.), *Understanding American Jewry* (pp. 272-294). New Brunswick, NJ: Transaction.

1982.5   "The Academic Mind at the Top: The Political Behavior and Values of Faculty Elites." *Public Opinion Quarterly* (Summer), pp. 143-168.

1982.6   "The Thugs and Susan Sontag." *American Spectator* (June), pp. 30-32.

1982.7   "Social Mobility in Industrial Societies." *Public Opinion* (June/July), pp. 41-44.

1982.8   "Democracy at the Polls: An Expository Review." *Electoral Studies, 1,* pp. 107-115.

1982.9   "Failures of Extremism." *Society* (November/December), pp. 48-56.

1982.10   "No Room for the Ins: Elections Around the World." *Public Opinion* (October/November), pp. 41-43.

1982.11   "Antisemitism Today: A Symposium." *Patterns of Prejudice* (October), pp. 37-38.

1983.1   "El Socialismo en America." *Revista de Occidente* (January), pp. 25-45.

1983.2   "Socialism in America." In Paul Kurtz (Ed.), *Sidney Hook: Philosopher of Democracy and Humanism* (pp. 47-63). Buffalo, NY: Prometheus.

1983.3   "Radicalism or Reformism: The Sources of Working-Class Politics." *American Political Science Review* (March), pp. 1-18.

1983.4   "Plus ca Change." *New Republic* (March 28), pp. 28-32.

1983.5   (With William Schneider) "Is There a Legitimacy Crisis?" *Micropolitics* (Spring), pp. 1-36.

1983.6   "The Congressional Candidate." *Journal of Contemporary Studies* (Summer), pp. 87-105.

1983.7   (With William Schneider) "Confidence in Confidence Measures." *Public Opinion* (August/September), pp. 42-44.

1983.8   (With William Schneider) "The Decline of Confidence in American Institutions." *Political Science Quarterly* (Fall), pp. 379-402.

1983.9   "Les Transformations Ideologiques aux Etats-Unis." *Politique* (Quebec) (Autumn), pp. 5-26.

1983.10   "Roosevelt and the Protest of the 1930s." *Minnesota Law Review* (December), pp. 173-198.

1984.1   "The Economy, Elections, and Public Opinion." In John Moore (Ed.), *To Promote Prosperity* (pp. 393-429). Stanford, CA: Hoover Institution Press. (Also published in *Tocqueville Review* [Fall-Winter], pp. 431-471.)

1984.2   "George Gallup: 1901 to 1984." *Public Opinion* (August/September), pp. 2-4.

1984.3   "China in Transition: A Travel Memoir, May-June 1984." *PS, 14*(4), pp. 765-777.

1984.4   "Foreword." In Jewel Bellush & Bernard Bellush, *Union Power and New York* (pp. vii-ix). New York: Praeger.

1985.1   "Canada and the United States: The Cultural Dimension." In Charles F. Doran & John H. Sigler (Eds.), *Canada and the United States: Enduring*

Friendship, Persistent Stress (pp. 109-160). Englewood Cliffs, NJ: Prentice-Hall.

1985.2   (With Earl Raab) "The American Jews, the 1984 Elections, and Beyond." *Tocqueville Review,* 6(2), pp. 401-419. (Also published in William Frankel [Ed.], *Survey of Jewish Affairs, 1985* [pp. 141-157]. Cranbury, NJ: Associated University Presses.)

1985.3   "The Elections, the Economy and Public Opinion: 1984." *PS, 18*(1), pp. 28-38.

1985.4   "Feeling Better: Measuring the Nation's Confidence." *Public Opinion* (April/May), pp. 55-61.

1985.5   (With Earl Raab), *The Political Future of American Jews.* New York: American Jewish Congress.

1985.6   (With Mikhail Bernstam), "Punishing Russia." *New Republic* (August 5), pp. 11-12.

1986.1   "Beyond 1984: The Anomalies of American Politics, *PS, 19*(2), pp. 222-236.

1986.2   "Labor Unions in the Public Mind." In S. M. Lipset (Ed.), *Unions in Transition: Entering the Second Century* (pp. 287-321). San Francisco: Institute for Contemporary Studies.

1986.3   "North American Labor Movements: A Comparative Perspective." In S. M. Lipset (Ed.), *Unions in Transition: Entering the Second Century* (pp. 421-452). San Francisco: Institute for Contemporary Studies.

1986.4   "The Sources of Public Interest Activism." *Public Relations Quarterly* (Fall), pp. 9-13.

1986.5   "Historical Traditions and National Characteristics: A Comparative Analysis of Canada and the United States." *Canadian Journal of Sociology* (Summer), pp. 113-155.

1986.6   "Jewish Survival and Secular Humanistic Judaism" (interview). *Secular Humanistic Judaism* (February), pp. 28-38.

1986.7   "The Reagan Factor." *New Society* (October 10), pp. 17-19.

1987.1   "The Confidence Gap During the Reagan Years: 1981-1987." *Political Science Quarterly* (Spring), pp. 1-23.

1987.2   "Tradition and Modernity in Japan and the United States." *International House of Japan (IHJ) Bulletin* (Winter), pp. 1-7.

1987.3   "Ken Arrow—Success Without Pressure: An Interview." In G. R. Feiwel (Ed.), *Arrow and the Foundations of the Theory of Economic Policy* (pp. 693-700). New York: New York University Press.

1987.4   "Blacks and Jews: How Much Bias?" *Public Opinion* (July/August), pp. 4-5, 57-58.

1987.5   (With Larry Diamond and Juan Linz) "Building and Sustaining Democratic Government in Developing Countries: Some Tentative Findings." *World Affairs, 150* (Summer), pp. 5-19.

1987.6   "The Expansion of Democracy: The Middle Classes." *Commonwealth* (August 31), pp. 372-374.

1988.1   "Is America Conservative? A Comparative Perspective." *Aus Politik und Zeitgeschichte* (February).

1988.2   "The Expansion of Democracy." *Temple University Law Review, 60* (Winter), pp. 985-992.

1988.3   "Preface." In S. M. Lipset, *Revolution and Counterrevolution: Change and Persistence in Social Structures* (3rd ed., pp. vii-xxiii). New Brunswick, NJ: Transaction.

1988.4   "Vote for the Other Guy: The Counterintuitive Character of Recent American Politics." In Dennis Bark & Annalise Anderson (Eds.), *Thinking About America: The United States in the 1990s.* Stanford, CA: Hoover Institution Press.

1988.5   "Israel and Palestine in the Year 2000." *The World & I* (May), pp. 46-49.

1988.6   (With Larry Diamond and Juan Linz), "Democracy in Developing Countries: Facilitating and Obstructing Factors." In Raymond D. Gastil (Ed.), *Freedom in the World: Political Rights and Civil Liberties 1987-1988* (pp. 229-258). New York: Freedom House.

1988.7   (With Daniel Frei and Frederick C. Turner), "Global State of Mind: A Comparative Study of National and International Identification." *The 40th ESOMAR Marketing Research Congress—Joint ESOMAR/WAPOR Session, Social and Opinion Research,* pp. 431-451.

1988.8   "The Failure of the American Socialist Movement." In Jean Heffer & Jeanine Rovet (Eds.), *Why Is There No Socialism in the United States?* (pp. 23-35). Paris: Editions de L'Ecole des Hautes Etudes en Sciences Sociales.

1988.9   "Introduction." In Svein S. Andersen, *British and Norwegian Offshore Industrial Relations: Pluralism and Neo-Corporatism as Contexts of Strategic Adaptation* (p. xiii). Aldershot: Avebury.

1988.10 "Reflections on a Research Agenda: Canada and the United States." *International Council for Canadian Studies Newsletter, 6*(2), pp. 24-32.

1988.11 "Neoconservatism: Myth and Reality." *Society* (July/August), pp. 29-37. (Also produced as a pamphlet from conference proceedings; John F. Kennedy Institut für Nordamerikastudien, Freie Universität Berlin.)

1988.12 "Israel at 40." *San Jose Mercury* (May 8).

1988.13 "Vote for the Other Guy." *Public Opinion, 11* (July/August), pp. 2-5.

1988.14 "Jewish Disunity Is Good for Us." *Moment, 13* (September), pp. 58-59.

1988.15 "A Reaffirming Election 1988." *International Journal of Public Opinion Research, 1* (Winter), pp. 25-44.

1989.1   "A Unique People in an Exceptional Country." In S. M. Lipset (Ed.), *American Pluralism and the Jewish Community: Essays in Honor of Earl Raab* (pp. 3-29). New Brunswick, NJ: Transaction.

1989.2   "A Singularidade Americana Reafirmada." *Revista de Historia Economica e Social* (September/December), pp. 1-39.

1989.3   (With Larry Diamond and Juan Linz) "Preface." In Larry Diamond, Juan Linz, & S. M. Lipset (Eds.), *Democracy in Developing Countries* (Vols. 2-4, pp. ix-xxvii). Boulder, CO: Lynne Rienner.

1989.4   "Liberalism, Conservatism and Americanism." *Ethics and International Affairs, 3,* pp. 205-218.

1989.5 "Are American Jews Drifting to the Right?" *Israeli Democracy, 3* (Spring), pp. 39-42.
1989.6 "Why Youth Revolt." *New York Times* (May 24).
1989.7 "Looking at the Eighties." *The World & I* (December), pp. 120-125.
1990.1 "The Work Ethic: Then and Now." *Public Interest* (Winter), pp. 61-69.
1990.2 "Political Renewal on the Left: A Comparative Perspective." Progressive Policy Institute Pamphlet, January.
1990.3 "Politics and Society in the USSR: A Traveller's Report." *PS, 23* (March), pp. 20-28.
1990.4 "Jewish Fear, Black Insensitivity." *New York Times* (March 9), p. A13.
1990.5 "The Nature and Sources of Jewish Identity." *Bulletin* of the Wilstein Institute (Winter), pp. 1, 9.
1990.6 "The Death of the Third Way." *National Interest, 20* (Summer), pp. 25-37.
1990.7 "Trade Unionism in Canada and the United States: A Reply to Bowden." *Canadian Review of Sociology and Anthropology, 27,* pp. 1-5.
1990.8 "American Values and the Market System." In Thomas R. Dye (Ed.), *The Political Legitimacy of Markets and Governments* (pp. 107-121). Greenwich, CT: JAI.
1990.9 "An Exchange With Herbert Stein." *National Interest, 21* (Fall), pp. 109-115.
1990.10 "A Unique People in an Exceptional Country." *Society, 28* (November/December), pp. 4-13.
1990.11 "The Values of Canadians and Americans: A Reply to Baer, Grabb and Johnston." *Social Forces, 69* (September), pp. 267-272.
1990.12 "Anti-Incumbency in Canada." *American Enterprise, 1* (November/December), pp. 22-23.
1991.1 "No Third Way: A Comparative Perspective on the Left." In Daniel Chirot (Ed.), *The Crisis of Leninism and the Decline of the Left* (pp. 183-232). Seattle: University of Washington Press.
1991.2 "American Exceptionalism Reaffirmed." In Byron Shafer (Ed.), *Is America Different? A New Look at American Exceptionalism* (pp. 1-45). London: Oxford University Press.
1991.3 (With Reinhard Bendix) "The Political Consequences of Social Mobility" (introduction to expanded ed.). In S. M. Lipset & R. Bendix, *Social Mobility in Industrial Society.* New Brunswick, NJ: Transaction.
1991.4 "In and Out of the Ghetto." *Times Literary Supplement* (May 31), p. 5.
1991.5 "The Politics of the United States." In *Oxford Companion to Politics of the World.* New York: Oxford University Press.
1991.6 "Two Americas, Two Value Systems: Blacks and Whites." In Aage Sorensen & Seymour Spilerman (Eds.), *Social Theory and Social Practice: Essays in Honor of James S. Coleman.* New York: Praeger.
1991.7 [Review of Donald L. Horowitz, *A Democratic South Africa?*] *Times Literary Supplement* (September 20), pp. 9-10.
1991.8 "The Memory of the Holocaust." *Dimensions, 6*(2), pp. 8-10.
1991.9 "Canada and the United States: The Great Divide." *Current History* (December), pp. 432-437.

Index

Adams, John, 208, 211
Affirmative action, 285-289
Africa, 41, 123, 124, 127
Agrarian socialism, x, 8
Albania, 159
Almond, Gabriel, 117
American Dream, 310
American exceptionalism, 8-12
American Federation of Labor (AFL), 253, 254, 255, 258-263, 265, 269
Argentina, 94, 141, 142, 145, 146, 150, 163
Associations, 7, 48, 59, 61, 123-125, 157, 163-175, 184
  properties of, 171-175
  public, 157, 159
Austria, 175
Autarkic economies, 142
Autarkic industrialization, 144-146, 151
Authoritarian systems, 48, 53-54, 58, 125, 140-141, 149, 150, 159, 160, 163, 165

Belgium, 19, 25
Ben Gurion, David, 212-213, 215-218, 219, 220, 221
Benin, 159
Bolivia, 159
Booth, J. A., 118
Borda, Jean Charles de, 20

Borochov, Dov, 212-213
Botswana, 123, 127
Brazil, 85, 94, 120, 121, 141, 148, 184
Brown, Jerry, 326
Buchanan, Patrick, 326
Bulgaria, 98, 215
Burma, 162
Bush, George, 318, 319, 326, 327
Business associations, 173

Capitalism, 7, 140-152, 214, 233, 242
  and labor organizations, 251
  dimensions of, 142
Capitalist transition, 149-151
Carter, Jimmy, 319
Central America, 41, 53
Chaos theory, 6, 47-66
Cheng, T. J., 119
Chile, 94, 102, 127, 141, 142, 145-146, 150
China, 86, 124
CIO, *See* Congress of Industrial Organizations
Citizenship, 160
Civil society, 123-125, 126, 163-164
Class, 18-19, 251, 259, 276-279, 280, 297-310
  class conflict, 254, 260
  structure, 119-121, 126, 186
Classical doctrine of democracy, 31

Clinton, Bill, 326, 327
Cold War, 82, 215-218, 219
Collective action, 148, 163-175, 299-310
Communism, 18-20, 183, 260-262
Communist Party (U.S.), 260-261, 282
Communitarianism, 70, 72, 73
Competition (political), 4, 13, 28-44, 183, 184, 325
　models of, 28-40
　risk in, 41, 42-43
　strategy in, 36-40
Competitive industrialization, 144-145, 146-148, 151
Competitive model of democracy, 28-35
Condorcet, Marquis de, 20-21
　Condorcet paradox, 21
The Confidence Gap, 315, 328
Conflict (political), 12-13
Congress of Industrial Organizations (CIO), 251, 253, 254, 255, 256, 258-269
　origins of, 259-269
　radical elements, 260-262, 263-265
Consensus model of democracy, 37-38
Constitutions, 161-162
Continental Divide, 9, 294, 296-297
Cooperative Commonwealth Federation (CCF) (Canada), ix, x
Corn Laws (Britain), 22-23
Corporatism, 183
Corse, Sarah, 297
Costa Rica, 94, 102, 118, 123, 127, 159
Croatia, 18, 20
Cutright, P., 103-104
Czech-Israeli arms deal (1947), 216
Czechoslovakia, 20, 59, 98, 141, 216-217

Dahl, Robert A., 28, 199
Debs, Eugene, 267, 276
Decisionmaking, 18-25
Democracy, 17-26, 27-44, 51-52, 70-78, 93-128, 140-152, 156-176, 182-201
　and labor organizations, 250-269
　measurement of, 252-253, 255-257
　possible determinants of, 1, 3, 4, 5-8, 103-106, 114-115, 116-117, 125-127, 200
Democratic consolidation, 7, 156-176
Democratic Party (U.S.), 238-239, 278, 282, 318, 319, 324, 331

Democratic transition, 6, 13, 48, 50-51, 54, 62-63, 66, 156-176, 182-184, 193, 198
Dependency theory, 114-115
Development (economic), 5, 6, 82-89, 92-128, 140-148, 182
　trade-offs of, 114-115
　variables of, 103-106
Dominican Republic, 102, 119
Downs, Anthony, 28, 29-31, 32-33, 35, 43-44
　Downsian model, 29-31, 32-33
Duke, David, 326
Durkheim, Émile, 300, 307

Eastern Europe, 18, 41, 58, 102-103, 124, 140, 163, 169, 198, 214, 216
East Germany (German Democratic Republic), 58, 141
An Economic Theory of Democracy (Downs), 28
Education, 10, 117, 228, 238, 275-291, 298-299
Ehrenhalt, Alan, 321
Electoral politics, 12, 29-44, 121-122, 164-165
Elites, 48-66, 148, 194-197
　politics of, 63-65, 66
European Community (EC), 18, 20, 25, 121, 174
Export-led industrialization, *See* Competitive industrialization

Fascism, 183
Federalism (American), 211-212
The First New Nation, 4, 9, 11, 294, 295, 296-297
Foreign aid, 83-84
Foster, William Z., 256, 267
France, 115, 210, 211
　institutions of, 298
　revolution (1789), 20
Freedom House, 97, 98

Gambia, 100, 101
Game theory, 35, 47-66
Geertz, Clifford, 306, 309
"General will", 20-21, 26, 31-32
Germany, 18, 53, 189, 191, 193

social policy of, 231
Ghana, 123
GNP. *See* Gross National Product
Goldwater, Barry, 327
Great Britain, 22-23, 210, 211, 214, 215
    democracy in, 22
    welfare state in, 228, 232, 240
Greece, 98, 103, 120, 176
Gross National Product (GNP), 100-102
Gutman, Herbert, 297

Haiti, 100, 159, 162
Hamilton, Alexander, 208, 211-212, 219, 220
    Hamiltonian ideology, 211-212, 213, 218
    See also Federalism
Harrod, Roy, 22
Hashomer, Hatzair, 213, 214
HDI. *See* Human Development Index
Hollenbach, David, 74
Holocaust, 214-215
Homans, George, 297
Huber, Joan and William Form, 301-302
Human Development Index (HDI), 100-103, 126
Hungary, 98, 215, 216-217

Ideology, 183, 184, 301-302, 320
Immigration, 283-284, 295, 297
Import-substituting industrialization, 114-115,
    145-146, 149-150
    See also Autarkic industrialization
India, 95, 100, 118, 120, 123, 127, 141, 159
Individualism, 11, 275-276, 277, 294, 298-
    29, 307
Indonesia, 125, 306, 308, 309
Inkeles, Alex, 117-118
Institutions, 48, 315, 329
    See also Associations
    social, 7, 8, 192-194, 279, 295
Intelligentsia, 146, 208
International Typographical Union (ITU), 17,
    19, 250-251, 258
Iran-Contra affair (U.S.), 316
Israel, 25, 208-209, 212-221
    foreign policy of, 10, 209, 212-221
    ideological forces in, 212-215
    non-identification policy of, 213-214, 217,
    218-219

political system of, 212
war for independence, 213
Italy, 173

Jackman, Mary and Robert, 304
Jamaica, 102, 118
Japan, 175
Jay, John, 211
    Jay Treaty (1794), 211
Jefferson, Thomas, 208, 211-212, 219, 220
    Jeffersonian ideology, 210, 211, 213, 215
Jennings, W. Ivor, 199

Kaldor, Nicholas, 22-23
    "compensation principle", 22-23, 25-26
Khrushchev, Nikita, 84
Korea, 217
Kuwait, 102

Labor movement in United States, 10, 233-
    234, 240-241, 250-269, 281
    See also United States—Trade unions
Labor Unions, 6, 17-18, 145-146, 184
    Communist influence on, 260-262, 263,
    264, 267-268
    constitutions of, 252-257
    factions within, 257-267
    internal structure of, 255-269
Lane, Robert, 301-303
Latin America, 114, 119, 140, 141, 148, 185, 192
Legitimacy, 8, 47, 51, 182, 183, 194, 275, 310
Lenin, V. I., 81, 84, 149, 161
    Leninism, 5, 81-85, 88-89
Lewis, John L., 263-264
Liberal Party (Great Britain), 232
Libertarianism, 71-72
Lipset, Seymour Martin, ix-xi, 1-13, 17, 27-
    28, 42, 47, 52, 75, 93-96, 102, 109,
    110, 114, 115, 116, 117, 121-122, 123,
    125-128, 140, 156, 182, 192, 200, 208,
    227, 251, 294, 315, 328
"Logrolling", 24-26

Madison, James, 169-170, 208, 211, 257
Mann, Michael, 301

Maoism, 86
Mapai Party (Israel), 213-217, 221
Mapam Party (Israel), 213-217
Market economy, 142
Marx, Karl, 141, 143, 148, 152
    Marxism, 81, 166-167, 183, 213
Mauritius, 102
McClosky, Herbert and John Zaller, 302
Meirson, Golda, 216-217
Mexico, 87, 118
Meyer, John, 296
Minority groups, 4, 17-18, 19, 20
    in Belgium, 19
    in Canada, 19
Modernization theory, 84-85, 93
Mongolia, 159
Morocco, 306, 308, 309
Murray, Phil, 264, 267

National Sovereignty, 80-82
Nation-State, definitons of, 20
National Identity, 183, 200, 296-298
Neocorporatism, 166-169
New Deal (U.S.), 229-230, 232-233, 239-
    240, 243, 282
Nigeria, 122, 123, 124, 310
Norway, 175
Novak, Michael, 72

OECD Nations, 83, 88
Olsen, M. E., 103
"Omnibus Bill", 24-25, 26
OPEC nations, 87
Oppostition (political), 48-63, 65-66
Organizations. *See* Associations
Ostrogorski, M., 21

Pacts (political), 43-62
Pakistan, 100, 120
Papua-New Guinea, 159
Paradox of collective action, 61
Parsonian Model, 294, 295
"Partial regimes", 160-163
Participation, 252, 256
Parties (political), 8, 29-31, 146, 157, 160,
    164, 165, 183, 184-191, 200, 285

church-based, 184-185, 193
competition of, 29-43
fragmentation, 36, 165, 257-268
mass-based, 184-187
Party discipline, 188-190
Payoff variability, 36, 37-38, 42
Perot, Ross, 326, 327, 328
Peru, 119, 184
Phillippines, 118, 124, 163
Physical Quality of Life Index (PQLI), 95,
    100, 102, 107, 126
Player indeterminacy, 36, 40, 42
Pluralism, 74-78
Poland, 87, 98
Political campaigns, 186-187, 318-321, 326-
    328
Political culture, 117-119, 126
Political leadership, 195-197, 315-331
Political Man, x, 2, 3, 27, 43, 47
Political violence, 118
Polyarchy. *See* Democracy
Portugal, 98, 103, 120, 141, 159, 173, 174,
    176
Powell, G. B., 118
PQLI. *See* Physical Quality of Life Index
Private ownership, 142
Professionalism (political), 11-12, 187, 195,
    315-331
Proportional representation, 187-190
Protest, 57-60
    psychology of, 58
Przeworski, Adam, 42, 51
Public assistance, administration of, 230
    See also Social policy

Race
    and education, 287-289
    and ideology, 305-306
    relations, 285-286
Rainwater, Lee, 305
Rationality,
    collective, 144
    individual, 143, 144
Reagan, Ronald, 316, 320, 328
Republican Party (U.S.), 239, 318, 324
Religious images, 306-309
Representation, 7, 157, 189-190, 255
Representativeness (in Downsian Model), 30

Reuther, Walter, 281
Revolution and Counterrevolution, x
Rimlinger, Gaston, 232
Robbins, Lionel, 22
Romania, 99, 215, 216
Rousseau, Jean Jacques, 20, 32

Scandinavia, welfare state in, 228, 234
Schumpeter, Joseph, 28, 31-34, 35, 43-44, 144
   Schumpeterian model, 31-33, 34, 35, 186, 190
Self-determination, 80-82, 84, 88-89, 198-199
Seligson, M.A., 118
Serbia, 18, 20
Singapore, 98, 102, 123
Skowronek, Stephen, 236
Slavery, 285
Slovenia, 18
Smith, Adam, 79, 140-141, 143
Social Democrats (Israel), 212-213
   institutions of, 212
Socialist Party of America (U.S.), 261, 282
Social policy in United States, 9-10, 228-246, 285
   theory of development, 231-234
Social Security Act (U.S.), 229-230, 232, 233, 239-240
Socialism, 209, 214, 278, 280, 284
Solomon Islands, 100
South Africa, 124
South America, 41, 58
Southern Europe, 41, 172, 176, 185
South Korea, 85, 103, 106, 121, 125, 147
Soviet Union (USSR), 18, 20, 25, 82-83, 98, 102-103, 106, 124, 198, 214, 215-216, 219
Spain, 98, 103, 120, 125, 141, 168, 173, 174, 176, 195
Spanish Confederation of Employers (CEOE), 174
Sri Lanka, 95, 100, 102, 118, 123
Stalin, Josef, 216
State and society, 121-123, 126, 197-200, 227-228
State formation, United States, 235-240
St. Augustine, 74
Steinbeck, John, 283-284

Strategic interaction, 48
Strategy determinacy, 36, 39-40, 42
Structural cleavage, 17-26
Suppression, 50, 51-54, 57-60
Sweden, 115, 175
Switzerland, 19, 157

Taiwan, 103, 106, 119-120, 123, 124, 125, 147
Thailand, 125
Third World, 82-84, 85, 87, 164
Tito, 17-18, 183
Tocqueville, Alexis de, 3, 123
Toleration (Political), 50-51, 54-57, 60-63
Turkey, 118-123

Uganda, 123
Unemployment insurance, 229, 318
Union Democracy, ix, x, 6, 17, 250-251
United Automobile Workers (UAW), 252, 264-265, 266
United Arab Emirates, 102
United Nations, 216, 217, 219
United States, 21-22, 71, 75, 76-77, 82, 115, 175, 197, 208-212, 215-216, 217, 218-221, 227
   American Revolution, 211, 213, 219, 235
   Civil War, 239
   congress, 189, 243, 319, 322-324
   courts, 236-237, 239, 255, 285
   democracy in, 21, 74, 315-331
   federalism in, 211-212
   foreign policy of, 10, 209-212
   Korean War, 217
   neutrality of, 210-212, 213, 218-219, 220
   political parties, 237-238
   public opinion in, 11-12
   social policy, 9-10, 228-246, 285
   suffrage, 244-245
   territorial expansion of, 210, 220, 221
   trade unions in, 240-241, 250-269, 278, 281
   values of, 11, 295-310
   Vietnam War, 329
Uruguay, 94, 102, 127, 141, 142, 145, 146, 148, 150

Valenzuela, Samuel, 55

Venezuala, 127
Verba, Sidney, 117
Veterans' Benefits, 228
Virtue, 70-78
   community, 70-72-73
Voluntarism, 124-125, 165-166, 294, 307-310
Voting, 18-19, 33-34, 186, 188, 319
   for incumbents, 319
   in divided systems, 22-26
Voter initiatives
   term limitations, 324-325

Washington, George, 211
Watergate, 327
Wealth, Distribution of, 100-102
Weber, Max, 143

Welfare state, history of, 228-230
Westminster model of democracy, 37-38
Wicksell, Knut, 23-24
   "taxation principle", 23-24
Wilson, Woodrow, 80-81
   Wilsonianism, 5, 80-85, 88-89
Wolfe, Tom, 299
Womens' political organizations, 241-242, 243

Yishuv, 214
Yugoslavia, 17-18, 19, 20, 25, 183

Zionism, 208-209, 212-218, 219-221
   factions of, 212
   Marxist influence on, 212-213

About the Authors

James S. Coleman is Professor of Sociology and Education at the University of Chicago and President of the American Sociological Association. His numerous published works include *The Adolescent Society, Introduction to Mathematical Sociology, The Asymmetric Society, Foundations of Social Theory,* and *Equality and Achievement in Education.* The recipient of numerous fellowships and honorary doctorates, he is a member of the National Academy of Sciences, the American Academy of Arts and Sciences, the National Academy of Education, and the Royal Swedish Academy of Education. His current interests are in the social theory of norm formation and in the functioning of schools.

Larry Diamond is Senior Research Fellow at the Hoover Institution and coeditor of the *Journal of Democracy.* He is author of *Class, Ethnicity and Democracy in Nigeria,* editor of *The Democratic Revolution: Struggles for Freedom and Pluralism in the Developing World,* and coeditor, with Juan J. Linz and Seymour Martin Lipset, of the four-volume *Democracy in Developing Countries.* He has written extensively on democratic politics, authoritarianism, ethnicity, and corruption in Africa, the global diffusion of democracy, and U.S. and international policies to promote democracy. He has served as a consultant to the Asia Foundation and the Agency for International Development, and has been a Fulbright Visiting Lecturer at Bayero University, Kano, Nigeria.

Amitai Etzioni is a Professor at George Washington University. He is the author of numerous books and articles, most recently *The Moral Dimension: Toward a New Economics.* Before taking his position at George Washington, he taught for 20 years in Columbia University's Sociology Department, was a Ford Foundation Professor at the Harvard Business School, a Guest Scholar at the Brookings Institution, and senior adviser in the Carter White House. He has been Director of the Center for Policy Research since 1968.

Juan J. Linz is Sterling Professor of Political and Social Science at Yale University. He has written dozens of articles and book chapters on authoritarianism and totalitarianism, fascism, political parties and elites, and democratic breakdowns and transitions, in Spain and in comparative perspective. His English-language publications include the four-volume work, *The Breakdown of Democratic Regimes,* which he edited with Alfred Stepan, and "Totalitarian and Authoritarian Regimes," in the *Handbook of Political Science.* Currently he is writing a book with Alfred Stepan, *Democratic Transitions and Consolidation: Eastern Europe, Southern Europe and Latin America,* and editing with Arturo Valenzuela a study of parliamentary versus presidential government. In 1987, he was awarded, in Spain, the Premio Principe de Asturias in the Social Sciences.

Gary Marks is Associate Professor of Political Science at the University of North Carolina at Chapel Hill. He is the author of *Unions in Politics: Britain, Germany, and the United States in the Nineteenth and Early Twentieth Centuries,* coauthor with Seymour M. Lipset of *Why Is There No Socialism in the United States? A Comparative Perspective* (forthcoming), and has written a number of articles on political economy in Western Europe and the European Community. He is currently a Fellow at the Center for Advanced Study in the Behavioral Sciences at Stanford, where he is writing on the European Community and the future of the state in Western Europe.

Amos Perlmutter is Professor of Political Science and Sociology at American University, Washington, D.C. A native of Israel and an American citizen, he specializes in comparative and international politics, and the role of the military, with an emphasis on Israel and the Middle East. He has published 13 books, the most recent of which is *The Life and Times of Menachem Begin,* and has completed a book on the FDR-Stalin war relationship, 1941-1945. He is editor of the *Journal of Strategic Studies* and *Security Studies.*

Philippe C. Schmitter is Professor of Political Science and Director of the Center for European Studies at Stanford University. Previously, he taught at the European University Institute in Florence and at the University of Chicago, and he has also held several visiting appointments in Europe and Latin America. He has authored and edited numerous works on interest representation and corporatism, and on democratic transition and consolidation.

William Schneider is a Resident Fellow at the American Enterprise Institute and Thomas P. O'Neill, Jr., Visiting Professor of American Politics at Boston College. One of the country's leading political commentators, he is a political analyst for CNN and a contributing editor to the *Los Angeles Times, National Journal,* and *The Atlantic,* where his essays and columns frequently appear. He is coauthor with Seymour Martin Lipset of *The Confidence Gap: Business, Labor, and Government in the Public Mind,* a second edition of which was published in 1987.

Theda Skocpol is Professor of Sociology at Harvard University and Cochair of the Working Group on States and Social Structures, sponsored by the Russell Sage Foundation. She is the author of *States and Social Revolutions,* editor of *Vision and Method in Historical Sociology,* and coeditor of *Bringing the State Back In* and *The Politics of Social Policy in the United States.* Among her works in progress are two books on the politics of social provision in the United States: from the 1870s to the 1920s, *Protecting Soldiers and Mothers,* and from the 1930s to the 1990s, *Social Security Against Welfare.* She is a member of several editorial boards, including those of *World Politics* and the *Journal of Historical Sociology.*

Judith Stepan-Norris is Assistant Professor of Sociology at the University of California, Irvine. She is currently working on a case study of union democracy, which is part of a larger project on the role of the Left in organized labor in the United States.

Kaare Strom is Associate Professor of Political Science at the University of California, San Diego. A native of Norway, he has previously taught at Michigan State University, the University of Bergen, and the University of Minnesota. He is the author of *Minority Government and Majority Rule,* as well as of a number of articles in the *American Political Science Review, American Journal of Political Science, European Journal of Political Research,* and other scholarly journals. His research interests are in government coalitions, party organization and behavior, and political competition.

Ann Swidler is an Associate Professor of Sociology at the University of California, Berkeley. She is coauthor of *Habits of the Heart* and *The Good Society* and author of *Organization Without Authority: Dilemmas of Social Control in Free Schools* and *Talk of Love: How Americans Use Their Culture* (forthcoming). Previously, she taught at Harvard University and Stanford University.

Martin Trow has been a faculty member of the University of California at Berkeley since 1957, first in the Department of Sociology and since 1969 in its Graduate School of Public Policy. From 1976 to 1988 he was Director of Berkeley's Center for Studies in Higher Education. As a Ph.D. student at Columbia University, he coauthored *Union Democracy* with Seymour Martin Lipset and James S. Coleman. Since then he has authored and edited many books and articles on issues in political sociology and comparative education. He is currently Chairman of the University of California's Academic Senate and a member of its Board of Regents. He is a member of the National Academy of Education and a Foreign Member of the Swedish Academy of Sciences.

Carlos H. Waisman is Professor of Sociology at the University of California, San Diego. He is the author of *Modernization and the Working Class: The Politics of Legitimacy*; *Reversal of Development in Argentina: Counter-revolutionary Policies and Their Structural Consequences*; and *From Military Rule to Liberal Democracy in Argentina*. His central interest has been the consequences of different patterns of industrialization for political institutions and legitimacy. He is now studying the twin capitalist and democratic revolutions that are transforming much of the contemporary world.

Immanuel Wallerstein is Distinguished Professor of Sociology and Director of the Fernand Braudel Center for the Study of Economics, Historical Systems, and Civilizations at the State University of New York at Binghamton. He is the author of *The Modern World-System* (3 vols.), *Unthinking Social Science, Geopolitics and Geoculture,* and *Historical Capitalism.*

Maurice Zeitlin is Professor of Sociology at the University of California, Los Angeles. Among his books are *Revolutionary Politics and the Cuban Working Class, The Civil Wars in Chile, Landlords and Capitalists* (with R. E. Ratcliff), and, most recently, *The Large Corporation and Contemporary Classes.* "During the quarter century since Lipset signed off on my dissertation," says Zeitlin, "Lipset's writings have continued to give me both inspiration and aggravation, in unequal parts, usually (but not always) much more of the former than the latter!"